The Phonology of Standard Chinese

THE PHONOLOGY OF THE WORLD'S LANGUAGES

General Editor: Jacques Durand

———

The Phonology of Danish
Hans Basbøll

The Phonology of Dutch
Geert Booij

The Phonology of Standard Chinese
San Duanmu

The Phonology of Polish
Edmund Gussmann

The Phonology of English
Michael Hammond

The Phonology of Norwegian
Gjert Kristoffersen

The Phonology of Portuguese
Maria Helena Mateus and Ernesto d'Andrade

The Phonology and Morphology of Kimatuumbi
David Odden

The Lexical Phonology of Slovak
Jerzy Rubach

The Phonology of Hungarian
Péter Siptár and Miklós Törkenczy

The Phonology of Mongolian
Jan-Olof Svantesson, Anna Tsendina, Anastasia Karlsson, and Vivan Franzén

The Phonology of Armenian
Bert Vaux

The Phonology and Morphology of Arabic
Janet Watson

The Phonology of Catalan
Max Wheeler

The Phonology of German
Richard Wiese

In preparation

The Phonology of Icelandic and Faroese
Kristján Árnason

The Phonology of Tamil
Prathima Christdas

The Phonology of Italian
Martin Krämer

The Phonology of Spanish
Iggy Roca

The Phonology of
STANDARD
CHINESE

Second Edition

San Duanmu
(端 木 三)

OXFORD
UNIVERSITY PRESS

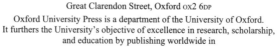

OXFORD
UNIVERSITY PRESS

Great Clarendon Street, Oxford OX2 6DP

Oxford University Press is a department of the University of Oxford.
It furthers the University's objective of excellence in research, scholarship,
and education by publishing worldwide in

Oxford New York

Auckland Cape Town Dar es Salaam Hong Kong Karachi
Kuala Lumpur Madrid Melbourne Mexico City Nairobi
New Delhi Shanghai Taipei Toronto

With offices in

Argentina Austria Brazil Chile Czech Republic France Greece
Guatemala Hungary Italy Japan Poland Portugal Singapore
South Korea Switzerland Thailand Turkey Ukraine Vietnam

Oxford is a registered trade mark of Oxford University Press
in the UK and in certain other countries

Published in the United States
by Oxford University Press Inc., New York

British Library Cataloguing in Publication Data

Data available

Library of Congress Cataloging in Publication Data

Data available

Typeset by SPI Publisher Services, Pondicherry, India
Printed in Great Britain
on acidfree paper by
Biddles Ltd., King's Lynn, Norfolk

ISBN 978-0-19-921578-2
978-0-19-921579-9

1 3 5 7 9 10 8 6 4 2

CONTENTS

NOTES ON TRANSCRIPTION

Chinese examples are transcribed either in Pinyin or in phonetic symbols (see Appendix for the correspondence between Pinyin and phonetic symbols). Unless otherwise noted, phonetic symbols will follow the International Phonetic Alphabet. Also, phonetic symbols will mostly be given in square brackets, unless they appear in a table, a list, a feature diagram, or a syllable diagram. Examples in Pinyin are italicized when cited in text, but not when cited in isolation in a numbered example. English examples cited in text are also italicized, unless they are in phonetic symbols, in which case they are given in square brackets.

The four full tones in Standard Chinese are indicated with the digits 1 to 4 (in either Pinyin or phonetic transcriptions). For example:

(1) [ma1] 'mother' has the first tone (a high level)
     [ma4] 'to scold' has the fourth tone (a fall)

A level tone representation (in terms of H and L) is used when it is relevant. When they are not relevant, tones are omitted.

Unless noted otherwise, phonetic transcriptions are given in square brackets at any level of detail. For example, three ways to transcribe the word for 'melon' are shown in (2).

(2) [kua]   indicating the phonemes
     [kʷa]   indicating the sounds but not their (predictable) lengths
     [kʷaa] indicating the sounds and their (predictable) lengths

Which degree of detail is transcribed will be noted when relevant.

A hyphen is sometimes used to indicate syllable boundaries, especially for a polysyllabic word or compound. For example, *Chi-ca-go* L-H-L shows that the word has three syllables and that their tones are, respectively, L, H, and L.

The translation of an example is given in single quotation marks. When relevant, both a word-for-word translation and a regular translation are given for a Chinese example. The translations are given either on the same line, as in (3), where the regular translation is in parentheses, or on separate lines, as in (4), where only the regular translation is in quotation marks.

(3)   gao-xing   'high-mood (glad)'

(4)   gao-xing
      high-mood
      'glad'

An asterisk means a bad form (in Standard Chinese) and a question mark means a marginal form. For example, *[pʷa] does not occur and *?yi ge bei* 'one cup' is marginal.

A slash is used between alternative words. For example, *very/more/most difficult* is an abbreviation for *very difficult, more difficult,* and *most difficult.* Similarly, *mai/*gou-mai zhi* means *mai zhi* (a good expression) and **gou-mai zhi* (a bad expression).

Sometimes square brackets are used to indicate syntactic boundaries, such as [*xiao* [*huo che*]] '[small [fire car]] (small train)'. When confusion may arise, a note will be given as to whether the brackets indicate phonetic symbols or syntactic boundaries.

FEATURES, ABBREVIATIONS, AND SYMBOLS

Features (each feature may be preceded with a + or − sign)

[ant]   [anterior]
[asp]   [aspirated]
[bk]   [back]
[stop]
[fric]   [fricative]
[hi]   [high]
[lat]   [lateral]
[lo]   [low]
[nas]   [nasal]
[rd]   [round]
[voi]   [voice]

Articulators

Cor   Coronal
Dor   Dorsal
Lab   Labial
SP   Soft palate
TR   Tongue root
VC   Vocal cords

Alternative feature terms

[−anterior] = [+retroflex]
[+anterior] = [−retroflex]

Other frequent abbreviations or symbols in this book

A   adjective
C   (*a*) consonant; (*b*) coda
G   glide
H   (*a*) high tone; (*b*) heavy syllable
L   (*a*) low tone; (*b*) light syllable
M   modifier
m   mora
N   (*a*) noun; (*b*) nucleus

O   (*a*) object; (*b*) onset
S   (*a*) syllable; (*b*) subject; (*c*) strong (metrical position)
SC   Standard Chinese
V   (*a*) vowel; (*b*) verb
W   weak (metrical position)
*   a bad form
Ø   an empty element (e.g. an empty onset, or an empty beat)
→   change to (e.g. A → B means A changes to B)

PREFACE TO THE SECOND EDITION

In one sense, this is not just a new edition but a new book because most chapters have been substantially revised or completely re-written. For example, in Chapter 2 I have adopted a simpler theory of feature structure, using just two stricture features, [fricative] and [stop]. In Chapter 3 I have dropped a dissimilation constraint and treated more syllable types as accidentally missing. In Chapter 4 I argue that the syllable onset is optional, rather than obligatory. In Chapter 6, I have proposed the Information-Stress Principle, from which all major properties of phrasal stress are derived. In addition, I have adopted the position that limits the number of stress levels by not assuming higher levels beyond the syllabic foot (Gussenhoven 1991). Moreover, I have revised the metrical analysis of many Chinese expressions; the new analysis assumes final stress in some disyllabic units and is more consistent with previous stress judgements such as Hoa (1983). The changes in Chapter 6 in turn affect other chapters. For example, in Chapter 8, the lack of the [V–O N] word order in compounds is not analysed in terms of initial stress, but in terms of a constraint against a compound-internal phrase. Besides revising existing chapters, I have also added a chapter on rhythm in poetry. In addition, I have changed many section titles so that they are more informative of their contents.

In another sense this book has changed little, because the theoretical goals and the basic proposals remain the same. In particular, the phonology of Chinese is analysed in terms of general phonological principles, and changes made to the analysis of Chinese usually reflect changes made to general phonological principles. For example, revisions to feature analysis in Chapter 2, syllable analysis in Chapter 4, and stress analysis in Chapter 6 are motivated by changes that are needed, in my view, for feature theory, syllable theory, and stress theory in general.

In the preparation of the second edition I have benefited from discussions and correspondences with many colleagues, students, and some reviewers. In particular, I would like to thank François Dell for discussions on stress, Bingfu Lu, Waltraud Paul, Hongjun Wang, Zheng Xu, and Ren Zhou for discussions on compounds, Nigel Fabb, Chris Golston, Morris Halle, and Yuchau Hsiao for discussions on poetic rhythm, Jun Da and James Myers for discussions on frequency, Hui-Ju Hsu and Chin-Cheng

Lo for discussions on Taiwanese Mandarin, Nathan Stiennon and Li Yang for some joint work on stress and poetry, and Ik-sang Eom, Chen Qu, and Hsin-I Hsieh for proofreading and comments. I would also like to thank the Linguistic Editor at Oxford, John Davey, for his gracious patience.

I am grateful to the Chiang Ching-kuo Foundation for International Scholarly Exchange and to the Center for Chinese Studies, University of Michigan, who provided grants to support the work on Chinese poetry.

A consuming project like this inevitably takes a toll on one's family, and I thank Yan, Youyou, and Alan for their understanding and support.

Ann Arbor   S.D.
2007

PREFACE

Once at a party I met a geologist. After introducing himself, he said, 'What do you study?'

I said, 'Linguistics.'

He said, 'Which language?'

I have heard this question many times. We know that languages are different. For example, a cat is called [kæt] in English but [mau] in Chinese. Such differences are arbitrary in the sense that any language could have chosen any sound to refer to an object. Since linguists study languages, they must be studying some language or other.

But for a modern linguist there is another side to the story. It is true that different languages can use different sounds to refer to an object, yet most variation also ends there. Beyond the lexicon, languages are strikingly similar. Thus, for a modern linguist, similarities among languages are far more interesting than their differences.

An analogy may illustrate the point. The landscapes of different countries may look quite different, but for a geologist all landscapes can be studied with the same physical principles. Likewise, languages of different countries may appear quite different, but for a modern linguist all languages can be studied with the same linguistic principles. So to ask a linguist 'Which language do you study?' is like asking a geologist 'Which country do you study?' Although geological facts can differ from one country to another and a geologist may focus on the facts of a particular country, yet the goal is to find principles that apply to the science in general. Similarly, a linguist may focus on the facts of a given language, but the goal is also to find principles that hold for all languages. Because of this, the subject matter of a geologist is not delimited by the borders of a given country. For example, a volcanologist is interested in volcanoes anywhere. Similarly, the subject matter of a linguist is not delimited by the speakers of a given language. For example, a tone specialist is interested in tone in any language.

But what is the evidence that patterns of language are more like principles of geology and less like social customs, such as colours of a costume, rituals of a wedding, rules for sports, or ways to celebrate a holiday? This is an age-old question, but considerable evidence has been gathered in the past few decades, especially since the rise of generative linguistics. Many patterns have been discovered that hold for all human languages. For example, all languages use a small set of consonants and vowels to make all words. All consonants and vowels can be decomposed into a small number of features according to articulatory mechanisms. All languages obey similar rhythmic requirements, such as a preference for a stressed syllable to be followed by an unstressed one. All contour tones (e.g. rise, fall, rise–fall, and fall–rise) are made of level tones (high and low). And so on. Such evidence suggests that much of our linguistic ability is not learned but innate, as argued by Chomsky (1986). In other words, the ability to talk is like the ability to walk. Both are determined biologically.

In many respects, Chinese is dramatically different from Indo-European languages. In this book I present many fascinating facts about the sound system of Standard Chinese. I also demonstrate that under a careful analysis, Chinese observes the same linguistic principles as other languages do.

Ann Arbor   S.D.
2000

ACKNOWLEDGEMENTS

This book is a distillation of my research on Chinese phonology in the past fifteen years, during which I benefited from numerous teachers, colleagues, and students—too many to list here. Nevertheless, I would like to thank Morris Halle, my mentor at MIT, and my colleagues at the University of Michigan for sharing a great research and teaching environment.

Some ideas offered here have appeared in my previous presentations and publications. In particular, I would like to thank the following for permission to reproduce published material: John Benjamins Publishing Company (Duanmu 1999*b*); Kluwer Academic Publishers (Duanmu 1999*a*); and Mouton de Gruyter (Duanmu 1998; 1999*c*).

The present ideas may differ from my earlier works though. For example, although I have previously discussed the topics of Chapter 9 (Duanmu 1990) and Chapter 11 (Duanmu 1989), the present analyses are quite different.

The Office of the Associate Provost for Academic and Multicultural Affairs and the Center for Chinese Studies, University of Michigan, provided partial support in the summer of 1998, which facilitated the completion of this book.

PREFACE TO THE PAPERBACK EDITION

Two changes have been made in this edition: (1) typographical corrections and minor stylistic revisions, and (2) a new chapter on theoretical implications (Chapter 13).

I benefited from discussions with John Davey, Ik-sang Eom, Yen-hwei Lin, Jeff Steele, and Jie Zhang. I thank them for their comments.

Ann Arbor   S.D.
2002

1

Introduction

1.1. CHINESE, ITS SPEAKERS, AND ITS DIALECTS

There are some fifty ethnic groups in China, the largest of which is Han, with over 90 per cent of the total population. The native language of the Han people is called *Hanyu* 'the Han Language' or *Zhongwen* 'Language of China'. The broader sense of the English word *Chinese* refers to anyone from China. The narrower sense of the word refers to the Han people or their native language. There are over 1,000 million native speakers of Chinese (including some non-Han groups such as Hui and Man), who make up about a fifth of the world's population today. In this regard, Chinese is the largest language in the world.

Chinese can be divided into several dialect families. Each family in turn consists of many dialects. Yuan (1989) divides Chinese into seven dialect families. The Mandarin family (or the Northern family) is the largest, with over 70 per cent of the speakers. The second largest, at about 8 per cent, is the Wu family, spoken in the area around Shanghai and the province of Zhejiang. Other families make up from 2 to 5 per cent each. The Yue family is spoken in the provinces of Guangdong and Guangxi, and in Hong Kong. The best-known Yue dialect is Cantonese, which is heard in many traditional Chinatowns overseas. The Min family is spoken in Fujian, part of Guangdong, and Taiwan, where it is often called Taiwanese. The Hakka family is centred near the borders of Guangdong, Fujian, and Jiangxi, along with scattered pockets in other parts of China and South East Asia. The remaining two families, Xiang and Gan, are spoken in the provinces of Hunan and Jiangxi, respectively.

A striking aspect of Chinese is the lack of intelligibility across dialect families, that is, speakers from different dialect families often cannot understand each other. Because of this, it is often said that Chinese dialects are in fact separate languages. However, all Chinese dialects share the same written language and essentially the same grammar. In addition, the sounds of one dialect can be related to those of another through systematic rules. For example, [ai] in Chengdu is related to [e] in Shanghai, so that [lai] 'come' in Chengdu is [le] in Shanghai. Likewise, Beijing and Chengdu have similar phonemes, but two of their tones have switched; low and falling in Beijing are falling and low in Chengdu. Thus, [ma (low)] is 'horse' in Beijing but 'to scold' in Chengdu, and [ma (falling)] is 'to scold' in Beijing but 'horse' in Chengdu. Such systematic rules enable speakers of one dialect to understand other dialects rather quickly. This happens, for example, to many college freshmen every year. No matter where a student goes to school, she or he can usually understand the local accent in just a few months. In this regard, for a Chinese speaker to learn a new dialect is like for an English speaker to learn Pig Latin. Although the new dialect appears to be unintelligible at first sight, one quickly realizes the correspondence rules and begins to understand the speech.

1.2. HISTORY

Not much is known for certain about Chinese history before 800 BC. The first Chinese emperor was believed to be Huang Di (about 2600 BC), at whose time there were reportedly some 10,000 states, and during the Xia Dynasty (about 2100 to 1700 BC) there were still 3,000 states. At the beginning of the Zhou Dynasty (about 1100 BC), the emperor reportedly divided land among 800 lords, who were perhaps heads of tribes. One can only guess that those communities probably spoke different dialects (or different languages).

Systematic records of Chinese history began from the Dong Zhou period (770 BC on), and linguistic diversity was immediately evident: the emperors appointed field linguists, known by their transportation as *youxuan shizhe* 'officials on light carriages', who regularly travelled the country to collect and archive samples of *fangyan* 'regional speech'.

Alongside regional speech, a common form of Chinese also existed. It was called *yayan* 'refined speech' in the Chunqiu period (722–482 BC), *tongyu* 'common speech' in the Han Dynasty (206 BC–AD 220), *tianxia tongyu* 'common speech under the heaven' in the Yuan Dynasty (1206–1368), and *guanhua* 'language of the officials' or 'Mandarin' since the Ming Dynasty (1368–1644).

Chinese emperors made several efforts to standardize the language. The first came from the emperor Shi Huang Di of the Qin Dynasty (221–206 BC), who unified the orthography of Chinese characters (a character is basically a monosyllabic word written as one graphic unit). During the Liu Chao period (AD 222–589), Chinese scholars began to produce the so-called *yunshu* 'rhyming books', which divided characters into different groups according to how they rhymed in verse. Characters in the same group rhymed with each other, those in different groups did not. Numerous rhyming books were written then, many of which were influenced by dialectal pronunciations. In AD 751, with the consent of the emperor Xuan Zong of the Tang Dynasty, Sun Mian wrote the first official rhyming book *Tangyun* (based on an earlier work *Qieyun* by Lu Fayan in AD 601). Subsequent emperors ordered several editions of the official rhyming book. The official rhyming books had a great influence on the literary tradition in two ways; they were used in exams for recruiting government officials, and besides grouping characters into rhyming categories, they explained the meanings and the shapes of the characters, complete with references to the sources. In this regard, rhyming books served the functions of dictionaries.

The earliest-known written Chinese dates back to the Shang Dynasty (between 1700 and 1100 BC). Some was carved on tortoise shells and animal bones and is known as *jiaguwen* 'shell-bone language'. Some was inscribed on metal instruments and is known as *jinwen* 'metal language'. With regard to the basic lexicon, grammar, and character shapes, *jiaguwen* and *jinwen* were already consistent with later Chinese.

The early style of written Chinese is called *wenyan* 'written language' and has largely remained unchanged throughout history. It differs considerably from modern spoken Chinese. The main characteristic of *wenyan* is its terseness in the use of words. As an example, consider a quotation from Confucius, shown in (1), where Q is a question marker and a hyphen indicates a possible compound (see Chapter 5).

(1) You peng zi yuan-fang lai bu yi le hu
    have friend from far-place come not also joy Q
    'If you have friends coming from far away, isn't it also a joy?'

The same sentence in modern Chinese is a lot longer, shown in (2), which uses sixteen syllables, compared to ten in (1).

(2) ruguo you pengyou cong yuan-fang lai bu shi ye hen kuaile ma
    if have friend from far-place come not be also very joy Q
    'If you have friends coming from far away, isn't it also a joy?'

Some people believe that *wenyan* reflects the spoken language in the past, and the fact that it differs from spoken Chinese today is because the spoken language has changed but the written language has not. However, it is likely that even at the beginning the written language was considerably condensed. The reason is that the earliest writings were inscribed on metals, shells, bones, and bamboo sticks, which was highly time consuming. In addition, space on such materials was limited. Understandably, redundant words were omitted, as one does in a telegram or an instant message. This is especially evident in *jiaguwen*, whose style can at best be called telegraphic. After the invention of ink and paper, writing became easier, but because of the reverence for ancient tradition, the early written style was largely preserved until the twentieth century.

1.3. STANDARD CHINESE

Around the turn of the twentieth century, in conjunction with the movement to abolish the imperial establishment, some intellectuals began a campaign for language reform. The campaign accelerated with government support after the Republic of China was founded in 1912. The People's Republic of China (founded in 1949) continued to support the reform. Over a period of half a century, three goals have been achieved: a standard spoken language, an alphabetic writing system, and vernacular writing.

1.3.1. Standard Spoken Chinese

The official body for language reform set up by the Republic of China proposed that a standard spoken Chinese be adopted. It was called *Guoyu* 'National Language' and was based on the pronunciation of the Beijing (Peking) dialect. The People's Republic of China adopted the standard pronunciation, although the name was changed to *Putonghua* 'Common Speech'. In this book I use Standard Chinese (SC) to refer to Guoyu (a term still used in Taiwan) or Putonghua. In Singapore, SC is called *Huayu* 'Chinese Language'. Other terms for SC are Beijing Mandarin, Standard Mandarin, Mandarin Chinese, or simply Mandarin.

Standard Chinese has been the official language of China for a few decades. It is used in schools and universities and on national radio and television broadcasts (although regional stations still air some programmes in local dialects). But unlike some standard European languages, such as the Received Pronunciation of British English, SC does not carry a superior social prestige. Instead, many Chinese see SC as a practical tool, not a symbol of status. Naturally, many people spend only as much effort learning SC as will make them understood, and do not bother with the accent they still have. This includes government leaders, academics, and the average person. In addition, many speakers in the Mandarin dialect family see little need to modify their pronunciation, because their dialect is often closer to SC than what is attempted by people from other dialect families. As a result, most SC speakers, or most of those who think they are speaking SC, do not have a perfect pronunciation. According to a recent survey (Chinese Ministry of Education 2004), 53 per cent of the people on Mainland China can speak SC, and of these, 20 per cent are fluent. This puts the number of fluent SC speakers at about one tenth of the Chinese population (about 130 million). However, since SC is the only dialect that Chinese speakers share, it will be the focus of this book.

Although SC is based on the Beijing dialect, there are two differences; SC has absorbed many expressions from other dialects, and it has excluded some local vocabulary from the Beijing dialect. The first difference has little effect on the sound system of SC, because words absorbed from other dialects are usually adapted to the Beijing pronunciation. For example, both syllables in the Shanghai word [pʲeˀ se] 'pauper' are ill-formed in Beijing (Beijing does not have glottalized vowels like [eˀ], and the rhyme [e] does not occur after [s]). When the word is adopted by SC, they are pronounced as [pʲe san], both of which are good syllables in Beijing. The second difference does influence the sound system of SC, and as a result SC has a slightly smaller syllable inventory than Beijing. For example, in SC the syllable [tʷei] does not occur with the third tone, but Beijing has the word [tʷei3] 'to cancel', as in the expression [tʷei3 tʂaŋ4] 'to cancel a debt'. Similarly, SC does have the syllable [tʰen] with any tone, but Beijing has the word [tʰen4] 'not hurry when one should'. According to Z. Liu (1957a, 1957b), ignoring the retroflex suffix, merged syllables, and unstressed syllables, Beijing has 432 syllables excluding tone, which is about 30 more than SC, and 1,376 syllables including tone, which is about 80 more than SC. A further difference between SC and Beijing is that the latter uses the [ɚ] suffix extensively (see Chapter 9), whereas SC uses it much less. Thus, people who have heard SC only over the radio and TV may have trouble understanding Beijing speakers when they visit the city for the first time.

1.3.2. Alphabetical writing and Pinyin

According to Ni (1948), the first alphabetical writing system for Chinese was designed by the Italian missionary Matteo Ricci and published in 1605 in Beijing (but the record was lost). Subsequently, other missionaries designed various other alphabetical systems, often to aid foreigners to learn Chinese. However, alphabetical writing did not attract the attention of Chinese intellectuals until after the Opium War (1840–2).

Many proponents of language reform around the turn of the nineteenth century believed that alphabetical writing was a key to the strength of a modern nation. Therefore, besides proposing a standard spoken language, they also proposed to establish an alphabetical writing system. The first Chinese design was published by Gangzhang Lu in 1892. In the next two decades some thirty designs were proposed. The system adopted by the Republic of China in 1928 is called *Guoyu Luomazi* 'National Language Romanization'. The system adopted by the People's Republic of China in 1958 is called *Hanyu Pinyin Fang'an* 'Chinese Spelling System', or 'Pinyin' for short. A main difference between the two systems is that Guoyu Luomazi uses letters to spell tones, whereas Pinyin marks tones with separate diacritics.

Because SC has a large number of homophones, and because of the difficulty in defining the word in Chinese, the alphabetical system is not yet an independent working orthography.

1.3.3. Vernacular writing

Before the twentieth century, written Chinese largely maintained the style of the earliest written texts (except for a small body of popular literature, which was written in a spoken style). The style is characterized by an extreme conciseness in the use of words, along with a preference for classical vocabulary. It departs considerably from how Chinese is spoken and creates great difficulty for literacy and mass communication. The Vernacular Movement, or *Baihuawen Yundong* 'Movement for Plain Speech Writing', urges people to write Chinese the way it is spoken. Most modern writing is now in the vernacular style.

1.4. PHONOLOGICAL LITERATURE ON SC

Chinese phonology has been studied for over 1,700 years since the appearance of the first rhyming books in the third century. This tradition can be divided into three periods: traditional literature before the twentieth century, the standardization effort in the twentieth century, and the generative influence since the late 1950s.

Before the twentieth century, the focus was on the rhyming categories of syllables, because the dominant interest was in composing proper literary works (especially at official exams) and in preserving or reconstructing what was thought to be the original Chinese.

The standardization movement reached a turning point after the founding of the Republic of China in 1912. Many of the active scholars had a western education and they introduced to China modern techniques of analysis, such as articulatory phonetics, acoustic phonetics, and phonemics. Since then many descriptive works have been published, mostly in Chinese, on SC and other dialects. But because of its specific goals, the standardization literature has limitations from a broader linguistic perspective. For example, many syllable types are missing in SC. For the purpose of standardization, this fact need not be addressed (and it often is not). But from the viewpoint of linguistic theory, the fact calls for an explanation. Similarly, SC has four tones on full syllables. For the purpose of transcription and teaching, they can simply be indicated by the digits 1 to 4 after each syllable, as in [man1, man2, man3, man4], or by diacritics over the nuclear vowel, as in [mān, mán, mǎn, màn], both being widely used options. However, from the viewpoint of linguistic theory, one would like to know the composition of the tones in terms of universal tone features which represent not only SC tones but tones in other languages as well. In addition, one would ask where exactly the tones fall: On the entire syllable? On the voiced part of the syllable? On the nuclear vowel only? Or on the nuclear vowel and the coda? Moreover, since the 1960s, there have been important advances in phonological theory, which are not reflected in the standardization literature.

Since the 1950s, generative linguistics has significantly changed the field of phonology. In particular, a number of insights have been gained through a series of theoretical developments, such as distinctive features and feature geometry, underspecification, multi-tiered phonology, syllable structure, metrical phonology, and Optimality Theory. Many issues in Chinese that had not been raised before have attracted attention, such as the feature representation of tones (e.g. W. Wang 1967; Woo 1969; Yip 1980; Bao 1990a; Chan 1991; Duanmu 1994), the interaction between tone and syntax (e.g. C. Cheng 1973; Shih 1986; Chen 1987; Selkirk and Shen 1990; H. Zhang 1992), the analysis of language games (e.g. Yip 1982; Bao 1990b), the feature analysis of affixation and segmental changes (e.g. Y. Lin 1989; Y. Yin 1989; J. Wang 1993), the analysis of syllable structure (Cheung 1986; Duanmu 1990; Chung 1996; Goh 1997), and the interactions among syllable, stress, and tone (e.g. Duanmu 1990, 1993, 1999a; Ao 1993; Yip 1992, 1994). Such works prepared the ground for a monograph that examines the entire phonology of SC from a theoretical perspective.

1.5. GOALS OF THIS BOOK

This book has three goals. First, I offer a systematic description of major phonological facts in SC. Many facts are either new or not fully treated in traditional literature, such as missing syllable patterns, properties of compounds, stress, word-length variation, word-order variation, and prosody in poetry. Secondly, I offer a theoretical analysis of the facts. I show that like other languages SC observes general linguistic principles. In addition, I show that the analysis of SC has implications for several areas of linguistic theory, such as syllable structure, metrical phonology, tone, and phonology–syntax interaction. Thirdly, I aim to present the facts and the analysis in a non-technical way, so that they are accessible to a broad audience, that is, to anyone who is familiar with the basic terms in a phonetic table. Theoretical background to be assumed in a given chapter will be introduced in advance and in plain terms.

2

The sound inventory

2.1. WHAT IS A SOUND?

This chapter addresses two questions: How many sounds are there in Standard Chinese? and, What sounds are they? The questions may seem simple, but the answers require an understanding of what a sound is, how sounds are counted, and how sounds are represented. I will therefore start with a discussion of the theories involved.

Speech is, at some level, made of a sequence of sounds (consonants and vowels). For example, there are three sounds (or segments) in the English word *miss* [mɪs], whose boundaries are easy to identify phonetically. However, sometimes the case is less obvious. For example, is the long vowel [iː] one sound or two? Since it has no internal boundary, it looks like one sound. On the other hand, it is much longer than a short vowel, so it is like two sounds in terms of duration. Similarly, the diphthong [ai] is like two sounds in terms of duration, but it is like one sound for lack of an internal boundary. A sound like [pʰ] presents another kind of problem. It is like two sounds because there is a phonetic boundary between [p] and [ʰ]. In addition, the duration of [pʰ] seems to be longer than that of [p]. However, phonetic studies show that the vowel that follows [pʰ] is shorter than the vowel that follows [p]. As a result, a syllable like [pʰai] 'send' in SC is not appreciably longer than a syllable like [pai] 'defeat'. Therefore, in terms of total syllable duration [pʰ] is still like one sound.

In this study I assume that a sound is defined in terms of two factors, stated in (1). First, in normal context a sound is uttered in one unit of time (or 'timing slot', see below), which is on average about 60–80 milliseconds (ms). Secondly, it is uttered with at most one gesture (or value) for each feature at each articulator (see the 'No-Contour Principle', below).

(1) A sound is articulated:
    (*a*) in one time unit (one timing slot)
    (*b*) with at most one value for each feature at each articulator

The definition in (1) assumes that articulatory gestures are organized into temporally coordinated units (at least at some level), departing from the view of Goldsmith (1976), which does not assume such a temporal coordination (what Goldsmith calls the 'absolute splicing hypothesis'). By this definition, [iː] is two sounds because it takes two time units. Similarly, [ai] is two sounds because it takes two time units and two gestures for the height of the tongue, first [+low] and then [−low]. For [pʰ], there is no evidence that it needs two time units (e.g. [pʰai] and [pai] have similar duration). In addition, there is just one gesture for [ʰ] (spread glottis), made at the same time as [p], even though the aspiration continues after [p]. Thus, there is no need to analyse [pʰ] as two sounds, especially if we count the start of the oral release as the start of the vowel.

Affricates, contour tones, and pre- and post-nasalized stops may complicate the definition of a sound. I will discuss affricates in section 2.4.1, contour tones in Chapter 10. For further discussion, see Duanmu (1994), who also addresses pre- and post-nasalized stops.

2.2. PHONEMICS

Phonemics is the technique for deciding the number of sounds, or phonemes, in a language (Pike 1947). Since speech sounds vary from person to person and from context to context for the same person, we must decide which differences are important and which are not. There are three basic elements of phonemics: the minimal pair, complementary distribution, and phonetic similarity. In addition, I discuss over-analysis, under-analysis, phonemic economy, and the notion of 'sound'. The discussion applies to what Chomsky (1964) called 'taxonomic phonemics' and 'systematic phonemics'.

2.2.1. The minimal pair

The minimal pair is a pair of words that are identical in pronunciation except for one sound. The minimal pair is a criterion for deciding which differences must be recognized. For example, consider the SC words in (2) (where tones are omitted).

(2)   (a) A minimal pair
         [mai] 'buy'
         [nai] 'milk'

(b) Not a minimal pair
   [ma]   'hemp'
   [min] 'people'

In (2a) the words differ only in the first sound, which is [m] in one and [n] in the other. Since [m] and [n] can distinguish words, they must be recognized as different sounds and represented by separate symbols. In other words, the difference between [m] and [n] is contrastive, and contrastive differences must be represented by different phonemes. When two words differ in more than one sound, as seen in (2b), no specific conclusion can be drawn. What we know here is that [a] and [in] are different. However, since [in] is not a single sound, we cannot represent it with one symbol. Nor can we tell whether [a] can contrast with [i] or [n].

Central to the idea of the minimal pair is the assumption that we know what is one sound and what is more than one sound. But the difference is not always straightforward. For example, a long vowel or a diphthong has been analysed as one sound in some studies but two in others. Similarly, consider the SC words in (3).

(3) [pʰai]   'row'
     [pai]   'white'

Whether (3) is a minimal pair or not depends on whether [pʰ] is one sound. Many studies consider [pʰ] to be one sound, but some consider it to be two, [p] and [h], such as Hockett (1947) and Martin (1957). The two approaches lead to different results. For example, excluding palatals and retroflexes, the first approach postulates eight oral stops and affricates for SC, [p, pʰ, t, tʰ, ts, tsʰ, k, kʰ], but the second postulates only four, [p, t, ts, k, (h)], where [h] is independently related to the velar fricative. I will return to this issue later.

2.2.2. Complementary distribution

The complementary distribution criterion decides which phonetic differences need not be represented by separate phonemes. The distribution of a sound refers to all the environments it can occur in. For illustration, consider the SC words in (4).

(4) Complementary distribution (tones ignored)

   [tʰa] 'he'   [wa] 'dig'   [ja] 'duck'
   [tʰɤ] 'special' [wo] 'I'   [je] 'leaf'

In SC, [a] can occur after [tʰ, w, j]. In contrast, [ɤ] can occur after [tʰ] but not after [w, j], [o] can occur after [w] but not after [tʰ, j], and [e] can occur after [j] but not after [tʰ, w]. With respect to [tʰ, w, j], therefore, the distribution of [a] is complete, but the distributions of [ɤ, o, e] complement one another. Because of this, [ɤ, o, e] are said to be in complementary distribution, in that the distribution of one does not overlap with the distribution of another. Sounds in complementary distribution can be represented by the same phoneme for two reasons; their distributions added together are only as large as a sound with complete distribution, and the variation among them is predictable from the environment so that there is no need to write them with different symbols. Thus, [ɤ, o, e] in SC can be represented with just one phoneme.

2.2.3. **Phonetic similarity**

The phonetic-similarity condition states that sounds represented by the same phoneme should be phonetically similar. If two sounds are quite different, they should be represented by different phonemes, even if they are in complementary distribution. For example, in English [h] and [ŋ] are in complementary distribution, because [h] only occurs before a vowel, and [ŋ] only occurs after a vowel. However, since [h] and [ŋ] are phonetically quite different, they are analysed as separate phonemes.

As Pike (1947: 63) points out, phonetic similarity is a vague notion which may be interpreted differently in different studies. For example, some studies of SC consider [e, o, ɤ] to be a single sound underlyingly, but the Pinyin system uses two symbols for them, *e* for [e, ɤ] and *o* for [o] (see H. Wang 1999: 38 for other views).

2.2.4. **Over-analysis**

Sometimes phonologists knowingly split a sound into two in order to achieve better phonemic economy, that is, to minimize the number of phonemes. Chao (1934) calls it 'over-analysis'. For example, in SC the combination [sw], as in [swan] 'sour', is phonetically one sound. The reason is that the lip rounding of [w] occurs at the same time as [s], and the following vowel 'starts almost as soon as the tongue leaves the [s]-position without leaving any appreciable duration for the [u] or [w] to stand alone' (Chao 1934: 42). In contrast, the combination [sw] in English, as in *sway*, is phonetically two sounds, in that the lip rounding of [w] occurs after [s]. In other words, since the SC [sʷ] and the English [sw] are phonetically different, their phonological analysis should also be different, namely, [sʷ] is one sound and [sw] is two. However, since [ʷ] occurs with many consonants in SC, to consider [Cʷ] as one sound would mean to recognize a new series of consonants [sʷ, tʷ, lʷ, nʷ, kʷ, …], in addition to the basic series [s, t, l, n, k, …]. If [Cʷ] is analysed as two sounds, then we need to recognize only the basic series [s, t, l, n, k, …], plus [u] or [w], which is independently needed. In general, if a feature F can appear on n phonemes, one can set up just n+1 phonemes (n phonemes without F plus F itself), instead of setting up $2n$ phonemes (n phonemes without F and n phonemes with F), provided one considers F to be a separate sound. A hypothetical example is shown in (5).

(5)   Regular analysis   Over-analysis
      Phonetic   [t, d, k, g, tʷ, dʷ, kʷ, gʷ]   [t, d, k, g, tʷ, dʷ, kʷ, gʷ]
      Representation   [t, d, k, g, tʷ, dʷ, kʷ, gʷ]   [t, d, k, g, tw, dw, kw, gw]
      Phonemes   [t, d, k, g, tʷ, dʷ, kʷ, gʷ]   [t, d, k, g, w]

In the regular analysis, [tʷ, dʷ, kʷ, gʷ] are single sounds, and there is a total of eight phonemes. In the over-analysis, [tw, dw, kw, gw] are each made of two sounds, and there is a total of five phonemes. Since over-analysis uses fewer phonemes, it is considered to be more economical. Because of over-analysis, most studies of SC consider a consonant–glide combination to be a cluster of two sounds, even though it is phonetically a single sound. I will return to this point.

Over-analysis has also been applied to vowels and glides. For example, Hartman (1944) and Hsueh (1986) treat the SC glide [ɥ] as [jw], and the high vowels [i, u, y] as [ji, wɨ, jwɨ], where [ɨ] is a central high vowel. I will return to this proposal below.

2.2.5. Under-analysis

Sometimes phonologists knowingly analyse two sounds as one in order, again, to achieve better phonemic economy. Chao (1934) calls this 'under-analysis'. For example, SC has full and weak syllables (see Chapter 4). In full syllables, a vowel is long when there is no consonant after it and short when there is (see Woo 1969; Howie 1976). However, since vowel length is predictable, it need not be represented. This is shown in (6).

(6)   Regular analysis   Under-analysis
      Phonetic   [maː], [man]   [maː], [man]
      Representation   [maː], [man]   [ma], [man]
      Vowel phonemes   [aː], [a]   [a]

Under-analysis ignores the length of [aː] and represents it the same way as [a]. Thus, under-analysis postulates only one vowel [a]. In contrast, the regular analysis postulates two vowels, [aː] and [a].

Another case of under-analysis is proposed by You *et al.* (1980). They argue that the syllable structure in SC can be simplified to CGV if we treat diphthongs, such as [ai] and [au], and VC rhymes, such as [an] and [in], as a single phoneme each, which they call a 'rhyme phoneme'. The proposal would create over a dozen new phonemes, but syllable structure would now be more consistent than previously thought. However, I will argue in Chapter 4 that syllable structure in SC is already quite simple and consistent, and so there is no need for under-analysis.

2.2.6. Phonemic economy

Pike (1947) calls phonemics 'a technique for reducing languages to writing'. The writing Pike refers to is an alphabetical writing system in which each letter is a phoneme. Naturally, it is thought, the fewer phonemes the better. An analysis with fewer phonemes is said to have better phonemic economy. The desire to achieve better phonemic economy has often led scholars to ignore other considerations. We have seen two cases above, over-analysis and under-analysis, which reduce the phonemic inventory by blurring the notion of a sound. However, it is not obvious what the importance of phonemic economy is or how it should be measured. If the goal is to save fonts for the printer, it is a trivial matter, and counting the phonemic inventory is enough. If phonemic economy makes claims about the organization of sounds in the speaker's mind, then it is a different matter, and the measurement of economy is more complicated. For example, compare the analyses in (7).

(7)	Regular analysis	Over-analysis
Phonetic	[t, d, k, g, t^w, d^w, k^w, g^w]	[t, d, k, g, t^w, d^w, k^w, g^w]
Representation	[t, d, k, g, t^w, d^w, k^w, g^w]	[t, d, k, g, tw, dw, kw, gw]
Inventory	8	5
Surface	8	12

To utter the same set of sounds, the speaker would make eight sounds in the regular analysis but twelve in the over-analysis, since [tw, dw, kw, gw] represent two sounds each. Thus, with regard to production, the regular analysis is more economical in that the speaker utters fewer sounds. In addition, the over-analysis must assume consonant clusters (e.g. [tw]) and a lack of transparency between the phonological representation and the phonetic output (e.g. [tw] are two sounds in the representation but one sound [t^w] phonetically). In contrast, the regular analysis does not have such problems. Thus, it is not clear whether the over-analysis gains better economy overall.

Sometimes phonemic economy is extended to the analysis of the syllable. A maximal Chinese syllable is CGVC or CGVG. The status of the medial G is unclear. For example, Chan (1985: 67–8) suggests that although [kw] is phonetically the same in both Cantonese and SC, it should be analysed as one sound in Cantonese but two in SC. The reason is that [k^w] and [k^{hw}] are the only CG combinations in Cantonese, and counting them as single sounds can eliminate three syllable types, CGV, CGVG, and CGVC. In contrast, SC has many CG combinations, and counting CG as two sounds can reduce the consonant inventory by about thirty (no need to set up the series C^j, C^w, and C^ɥ), with an increase of only three syllable types (that is, adding CGV, CGVC, and CGVG). A similar argument is made by R. Li (1983).

There are several problems with this reasoning. First, it assumes that two series of consonants, say C and C^w, are twice as complicated as one series. The assumption is correct if phonemes are the minimal units of speech. However, if distinctive features are the basic building blocks of sounds (see below), then adding a C^w series to the C series may only involve one more feature, say [+round] for [^{w}]. Secondly, comparing phoneme count with syllable count is like comparing apples with oranges; they do not have the same unit of measurement. For example, what is the basis for deciding whether adding ten consonants is more (or less) costly than adding three syllable types? Third, there is the issue of the generality of linguistic structure. For example, in most languages the syllable is divided into onset and rhyme, where the rhyme starts with a nuclear vowel. If one is to postulate a rhyme that starts with a glide, one needs to provide independent evidence for it. An apparent reduction in the consonant inventory of a particular language is no compelling evidence.

2.3. USING SYLLABLE STRUCTURE IN PHONEMIC ANALYSIS

The problems with under-analysis and over-analysis can be resolved without compromising phonemic economy if we take syllable structure into consideration. Every syllable has a nucleus, usually filled by a vowel. The part before the nucleus is called the onset, the part after it, the coda.

The nucleus and the coda together are called the rhyme. For example, in [man] the onset is [m], the nucleus is [a], the coda is [n], and the rhyme is [an]. In [mai] the onset is [m], the nucleus is [a], the coda is [i], and the rhyme is [ai]. A syllable with a nuclear vowel but without a coda conso-nant is called an open syllable, such as [ma] (with a short [a]) or [maa] (with a long [a]). A syllable with a nuclear vowel and a coda consonant is called a closed syllable, such as [man]. A syllable like [mai], where [i] is in the coda, can also be called a closed syllable. More discussion of the syllable is given in Chapter 4. A slightly simplified representation of [ma:] and [man] in SC is shown in (8).

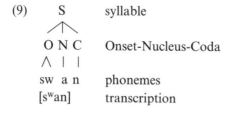

(8)   S   S   syllable
       ONC   ONC   Onset-Nucleus-Coda
       m a n   m a   phonemes
       [man]   [ma:]   transcription

In (8) there is one vowel phoneme [a], in agreement with under-analy-sis. However, given the syllable structure, the predictable vowel length is also represented. In [man] the vowel is associated with the nucleus, and so it is realized as a short vowel. In [ma:] the vowel is associated with both the nucleus and the coda, and so it is realized as a long vowel. Thus, the analysis captures both phonemic economy and phonetic accu-racy. Now consider the representation of [sʷan] 'sour' in SC, shown in (9).

(9)   S   syllable
       O N C   Onset-Nucleus-Coda
       sw a n   phonemes
       [sʷan]   transcription

In (9) there are four phonemes, in agreement with over-analysis. How-ever, since [sw] share one onset slot, they are realized as a single sound [sʷ]. The analysis again captures both phonemic economy and phonetic accuracy. In (9) I have assumed that two sounds can merge into one. Which sound pairs can merge and which cannot is specified in feature theory, which concerns the representation of speech sounds, to which we now turn.

2.4. FEATURES AND THE REPRESENTATION OF SOUNDS

A fundamental discovery in phonology is that speech consists of a sequence of sounds (besides prosodic structures such as the syllable and stress), despite various phonetic interactions between neighbouring sounds. Each sound in turn is made of more basic elements called 'features' (or 'distinctive features'). In this section I discuss feature theory, including the representation of complex sounds and length. I also discuss the theory of underspecification.

2.4.1. **Phonological features**

The feature property of speech sounds has been recognized in traditional phonetic tables, where each sound can be uniquely referred to by its articulatory features. For example, [p] is a voiceless labial stop, [u] is a back high rounded vowel.

There are three motivations for using phonological features. First, features indicate how sounds are made. For example, [p] is made when the vocal cords are not vibrating (voiceless) and the lips (labial) are closed (stop). Secondly, features can show similarities and differences between sounds. For example, [p] is a 'voiceless labial stop' and [b] is a 'voiced labial stop'. Thus, the two sounds are similar in two features and differ in one. Thirdly, features can reveal natural classes of sounds. For example, the English plural suffix is [s] when added to *map, cat, back, fourth*, etc., and [z] when added to *job, food, mug, pen, mom, pill, bee, cow*, etc. In the former case the words end in [p, t, k, θ], which belong to the class 'voiceless', and in the latter case the words end in [b, d, g, n, m, l, i, u], which belong to the class 'voiced'.

Jakobson *et al.* (1952) define features in both acoustic and articulatory terms. Later works have focussed on articulatory definitions. In addition, a distinction can be made between articulators and features. Articulators are movable parts in the vocal tract that participate in speech production. For example, the articulator for [t] in English is Coronal (tongue tip), instead of alveolar, since it is the tongue tip that initiates the closure. Features are gestures made by articulators. In the present study I assume the feature structure (also called feature geometry) in (10), based on the works of Clements (1985), Sagey (1986), Halle and Clements (1983), Ladefoged and Halle (1988), McCarthy (1988), Steriade (1989), Kenstowicz (1994), Keyser and Stevens (1994), Halle (1995), Padgett (1995), and Halle (2005).

By convention, features are placed in brackets and written under the articulators that make them. Features for tone will be discussed in Chapter 10.

(10)

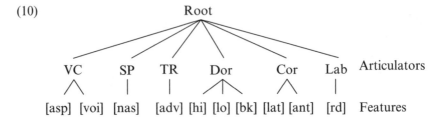

In (10) there are six articulators: Vocal-cords, Soft-palate, Tongue-root,
Dorsal (tongue body), Coronal, and Labial. The features [aspirated],
[voice], and [nasal] have also been called [spread (vocal cords)], [slack
(vocal cords)], and [lowered (soft palate)] respectively. I use [aspirated],
[voice], and [nasal] on grounds of familiarity. The articulator Tongue-
root and its feature [advanced] are not relevant for Chinese and will be
ignored.

Besides the features in (10), there are some that can be made by more than
one articulator. They have been called manner features, stricture features,
major-class features, and articulator-free features. Commonly used manner features are [consonantal], [sonorant], [strident], [fricative], and [stop]
(or [continuant]). For present purposes, only two are needed, [fricative]
and [stop], following Padgett (1995) (Coleman 1996 also argues against
the manner feature [consonantal], but for somewhat different reasons). In
(11) I list some traditional terms and their translations in feature structure
(see Chomsky and Halle 1968; Halle and Clements 1983; Steriade 1989;
Clements and Hume 1995; Halle 1995; Padgett 1995; and others).

(11)   Traditional terms   Feature structure
       stops   [+stop]
       sonorants   [−stop, −fricative]
       fricatives   [+fricative]
       affricates   [+stop, +fricative]
       dentals   Coronal-[+ant]
       retroflexes   Coronal-[−ant]
       palatals   Coronal and Dorsal–[−back]

The translations between traditional terms and feature structure are mostly
transparent, although a note is needed for affricates and palatals. Affricates are [+stop, +fricative], instead of strident stops (Steriade 1989). It
may seem contradictory for a sound to be both [+stop] and [+fricative],

if [+stop] means that the vocal tract is fully closed and [+fricative] means that it is not. I suggest that [stop] is a gesture for centre closure and [fricative] for edge closure. For example, in [t] the force of closure is applied at the centre of the tongue tip. In [s] the force of closure is applied at the edges of the tongue tip (or blade). In the affricate [ts] the force of closure is applied at both the centre and the edges of the tongue tip. Palatals are represented as Coronal and [−back] under Dorsal (Clements and Hume 1995). A palatal may also have the feature [+ant] under Coronal, since in SC palatals there is both a dental contact (by the tongue tip) and a palatal closure (by the tongue body) at the same time.

2.4.2. Complex sounds and the No-Contour Principle

Some sounds use only one articulator, such as [ʔ], which uses Vocal-cords. Some sounds use more, such as [gʷ], which uses Vocal-cords, Dorsal, and Labial. We can call a sound that uses one oral articulator (i.e. Labial, Coronal, or Dorsal) a simple sound, and one that uses two or three oral articulators a complex sound. Some examples are given in (12).

(12)
Sounds	Simple/complex	Oral articulators
[p]	simple	Labl-[+stop]
[t]	simple	Cor-[+stop]
[k]	simple	Dor-[+stop]
[k͡p]	complex	Dor-[+stop], Lab-[+stop]
[kʷ]	complex	Dor-[+stop], Lab-[+round]
[tɕ]	complex	Dor-[+stop, +fric], Cor-[+stop, +fric]
[tsʲ]	complex	Dor-[−back], Cor-[+stop, +fric]

When a sound has two (or more) oral articulators, the one that has greater closure, that is, the one that has [+stop] or [+fricative], is often called the major (or primary) articulator, and the one that has less constriction, the minor (or secondary) articulator. For example, in [kʷ], Dorsal is the major articulator and Labial is the minor articulator. A sound can have two (or more) major articulators. For example, in [tɕ] both Dorsal and Coronal are major articulators. Since the major articulator is indicated with the presence of the feature [+stop] or [+fricative] (Keyser and Stevens 1994; Padgett 1995), there is no need to indicate it in other ways, such as a pointer (Sagey 1986), an asterisk (Kenstowicz 1994), or a special label called 'designated articulator' (Halle *et al.* 2000; Halle 2005).

Some studies propose another kind of complex segment, the so-called 'contour segments' or 'contour sound', in which a feature can take two or more values. Such a feature is called a 'contour feature'. For example, Sagey (1986) proposes (13) for a short contour tone.

(13)   Laryngeal

      ⌒

  [+H] [−H]

The articulator Laryngeal (similar to Vocal-cords in the present analysis) executes the tone feature [H] twice, first [+H] (a high tone) and then [−H] (a low tone). The result is a falling tone on a single (short) sound. However, Duanmu (1994) has argued for a constraint called the No-Contour Principle, rephrased in (14), where F is any feature. It rules out contour features and contour sounds in general, including short contour tones.

(14)   *No-Contour Principle*

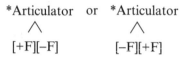

    *Articulator   or   *Articulator

      ⋀   ⋀

    [+F][−F]   [−F][+F]

I will show in Chapter 10 that as far as SC is concerned, there is no evidence for contour segments.

2.4.3. Length and diphthongs

Many languages have short and long sounds, such as [t] vs. [tt], or [a] vs. [aa] (or [aː]). The length of a sound can be represented either by timing slots, as in (15a), or by moras, as in (15b), where a mora is an alternative measure of length and is essentially a segment slot in the rhyme (see Broselow 1995 for a review of the two approaches).

(15)   (a) Timing slot representation of length

X	XX	X	XX	timing slot tier
|	V	|	V	
t	t	a	a	feature structure tier
[t]	[tt]	[a]	[aa]	transcription

    (b) Moraic representation of length

	m	m	mm	mora tier
	|	|	V	
t	t	a	a	feature structure tier
[t]	[tt]	[a]	[aa]	transcription

Each symbol on the feature structure tier is an abbreviation of a feature tree. The timing-slot representation indicates length directly; a short sound has one timing slot and a long sound has two (or sometimes three). In contrast, the moraic representation highlights the function of the mora, which plays a role in prosodic phonology. However, the moraic representation does not indicate length in a consistent way. For example, [tt] is longer than [a], but they both have one mora, and [tt] and [aa] have the same length, yet [tt] has one mora but [aa] has two. Consider also the representation in (16).

(16)
```
   mm  mm      mmmm      mm     mora tier
   | |  | |     | | | |     | |
  wɛ t  læ b   hɑ t ʌ b   t ʌ b
```
[wɛt.læb]   [hɑt.tʌb]   [tʌb]   transcription

'wet-lab'   'hot-tub'   'tub'

In *wet-lab* and *tub*, [t] is short, yet it has a mora in the former and no mora in the latter. In addition, [t] is short in *wet-lab* and long in *hot-tub*, yet it has one mora in both cases. In order to keep a more accurate representation of length, I will use timing slots in this study. The mora count can be inferred by interpreting each timing slot in the rhyme as a mora. Example (17) shows the representation of [pan], [paa], and [pai].

(17)
```
   S          S          S       syllable tier
   /\         /\         /\
  Xmm        Xmm        Xmm      timing slot/mora tier
  | | |       | ⋁        | | |
  p a n      p a        p a i    feature structure tier
  [pan]      [paa]      [pai]    transcription
```

Here [p], [a], [n], and [i] each have one unit of time (short), and [aa] has two (long). In addition, [p] has no mora, [a], [n], and [i] have one each, and [aa] has two.

2.4.4. Underspecification

It has been common practice to omit predictable features. For example, it suffices to call [u] a high back rounded vowel without saying that it is voiced, unaspirated, oral, etc. There is, nevertheless, a tacit assumption that, if one wants to, one can fully specify every feature for every sound, or fill in the unspecified features by redundancy rules (Halle 1962).

Underspecification theory claims that some features not only can but must be unspecified (for a review, see Steriade 1995). The evidence comes from two phenomena. The first is the transparency phenomenon: certain sounds allow certain features to pass through them in assimilation or harmony processes. A classic example is Turkish, shown in (18).

(18) Root   Pl.   Gen.   Pl. Gen.

      ip   ip-ler   ip-in   ip-ler-in   'rope'
      son   son-lar   son-un   son-lar-ɯn   'end'

In the plural column, the suffix vowel gets its values for [back] from the vowel of the root. In the genitive column, it gets its values for both [back] and [round] from the vowel of the root. In the plural genitive column, the genitive suffix can get values for [back] from the root vowel but not for [round], because the vowel in the plural suffix is [−round], which is itself passed on to the genitive suffix. The underspecification analysis is that features can pass through sounds that are not specified for them but not through sounds that are. In (18) consonants are unspecified for [back] and [round], so these features can pass through them. The vowel in the plural suffix is specified for [−round] but unspecified for [back], so it can acquire [−back] or [+back] and pass it on. The second phenomenon is that specified features resist change. For example, the vowel of the genitive suffix is specified for [+high], and it remains so no matter what the preceding vowel is. In general, the more specified a sound is, the less change it undergoes, and vice versa. The variation of the SC mid vowel is another case, shown in (19).

(19) Variant   Environment   Example
      [o]   after labial   [wo]   'I'
      [e]   after palatal   [je]   'leaf'
      [ɤ]   otherwise   [tʰɤ]   'special'

Since the mid vowel can change its backness and rounding but not its height, we can specify it as [−high, −low] (which means mid). This also agrees with the fact that there is only one mid vowel in SC, and therefore it does not contrast with any other vowel in [back] or [round]. Its surface [round] and [back] values can come from a neighbouring sound, as in [wo] and [je]. The [+back] feature in the [ɤ] variant can be assigned as a default value.

2.5. GLIDES

Let us now consider the sounds in SC. I start with glides. SC has three glides, [j, w, ɥ], as in [jan] 'smoke', [wan] 'curved', and [ɥan] 'round'.

The glides do not contrast with the corresponding high vowels [i, u, y], and the two sets can be treated as variants of each other. I will use the vowel symbol when the sound is the main vowel or the second part of a diphthong, such as [u] in [mu] 'wood' and [mau] 'cat'. I will use the glide symbol when the sound precedes the nuclear vowel, such as [w] in [wai] 'outside' and [sʷan] 'sour'.

When [w] occurs initially without a consonant, many Beijing speakers pronounce it as a labio-dental [ʋ] (J. Shen 1987; M. Hu 1991). According M. Hu (1991: 244–5), at least 90 per cent of Beijing speakers use [ʋ] to various degrees. The choice between [w] and [ʋ] depends on the main vowel. Chao (1927: 2) suggests that [ʋ] is better than [w] before [əi], but both [w] and [ʋ] can be used before other vowels. M. Hu (1991: 244–5) suggests that [w] is used before a low vowel, [ʋ] before a high vowel; however, he considers [o] to be a low vowel and [ə] a high vowel. J. Shen (1987) reports that [ʋ] can occur before any vowel except [o], before which [ʋ] is rare (J. Shen also reports that [wu] rarely becomes [ʋu]; in the present analysis, [ʋu] is underlyingly [u], so it is not included here). This is shown in (20) (see below for the transcription of the vowels).

(20) [wo]/*[ʋo]   'I'
      [wəi]/[ʋəi]   'tail'
      [wən]/[ʋən]   'literary'
      [wəŋ]/[ʋəŋ]   'Weng' (a name)
      [wa]/[ʋa]   'tile'
      [wai]/[ʋai]   'outside'
      [wan]/[ʋan]   'late'
      [waŋ]/[ʋaŋ]   'king'

The lack of *[ʋo] is due to the fact that [w] and [o] share the feature [+round] (see Chapter 3). It is worth noting that SC speakers other than those from Beijing generally do not use [ʋ]. It is also common for Beijing speakers of English to replace [w] with [ʋ], such as [ʋei] for *way*.

It has been proposed that [ɥ] can be reduced to [jw], articulated simultaneously (Hartman 1944; Hsueh 1986). In terms of feature representation, [ɥ] indeed contains the components of [j] and [w].

2.6. CONSONANTS

SC has nineteen consonants. In addition, there are three palatals and some syllabic consonants, to be discussed in separate sections. Also, in a syllable that begins with a vowel, there is sometimes a consonant-like articulatory gesture before the vowel. This gesture has been called the 'zero onset' (Chao 1968), which I discuss in Chapter 4. Example (21) shows the nineteen consonants in phonetic symbols.

(21)

	Labial	Dental	Retroflex	Velar
Stop	p, pʰ	t, tʰ		k, kʰ
Affricate		ts, tsʰ	ʈʂ, ʈʂʰ	
Fricative	f	s	ʂ, ʐ̩	x
Nasal	m	n		(ŋ)
Liquid		l		

The aspirated sounds [pʰ, tʰ, kʰ, tsʰ, ʈʂʰ] are often [pˣ, tˣ, kˣ, tsˣ, ʈʂˣ] before a back vowel. All nineteen consonants except [ŋ] can occur in onset position. For some speakers [ŋ] can occur initially as a variant of the 'zero onset', to be discussed below. In coda position, only [n] and [ŋ] can occur, where their oral closure is often incomplete (Y. Xu 1986; J. Wang 1993).

In some studies, such as M. Fu (1956), L. Wang (1979), and Duanmu (2000), the sound [ʐ̩] is transcribed as [r]. I choose [ʐ̩] here because the relation between [ʂ] and [ʐ̩] is similar to that between [s] and [z]. For example, in the syllable [sz] 'die', the rhyme is the voiced version of the onset, and in the syllable [ʂʐ̩] 'history', the rhyme is also the voiced version of the onset. In addition, in casual speech [sz] 'die' can undergo devoicing and become [ss], and [ʂʐ̩] 'history' can become [ʂʂ]. A criticism of this analysis is that [ʐ̩] is the only voiced obstruent; all other stops and fricatives are voiceless. A possible answer is that the distinction between [ʂ] and [ʐ̩] is not in voicing but in aspiration, [ʂʰ] and [ʂ] respectively. Another criticism of this analysis of [ʐ̩] is that [ʐ̩] does not have much friction and is therefore not like a fricative (M. Fu 1956; L. Wang 1979). A possible answer to this objection is that an unaspirated fricative always has much less friction than its aspirated counterpart; in other words, we expect [ʂ] (written as [ʐ̩] here) to have less friction than [ʂʰ].

The retroflex series [ʈʂ, ʈʂʰ, ʂ, ʐ̩] is a major characteristic of SC speakers from Beijing. SC speakers from other places often do not have [ʈʂ, ʈʂʰ, ʂ, ʐ̩] in their native dialects, so they often replace [ʈʂ, ʈʂʰ, ʂ, ʐ̩] with the dentals [ts, tsʰ, s, z], or they may use [ʈʂ, ʈʂʰ, ʂ] for [ts, tsʰ, s] in hypercorrection. For them there is no distinction between pairs like [tsai] 'again' and [ʈʂai] 'debt', [tsʰa] 'wipe' and [ʈʂʰa] 'fork', and [sa] 'sprinkle' and [ʂa] 'stupid'.

The unaspirated stops and affricates [p, t, k, ʈʂ, ts] can become voiced [b, d, g, ɖʐ̩, dz] when they occur in an unstressed syllable, such as [tsʷəi pa] → [tsʷəi ba] 'mouth' (M. Fu 1956: 3; Dong 1958: 75). It is possible to represent [p, t, k, t̺ʂ, ts, pʰ, tʰ, kʰ, t̺ʂʰ, tsʰ] as [b, d, g, d̺ʐ, dz, p, t, k, t̺ʂ, ts] instead; however, I do not explore the alternative here.

The place of constriction in the SC dentals is generally more forward than that in the corresponding American English sounds. I remember once seeing Professor Joan Morley demonstrate the American English [s]. She opened her mouth wide to show the alveolar closure by the tongue tip without stopping pronouncing [s]. The same cannot be done for SC speakers, for whom the tongue tip is usually on the lower teeth. Some studies call the SC [ts, tsʰ, s] dentals and the SC [t, tʰ, n, l] alveolars (Kratochvil 1968; Luo and Wang 1981). I follow Chao (1968) in treating them all as dentals. This agrees with the X-ray and palatographic study of D. Zhou and Wu (1963: 22), who found that the tongue tip in [ts, tsʰ, s] can be on either the upper or the lower teeth. In [t, tʰ, n, l] the tongue tip is generally on the upper teeth, although sometimes it is on the lower teeth, such as in the [n] of [an] (D. Zhou and Wu 1963: 39, and diagram 41). Luo and J. Wang (1981: 89) also note that the tongue tip in [ts, tsʰ, s] is generally on the lower teeth, and M. Fu (1956: 4) notes that some Beijing speakers use interdentals [t̪θ, t̪θʰ, θ] instead of the dentals [ts, tsʰ, s].

The place of [x] is variable. It is possible to consider [x] to be [h] instead, whose place is assimilated to the following vowel. On the other hand, [x] is a more symmetric choice in that every place of articulation has a fricative. If we choose [h], the velar place would lack a fricative and [h] would be the only glottal sound.

2.7. CONSONANT–GLIDE COMBINATIONS

A CG combination is made of a consonant C and a glide G. All CG combinations occur before the nuclear vowel. In most studies, including recent ones (e.g. H. Wang 1999: 128–9), CG is analysed as two sounds. However, as Chao (1934: 42) points out, this is over-analysis (see section 2.2.4), because phonetically CG is a single sound in SC. For example, in [sʷan] 'sour', [s] and [ʷ] are articulated at the same time. In contrast, [sw] in English words like *sway* are two sounds, in that the lip rounding of [w] occurs after [s]. As will be discussed in Chapter 4, the reason CG is a single sound in Chinese is that there is only one slot in the onset, which C and G must share. In what follows I will write CG as a single sound. Given eighteen consonants ([ŋ] does not occur initially) and three glides, there are fifty-four possible CG combinations, of which twenty-nine are found. This is shown in (22) and exemplified in (23), where a minus sign indicates a missing CG.

(22) CG combinations (in phonetic symbols)

	C	Cʲ	Cʷ	Cᶣ
labial	p	pʲ	–	–
	pʰ	pʰʲ	–	–
	m	mʲ	–	–
	f	–	–	–
dental	t	tʲ	tʷ	–
	tʰ	tʰʲ	tʰʷ	–
	n	nʲ	nʷ	nᶣ
	l	lʲ	lʷ	lᶣ
	ts	(tɕ)	tsʷ	(tɕʷ)
	tsʰ	(tɕʰ)	tsʰʷ	(tɕʰʷ)
	s	(ɕ)	sʷ	(ɕʷ)
velar	k	–	kʷ	–
	kʰ	–	kʰʷ	–
	x	–	xʷ	–
retroflex	tʂ	–	tʂʷ	–
	tʂʰ	–	tʂʰʷ	–
	ʂ	–	ʂʷ	–
	ʐ	–	ʐʷ	–

(23) CG combinations (examples, in phonetic symbols)

	C	Cʲ	Cʷ	Cᶣ
labial	p	pʲan 'change'	–	–
	pʰ	pʰʲan 'cheat'	–	–
	m	mʲan 'noodles'	–	–
	f	–	–	–
dental	t	tʲan 'store'	tʷan 'broken'	–
	tʰ	tʰʲan 'sky'	tʰʷan 'roll'	–
	n	nʲan 'year'	nʷan 'warm'	nᶣe 'cruel'
	l	lʲan 'link'	lʷan 'disorder'	lᶣe 'omit'

	ts	tɕan 'sharp'	tsʷan 'drill'	tɕʷan 'donate'
	tsʰ	tɕʰan 'owe'	tsʰʷan 'usurp'	tɕʰʷan 'persuade'
	s	ɕan 'thread'	sʷan 'garlic'	ɕʷan 'select'
velar	k	–	kʷan 'close'	–
	kʰ	–	kʰʷan 'broad'	–
	x	–	xʷan 'joyful'	–
retroflex	tʂ	–	tʂʷan 'brick'	–
	tʂʰ	–	tʂʰʷan 'boat'	–
	ʂ	–	ʂʷan 'bolt'	–
	ʐ	–	ʐʷan 'soft'	–

Although [pʷ, pʰʷ, mʷ, fʷ] are generally missing, there is an exception. For many SC speakers, they occur in [pʷo, pʰʷo, mʷo, fʷo]. I return to this case in Chapter 3. The missing CG combinations call for an explanation. There are two views on such matters. According to Blevins (2003), gaps in a language may be due to historical accidents, and it may be useless to try to account for them synchronically. Alternatively, it is possible that most of the gaps are due to phonological constraints. Before I discuss the solution, several remarks are in order. First, the lack of [fʲ] is probably accidental, since all other labials can combine with [j]. Secondly, where we expect palatalized dentals [tsʲ, tsʰʲ, sʲ] and [tsᶣ, tsʰᶣ, sᶣ] (shown in parentheses), we find palatals [tɕ, tɕʰ, ɕ] and [tɕʷ, tɕʰʷ, ɕʷ]. In addition, [nʲ] can become a palatal [ɲ], [nᶣ] a labialized palatal [ɲʷ]. For example, [nʲan] 'year' can be pronounced as [ɲan], [nᶣe] 'cruel' as [ɲʷe]. This is because palatalized dentals and palatals have the same articulators; I will return to this point. Finally, of the seven dentals, five can combine with [ᶣ] and two cannot. It is reasonable to assume that dentals can in principle combine with [ᶣ] and that the lack of [tᶣ, tʰᶣ] is due to independent reasons. If one assumes that dentals cannot in principle combine with [ᶣ], then there is no explanation for the presence of the other five combinations. Under these considerations, a generalization emerges, stated in (24), where a plus sign means a good combination and a minus sign, a bad one.

(24)   Generalization on CG combinations

	[j]	[w]	[ɥ]
labial	+	−	−
dental	+	+	+
velar	−	+	−
retroflex	−	+	−

In the present analysis, the pattern is explained as follows. First, consider the retroflex sounds. In a retroflex the tongue tip is curled back, which tends to push the tongue body back, yet [j] and [ɥ] require the tongue body to be fronted. The lack of retroflex [j] and retroflex [ɥ], therefore, is probably due to articulatory ease. (This is not to say that retroflex [j] is impossible, but that it is hard; retroflex [j] does occur in Russian, for example.) The other cases can be explained in terms of articulators in feature structure. In particular, if the articulators for glides are simply Dorsal for [j], Labial for [w], and Dorsal and Labial for [ɥ], then (24) can be translated into (25).

(25)   Articulator analysis of CG combinations

	[j]	[w]	[ɥ]
	Dor	Lab	Dor-Lab
Lab	+	−	−
Cor (dental)	+	+	+
Dor (velar)	−	+	−

Whenever there is a conflict between the articulators of C and G (i.e. when an articulator is found in both), the combination is bad. Otherwise the combination is good. This result is expected if CG is a single sound, in which each articulator can occur only once.

If glides have a more complex structure, the same conclusion can be drawn. Let us assume that the SC glides have the structures in (26).

(26)   SC glides

When C and G have different articulators, as in [p]+[j], all articulators can be kept. This is shown in (27).

(31)   Articulator analysis of CG combinations

	[j]	[w]	[ɥ]	
	Dor–Cor	Dor–Lab	Dor–Cor–Lab	
	|	|	|	|
	[–back]	[+round]	[–back]	[+round]
Lab	+	–	–	
Cor	+	+	+	
Dor	–	+	–	

I am not aware of any account of missing CGs in the traditional literature which over-analyses CG as a sequence of two sounds. However, a possible solution in the traditional approach is as follows; the lack of retroflex [j] and retroflex [ɥ] can be attributed to articulatory ease, similar to the present analysis; and the lack of other CG combinations can be attributed to articulator dissimilation, which prevents two identical articulators from occurring in a row, as stated in (32).

(32)   *Articulator dissimilation*
       Identical articulators cannot occur in succession.

While Articulator dissimilation can correctly rule out some missing CGs, it is hard to account for Cor+[j] and Cor+[ɥ], since [j] and [ɥ] also contain Cor. In addition, Articulator dissimilation fails elsewhere, such as CV, GV, or across syllables, as can be seen in (33).

(33)

Labial–Labial	Labial–Labial	Dorsal–Dorsal	Coronal–Coronal
CV	GV	CV	CVC.CV
[mu]	[wo]	[kɤ]	[çan.tai]
'female'	'me'	'song'	'present time'

Evidently, CG is the only 'sequence' to which Articulator dissimilation applies. The special status of CG remains a stipulation in the over-analysis. In contrast, in the present analysis there is no need for the stipulation. Since CG is a single sound, each articulator can only occur once. Since CV and GV are not single sounds, they are not subject to the same restriction.

A reviewer suggests that the lack of Lab [w] or Lab [ɥ] is due to perceptual reasons. In particular, there is not much transition of F2 in such clusters and salient transitions are preferred for perception. However, there is no Lab–Lab constraint against CV or GV, as seen in (33). If phonetic salience were the reason, one would expect CV and GV to be subject to the Lab–Lab constraint, too.

2.8. PALATALS AS CONSONANT–GLIDE COMBINATIONS

Besides the nineteen consonants in (21), most studies also list three palatals in SC, [tɕ, tɕʰ, ɕ], as in [tɕi] 'chicken', [tɕʰi] 'seven', and [ɕi] 'west'. Synchronically the palatal series is in complementary distribution with the velars [k, kʰ, x], the dentals [ts, tsʰ, s], and the retroflexes [tʂ, tʂʰ, ʂ], shown in (34).

(34)
Series	[tɕ, tɕʰ, ɕ]	[k, kʰ, x]	[ts, tsʰ, s]	[tʂ, tʂʰ, ʂ]
With [j, ɥ]/[i, y]	yes	no	no	no
Without [j, ɥ]/[i, y]	no	yes	yes	yes

The palatal series cooccurs with the prenuclear glides [j, ɥ] or the high vowels [i, y], but the other series do not. It is possible, therefore, to identify the palatal series with one of the other series. However, opinions differ as to which series the palatals should be identified with, or whether the palatals should be recognized as an independent series. For example, Hartman (1944) identifies the palatal series with the dental series without giving phonological evidence (see C. Cheng 1973: ch. 5 for a review). Chao (1934, 1968) identifies the palatal series with the velar series, but C. Cheng (1973) found Chao's arguments questionable. As a result, Cheng treats the palatals as an independent series. Hsueh (1986: 34–6) also identifies the palatal series with the velar series, based on some reduplication expressions, but the evidence does not seem to be strong either. In this section I argue instead that palatals are a special case of consonant–glide combinations. In addition, I will show that palatals have a special relation with dentals.

As seen in the CG combinations, six palatalized dentals, [tsʲ, tsʰʲ, sʲ] and [tsɥ, tsʰɥ, sɥ], are replaced by the palatals [tɕ, tɕʰ, ɕ] and [tɕʷ, tɕʰʷ, ɕʷ]. However, not all speakers do this. There are two varieties of pronunciation. Variety A uses palatalized dentals, variety B, palatals. This is exemplified in (35).

(35)
C+G	Variety A	Variety B	
[ts]+[j]	[tsʲan]	[tɕan]	'sharp'
[tsʰ]+[j]	[tsʰʲan]	[tɕʰan]	'owe'
[s]+[j]	[sʲan]	[ɕan]	'thread'
[ts]+[ɥ]	[tsɥan]	[tɕʷan]	'donate'
[tsʰ]+[ɥ]	[tsʰɥan]	[tɕʰʷan]	'persuade'
[s]+[ɥ]	[sɥan]	[ɕʷan]	'select'

Variety A is common among children and female speakers, as well as some males (S. Xu 1957; Cao 1987; M. Hu 1991: 230–43). According to Cao (1987), in a survey of 200 speakers in Beijing, 85 per cent of females and 29 per cent of males used variety A to various degrees. The presence of the two varieties suggests a link between palatalized dentals and palatals, which is revealed in a feature analysis. Consider [s]+[j] and [s]+[ɥ], shown in (36).

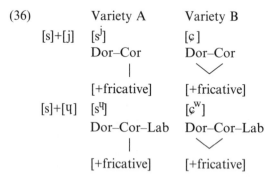

(36)   Variety A   Variety B

[s]+[j]   [sʲ]   [ɕ]
           Dor–Cor   Dor–Cor
              | ⌄
           [+fricative]   [+fricative]

[s]+[ɥ]   [sɥ]   [ɕʷ]
           Dor–Cor–Lab   Dor–Cor–Lab
              | ⌄
           [+fricative]   [+fricative]

In variety A, the major articulator (in this case, the one that performs [+fricative]) is Cor only. In variety B, both Cor and Dor are the major articulators. Thus, the two varieties use the same articulators but differ in whether Dor is a major or a minor articulator. The alternations between [tsʲ, tsʰʲ, tsɥ, tsʰɥ] and [tɕ, tɕʰ, tɕʷ, tɕʰʷ], as well as between [nʲ, nɥ] and [ɲ, ɲʷ], are explained in the same way.

  Besides being influenced by the prenuclear glide, SC consonants can also be palatalized, labialized, or both before a high vowel. This is exemplified in (37).

(37)   [li] → [lʲi]   'inside'
       [lu] → [lʷu]   'road'
       [ly] → [lᶣy]   'green'

In feature analysis, this can be seen as feature spreading from the high vowel to the consonant, shown in (38).

(38)   [l   i]   →   [lʲ   i]

       Root   Root   Root   Root
        | ⌒   ⌒   ⌒
       Cor   Dor Cor   Cor Dor Dor Cor
              | ⌄
            [–back]   [–back]

When the [−back] of [i] spreads to [l], it activates the articulator Dor in [l], whereby [l] becomes Cor and Dor, which is [lʲ]. Interestingly, palatals are also found before front vowels for variety B speakers when C is a dental stop, fricative, or affricate, as shown in (39).

(39) Variety A   Variety B

[nʲi]	[ɲi]	'you'
[tsʲi]	[tɕi]	'chicken'
[tsʰʲi]	[tɕʰi]	'seven'
[sʲi]	[ɕi]	'west'
[nᵁy]	[ɲʷy]	'female'
[tsᵁy]	[tɕʷy]	'tangerine'
[tsʰᵁy]	[tɕʰʷy]	'curved'
[sᵁy]	[ɕʷy]	'weak'

The pronunciation of variety A suggests that the original consonants in such words are dentals, which become palatalized (and labialized) through feature spreading from a high vowel, illustrated in (38). Variety B further changes Dor into [+stop] or [+fricative] according to the C, turning CG into a palatal. The two processes are compared in (40), using the word 'west'.

(40)   Underlying   Variety A   Variety B
       [s   i]   →   [sʲ   i]   →   [ɕ   i]

       Root   Root   Root   Root   Root   Root
        | ╱╲   ╱╲   ╱╲   ╱╲   ╱╲
       Cor   Dor Cor   Cor Dor Dor Cor   Cor Dor Dor Cor
        | | | ╲╱   ╲╱   ╲╱
      [+fric][−back]   [+fric][−back]   [+fric][−back]

While there is a connection between dentals and palatals, there is also a connection between velars and palatals. Chao (1931, 1934, 1968) refers to a language game by Beijing speakers in which [k] changes to [tɕ] when it combines with [j] or [i]. In feature analysis, the change from [k]+[j] to [tɕ] can be represented in (41).

(41)   [k]   +   [j]   →   [kʲ]   →   [tɕ]
       Dor   Dor–Cor   Dor–Cor   Dor–Cor
        | | ╱╲   ╱╲
     [+stop]   [−back]   [−back][+stop]   [−back][+stop]

After the Dor of [k] merges with that of [j], the feature [+stop] further spreads from Dor to Cor. One might suggest that perhaps like dental+[j], velar+[j] also gives palatals in regular CG combinations. However, this cannot explain why palatals can alternate with palatalized dentals (cf. varieties A and B), but not with palatalized velars.

The articulatory relation between palatals on the one hand and palatalized dentals and palatalized dorsals, on the other, can also explain the fact that present-day palatals in SC come from two historical sources: palatalized dentals and palatalized dorsals. Two examples are shown in (42) (from L. Wang 1980: 79).

(42)   Historical   Present
       [kʲan] →   [tɕan] 'see'
       [tsʲan] →   [tɕan] 'arrow'

In addition, the articulatory analysis can account for the fact that in translation from English into Chinese both dentals and velars can turn into palatals, as noted by Y. Lin (1989: 46). Two examples are shown in (43), where [si] is translated into [ɕi] and [ki] is translated into [tɕi].

(43)   'Wisconsin' → [wəi sz kʰaŋ ɕin]
       'Kentucky' → [kʰən tʰa tɕi]

In the present analysis, palatals, palatalized dentals, and palatalized velars have the same articulators, Cor and Dor, which explains both the historical facts and the translation facts.

2.9. SYLLABIC CONSONANTS

SC has three syllabic nasals, [m], [n], and [ŋ], which mostly occur in interjections, such as [hm] (showing contempt), [hŋ] (showing contempt), [m] ('yes'), [n] ('yes'), and [ŋ] ('yes'). Although such words have a somewhat marginal status, they have been included in some dictionaries, such as *Xiandai Hanyu Cidian* (Chinese Academy of Social Sciences Institute of Linguistics 1978).

More productive are the syllabic consonants [z] and [z̩], which do not contrast with each other: [z] occurs after the dentals [ts, tsʰ, s], [z̩] after the retroflexes [tʂ, tʂʰ, ʂ, ʐ]. This is exemplified in (44).

(44)   [z] after [ts, tsʰ, s]:   [tsz]   [tsʰz]   [sz]
                                       'self'   'word'   'silk'

       [z̩] after [tʂ, tʂʰ, ʂ, ʐ]:   [tʂz̩]   [tʂʰz̩]   [ʂz̩]   [ʐz̩]
                                       'know'   'eat'   'poem'   'sun'

Neither [z] nor [ʐ] occurs after the palatals [tɕ, tɕʰ, ɕ], or after any other consonant. Some linguists, perhaps since Karlgren (1915–26), consider [z] and [ʐ] to be 'apical vowels'. There are three reasons. There seems to be an assumption that every syllable must have a vowel—this view has been reiterated in Cheung (1986), Hsueh (1986), and Coleman (1996, 2001); secondly, some researchers argue that [z] and [ʐ] are phonetically like a vowel. For example, Howie (1976: 10) argues that [z] and [ʐ] have formants, which is a property of vowels. In addition, C. Cheng (1973: 13), citing the X-ray study of D. Zhou and Wu (1963), notes that the back of the tongue is raised in [z], similar to a vowel articulation. Thirdly, it has been suggested that [z] and [ʐ] are in complementary distribution with [i] and so they can be analysed as allophones of the same phoneme. Since [i] is a vowel, it is better to consider [z] and [ʐ] to be vowels, too.

On the other hand, there are reasons to consider [z] and [ʐ] consonants (see Dong 1958: 37; Chao 1968: 24; E. Pulleyblank 1984; Ramsey 1987; Wiese 1997: 239–44). First, [z, ʐ] are a voiced prolongation of the preceding consonant. Syllabic [z] is similar to a voiced [s], syllabic [ʐ], to the onset [ʐ]. Secondly, having formants or a dorsal articulation is not an exclusive property of vowels. For example, [l] has formants and [k] and [x] have dorsal articulation, but they are all consonants. With regard to [z], D. Zhou and Wu's (1963: 35) X-ray study indeed shows a somewhat raised back of the tongue, but the same is also true of [ts], [tsʰ], and [s] (*ibid.*: 31–2). As for [ʐ] (*ibid.*: 35), there is no raising of the back of the tongue. Thus, phonetic evidence does not show that [z] and [ʐ] are vowels. Finally, [z, ʐ] are articulated quite differently from [i]; for example, while [z] and [ʐ] can barely rhyme with each other in poetry, neither rhymes with [i] (see Chao 1927). Thus, even if [z, ʐ] are in complementary distribution with [i], they need not be analysed as variants of the same vowel.

2.10. VOWELS

If we exclude the two 'apical vowels', discussed under syllabic consonants above, and the retroflex vowel, to be discussed below, SC has five vowel phonemes, shown in (45) (I denote the mid vowel as [ə] and the low vowel as [a]).

(45)   SC vowel phonemes

high	[i	y	u]
mid	[ə]		
low	[a]		

Some researchers have proposed to reduce the vowel inventory further. For example, J. Wang (1993) suggests that the high vowels are glides underlyingly; if so there are just two vowels. The most extreme proposal is made by E. Pulleyblank (1984), who suggests that [i, y, u] are glides, [ə] is not specified at the underlying level, and [a] is a pharyngeal glide instead of a vowel. If so, SC has no vowel at all. I will, however, not pursue such approaches here.

A SC vowel can carry one of four tones to distinguish different words. Some examples are shown in (46), where the digits 1 to 4 denote the four tones.

(46)   Tone 1:   [ma1] 'mother'   [ɕi1] 'west'
       Tone 2:   [ma2] 'hemp'   [ɕi2] 'mat'
       Tone 3:   [ma3] 'horse'   [ɕi3] 'wash'
       Tone 4:   [ma4] 'scold'   [ɕi4] 'thin'

Some studies (e.g. M. Fu 1956: 12; J. Zhang 1957: 15) analyse [a1, a2, a3, a4, i1, i2, i3, i4, . . .] as separate vowel phonemes. Their assumption is that the tone of a syllable falls on the nuclear vowel alone, but I will argue in Chapter 10 that the assumption is incorrect. In what follows I analyse tones separately in order to keep the vowel inventory small.

2.10.1. High vowels

[i] and [u] are ordinary high vowels, similar to those in English. [y] is a front, high, rounded vowel. A minimal contrastive triplet is shown in (47).

(47)   [li]   [ly]   [lu]
       'force'   'filter'   'road'

[i] and [u], but not [y], can serve as the second part of a diphthong, as in [lai] 'come' and [lau] 'work'. All three high vowels can occur before a non-high vowel, in which case they are written as glides, as shown in (48).

(48)   [jan]   [ɥan]   [wan]
       'smoke'   'grievance'   'curve'

As discussed in section 2.5, [w] can alternate with [ʋ] for many Beijing speakers. The high vowels can also occur in CG combinations, where they are represented as glides, as shown in (49).

(49)   [lʲe]   [lᶣe]   [kʷa]
       'crack'   'omit'   'melon'

Some studies propose that [y] can be replaced by [iu] (see Hartman 1944; Hockett 1947; Martin 1957; Hsueh 1986), which I do not pursue. Otherwise there is little controversy in the analysis of the high vowels.

2.10.2. The mid vowel

The mid vowel has several variants and there is some disagreement on how to transcribe them. According to S. Xu (1980: 184), there are five variants, shown in (50), where [E] denotes a vowel that is higher than [ɛ] but lower than [e] (S. Xu 1980: 33).

(50)   Variants of the mid vowel

Variant	Sample	Environment
[o]	[wo] 'I' [pʷo] 'wave'	In open syllables, after labials
[E]	[jE] 'leaf' [ɥE] 'crack'	In open syllables, after palatals ([j], [ɥ], [Cʲ], or [Cʲ])
[ɤ]	[kɤ] 'song' [sɤ] 'colour'	In open syllables, not after a labial or a palatal
[e]	[fei] 'fly' [kei] 'give'	Before [-i]
[ə]	[kəu] 'dog' [mən] 'door' [məŋ] 'dream'	Before [-u, -n, -ŋ]

Chao (1968) and C. Cheng (1973) do not distinguish [E] and [e], and they write [e] for both cases. J. Wang (1993) does make the distinction, but she writes [e] for S. Xu's [E] and [ə] for S. Xu's [e]. For S. Xu's [ə], Chao (1968: 24) distinguishes three variants, shown in (51).

(51)

Environment	S. Xu	Chao	
before [n]	[mən]	[mən]	'door'
before [u]	[kəu]	[kou]	'dog'
before [ŋ]	[məŋ]	[mʌŋ]	'dream'

Several other researchers also write [ou] for S. Xu's [əu], although M. Fu (1956: 6) points out that [ə] is only 'slightly round' in [əu]. On the other hand, Chao's distinction between [ə] and [ʌ] is not recognized by others. M. Fu (1956: 6) suggests that the mid vowel is [ɤ] after a labial, such as [wɤ] 'I'. S. Xu (1980: 54) also acknowledges that the vowel in what he (and most others) writes as [wo] is a 'neutral vowel' [ə] and is not fully rounded. The difference in transcription may in part reflect variation among SC speakers, since I have heard both [o] and [ɤ] after labials, such as [pʰʷo] and [pʰɤ] for 'slope'; it is especially common to use [ɤ] after labials in north east China. C. Cheng (1973: 21) suggests that the difference between [ɤ] in an open syllable and [ə] in a closed one is not so much in quality as in length. As I will argue in Chapter 4, full syllables in SC have two timing slots in the rhyme, so that a vowel is long in an open syllable and short in a closed syllable. If so, the difference between [ɤ] and [ə] can be represented in (52).

(52)   [ɤ]   [ən]   S. Xu's transcription

     XX   XX   length representation (X = timing slots)
     V | |
     ə   ə n

What we can conclude so far is that the mid vowel can change its frontness, and possibly its rounding, but not its height. Therefore, following underspecification discussed earlier, it can be represented as [−high, −low] underlyingly, without specifying [back] or [round]. The surface variants of the mid vowel are discussed at greater length in Chapter 3.

While most analyses assume that all mid-vowel variants in SC belong to the same phoneme, there are some cases that complicate the picture. In SC there is an interjection [o] (or [ʔo]) 'I see', which contrasts with [ɤ] (or [ʔɤ]) 'goose'. If interjections are treated as words, then [o] and [ɤ] (or [ʔo] and [ʔɤ]) form a minimal pair, and so [o] and [ɤ] must be analysed as different vowels. Similarly, there is an interjection [e] (or [ʔe]) 'hello'. If it is also treated as a word, then we have a minimally contrastive triplet [o]-[ɤ]-[e] (or [ʔo]-[ʔɤ]-[ʔe]), which means that [o], [ɤ], and [e] are three different mid vowels. Some linguists indeed consider there to be two or more mid vowel phonemes in SC (H. Wang 1999: 38). But if [o], [ɤ], and [e] are indeed different vowel phonemes, we need to explain why they are mostly in complementary distribution except for a few interjections. Perhaps it is unrealistic to expect the phonemes of a language to be perfectly clear and evenly distributed.

2.10.3. **The low vowel**

Like the mid vowel, the low vowel has several variants, and there is again some disagreement on their surface values. According to S. Xu (1980: 183), the low vowel has five variants, shown in (53), where [A] is a central low vowel, [ɑ] a back low vowel, [a] a front low vowel, [æ] a vowel between [a] and [ɛ], and [ɐ] a central mid low vowel (S. Xu 1980: 33).

(53) Variants of the low vowel (S. Xu 1980)

Variant	Sample	Environment
[A]	[pA] 'eight' [jA] 'duck'	In open syllables
[ɑ]	[tʰɑu] 'peach' [tʰɑŋ] 'sugar'	In closed syllables, before [u] or [ŋ]
[a]	[kʰai] 'open' [san] 'three'	In closed syllables, before [n] or [i] and not after a palatal
[æ]	[jæn] 'salt' [pʲæn] 'side'	In closed syllables, before [n] and after [j] or [Cʲ]
[ɐ]	[ɥɐn] 'round' [ɕʷɐn] 'select'	In closed syllables, before [n] and after [ɥ] or [Cᶣ]

M. Fu (1956) and Dong (1958) propose different values for the low vowel in an open syllable or before [u] and [ŋ]. In (54) I compare their proposals with S. Xu's.

(54)

	Before [u] or [ŋ]	In open syllables
S. Xu (1980)	back	central
M. Fu (1956)	central	back
Dong (1958)	back	back

M. Fu (1956: 6) also suggests a difference in the low vowel between [jaŋ] 'sheep' and [paŋ] 'help', which is not shared by other studies. With regard to the three non-back values distinguished by S. Xu, there is again disagreement. In (55) I compare four proposals (the underscore in the top row indicates the location of the low vowel; [a] is front in all transcriptions).

(55)

	[j_n]	[ɥ_n]	[_i]/[_n]
S. Xu (1980)	[æ]	[ɐ]	[a]
M. Fu (1956)	[ɛ]	[ɛ]	[a]
Chao (1968)	[ɛ]	[a]	[a]
Y. Lin (1989)	[ɛ]	[a]([ɛ])	[a]

Unlike S. Xu and most others, J. Wang (1993) argues that the low vowel is unspecified for frontness in a closed syllable (see Chapter 3). Overall, the low vowel remains low and unrounded, but can probably change its backness. Therefore, it can be represented as [+low, –round] underlyingly. I return to the analysis of its variants in Chapter 3.

2.10.4. The retroflex vowel

Besides the five vowels [i, u, y, ə, a], SC also has a so-called retroflex vowel, which I transcribe as [ɚ], although it has also been transcribed as [r]. It occurs in two cases: in words without a suffix, [ɚ] only occurs in the syllable [ɚ], which is sometimes pronounced as a diphthong [aɚ]; and, [ɚ] can occur as a suffix and replace the coda of the syllable it attaches to (see Chapter 9). The two cases are illustrated in (56).

(56) (a) Words without suffixes: in [ɚ] (or [aɚ]) only
          [ɚ2]   [ɚ3]   [ɚ4]
          'son'   'ear'   'two'
      (b) The [ɚ] suffix
          Unsuffixed   [kan1] 'dried food'
          Suffixed   [kaɚ1] 'dried food'

The retroflex vowel [ɚ] and the retroflex consonant [ʐ] are not phonetically identical. Phonologically, they are mostly in complementary distribution: [ʐ] occurs in the onset and the nucleus, whereas [ɚ] mostly occurs in the coda. Chapter 9 discusses [ɚ] further.

2.10.5. Diphthongs

In feature theory a diphthong is analysed as a combination of two vowels. Ignoring prenuclear glides, which in the present analysis are in the onset (see also Chapter 4), and the retroflex vowel, SC has four diphthongs. They are made by combining the mid or the low vowel with the high vowels [i] or [u], shown in (57). The high vowel [y] does not occur in a diphthong.

(57)   [i]   [u]
      mid   əi   əu
      low   ai   au

As discussed above, there is some disagreement on the surface values of the diphthongs, to which I return in Chapter 3.

Many analyses of SC also list triphthongs, which consist of a diphthong and a prenuclear glide. But if the prenuclear glide is in the onset, as I suggest, SC has no triphthongs.

2.10.6. Vowel length

SC has full syllables and weak syllables (see Chapter 4). Phonetically, full syllables have similar duration. This means that a vowel is long in full open syllables, such as [maː], and short in full closed syllables, such as [man] or [mai]. It also means that vowel length is not contrastive in full syllables, since it is predictable from syllable structure.

Weak syllables are shorter than full syllables. According to Woo (1969) and M. Lin and Yan (1988), a vowel in a weak CV syllable is about half as long as one in a full CV syllable. However, vowel length is not contrastive here either, since vowels carry tone in full syllables but are generally toneless in weak syllables. An example is given in (58).

(58) [kɤɤ kɤ] 'brother'
        V
        H

The first syllable has a long vowel, as well as a high tone. The second syllable has a short vowel and no tone. To distinguish the two vowels, we only need to mention one difference, either length or tone. Since tone must be assumed for SC anyway, most studies choose to ignore length, and transcribe the word as (59) instead.

(59) *Representation omitting length*

     [kɤ kɤ] 'brother'
      |
      H

However, it is important to keep in mind that vowels are long in full CV syllables. This fact is especially relevant when we discuss syllable weight and stress in Chapter 6.

2.11. HOW MANY SOUNDS ARE THERE IN STANDARD CHINESE?

I have introduced all the sounds in SC (except the 'zero onset', to be discussed in Chapter 4). Let us now consider how many phonemes there are. Example (60) summarizes the types of sound discussed so far.

(60)

Type	Number	Comment
glides	3	same as high vowels
consonants	19	excluding palatals
CG combinations	29	including palatals

syllabic consonants	2	[z, z̩], in complementary distribution
vowels	6	including a retroflex vowel

The sounds are not all surface phones, since some represent two or more variants each. For example, each unaspirated stop or affricate also has a voiced variant, and the mid vowel represents at least four variants, [o, e, ə, ɤ]. The sounds are not all phonemes either. For example, there is overlap between vowels and glides and among consonants, glides, and CG combinations.

I propose that there are three levels in the analysis of SC sounds: the underlying level, the syllabic level, and the phonetic level. The analysis is shown in (61), using [ə] for the mid vowel and [a] for the low vowel.

(61)   Analysis of SC sounds

Level	Sounds	Comments
Underlying	19 consonants	[p, pʰ, f, m, t, tʰ, ts, tsʰ, s, n, l, tʂ, tʂʰ, ʂ, z̩, k, kʰ, x, ŋ]
	6 vowels	[i, u, y, ə, a, ɚ]
Syllabic	glides	high vowels in the onset
	CG combinations	C and G sharing one onset slot
	syllabic consonants	empty rhyme slots filled by C
Phonetic	allophones	e.g. [o, e, ə, ɤ] for the mid vowel

The twenty-five underlying phonemes are assumed in most studies and need little comment. The analysis of allophones will be discussed in Chapter 3. Let us now focus on the syllabic level. I will propose in Chapter 4 that a full SC syllable has three timing slots, shown in (62), where each slot in the rhyme counts as a mora and where the first rhyme slot is the nucleus and the second the coda.

(62)   *Full syllable in SC*
```
     S      Syllable
    /\
   O  R     Onset/Rhyme
   |  /\
   X  XX    timing slots
```

When a high vowel occurs before a non-high vowel, the latter is linked to the nucleus and the high vowel must be linked to the onset. This is because a non-high vowel cannot be in the coda in SC; it cannot be in the onset either, because otherwise there is no place for the preceding high vowel to go. An example is shown in (63), where I have omitted the onset–rhyme labels.

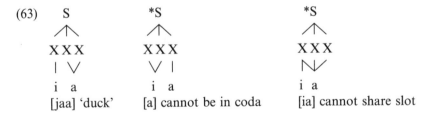

(63)   S   *S   *S

    X X X   X X X   X X X

    i   a   i   a   i   a

   [jaa] 'duck'   [a] cannot be in coda   [ia] cannot share slot

In the well-formed structure, the high vowel in the onset is transcribed as a glide. In addition, because there are two slots in the rhyme, [a] is linked to both and becomes a long vowel. It is important to note that [ia] cannot share a timing slot. The reason is that the features of [i] and [a] are in conflict, because [i] is [+high, −low] and [a] is [−high, +low], which cannot both occur in the same sound (see section 2.4.2, and Duanmu 1994). Next consider CG combinations, exemplified in (64).

(64)   S

    XXX

   l i a   [lʲaa] 'two'

Underlyingly, there are three sounds, [l, i, a]. Again, [a] must be linked to the nucleus (and extended to the coda). [l] and [i] must then share the onset slot, giving a complex sound [lʲ]. [lʲ] can be represented as a single sound because [l] and [i] do not have conflicting features. In fact, as discussed in Section 2.7, only those CG combinations that can form a complex sound are found in SC.

Next, consider the syllabic consonants [z, z̩]. Some studies, such as M. Fu (1956), L. Wang (1980), and S. Xu (1980), suggest that they are in complementary distribution with [i], as shown in (65). If so, [i, z, z̩] can be seen as variants of the same phoneme.

(65) Variant Environment

    [z]   Only after [ts, tsʰ, s]
    [z̩]   Only after [tʂ, tʂʰ, ʂ, z̩]
    [i]   Not after [ts, tsʰ, s] or [tʂ, tʂʰ, ʂ, z̩]

However, in the present analysis [i] can occur also after [ts, tsʰ, s], which become palatalized for some speakers and palatals for others, as shown in (66).

(66)   Underlying   Variety A   Variety B
        [tsi]   [tsʲi]   [tɕi]   'chicken'
        [tsʰi]   [tsʰʲi]   [tɕʰi]   'seven'
        [si]   [sʲi]   [ɕi]   'west'

Thus, there seem to be underlying minimal pairs, such as [sz] 'silk' and [si] 'west'. If this is accepted at least [z] and [i] are not in complementary distribution and cannot be analysed as variants of the same phoneme.

An alternative analysis is to consider syllabic [z, z̩] to belong to a separate phoneme (see e.g. C. Cheng 1973). Still another analysis, which I prefer, is to assume that syllabic [z, z̩] do not come from an underlying phoneme but are triggered by an empty nuclear slot (see E. Pulleyblank 1984; Y. Lin 1989; Wiese 1997; among others). The analysis of [tszz] 'word' is shown in (67) (only relevant nodes of feature geometry are shown).

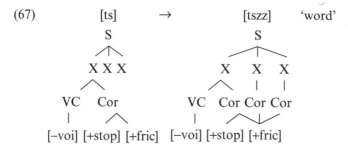

(67)   [ts]   →   [tszz]   'word'
               S   S
              ⟨VC Cor⟩   ⟨VC Cor Cor Cor⟩
           [−voi] [+stop] [+fric] [−voi] [+stop] [+fric]

The word starts with the affricate [ts], which has two articulators, Vocalcords, which dominates the features [−voice], and Coronal, which dominates [+stop] and [+fricative]. Assuming that the nucleus does not allow [+stop] or [−voice], [ts] must be linked to the onset. Next, the empty slots in the rhyme trigger the spreading of [+fricative], which activates Coronal. The result is [ts] in the onset and [zz] in the rhyme. On this analysis, 'silk' and 'west' are [s] → [sz] and [si] → [sʲi]/[ɕi], respectively, where the syllabic [z] is not underlyingly contrastive with [i].

Since not every SC consonant can be followed by a syllabic consonant, the above analysis must explain which consonants can spread to the nucleus and which cannot. The set that allows spreading is [ts, tsʰ, s, tʂ, tʂʰ, ʂ, ʐ̩], all of which share Coronal-[+fricative]. The last has also been called a Coronal fricative in some analyses, although others considered it to be a semivowel, such as M. Fu (1956: 3).

Similar to the treatment of the syllabic [z] and [z̩], it has been proposed that the zero onset can be treated as an obligatory onset slot (Duanmu 1990, 2000), though I will argue in Chapter 4 that the onset slot is not required but optional. Therefore, the zero onset effect is available only when a full syllable occurs in initial position, but not when it occurs after another full syllable.

In summary, the present analysis proposes nineteen consonants and six vowels for SC, including a retroflex vowel [ɚ], which has limited distribution. Like the traditional analysis, the present one considers a CG combination to be two sounds underlyingly. But unlike the traditional analysis, we consider a CG combination to be one sound at surface, which has several merits: it assumes fewer phonemes by excluding palatals and the zero onset; it agrees with the fact that a CG combination is phonetically a single sound; and it offers a better account of the cooccurrence restrictions on CG combinations and the lack of such restrictions on CV combinations. These merits are achieved by combining phonemic analysis with two other theories: (*a*) syllable theory and (*b*) feature theory.

2.12. FEATURE CHARTS FOR STANDARD CHINESE SOUNDS

In Tables 2.1 and 2.2 I show the features and articulators of SC consonants and vowels (using [ə] for the mid vowel and [a] for the low vowel), with some degree of underspecification. Table 2.1 specifies the stricture features [stop] and [fricative] for most of the consonants, because these features generally do not change; however, [stop] is unspecified for [n] and [ŋ] because they need not have oral closure in coda position (Y. Xu 1986; J. Wang 1993). No other stricture features are used, such as [consonantal], [sonorant], or [strident], since they are not needed for SC. For other features, I have put predictable values in parentheses. In addition, values that do not apply or are subject to change are left empty. For example, I have put values of [voice] in parentheses for aspirated obstruents and sonorants, because aspirated obstruents are all unvoiced and sonorants are usually voiced. The voice values for unaspirated stops and affricates are left empty, because these sounds can become voiced in an unstressed syllable. In addition, since the feature [ant] applies to Coronal consonants only, non-Coronals are not specified for this value. In Table 2.2, [back]

TABLE 2.1 *Features of SC consonants*

	p	pʰ	f	m	t	tʰ	ts	tsʰ	s	n	l	tʂ	tʂʰ	ʂ	ʐ̩	k	kʰ	x	ŋ
[stop]	+	+	−	+	+	+	+	+	−	−	−	+	+	−	−	+	+	−	−
[fric]	−	−	+	−	−	−	+	+	+	−	−	+	+	+	+	−	−	+	−
[voice]	(−)	(−)	(−)	(+)	(−)	(−)	(−)	(−)	(−)	(+)	(+)	(−)	(−)	(−)	(+)	(−)	(−)	(−)	(+)
[asp]	−	+			−	+	−	+	+			−	+	+	−	−	+	+	
[nasal]				+						+									+
[ant]					+	+	+	+	+	+	(+)	−	−	−	−				
[lat]											(+)								
Dor																√	√	√	√
Cor					√	√	√	√	√	√	√	√	√	√	√				
Lab	√	√	√	√															

Notes: '( )' indicates predictable values of features; changeable or irrelevant values are left empty; '√' indicates the presence of an articulator; [x] can be analysed as [h] underlyingly, in which case its articulator will be Vocal-cords; [ʂ, ʐ̩] can be transcribed as [ʂ, ʐ] respectively.

TABLE 2.2 *Features of SC vowels*

	i	u	y	ə	a
[high]	+	+	+	−	(−)
[low]	(−)	(−)	(−)	−	+
[back]	−	+	−		
[round]	−	+	+		(−)
Dor	√	√	√	√	√
Cor	√		√		
Lab		√	√		

and [round] are not specified for [ə], because its backness and rounding can change. In addition, [a] is unspecified for [back] and [round] because [a] can probably change [back] (more to be discussed in Chapter 3) and the feature [−round] can be assigned to it as a default value. It should be noted that Tables 2.1 and 2.2 are not meant to be minimally specified. A radical underspecification approach (e.g. Archangeli 1988) can leave out many additional values.

3

Combinations and Variation

3.1. INTRODUCTION

In this chapter I discuss how SC sounds combine to make full syllables that do not contain the retroflex suffix, and how they vary in different environments. Light syllables and syllables with the retroflex suffix are discussed in later chapters.

A puzzling fact about SC is that the majority of expected syllables are missing, a fact that has rarely caught the attention of Chinese scholars. For example, H. Wang (1999: 283) says that Chinese does not have many gaps in its syllable inventory. To appreciate the enormity of the number of syllables that are missing, consider two ways of counting them. First, let us assume that there is no restriction on consonant–vowel combinations. Ignoring syllabic consonants, a full SC syllable can be made of up to four sounds CGVX, where C is a consonant, G a glide, V a vowel, and X a glide or a consonant. Given nineteen Cs, three Gs, and five Vs in SC (excluding the retroflex V [ɚ], see Chapter 2), there are twenty choices for C (nineteen consonants or no C), four choices for G (three glides or no G), five choices for V (not counting the retroflex vowel [ɚ]), and twenty-three choices for X (three glides, nineteen consonants, or no X). This gives $20 \times 4 \times 5 \times 23 = 9{,}200$ syllables, which is roughly the number of monosyllables that occur in English. However, in SC only about 400 are used, hardly 5 per cent.

A major difference between English and Chinese is that, in Chinese, only a few sounds can occur in the coda of a syllable. Such language-specific restrictions, or phonotactic constraints, are quite common and, beyond historical accidents, there is little explanation to offer, just as there is little explanation of why English uses more than ten vowels while SC uses just five. Nevertheless, given the phonotactic constraints, there is still a large number of missing syllables in SC. Specifically, the C slot can be filled by one of eighteen consonants (or left unfilled), the G slot can be filled by one of three glides (or left unfilled), and the X slot can be filled by one of [i, u, n, ŋ] (or left unfilled). This still gives $19 \times 4 \times 5 \times 5 = 1,900$ syllables, about five times the actual size of 400. For example, *[pjəu], *[fje], *[wau], and *[ɥai] are absent in SC. Some missing forms are probably accidental gaps. For example, SC has [mje] 'wipe out' and [pʰje] 'skim', so *[fje] is probably an accidental gap. However, it is possible that not all gaps are accidental. If we consider only GVX, there are $4 \times 5 \times 5 = 100$ forms, of which only 35, or a third, are found. Some missing syllables have been studied before (e.g. Y. Lin 1989; Duanmu 1990), but a systematic account is lacking. In this chapter I will focus on GVX forms, the understanding of which can provide some insight into the analysis of how SC sounds vary. I start with some theoretical background.

3.2. PHONETICS AND PHONOLOGY: WHAT IS RELEVANT?

Phonetically, speech is infinitely variable. No two people pronounce the same word alike. Even for the same person, the utterance of the same word may vary from moment to moment. Evidently, phonology cannot deal with all of the details.

The line that is often drawn between phonetics and phonology is whether a variation is, or can be, contrastive. For example, [m] and [n] are contrastive in SC because they distinguish words like [mi] 'rice' and [ni] 'you'. The difference between [o] and [e] is not contrastive in SC (see Chapter 2 and below), but can be contrastive in other languages, such as English. Therefore, a phonological analysis of SC should also account for the variation between [o] and [e].

The presence of a phonetic variation, even if systematic, is no guarantee that it is phonologically relevant. For example, in many languages, a low vowel has a lower pitch than a high vowel, but there is no known phonological consequence that follows from it. Therefore, such pitch variation falls outside the domain of phonology. If there is a language in which the loss of a vowel-height contrast can lead to a tonal contrast, then the correlation between pitch and vowel height will be a phonological issue.

Even for phonologically relevant distinctions such as lip rounding it can still be difficult to decide when a phonetic cue is strong enough to be recognized. For example, consider *coral* and *quarrel* in English, shown in (1).

(1) [kɔrəl]   'coral'
     [kʷɔrəl]   'quarrel'

In *coral*, the lips are somewhat rounded for [k], but we cannot call it [kʷ] because it is still different from the [kʷ] in *quarrel* (assuming, following Golston and Kehrein 1999, that no language contrasts [kʷ] and [kw]). As a result, we must consider [k] in *coral* to be unrounded. But in *cool*, the lips are also rounded for [k]. Can we call it [kʷ]? The answer is less obvious because there is no word pair in English where [kul] and [kʷul] contrast.

The difficulty in deciding whether a phonetic detail is relevant can affect phonological analysis. For example, there are two transcriptions of the British English pronunciation of the diphthong in *go*, shown in (2).

(2)   Jones (1950):   [gou]   'go'
        Gimson (1979):   [gəu]   'go'

Apparently, the first part of the diphthong is somewhat rounded, but perhaps not as much as the vowel in *or*. The same disagreement exists for the corresponding diphthong in SC, shown in (3).

(3)
	Underlying	Surface	
C. Cheng (1973):	[kəu]	[kou]	'dog'
J. Wang (1993):	[kəu]	[kəu]	'dog'

Let us assume that the SC mid vowel is underlyingly [ə] (see Chapter 2). For C. Cheng (1973) there is a phonological rule that changes [ə] to [o] before [u], shown in (4), but for J. Wang (1993) there is no such rule.

(4)   C. Cheng (1973):   [ə] → [o]/__[u]
                       ([ə] changes to [o] when it occurs before [u])

       J. Wang (1993):   no rule required

Such differences cannot be resolved phonetically, because both analyses agree that [ə] is somewhat rounded before [u]. They differ in whether the rounding is phonologically relevant. For C. Cheng (1973) it is; for J. Wang (1993) it is not, just as the rounding of [k] in 'coral' does not make it [kʷ]—uncertainties of this kind have given rise to considerable disagreement in both the transcription and the analysis of SC sounds.

3.3. THE RULE-BASED APPROACH

The rule-based analysis has been the standard practice in phonology for many years. In this analysis, an utterance starts from an underlying representation (UR), which then undergoes a set of ordered rules to arrive at the

surface representation (SR). For illustration, consider the transcription of
the SC mid vowel in (5) (which differs somewhat from what I will argue
for below) and the analysis based on it, given in (6) and (7). The analysis
is similar to what is offered by C. Cheng (1973), which was also adopted,
with minor variations, by Chen (1984) and Steriade (1988).

(5)   The SC mid vowel (C. Cheng 1973)

    [e]: [ei], [je], [ɥe] (*[ɥö]), [wei] (*[woi])
    [o]: [ou], [wo], [jou] (*[jeu])
    [ə]: Elsewhere, e.g. [kə]

(6)   Analysis of (5)

    (*a*) UR: [ə]
    (*b*) Ordered rules:

        1. (*a*) [ə] → [−back] / __[−back]
            ([ə] becomes front before a front vowel)
          (*b*) [ə] → [+round] / __[+round]
            ([ə] becomes round before a round vowel)
        2. [ə] → [−back] / [−back]__
          ([ə] becomes front after a front vowel)
        3. [ə] → [+round] / [+round]__
          ([ə] becomes round after a round vowel)

(7)   Derivations (illustration of the analysis)

UR	[əi]	[jə]	[ɥə]	[wəi]	[əu]	[wə]	[jəu]	[kə]
(6.*b*.1)	ei	–	–	wei	ou	–	jou	–
(6.*b*.2)	–	je	ɥe	–	–	–	–	–
(6.*b*.3)	–	–	–	–	–	wo	–	–
SR	[ei]	[je]	[ɥe]	[wei]	[ou]	[wo]	[jou]	[kə]

First, consider the UR of the mid vowel. Both [e] and [o] are predictable
from the environment: [e] occurs next to a front vowel or glide, [o] next to
[u] or [w]. In contrast, [ə] is not predictable, so [ə] must be the underlying
form. Next consider the rules. We see that [ə] can assimilate in frontness
(cf. [je] and [ei]) and rounding (cf. [wo] and [ou]) from either direction.
This gives rise to two pairs of assimilation rules, one to the right and one
to the left. Second, we see that [ə] is more prone to the influence from
the right than from the left (cf. [wei] not *[woi], and [jou] not *[jeu]).
This means that (6.*b*.1) should apply first. Finally, we see in [ɥe] that if
the conditions for both frontness and rounding are present, only frontness
assimilation takes place. This can be accounted for by ordering (6.*b*.2)
before (6.*b*.3). Example (7) shows that the analysis derives the correct
surface forms. For example, consider [wəi]. First, (6.*b*.1) changes it to

[wei]. When (6.*b*.3) comes along, the target vowel is no longer [ə] but [e], so (6.*b*.3) cannot apply. The output is therefore [wei].

3.4. THE CONSTRAINT-BASED APPROACH

The constraint-based analysis was introduced to syntax by Chomsky (1981) and was later adopted in phonology, where it is known as Optimality Theory (Prince and Smolensky 1993). In this approach, a grammar consists of a set of constraints instead of a set of ordered rules. In addition, the constraints can be in conflict with each other, and so they must be ranked. Moreover, all possible surface forms (output candidates) of an underlying form (input) are evaluated at the same time, and the best candidate is the actual surface form. Some researchers, such as Burzio (1996), propose that even the underlying form is not needed, which I will not pursue here.

For illustration, let us consider how the data in (5) can be analysed in Optimality Theory. The analysis exemplified here is similar to that of Y. Lin (1997): the underlying form of the mid vowel is still [ə], as in the previous analysis, and the four assimilation rules can be stated as four constraints, shown in (8) and (9).

(8)   Nucleus–coda harmony (NC-harmony)
     (*a*) The nucleus and the coda must agree in frontness (same as (6.*b*.1.*a*))
     (*b*) The nucleus and the coda must agree in rounding (same as (6.*b*.1.*b*))

(9)   Glide–nucleus harmony (GN-harmony)
     (*a*) The prenuclear glide and the nucleus must agree in frontness (same as (6.*b*.2))
     (*b*) The prenuclear glide and the nucleus must agree in rounding (same as (6.*b*.3))

Next consider the ranking of the constraints, using the input [wəi] for illustration. If NC-harmony is ranked above GN-harmony (NC-harmony >> GN-harmony), the result is in (10), which is called a tableau—a table showing the evaluation of candidates against ranked constraints.

(10)   Analysis of [wei] when NC-harmony>>GN-harmony

	/wəi/	NC-harmony	GN-harmony
	[wəi]	*!	*
√	[wei]		*
	[woi]	*!	

Notations

Input:	/.../
Constraints:	top row
Violation:	*
Fatal violation:	*! (evaluation irrelevant thereafter)
Candidates:	[ ]
Best candidate:	√

Three candidates are compared: [wəi] violates both constraints, [wei] violates GN-harmony, and [woi] violates NC-harmony. Since NC-harmony is more important, [wei] is the best candidate. If the ranking is reversed, the result will be wrong, as shown in (11).

(11) Analysis of [wei] when GN-harmony >> NC-harmony

/wəi/	GN-harmony	NC-harmony
[wəi]	*!	*
[wei]	*!	
*√ [woi]		*

This time the best candidate is predicted to be [woi], which is wrong (indicated by *√). Thus, the correct ranking should be NC-harmony >> GN-harmony, as in (10).

In the above illustration the constraints correspond to the rules of the traditional analysis, and the ranking of the constraints correspond to the ordering of the rules. However, sometimes the translation between rules and constraints is not so obvious. Consider the analysis of [ɥe]. In the rule-based approach the frontness assimilation applies before the rounding assimilation. If we translate this ordering with the constraint ranking in (12), we get the analysis in (13).

(12) (*a*) GN-[back]: The prenuclear glide and the nucleus must agree in [back].
      (*b*) GN-[round]: The prenuclear glide and the nucleus must agree in [round]
      NC-harmony >> GN-[back] >> GN-[round]

(13) Analysis of [ɥe] by (12)

/ɥə/	NC-harmony	GN-[back]	GN-[round]
[ɥə]		*!	*
[ɥe]			*!
*√ [ɥö]			

Since [ɥö] violates no constraint, it is predicted to be the output, but it is not. The correct output should be [ɥe]. Thus, translating the rule ordering 'the frontness assimilation applies before the rounding assimilation' into the constraint ranking 'GN-[back] >> GN-[round]' does not work here. The solution is to propose a new constraint, Avoid-[ö], and rank it above the two GN-harmony constraints, as shown in (14), where curly brackets indicate that GN-[back] and GN-[round] have the same ranking.

(14)   Avoid-[ö]: Avoid the vowel [ö]

      NC-harmony>>Avoid-[ö]>>{GN-[back], GN-[round]}

The new analysis of [ɥe] is shown in (15), which gives the correct result.

(15)   Analysis of [ɥe] by (14)

	/ɥə/	NC-harmony	Avoid-[ö]	{GN-[back],	GN-[round]}
	[ɥə]			*	*!
√	[ɥe]				*
	[ɥö]		*!		

These examples show that a rule-based analysis is quite different from a constraint-based analysis. In what follows I will make use of phonological constraints.

3.5. THE DATA

Compared with languages like English, SC has a small syllable inventory. There are about 1,300 syllables including tone, or about 400 syllables ignoring tone (the specific numbers depend on whether you include some interjections and rare words). A full SC syllable can consist of up to four underlying sounds, CGVX, where CG is phonetically realized as a single sound (see Chapters 2 and 4). If we ignore C and consider just (G)V(X) (G and X are optional in some syllables), then there are only thirty-five actual combinations.

3.5.1. Transcriptions

There is some disagreement on the transcription of the thirty-five (G)V(X) combinations. In (16) I show the analyses of Chao (1968), S. Xu (1980), C. Cheng (1973), and Y. Lin (1989). The item [iai] is included, even though there is only one such word, [iai] 'cliff', which is a literary word and which is sometimes pronounced as [ia] or [ai].

(16)

Chao	S. Xu	C. Cheng	Y. Lin
i	i	i	i
u	u	u	u
y	y	y	y
ʌ	ʌ	ɑ	ʌ
iʌ	iʌ	ia	iʌ
uʌ	uʌ	uɑ	uʌ
ɤ	ɤ	ɤ	ɤ
iɛ	iɛ	ie	ie
yɛ	yɛ	ye	ye
uo	uo	uo	uo
ai	aɪ	ai	ʌi
iai	iaɪ	iai	iʌi
uai	uaɪ	uai	uʌi
ei	eɪ	ei	ei
uei	uəɪ	uei	uei
ɑu	ɑʊ	ɑu	ɑu
iɑu	iɑʊ	iɑu	iɑu
ou	əʊ	ou	ou
iou	iəʊ	iou	iou
in	in	in	in
yn	yn	ün	ün
ən	ən	ən	ən
uən	uən	uən	uən
an	an	an	ʌn
uan	uan	uan	uʌn
yan	yɐn	yan	yɐn
iɛn	iæn	iɛn	iɛn
ʌŋ	əŋ	əŋ	əŋ
uʌŋ	uʊŋ	uəŋ	uəŋ
iŋ	iŋ	iŋ	iŋ
ɑŋ	ɑŋ	ɑŋ	ɑŋ
iɑŋ	iɑŋ	iɑŋ	iɑŋ
uɑŋ	uɑŋ	uɑŋ	uɑŋ
ʊŋ	ʊŋ	uŋ	ʊŋ
iʊŋ	iʊŋ	yəŋ	yəŋ

In (16), [a] is a front low vowel, [ʌ] is a central low vowel, and [ɑ] is a back low vowel. For ease of comparison, I have made three minor adjustments in the phonetic symbols: Cheng and Lin used [ü] for the high front rounded vowel—I have changed it to [y]; Chao used a small omega symbol for the lax high back rounded vowel—I have changed it to [ʊ]; and Lin used [a] for a 'central low vowel', which I have changed to [ʌ] to be consistent with Chao and Xu. In addition, C. Cheng and Lin consider [ʊən] to be a variant of [ʊŋ], but Chao lists them separately. I follow Chao and will give reasons below.

The variation in transcription is in part influenced by the analyses of the researchers. For example, C. Cheng proposes a rule by which non-high vowels are fronted by [i]; the rule predicts that the low vowel is front in [ia] but back in [ɑ], as he transcribes. However, other researchers do not find such a difference in the low vowels. In the analysis of Lin, the low vowel is not assimilated to [i], so it is predicted to be 'central' in [ʌ], [iʌ], and [ʌi].

3.5.2. **Rhyming groups**

A rhyming group is a group of syllables that rhyme with each other. In Chinese, two full syllables rhyme if they have the same nuclear vowel and coda but differ in the onset consonant or the prenuclear glide. Thus, rhyming groups offer important evidence for the qualities of (G)V(X) items. Most studies on rhyming groups deal with historical Chinese. The first to deal with SC is probably Chao (1927), although it also contains a remnant of older Chinese—it kept the Ru tone category, which is lost in SC but present in many other dialects. Perhaps Chao's intention was for the poet's work to be appreciated not only by speakers of SC but also by speakers of other dialects. *Shiyun Xinbian*, compiled by Shanghai Guji Chubanshe (1989), offers a similar analysis of SC, except that [in, yn] and [ən, uən] are separate in Chao (1927) but grouped together in *Shiyun Xinbian*. L. Wang (1980: 22–4) also suggests that [ən, uən, in, yn] form a rhyming group and that they can be considered [ən, uən, iən, yən] underlyingly; this view is shared by Chen (1984). However, the rhyming groups L. Wang refers to are not based on SC, but on an opera tradition that originated from the Huguang region (now the provinces of Hunan and Hubei). In what follows I use Chao's analysis, according to which SC has seventeen rhyming groups (ignoring tone, syllabic consonants, and retroflex rhymes). In (17) I show how the thirty-five (G)V(X) items are grouped, using Chao's (1968) transcription.

(17)   Phonetic transcriptions of 17 rhyming groups in SC (Chao 1927, 1968)

i		
u		
y		
ʌ	iʌ	uʌ
ɤ		

iɛ	yɛ		
uo			
ai	iai	uai	
ei	uei		
ɑu	iɑu		
ou	iou		
in	yn		
ən	uən		
an	iɛn	uan	yan
ʌŋ	iŋ	uʌŋ	
ɑŋ	iɑŋ	uɑŋ	
ʊŋ	iʊŋ		

Many analyses treat [ɤ, ɛ, o] as allophonic variants of the same phoneme (see Chapter 2), and some further claim that [ɤ, ɛ, o] form a rhyming group (e.g. Hsueh 1986). However, I agree with Chao that for most SC speakers [ɤ, ɛ, o] do not rhyme. In particular, as far as I am aware, [ɤ] and [ɛ] do not rhyme, such as [kɤ] 'brother' and [tʲɛ] 'father', nor do [ɛ] and [o] rhyme, such as [tʲɛ] 'father' and [kʷo] 'pot'. However, [ɤ] and [o] occasionally seem to rhyme, as seen in the following verse lines (cited in Duanmu 1990, from the 1989 Spring Festival Gala TV Show, CCTV, Beijing, transcribed phonetically).

(18) tçin   tçʰin   tçe-xʷən   xai   tʂʰu   tʷo (or [tʷɤ])
      close kin   marry   bad   effects many
      'Inbreeding marriages have many bad effects.'

      tʂɤ   jɑŋ   ça-tçʰy   lʲau-pu-tɤ
      this way   go-on   terrible
      'It will be terrible if such things go on.'

If the lines rhyme, then the rhyming syllables are [tʷo] and [tɤ], in which the surface vowels are different. However, for some SC speakers, especially those from northeast China, [tʷo] is pronounced as [tʷɤ], shown in parentheses in (18), which has the same surface vowel as [tɤ]. S. Xu (1980: 54) also observes that for some SC speakers [o] is a 'neutral vowel' [ə] and is not always rounded. I suspect that these lines were intended to be read with such a pronunciation. It is also possible that the lines in fact do not rhyme. Instead, what makes the lines rhythmic can be the template alone, which is SWSWSWØ for both lines (see Chapter 12).

It is interesting to note that although [ɛ, o, ɤ] come from the same underlying vowel, they do not rhyme with one another. Clearly, then, rhyming is based on surface forms. Given this, [ʌ], [iʌ], and [uʌ] must

(27)   [p]   +   [j]   →   [pʲ]
      Lab   Dor-Cor   Lab-Dor-Cor
      | | | |
   [+stop] [−back]   [+stop][−back]

When the articulator of C is the same as an articulator of G, as in [t]+[j], the two merge into one. This is shown in (28).

(28)   [t]   +   [j]   →   [tʲ]
      Cor   Dor-Cor   Cor-Dor
      | | | |
   [+stop]   [−back]   [+stop]   [−back]

Now consider [p]+[w], shown in (29).

(29)   [p]   +   [w]   →   ?[pʷ]
      Lab   Dor-Lab   Dor-Lab
      | | ⟋⟍
   [+stop]   [+round]   [+stop]   [+round]

It is theoretically possible to merge [p] and [w] into [pʷ]. The absence of [pʷ] suggests that SC disfavours merging articulators that both have their own features or it disfavours an articulator that dominates two features. Similarly, consider [k]+[j], shown in (30).

(30)   [k]   +   [j]   →   ?[kʲ]
      Dor   Dor-Cor   Dor-Cor
      | | ⟋⟍
   [+stop]   [−back]   [+stop] [−back]

Again, it is theoretically possible to merge [k] and [j] into [kʲ], which in fact occurs in some Chinese dialects. The absence of [kʲ] in SC suggests that it is too complex for SC.

    With this background, we return to the CG distribution pattern, analysed in (31). The general pattern is that when G has an articulator that has its own feature, it does not combine with C that has that articulator. Thus, [j] and [ɥ] do not combine with Coronal C, and [w] and [ɥ] do not combine with Labial C.

have the same surface vowel, as Chao, Xu, and Lin transcribe, instead of [ɑ], [iɑ], and [uɑ], as C. Cheng transcribes. Similarly, since [an], [uan], [yan], and [iɛn] rhyme, they ought to have the same surface vowel. It is not necessary to distinguish the low vowels in [an], [uan], [yɐn], and [iæn], as S. Xu does, nor the low vowels in [yan] and [iɛn], as Chao does.

Two other sets, [in, yn] and [ʌŋ, uʌŋ, iŋ], also need some comments. Since [in, yn] do not rhyme with [ən], there should be no [ə] in [in, yn]. In addition, since [in] and [yn] rhyme, they should have the same vowel. A better transcription, therefore, is [in] and [yin]. Similarly, since [ʌŋ, uʌŋ, iŋ] rhyme, they should have the same vowel, either [ʌŋ, uʌŋ, iʌŋ] or [əŋ, uəŋ, iəŋ]. This is supported by the fact that [iŋ] is indeed pronounced as [iəŋ], as noted by Chao (1927: 18), L. Wang (1980: 22), and Y. Lin (1989: 63). Under such considerations, (17) is revised in (19).

(19) Phonetic transcriptions of 17 rhyming groups in SC (revised)

i			
u			
y			
ʌ	iʌ	uʌ	
ɤ			
iɛ	yɛ		
uo			
ai	iai	uai	
ei	uei		
ɑu	iɑu		
ou	iou		
in	yin		
ən	uən		
an	ian	uan	yan
ʌŋ	iʌŋ	uʌŋ	
ɑŋ	iɑŋ	uɑŋ	
ʊŋ	iʊŋ		

There still remain some distinctions that do not seem to be necessary: [u, ʊ], [a, ʌ, ɑ], [ə, ʌ], [ɛ, e], and [ɤ, ə]. I return to these later.

3.5.3. Missing forms

Given four choices for G (three glides, plus one without G), five for V, and five for X (two high vowels, two nasals, one without X), there are 100 combinations of (G)V(X), of which only 35 actually occur, shown in (20). The top row indicates the choices for G, where [Ø–] means no glide.

The first column indicates the choices for X, where [−Ø] means no X. The second column indicates the underlying forms of V(X), using [ə] for the mid vowel and [a] for the low vowel.

(20)   Actual and missing (G)V(X) forms in phonetic symbols

		Ø-	j-	w-	ɥ-	
[-Ø]	i	+	(+)	−	−	[ji] = [i]
	u	+	−	(+)	−	[wu] = [u]
	y	+	−	−	(+)	[ɥy] = [y]
	ə	+	+	+	+	
	a	+	+	+	−	
[-n]	in	+	(+)	−	+	[jin] = [in]
	un	−	−	(+)	−	[wun] = [un]
	yn	−	−	−	(+)	[ɥyn] = [yn]
	ən	+	−	+	−	
	an	+	+	+	+	
[-ŋ]	iŋ	−	(+)	−	−	[jiŋ] = [iŋ]
	uŋ	+	+	(+)	−	[wuŋ] = [uŋ]
	yŋ	−	−	−	(+)	[ɥyŋ] = [yŋ]
	əŋ	+	+	+	−	
	aŋ	+	+	+	−	
[-i]	ii	(+)	(+)	−	−	[ii] = [i], [jii] = [ji]
	ui	−	−	(+)	−	[wui] = [ui]
	yi	−	−	−	(+)	[ɥyi] = [yi]
	əi	+	−	+	−	
	ai	+	+	+	−	
[-u]	iu	−	(+)	−	−	[jiu] = [iu]
	uu	(+)	−	(+)	−	[uu] = [u], [wuu] = [wu]
	yu	−	−	−	(+)	[ɥyu] = [yu]
	əu	+	+	−	−	
	au	+	+	−	−	

The 35 actual forms are indicated by '+', the other 65 by '−' or '(+)'. A form with (+) indicates one that does not contrast with another (indicated on the right-hand side) because of the constraints Merge and G-Spreading, to be discussed below.

There are two possible views on the missing forms. The first is that they are due to historical accidents or arbitrary choices of a dialect, and there is no further explanation. Another view is that the missing forms indicate systematic constraints on possible syllable structures. To support the second view, one should show that there are indeed reasonably natural constraints for most of the missing forms. I offer such an analysis in the next section.

3.6. RHYME-HARMONY, MERGE, AND G-SPREADING

The analysis I offer makes use of three constraints to rule out most non-occurring forms. They are shown in (21), where α is any feature value and $-\alpha$ is the opposite value.

(21) Rhyme-Harmony: VX cannot have opposite values in [round] or [back]:

$$*[+back][-back], *[-back][+back]$$
$$*[+round][-round], *[-round][+round]$$

Merge: Two tokens of the same feature merge into one long feature:

$$XX \rightarrow XX$$
$$|\ | \quad\ \lor$$
$$F_iF_i \quad F_i$$

G-Spreading: A high nuclear vowel spreads to the onset C:

$$[Ci] \rightarrow [C^ji], [Cu] \rightarrow [C^wu], [Cy] \rightarrow [C^\eta y]$$

Rhyme-Harmony rules out opposite values of [back], but if a sound is unspecified for [back], it can freely combine with [+back] or [−back]. In other words, [+back][∅ back], [−back][∅ back], [∅ back][−back], [∅ back][+back] are allowed. The same is true for [round].

There is a likely physical reason for Rhyme-Harmony and Merge: it is hard for an articulator to move fast enough to execute two opposite gestures in a rhyme (such as [+back][−back]), or the same gesture twice in a rhyme (such as [−back][−back]). If so, one might find similar constraints in other languages, a topic that is beyond the scope of the present study.

G-Spreading is an anticipatory process. I will argue in Chapter 4 that there is only one onset slot in the syllable, which can be filled by C, G, or C^G. G–Spreading does not apply when the onset is G or C^G. For example, G–Spreading does not require [wi] to become [ɥi] or [w^{j}i], or [t^{w}i] to become [t^{ɥ}i] or [t^{wj}i], or [ju] to become [ɥu] or [j^{w}u]. However, I will discuss some cases below where G–Spreading seems to occur when the onset already has a glide. Also, I will argue in Chapter 4 that the onset slot is optional, and G-Spreading does not apply when there is no onset. This explains why the English word [ist] *east* does not become [jist], the latter being a different word, *yeast*. The reason is that *yeast* has an onset while *east* does not.

Of the 25 VX rows in the GVX table, Rhyme-Harmony and Merge rule out nine, shown in (22), where I consider [n] to be [−back] in SC and [ŋ] to be [+back]. Since SC has only one mid vowel and one low vowel, they are unspecified for [back] or [round], and so they can combine with any glide or high vowel.

(22) VX rows ruled out by Rhyme-Harmony and Merge

    *row-[un]   differ in frontness
    *row-[in]   differ in frontness
    *row-[yŋ]   differ in frontness
    *row-[ui]   differ in rounding and frontness
    *row-[yu]   differ in frontness
    *row-[yi]   differ in rounding
    *row-[iu]   differ in rounding and frontness
    *row-[ii]   Merge, [ii] = [iː]
    *row-[uu]   Merge, [uu] = [uː]

Because all regular SC syllables are heavy, a rhyme with just [i] or [u] is in fact long [iː] and [uː] (see Chapter 4). Therefore, there is no contrast between [iː] and [ii], because the latter will change to [iː] under Merge. Similarly, there is no contrast between [uː] and [uu].

It can be seen that most of the rhymes in (22) contain a pair of high vowels. Y. Lin (1989: 59) suggests that SC has a constraint *[+high][+high] that prohibits two high vowels from occurring next to each other. In the present analysis, Lin's constraint is not necessary because the effect can be achieved by Rhyme-Harmony and Merge, which also rules out bad VN rhymes.

There remain 16 rows of rhymes, all of which satisfy Rhyme-Harmony. They are shown in (23). The mid vowel [ə] and the low vowel [a] are unspecified for rounding and frontness (see Chapter 2).

(23) Row   Comment

    [i]
    [u]
    [y]
    [ə]
    [a]
    [in]   both [−back]
    [yn]   both [−back]; [n] unspecified for [round]
    [ən]   [ə] unspecified for [back]
    [an]   [a] unspecified for [back]
    [uŋ]   both [+back]; [ŋ] unspecified for [round]
    [əŋ]   [ə] unspecified for [back]
    [aŋ]   [a] unspecified for [back]
    [əi]   [ə] unspecified for [back]

[ai]   [a] unspecified for [back]
[əu]   [ə] unspecified for [back]
[au]   [a] unspecified for [back]

The rhyme [in] is [−back][−back], and so it will undergo Merge. This is shown in (24), where I use '−B' for [−back].

(24)   i n → i n
       | | ∨
    −B−B   −B

The result is still [in], which does not overlap with another rhyme. Similarly, [yn] and [uŋ] will undergo Merge but will still remain separate rhymes.

The 16 rows contain 64 forms, listed in (25), where G-Spreading (G) accounts for six of them. The equivalent pairs under G-Spreading are listed on the right. For example, [u] and [wu] are equivalent, which means that [Cu] will become [Cʷu].

(25)   Cells ruled out by G-Spreading (G)

	Ø-	j-	w-	ɥ-	
i	+	G	−	−	[ji] = [i]
u	+	−	G	−	[wu] = [u]
y	+	−	−	G	[ɥy] = [y]
ə	+	+	+	+	
a	+	+	+	−	
in	+	G	−	+	[jin] = [in]
yn	−	−	−	G	[ɥyn] = [yn]
ən	+	−	+	−	
an	+	+	+	+	
uŋ	+	+	G	−	[wuŋ] = [uŋ]
əŋ	+	+	+	−	
aŋ	+	+	+	−	
əi	+	−	+	−	
ai	+	+	+	−	
əu	+	+	−	−	
au	+	+	−	−	

The 35 occurring forms are indicated by '+'. There are 23 non-occurring forms, indicated by '−', which I list in (26). About half of them seem to be accountable in some ways, and I have made some tentative comments on why they do not occur independently. For each pair of variants, such as [wi]–[wəi] or [ɥuŋ]–[juŋ], there seems to be no principled way to decide which variant is underlying and which is missing or derived.

(26) Forms   Comments

    wi   Variant of [wəi]
    ju   Variant of [jəu]
    win   Same as [yin] if G-Spreading applies to [win]
    ɥuŋ   Same as [juŋ] if G-Spreading applies to [juŋ]
    jy   wy   Same as [y] if G-Spreading applies to [jy, wy]
    jyn   wyn   Same as [yn] if G-Spreading applies to [jyn, wyn]
    ɥəu   ɥau   wəu   wau   [+round]–[+round] between onset and coda
    ɥi   ɥu   yn
    ɥəi   jəi
    jən   ɥən   ɥəŋ
    ɥaŋ   ɥai   ɥa

In SC [wi] is a variant of [wəi]; the variation is conditioned by tone, to be discussed below. Similarly, [ju] is a variant of [jəu], also conditioned by tone. In [win], [ɥuŋ], [jy], [wy], [jyn], and [wyn], there is a prenuclear G and a high nuclear vowel. If G-Spreading applies to the high nuclear vowel even if G is already occupied, these forms will become the same as some others (which can be occurring or non-occurring) and so not independently contrastive. In [ɥəu], [ɥau], [wəu], and [wau], both the onset and the coda are [+round], and there seems to be a dissimilation effect against that. It is interesting to note that [wau] is marginal in English, too, and only occurs in three words, *powwow*, *bowwow*, and *wow*. More frequent in English are *quote*, *quota*, *swollen*, *woeful*, and *wont*, etc., probably because some speakers use [wou] or [wo] (with one long [+round]) and some use [wəɯ]. So there does not seem to be a good reason to rule out [wau] and [wəu] completely. The syllable [jəi] is similar to [jei] in English, which only occurs in a marginal word *yea* and a few French borrowings such as *soigné*. Finally, it is interesting to note that 16 out of the 23 non-occurring forms, or 70 per cent, contain [y] or [ɥ].

It is possible that under G-Spreading [ɥuŋ] and [iuŋ] are identical. If so, the underlying form could be either [ɥuŋ] or [iuŋ], although I have assumed that it is the latter. The ambiguity may explain some confusion in the literature. In traditional Chinese phonology, syllables are sometimes grouped according to the prenuclear glide. The SC word 'use' is sometimes thought to be [juŋ] and grouped with the [j]-group (Chao 1968) and sometimes [ɥuŋ] and grouped with the [ɥ]-group (Hsueh 1986). The present analysis suggests that there is no simple way to resolve the ambiguity.

Duanmu (2003) proposes a rule called Triphthong Raising, according to which a form with three vowels [high][mid][high] is raised to [high][high][high]. The effect has been observed in SC (Zee 2003) and can be understood in terms of articulatory effort reduction. The rule accounts for the alternation in the pairs [wəi]–[wi] and [jəu]–[ju]. It can also account for the lack of [ɥəu], [wəu], [ɥəi], and [jəi], all of which contain [high][mid][high]. However, Triphthong Raising is not universal, because English uses [wi] 'we' and [wei] 'way' contrastively. Also, English uses [wou] quite often, as just seen.

In (27) I summarize the analysis of GVX forms.

(27) Summary of the analysis of GVX forms

Reason	Number of forms
Rhyme-Harmony	28
Merge	8
G-Spreading	6
Other missing ones	23
Occurring	35
Total	100

65% of all missing forms are accounted for
77% of all forms are accounted for

3.7. ALLOPHONIC VARIATIONS

Let us now consider surface variations of SC sounds, or allophonic variations. I focus on the G-Spreading effect and surface variations in the mid and low vowels.

3.7.1. **G-Spreading**

G-Spreading requires a high nuclear vowel to spread to the onset. As a result, there is a lack of contrast between many pairs of forms, such as [sin] vs. [sʲin] or [ɕin]. The process is graphically shown in (28), where O is the onset, N the nucleus, and C the coda. As will be discussed in Chapter 4, in a CGVX syllable both C and G are in the onset.

(28) [sin] → [sʲin] or [ɕin]

```
ONC     ONC
| | |    N |
s i n    s i n
```

Because of G-Spreading, there is no surface [sin] but only [sʲin], which is used by some speakers, and [ɕin], which has further undergone palatalization and is used by most speakers (see Chapter 2).

G-Spreading may also be responsible for the lack of contrast between [win] and [wʲin] or [ɥin], or between [juŋ] and [jʷuŋ] or [ɥuŋ], if it can apply, at least sometimes, when the onset already has G. Assuming that [ɥ] is a combination of [j] and [w], [juŋ] can be analysed as in (29).

(29) [juŋ] → [jʷuŋ] or [ɥuŋ]
      ONC   ONC
      | | | ⋈ |
      j u ŋ   j u ŋ

Chinese also lacks the contrast between V and GV, or VC and GVC, where V is a high vowel and G is the corresponding glide, such as the pairs in (30).

(30) Contrasts not found in Chinese

      [i]–[ji]   [u]–[wu]   [y]–[ɥy]
      [in]–[jin]   [uŋ]–[wuŋ]   etc.

One possibility is that every syllable has an onset, so that a high vowel is always preceded by G. For example, [in] is in fact [Øin], which has an empty onset Ø, and it becomes [jin] under G-Spreading, as shown in (31).

(31) [in] → [jin]
      ONC   ONC
      | | ⟍ |
      i n   i n

Another possibility, to be proposed in Chapter 4, is that an onset is not required for every syllable and Chinese does not use the empty onset. If so, Chinese simply lacks syllables like [ji], [wu], [ɥy], [jin], etc., because there is no onset slot for the high nuclear vowel to spread to.

3.7.2. Surface variation in vowels

First, consider the mid vowel. In an open syllable, where the vowel is long, the mid vowel has three values, shown in (32).

(32) Environment   Value
      After [j]   [eː]
      After [ɥ]   [eː]
      After [w]   [oː]
      Elsewhere   [ɤː]

The mid vowel is also [oː] after a labial consonant, to be discussed below. The three variants are phonologically different because they fall into three different rhyming groups. In addition, the variation is phonologically natural. In [eː] the mid vowel gets [–back] from the preceding [j] or [ɥ]. In [oː] the mid vowel gets [+round] (and possibly also [+back]) from the preceding [w]. Otherwise the mid vowel gets [+back] by default.

One problem for the above analysis is that, if the vowel can get [–back] and [+round] from the preceding glide, we would expect [ɥe] to surface as [ɥöː]. Instead, it surfaces as [ɥeː]. A possible answer, suggested by Y. Lin (1997), is that SC simply does not use the vowel [ö].

In closed syllables, the mid vowel may have different shades of variation in different environments, but there is no evidence that such variation is relevant or required. For example, the mid vowel is somewhat rounded in [əu], but there is no phonological evidence that it has become [o].

Let us now consider the analysis of other long vowels, which are [iː], [uː], [yː], and [aː]. There is no evidence that they undergo any phonologically relevant variation. It is easy to understand why the high vowels resist change. In SC the high vowels are probably specified for both [back] and [round] in order to contrast with each other, and specified features are generally resistant to change. However, the lack of change in the low vowel requires a different account. Since SC has only one low vowel, it need not be specified for [back] or [round]. If so, there seems to be no reason why it cannot change [back] and [round] according to the environment, as shown in (33).

(33) Environment   Possible change (not found)

    [ja]   [jæː] ([æː] = [–back, –round])

    [ɥa]   [ɥœː] ([œː] = [–back, +round])

    [wa]   [wɒː] ([ɒː] = [+back, +round])

    [xa]   [xɑː] ([ɑː] = [+back, –round])

Of the four hypothetical variants, only [ɑː] is close to the transcriptions (see (16)). It seems that SC simply chooses not to use [œː], [ɒː], and [æː].

3.8. TRANSCRIPTION OF SURFACE STANDARD CHINESE SOUNDS

As discussed in section 3.2, the transcription of surface sounds depends on which variations are phonologically relevant. This issue cannot always be resolved by looking at the phonetic values of the sounds. In this section I discuss the transcription of SC sounds in two parts; the first reflects obligatory phonological changes, the second, possible optional variations.

3.8.1. Required surface variations

The transcription in (34) shows the required surface variations of the 35 (G)V(X) forms in SC, listed by rhyming groups. Since vowel length is predictable (long in open syllables, short in closed syllables), it is omitted here. In the cases where G-Spreading has applied, such as [i] → [ji], it is assumed that there is an onset C. If there is no onset, G-Spreading will not apply.

(34)   Transcription of (G)V(X) forms (by rhyming groups, omitting vowel length)

Underlying (UR)				*Surface* (SR)					
i				ji					
u				wu					
y				ɥy					
a	ia	ua		ɑ	jɑ	wɑ	(a	ja	wa)
ə				ɤ					
iə			yə	je			ɥe		
uə				wo					
ai		uai		ai		wai			
əi		uəi		əi		wəi			
au	iau			au	jau				
əu	iəu			əu	jəu				
in			yin	jin			ɥin		
ən		uən		ən		wən			
an	ian	uan	yan	an	jan	wan	ɥan		
əŋ	iəŋ	uəŋ		əŋ	jəŋ	wəŋ			
aŋ	iaŋ	uaŋ		aŋ	jaŋ	waŋ			
uŋ	iuŋ			wuŋ	jʷuŋ				

The underlying sounds are as discussed in Chapter 2, where [ə] and [a] are unspecified for frontness and rounding. The low vowel in an open syllable can be [ɑ] if the default value for a long vowel is [+back, −round], otherwise it can be transcribed as [a]. The differences between the underlying and the surface transcriptions are summarized in (35).

(35)   Differences between UR and SR in (G)V(X) forms

   (a) [i, u, y]:   realized as [ji, wu, ɥy] under G-Spreading (when there is an onset); written as [j w ɥ] before the nuclear vowel;

   (b) [ə]:   changes to [e] after [j] or [ɥ] in an open syllable;
      changes to [o] after [w] in an open syllable;
      changes to [ɤ] (back and unrounded) in other open syllables;
      no necessary change otherwise;

   (c) [a]:   possibly changes to [ɑ] (back and unrounded) in an open syllable;
      no necessary change otherwise (but see below for nasal codas);

(*d*) [n, ŋ]:   no necessary change (but see below for coda position);

(*e*) [iuŋ]:   realized as [jʷuŋ] or [ɥuŋ] after G-Spreading.

Under G-Spreading, a high nuclear vowel will spread to the onset consonant, creating a secondary articulation on it, or palatalizing it. For example, underlying [mi] 'rice' is at surface [mʲiː], and underlying [ni] 'you' is at surface [nʲiː] or [ɲiː].

It has been observed that the nasals [n, ŋ] often do not have complete oral closure when they occur in the coda (Y. Xu 1986; J. Wang 1993), especially after the low vowel. If so, the rhyme may become a long nasalized vowel. Also, because [n] is [−back] and [ŋ] is [+back], they can affect the frontness of the low vowel, as shown in (36).

(36)   Underlying   Surface
       [ən]   [ən], [ə̃ː], or [ẽː]
       [əŋ]   [əŋ] or [ɤ̃ː]
       [an]   [æ̃ː]
       [aŋ]   [ɑ̃ː]

The analysis agrees with J. Wang's (1993) suggestion that the mid and the low vowels do not have values for [back] or [round] when they are short, but do when they are long. In addition, it explains why previous transcriptions often use a fronter low vowel before [n] and a backer low vowel before [ŋ]. Finally, it agrees with a well-known phonetic effect that low vowels are more likely to be nasalized (Whalen and Beddor 1989), which in turn may explain why nasal codas are more likely to be deleted after low vowels.

3.8.2. Optional surface variations

Besides the required variations, a number of variations may occur, as reflected in various previous transcriptions (see also (16)). These are summarized in (37).

(37)   Optional surface variations in (G)V(X) forms
       (*a*) Short [ə] or [a] may be somewhat rounded and backed before the coda [u].
       (*b*) Short [ə] or [a] may be somewhat fronted before the coda [i].
       (*c*) Vowels are nasalized before a nasal coda.
       (*d*) Short [a] may be raised between a high front vowel and the coda [n].

The optional variations may reflect optional phonological rules or constraints, by which such changes either take place or not. Or, SC phonology may have no requirements for such variations, leaving it open for individual speakers to decide what to do.

3.9. TONE AND VOWEL HEIGHT

It has been noted (e.g. L. Wang 1980: 15; S. Xu 1980: 75) that, when a syllable has a high tone (T1 or T2 in SC), the mid vowel tends to be deleted if it occurs after a glide and before a high vowel, as shown in (38).

(38) Underlying   With high tone   With low tone
     [wəi]   [wiː] 'danger'   [wəi] 'tail'
     [jəu]   [juː] 'superior'   [jəu] 'have'

L. Wang (1980: 15) also gives the example [uen] → [un] 'warm', which can be interpreted in the present analysis as [wən] → [wn], where the nasal becomes syllabic. There is no obvious phonological explanation for such variation. Phonetically, if tone is related to vertical larynx movement, then there is a possible answer. In a high tone, the larynx is raised, which possibly also pushes up the tongue root, giving a higher vowel. In a low tone, the larynx is lowered, which possibly also pulls down the tongue root, giving a lower vowel. The effect of tone on the height of other vowels may also exist, although there is no systematic study of it.

3.10. LABIAL ONSETS

As discussed above, the mid vowel has three variants in open syllables, repeated in (39).

(39) Environment   Value
     After [j] or [ɥ] [eː]
     After [w]   [oː]
     Elsewhere   [ɤː]

For many SC speakers, the mid vowel is [oː] in an open syllable after the labials [p, pʰ, m, f], where the labials become rounded, too. On the other hand, some speakers use [ɤː] in this environment, where the labial is not rounded. This is shown in (40).

(40) The mid vowel after a labial onset in SC
      Variety A   Variety B
      [pʷoː]   [pɤː]   'waves'
      [pʷʰoː]   [pʰɤː]   'slope'
      [mʷoː]   [mɤː]   'to touch'
      [fʷoː]   [fɤː]   'Buddha'

These words can be compared with the corresponding words in the Chengdu dialect (also a member of the Mandarin family), where the labials are not rounded but the vowel is, as shown in (41).

(41)   The vowel [o] after a labial onset in Chengdu
       [poː]   'waves'
       [pʰoː]   'slope'
       [moː]   'to touch'
       [foː]   'negate'

The patterns in Variety A raise two questions. First, SC labials are not rounded elsewhere, as seen in [ma] 'mother' and [mi] 'rice', instead of [mʷa] and [mʷi]. What then makes labials rounded before the mid vowel and cause it to become [oː]? Second, labials usually do not combine with [w] in SC, although coronals and dorsals do (see Chapter 2). For example, while both [tan] 'egg' and [tʷan] 'break' are found, there is only [pan] 'half' but no [pʷan], nor is there [pʰʷan], [mʷan], or [fʷan]. Why then could labials occur with [w] in Variety A? Some proposals have been made (e.g. Duanmu 1990; Duanmu 2000), but it remains unclear what the right answers are.

3.11. SUMMARY

In this chapter I have discussed variation of SC sounds, how they combine with each other, and how they should be transcribed. I have shown that phonological variations can be distinguished from phonetic variations. In particular, rhyming groups and the distribution of GVX forms can help determine which variations should be recognized phonologically. In addition, I have shown that most missing GVX forms can be accounted for by three constraints: Rhyme-Harmony, Merge, and G-Spreading. Finally, the analysis offers specific ways to transcribe SC sounds and syllable types and provides a solution to discrepancies in previous transcriptions.

4

The Syllable

4.1. SYLLABLE BOUNDARIES

Syllable boundaries in Chinese are mostly unambiguous, regardless of the dialect. The majority of Chinese words are monosyllabic. The maximal size of a syllable in SC is either CGVV or CGVC, where C is a consonant, G a glide, and VV either a long vowel or a diphthong. I refer to such syllables as CGVX, where CG is realized as a complex sound C^G (see below). In polysyllabic words, which are often foreign names, syllable boundaries are also unambiguous. In particular, the durational patterns and allophonic changes provide cues for word-medial syllable boundaries. Some examples in SC are shown in (1).

(1) Word-medial syllable boundaries

Sounds	Boundary	Gloss
[maaii]	[maa.ii]	'ant'
[maanau]	[maa.nau]	'amber'
[mæ̃nkuu]	[mæ̃n.kuu]	'Bangkok'

In 'ant' the length of [aa] indicates that the medial syllable boundary must be [maa.ii]. In 'amber' the length of [aa], its lack of nasalization, and its lack of fronting indicate that the medial syllable boundary must be [maa.nau]. In 'Bangkok' the first vowel is an allophone of [a]; its fronting to [æ] and its nasalization indicate that the medial syllable boundary is [mæ̃n.kuu]. In addition, the lack of word initial [nk] points to the same conclusion.

SC has no segmental prefixes. There is a suffix [ɚ] (diminutive), but it does not expand the syllable structure. Instead, the [ɚ] suffix replaces the coda of its host syllable, as in [njau] + [ɚ] → [njaɚ] '(little) bird' (see Chapter 9). The resulting syllable is still within CGVX.

Most Chinese words are stressed syllables; they are also called regular or full syllables. Unstressed syllables are usually grammatical words; they are also called weak syllables. Stressed syllables carry lexical tones and are longer than unstressed syllables, which do not carry lexical tones. In addition, unstressed syllables undergo rhyme reduction. I will argue that stressed and unstressed syllables have different structures, in that stressed syllables are heavy and unstressed syllables, light. Syllable structure can also be affected by casualness of speech and lengthening at pre-pause boundaries. We begin, however, with two controversial issues: (a) whether an onset is required and (b) whether G is an independent sound.

4.2. THE ONSET: OBLIGATORY OR OPTIONAL?

It has been observed that when a syllable begins with a non-high vowel, an onset of some sort is often added, most commonly [ʔ]. Two examples from SC are shown in (2), where [Ø] is what Chao (1968) calls a 'true vowel' onset.

(2) The zero onset effect

   [ʔɤɤ]/[ɣɤɤ]/[ŋɤɤ]/[Øɤɤ]   'goose'
   [ʔæ̃n]/[ɣæ̃n]/[ŋæ̃n]/[Øæ̃n]   'peace'

There are some speakers who use [ŋ] for such syllables throughout, so for them the onset has a real phoneme [ŋ]. However, for the majority of speakers the variation in (2) is found. It is worth noting that in onset position, [ʔ, ɣ, ŋ] occur only in such syllables, optionally, and they do not contrast with each other. The presence of such sounds has lead some linguists to conclude that every syllable has an onset, and those syllables that do not have a regular initial C or G have a 'zero onset' (Chao 1948, 1968; F. Li 1966).

We could propose that the zero onset is a variation of [ŋ], which is supported by two arguments. First, since [ŋ] occurs in codas independently, proposing an onset [ŋ] makes the distribution of [ŋ] complete. Second, [ŋ] is one of the variants of the zero onset. However, the proposal also has some drawbacks: there is no explanation why [ŋ] never occurs before the vowels [i, u, y] for any SC speaker, while the other two nasal onsets [n, m] do; deriving [ɣ, ʔ, Ø] from [ŋ] requires unnatural rules; and for most speakers the zero onset is not used when the syllable is not initial, to be seen shortly. The same criticisms apply to the proposal that the zero onset is a special consonant.

Duanmu (1990, 2000) proposes that the zero-onset effect is the result of an obligatory onset slot in the syllable structure, which needs to be filled

with something. The analysis of [an] 'peace' is shown in (3), where Ø is
the zero onset.

(3)   S
       ⟋⟍
       X X X
       | |
       a n   [Øan]   'peace'

The surface variants of the zero onset are what fills the empty onset slot.
When the nucleus has a high vowel, it is thought to spread to the empty
onset. There are two possible cases, exemplified in (4).

(4)   [Øii]   →   [jii]   or   [ʔʲii]   'one'
       S   S   S
      ⟋⟍   ⟋⟍   ⟋⟍
      X X X   X X X   X X X
       ⋁   ⋁   ⋁
       i   i   ʔ i

In [jii], spreading alone fills the onset; in [ʔʲii], the onset is filled by both
[ʔ] and spreading. The onset in (4) cannot be [ŋ] or [ɣ], presumably
because of a conflict in frontness ([i] is front and [ŋ] and [ɣ] are back).
The need for an onset is widely thought to be natural since Kahn (1976),
although the reason for the need remains unclear. The zero onset effect
is found in English, too. For example, vowel-initial words such as *out*
and *Ann* are often pronounced as [ʔaut] and [ʔæn], where an initial glottal stop is added.

However, there are two ways to look at the zero onset effect. One
is that it represents a real, intended position for a sound. The other is
that it is an unintended gesture: the vocal tract cannot assume the vowel
gesture all of a sudden, and the zero onset reflects an unintended state
before the vowel is pronounced. The two interpretations make different
predictions. According to the first, the zero onset effect should be present
whether there is a preceding syllable or not. According to the second, the
zero onset effect should go away when there is a preceding syllable. Evidence seems to support the second view. Consider the American English
examples in (5).

(5)   No glottal stop
      [rænaut]/*[rænʔaut]   'ran out'
      [kʰɪkaut]/*[kʰɪkʔaut]/*[kʰɪkʰaut]   'kick out'

When a vowel-initial word follows another word, the glottal stop cannot
be added. One might suggest that perhaps the final consonant of the first
word is shifted to the onset position of the second word, but that does not
seem to be the case. For example, in American English, [k] is aspirated
before a stressed vowel, yet in *kick out* the second [k] is not aspirated,
which suggests that it is still in the coda of the first word. The examples
in (6) illustrate the same point.

(6)   [tʰáini]   'tiny'
      [pətʰéɾo]   'potato'
      [ɪɹíz]/*[ɪtʔíz]/*[ɪtʰíz]   'It is.'
      [gɛɾǽn]/*[gɛtʔǽn]/*[gɛtʰǽn]   'Get Ann.'

In American English, [tʰ] and [ɾ] are allophones of the same phoneme. In
tiny, the initial [tʰ] is in the onset. In *potato*, the first [tʰ] is also in the onset
(there is no reason for the unstressed first syllable to need a coda). This
shows that in the onset of a stressed syllable, we should use [tʰ], not [ɾ].
Now, consider *it is* and *get Ann*. First of all, one cannot insert a glottal stop
before the word-initial vowels. In addition, [tʰ] is not used, even though
the following vowel is stressed. This suggests again that either syllables
do not need an onset, or the need is not strong enough for a vowel-initial
word to grab a consonant from across a word boundary. Finally, it is worth
noting that [ɾ] is not a geminate sound and so it should not be both in the
coda and in the onset at the same time.

   In Chinese, when an unstressed vowel-initial syllable follows a conso-
nant-final syllable, there is no glottal stop between the consonant and the
vowel either, to be discussed shortly. However, Chao (1968: 20) observes
that when a stressed vowel-initial Chinese syllable follows a consonant-
final syllable, the consonant does not directly link with the vowel. Instead,
the zero onset seems to intervene in between. Consider the example in (7)
from SC.

(7)   [mjǽn]+[au]   →   *[mjǽnau] (cf. English: *ran out* [rǽnaut])
      'cotton jacket'

Here [au] cannot directly link with [n], although it can in English. Duanmu
(1990, 2000) suggests the analysis in (8).

(8)   [mjǽn]+[Øau] → (*a*) [mjǽnʔau]
      'cotton jacket'   (*b*) [mjǽnɣau]
                          (*c*) [mjǽŋɣau]
                          (*d*) [mjǽŋŋau]
                          (*e*) *[mjǽnau]

In the analysis, various realizations of the zero onset intervenes between [n] and [au], so that [n] and [au] do not link with each other. In the case of (8c) and (8d), the zero onset further causes [n] to change to [ŋ].

However, as Y. Xu (1986) and J. Wang (1993) report, in connected speech none of the output forms in (8) is natural. Instead, when the words are spoken together the most natural pronunciation is (9), in which there is no nasal closure or any version of the zero onset.

(9)   [mjæ̃n]+[au] → [mjæ̃:au]
      'cotton jacket'

Y. Xu further points out that there is a three-way contrast in a VNV sequence—VN.V, V.NV, and VN.NV, which are exemplified in (10). For the sake of parallel comparison, 'overturn trouble' is a made-up phrase, semantically odd but phonologically natural (Y. Xu's original example was [pæ̃n.njæ̃n] 'half year', which has different tones from the other two examples).

(10)   Three-way contrast in VNV
         V.NV   [fa:]+[næ̃n]   → [fa:.næ̃n]   'raise trouble'
         VN.V   [fæ̃n]+[æ̃n]   → [fæ̃:.æ̃n]   'overturn case'
         VN.NV   [fæ̃n]+[næ̃n] → [fæ̃n.næ̃n]   'overturn trouble'

An oral closure is required for a nasal only when it is in the onset position. When a nasal coda occurs before vowel-initial full syllable, oral closure is not allowed. When a nasal coda occurs before a pause, oral closure is optional. When a nasal coda occurs before another nasal, it may add an additional duration for oral closure. Thus, there is no oral closure in VN.V, and the oral closure in VN.NV is longer than that in V.NV; in addition, VN.V and V.NV differ in the preceding vowel. In summary, there is no evidence for the zero onset, and the contrast between V.NV and VN.V shows that vowel-initial syllables cannot move a nasal coda into its own onset position. The examples in (11) also show the lack of the zero onset, even when the nucleus has a high vowel.

(11)   No zero onset
         [taa.ɤɤ]/*[taa.ʔɤɤ]/*ʔ[taa.ɣɤɤ]/*[taa.ŋɤɤ]   'big goose'
         [maa.æ̃n]/*[maa.ʔæ̃n]/*ʔ[maa.ɣæ̃n]/*[maa.ŋæ̃n]   'horse saddle'
         [taa.ii]/*ʔ[taa.jii]/*[taa.ʔii]/*[taa.ɣii]/*[taa.ŋii]   'big clothes (coat)'

In (11), [ʔ] cannot be added (unless one is speaking slowly), nor is there clear evidence for the presence of [ɣ] for the non-high vowels or [j] for the high vowel (although it may be hard to tell). For most speakers [ŋ] cannot be used either (except for those who always use [ŋ] before non-high vowels).

However, there is one case when VN.V does have oral closure, namely, when the second V is unstressed, such as the interjection [a]. Some examples are shown in (12).

(12)   Oral closure for N before unstressed V

[nǽn]+[a] → [nǽna]   'Hard!'
[tʰʲǽn]+[a] → [tʰʲǽna] 'Heavens!'
[mãŋ]+[a] → [mãŋa]   'Busy!'

Chao (1968) calls such cases 'linking', whereby the vowel of the second syllable is directly connected with the coda of the first. The result of linking is the auditory impression that the second syllable [a] now has an onset, so that it sounds like [na] and [ŋa] in the above examples. In Duanmu (1990, 2000) it was suggested that when linking happens the medial nasal is lengthened to a geminate and serves as both the coda of the first syllable and the onset of the second. It was further suggested that the same is true for glides and high vowels, so that VG.V changes to VG.GV, as shown in (13).

(13)   The geminate analysis

[nǽn]   +   [a]   →   [nǽnna]   'Hard!'
[tʰʲǽn]   +   [a]   →   [tʰʲǽnna] 'Heavens!'
[mãŋ]   +   [a]   →   [mãŋŋa]   'Busy!'
[xau]   +   [a]   →   [xauwa]   'Good!'
[tuu]   +   [a]   →   [tuuwa]   'Read!'
[pii]   +   [a]   →   [piija]   'Compare!'
[lai]   +   [a]   →   [laija]   'Come!'

However, in order to establish the geminate analysis, one needs to show evidence that (a) there is an increase in duration for the intervocalic nasal or glide and (b) there is a contrast between VN.a and VN.Na, or Vu.a and Vu.wa, or Vi.a and Vi.ja—but there is no such evidence. Therefore, a non-geminate analysis is sufficient, which is shown in (14).

(14)   The non-geminate analysis

[nǽn]   +   [a]   →   [nǽn.a]   'Hard!'
[tʰʲǽn]   +   [a]   →   [tʰʲǽn.a] 'Heavens!'
[mãŋ]   +   [a]   →   [mãŋ.a]   'Busy!'
[xau]   +   [a]   →   [xau.a]   'Good!'
[tuu]   +   [a]   →   [tuu.a]   'Read!'

[pii] + [a] → [pii.a] 'Compare!'
[lai] + [a] → [lai.a] 'Come!'

The non-geminate analysis is the same as that for *ran out* or *ran a* (*race*) in English, which we saw earlier. However, there remains a question: why does the nasal coda have oral closure before an unstressed vowel but not before a stressed vowel in SC? The answer seems to be a case of assimilation. Assuming that a nasal with no oral closure is more sonorous than one with oral closure, and that a stressed vowel is more sonorous than an unstressed one, it is plausible for a nasal coda to become more sonorous (lose oral closure) between two sonorous vowels.

One might still wonder why a nasal coda in English always has oral closure, whether the following vowel is stressed or not. I suggest that the answer lies in the frequency of use. English has more syllable types (about 10,000 monosyllables) than SC (about 400). Therefore, each syllable type is used much more frequently in SC than in English. According to Bybee (2001), frequent words are more likely to undergo reduction than infrequent words, which explains the difference between Chinese VN (frequent and reduced) and English VN (not frequent and not reduced). It is relevant to note that many Chinese dialects, Shanghai among them, have lost altogether nasal codas in which VN has become nasalized V or just V. Other Chinese dialects seem to be moving towards this direction as well.

Next we consider some cases that appear to require an obligatory onset slot. Duanmu (1990) offers some examples in SC that seem to support an empty onset; they are shown in (15).

(15) [tʰaa-Øa] → [tʰaa-ɦa] or [tʰaa-ja]   'Him!'
      [tʷoo-Øa] → [tʷoo-ɦa] or [tʷoo-ja]   'Many!'
      [xɤɤ-Øa]   → [xɤɤ-ɦa] or [xɤɤ-ja]   'River!'
      [ɕʲee-Øa] → [ɕʲee -ɦa] or [ɕʲee-ja]   'Shoe!'

The examples are meant to show that the zero onset (shown as [Ø]) triggers either [ɦ] or [j]. The occurrence of [ɦ] is not easy to confirm, since it is hard to distinguish [ɦ] from a simple transition from one vowel to another. In contrast, the occurrence of [j] is easy to detect. There are, however, two problems with the data: the forms with [ja] is not the preferred or most common pronunciation; and the use of [j] is hard to explain by the zero onset; for example, one might expect [w] after [oo] and [ɣ] after [ɤɤ] instead. I suggest that (15) be analysed as (16), where there is no zero onset or epenthetic [ɦ] or [j].

(16) [tʰaa-a] → [tʰaa-a]   'Him!'
      [tʷoo-a] → [tʷoo-a]   'Many!'
      [xɤɤ-a]   → [xɤɤ-a]   'River!'
      [ɕʲee-a] → [ɕʲee-a]   'Shoe!'

The interjection [ja] does occur in SC, but it is a separate word, which usually occurs phrase initially. An example is given in (17).

(17) [ja,   ɕa   ɕʷe   lə!]
      INT   fall   snow   ASP
      'Wow, it is snowing!'

Thus, the use of [ja] in (15) does not support an obligatory onset. Another
case of interest is shown by the examples in (18), which contrast with each
other.

(18) [muu3 wai4]   vs.   [muu3 ai4]
      mother outside   mother love
      'outside the mother'   'motherly love'

The two expressions are identical, including tones, except that the first one
has a medial [w] but the second one does not. Since the expressions do not
sound the same, we must represent them differently. One proposal is that
'love' has an obligatory onset; alternatively, we might say that 'love' lacks
an onset. The two analyses are compared in (19).

(19)   Onset optional   Onset required

      'outside the mother'   [muu.wai]   [muu.wai]
      'mother love'   [muu.ai]   [muu.Øai]

Since both analyses can represent the difference, there is no need to assume
that the onset is obligatory.

    Next consider the English words [ist] *east* and [jist] *yeast*, which contrast
with each other. There are again two possible analyses, shown in (20).

(20)   Onset optional   Onset required

      'east'   [ist]   [Øist]
      'yeast'   [Øist] → [jist]   [jist]

If English has G-Spreading, which spreads a high vowel to the onset (see
Chapter 3), we must assume that the onset is optional, so that *yeast* has it
but *east* does not. If we assume that the onset is required, then we must
assume that English has both [j] and [i] as separate phonemes and English
has no G-Spreading, or that G-Spreading can be used contrastively, so that
it applies in *yeast* but not in *east*.

The example in (20) raises a question for Chinese. If [ist] and [jist] can contrast in English, why do we not find similar contrasts in Chinese, such as [ii] vs. [jii], or [uu] vs. [wuu]? One possibility is that English does not require an obligatory onset but Chinese does, so that [ii] and [uu] always become [jii] and [wuu] in Chinese by G-Spreading. Another possibility is that, whereas English sometimes uses an empty onset, as in [Øist] yeast, Chinese simply does not use it at all. The preceding discussion on the lack of the zero onset favours the second possibility.

In summary, the zero onset effect in utterance-initial position is probably unintended, and in medial positions there is no evidence for the zero onset or for resyllabification across a word boundary. Moreover, as far as I am aware, there is no real phonological reason for a syllable to need an onset. For example, while the presence of the second rhyme slot increases the chance for a syllable to attract stress or to carry an extra tone, the presence of an onset slot does not. Given such considerations, I propose that the onset slot is optional for syllable structure. It is relevant to note that Poser (1984: 24–5) also argues that the onset is optional in Japanese, contrary to previous claims that vowel initial words starts with a glottal stop.

4.3. THE ANALYSIS OF CONSONANT–GLIDE

A syllable can be divided into an onset and a rhyme. It is clear that in CGVX, the rhyme includes VX only. This can be seen in words that rhyme in SC, exemplified in (21), where the common rhyming part is VX, or [æn].

(21)   Words that rhyme in Standard Chinese

[mæ̌n]	slow
[mjæ̌n]	noodles
[jæ̌n]	bright colored
[tæ̌n]	egg
[tjæ̌n]	shop
[wæ̌n]	ten thousand
[twæ̌n]	broken

More controversial is the analysis of the CG part. Some consider CG to share one onset slot (Cheung 1986; Duanmu 1990; Ao 1992; J. Wang 1993), some think that G shares the nuclear slot with V (Bao 1990*b*: 342;

Goh 2000), and some believe that G has its own slot. Within the third view, some consider G to be structurally closer to C (Firth and Rogers 1937; Bao 1990*b*: 328; J. Fu 1990; H. Wang 1999), others deem it to be structurally closer to V (R. Cheng 1966, 1968; C. Cheng 1973; L. Wang 1980; Ji 1988; Y. Lin 1989; Baxter 1992), and some think it is variably related to C or V (Chao 1934; R. Li 1983; Y. Lin 1989; Bao 1990*b*; J. Fu 1990). Evidence has been drawn from various sources, including phonemic economy, co-occurrence restrictions, and language games, but the interpretations of the evidence remain divided (see Duanmu 1990, 2000 for a review).

I want to argue that CG forms a single new sound C^G. The first argument comes from an observation by Chao (1934) that [sw] sounds quite differently in English (as in [swei] 'sway') and Chinese (as in [swei] 'age'). In English, [sw] sounds like two separate sounds, in that the rounding of [w] starts after [s]. In Chinese [sw] sounds like a single sound, in that the rounding of [w] starts at the same time as [s]. The simplest way to represent the difference, therefore, is to use [sw] (two sounds) for English and [s^w] (one sound) for Chinese (or C^G for Chinese CG in general). The second argument is that every CG (or C^G) in Chinese can be represented as a single sound in feature structure (see Chapter 2). Thus, there is no need for CG to be represented as two sounds. In addition, the C^G analysis automatically accounts for the absence of CG clusters that cannot be represented as a single sound. The third argument is that the presence of G does not increase the length of a syllable in any appreciable way. Rather, CVX and CGVX are more or less similar in duration. In addition, in CVX the onset C takes about a third of the total duration (Howie 1976). It is therefore better to use the same syllable structure for both, with just one onset slot, which can be filled by C^G.

The fourth argument is that sometimes CG alternates with C. For example, in SC, [nj] can alternate with [ɲ] (as in [njau]/[ɲau] 'bird'), [sj], with [ɕ] (as in [sjau]/[ɕau] 'small'). In terms of feature structure, the analysis is quite simple (see Chapter 2); see (22).

(22)   Sounds   Feature structure

   [ɕ]   Cor—[+fricative]
            Dorsal—[+fricative, –back]

   [s^j]   Cor—[+fricative]
            Dorsal—[–back]

   [ɲ]   Cor—[+stop]
            Dorsal—[+stop, –back]
            Soft-palate—[+nasal]

[nʲ]   Cor—[+stop]
               Dorsal—[–back]
               Soft-palate—[+nasal]

The difference between [ɕ] and [sʲ] is that the feature for Dorsal is [+fricative] in the former but not in the latter. Similarly, the difference between [ɲ] and [nʲ] is that the feature for Dorsal is [+stop] in the former but not in the latter.

The fifth argument is that when G is present, the zero onset cannot be used. This can be seen in the examples in (23).

(23)   Lack of zero onset when G is present
        [waa]   (*[ɦwaa]   *[ɣwaa]   *[ʔwaa]   *[ŋwaa])   'frog'
        [jaa]   (*[ɦjaa]   *[ɣjaa]   *[ʔjaa]   *[ŋjaa])   'crow'

If CG occupy two separate slots, the lack of the combination between a zero onset and a glide is unexpected. In contrast, if CG share a single slot, the lack of such a combination is expected.

The sixth argument for the C^G analysis is that there is simply no compelling evidence for assuming otherwise. For example, language games have often been used to argue for a particular analysis of CG, but as I will discuss below, language games do not offer conclusive evidence one way or another.

A common criticism against the C^G analysis is that it assumes too many phonemes. In particular, in the C^G analysis we must assume not only [p, t, k, s, f, …, j, w] but also [pʲ, tʲ, tʷ kʷ, sʷ, sʲ, fʲ, …]. In contrast, if CG is made of two sounds, we only need to assume the first set. However, it is a fact that C^G is phonetically a single sound, and all analyses should acknowledge that both [p, t, k, s, f, …, j, w] and [pʲ, tʲ, tʷ kʷ, sʷ, sʲ, fʲ, …] exist in SC. In addition, accepting the existence of [pʲ, tʲ, tʷ kʷ, sʷ, sʲ, fʲ, …] need not imply accepting them as additional phonemes. Rather, it is possible for two pho-nemes to merge into a single sound, as discussed in Chapter 2. Therefore, acknowledging [pʲ, tʲ, tʷ kʷ, sʷ, sʲ, fʲ …] as single sounds at the phonetic level need not imply an increase in the phonemic inventory. In fact, the C^G analy-sis assumes fewer phonemes than traditional analyses by deriving the pala-tals [tɕ tɕʰ ɕ] from CG combinations—that is from [ts tsʰ s] plus [j] or [ɥ].

4.4. STRUCTURE OF STRESSED SYLLABLES

In traditional transcriptions (e.g. R. Cheng 1966, 1968; C. Cheng 1973), a stressed syllable in SC can range from one to four sounds. Some examples are shown in (24).

(24) Traditional transcription

C	V	GV	VC	CV	VG
[m]	[ɤ]	[wa]	[an]	[ta]	[ai]
'yes?'	'goose'	'frog'	'peace'	'big'	'love'

CVG	GVG	CVC	CGV	CGVC	CGVG
[fei]	[wai]	[tʰan]	[kwa]	[xwaŋ]	[njau]
'fly'	'outside'	'sugar'	'melon'	'yellow'	'bird'

However, it is well known that all stressed syllables are long (e.g. Kratoch-vil 1968; Woo 1969; Howie 1976; M. Lin, Yan, and Sun 1984; M. Lin and Yan 1988). In addition, I have argued that CG is a single sound Cᴳ. Given such considerations, I offer the analysis in (25).

(25) Present analysis

[mː]	[ɤː]	[waː]	[ãn]	[taː]	[ai]
'yes?'	'goose'	'frog'	'peace'	'big'	'love'

[fei]	[wai]	[tʰãŋ]	[kʷaː]	[xʷãŋ]	[nʲau]
'fly'	'outside'	'sugar'	'melon'	'yellow'	'bird'

All the syllables have the rhyme VX, although some also have an onset and some do not. The full syllable structure is shown in (26).

(26) Structure for stressed syllables (onset is optional)

```
     σ
    /\
 (O) R      Onset–Rhyme
  |  /\
  X  X X   Timing slots
```

The structure can be abbreviated as (C)VX, where VX can be filled with a syllabic consonant, or as (O)NC (Onset–Nucleus–Coda). For illustration, some words are represented in (27).

(27) Sample representations

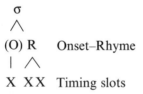

σ	σ	σ	σ	σ	σ
ONC	ONC	ONC	NC	NC	NC
nʲ a u	w a	f e i	a i	ɤ	m
'bird'	'frog'	'fly'	'love'	'goose'	'yes?'

When both CG are present, they share the onset slot. When only C or G is present, it occupies the onset slot alone. A single vowel is long because it occupies both rhyme slots. For the same reason, a syllabic consonant is also long. Syllabic consonants may seem to be marginal in SC, because they only occur as interjections. In fact, some scholars believe that every syllable must have a vowel (Cheung 1986; Hsueh 1986; Coleman 1996, 2001). However, in some dialects syllabic consonants can occur as lexical words. For example, in Shanghai, [ŋ] can mean 'fish' or 'five' depending on its tone. In addition, according to Ramsey (1987) and Duanmu (2000), fricatives can occur as syllabic consonants in SC, too. For example, the analysis of [sz̩] 'four' is shown in (28).

(28)   Syllabic consonant

s z   'four'

In traditional analyses, which assume that every syllable must have a vowel, the sound in the rhyme of 'four' has been thought to be a special kind of vowel, called an 'apical vowel', which is pronounced with a consonant-like gesture but serves as a vowel. But if consonants can serve as the rhyme of stressed syllables (consider [ŋ] 'fish' in Shanghai), there is no need to assume apical vowels.

4.5. STRUCTURE OF UNSTRESSED SYLLABLES

In traditional transcriptions, an unstressed Chinese syllable can range from one to four sounds. Some examples in Standard Chinese are shown in (29) (ASP is an aspect marker).

(29)   Traditional transcription

	Word		Example
V	[a]	interjection	[nan-a] 'hard-a (Hard!)'
CV	[lə]	ASP	[mai-lə] 'buy-ASP (bought already)'
CGV	[kwo]	ASP	[mai-kwo] 'buy-ASP (bought before)'
CVG	[tʰəu]	'head'	[mu-tʰəu] 'wood-head (wood)'
CGVC	[tʰjan]	'day'	[tʂʰwən-tʰjan] 'spring-day (spring)'

However, phonetic studies show that unstressed syllables are short and have a reduced rhyme (Woo 1969; M. Lin and Yan 1988). In particular, when VC and VG rhymes are unstressed, the coda is dropped and the rhyme duration is reduced by about 50 per cent. An example from M. Lin and Yan (1988) is shown in (30).

(30)   Rhyme reduction in unstressed syllables

[ti:]+[fãŋ] → [ti:.fə̃]   'land-direction (place)'

When [fãŋ] is unstressed, the coda [ŋ] is dropped, and the vowel (still nasalized) is reduced to a schwa. Similar observations have been made before. For example, Gao and Shi (1963: 84–5) gave the examples in (31).

(31)   [muu]   +   [tʰou]   →   [muu.tʰo]   'wood-head (wood)'
       [nau]   +   [tai]   →   [nau.te]   'head-bag (head)'

The expressions are pseudo-compounds. A pseudo-compound is a compound in structure but a single word in meaning. The second syllable of a disyllabic compound is often unstressed, and when it happens, its rhyme is shortened. In the present analysis, an unstressed syllable loses the second rhyme slot. Its syllable structure is shown in (32).

(32)   Structure for unstressed syllables (onset is optional)

σ
∧
(O)R   Onset/Rhyme
| |
X X   Timing slots

The structure can be abbreviated as (C)V, although V can be filled with a syllabic consonant. It can also be abbreviated as (O)N (Onset–Nucleus). Some sample words are represented in (33), where ASP is an aspect marker.

(33)   Sample representations

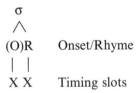

σ   σ   σ   σ
∧   ∧   ∧ |
ON   ON   ON   N
| | | | | | |
tʰ o   tʰʲ ə̃   l ə   a
'head'   'day'   ASP   interjection

4.6. LANGUAGE GAMES

Language games (also called secret languages) have sometimes been used as evidence in phonological analysis (e.g. Yip 1982; Bao 1990*b*). The assumption is that the phonology of a language game is basically the same as the phonology of the source language (see, however, Manaster-Ramer 1995, who questions the assumption). In this section I discuss some language games in Chinese and show that they are consistent with the syllable structure I propose.

The most popular language games in Chinese are Fanqie languages, in which a given syllable is first copied, then the onset of one of the syllables is modified, and finally the rhyme of the other syllable is modified. Following Chao (1931), which is the first detailed study of Fanqie languages, the output of the syllable [ma] 'mother' in a Fanqie language is used as the name of that language. Thus, Na-ma, Mai-ka, and Mo-pa will change [ma] 'mother' as in (34), where changed sounds are italicized.

(34) | Language | Input | | Reduplicate | | Onset change | | Rhyme change |
| --- | --- | --- | --- | --- | --- | --- | --- |
| Na-ma | [ma] | → | [ma-ma] | → | [*n*a-ma] | → | N/A |
| Mo-pa | [ma] | → | [ma-ma] | → | [ma-*p*a] | → | [m*o*-*p*a] |
| Mai-ka | [ma] | → | [ma-ma] | → | [ma-*k*a] | → | [m*ai*-*k*a] |

In Na-ma, only the first onset is changed; in Mo-pa and Mai-ka, both the first rhyme and the second onset are changed.

A problem in the analysis of Fanqie languages is the behaviour of the prenuclear G. In particular, sometimes the prenuclear G seems to be in the onset, sometimes it appears to be in the rhyme, and sometimes it seems to be in both. Consider the cases in (35).

(35) | Na-ma: | [tuei] | → | [nei-tuei] | 'correct' | (N. Liu 1944: 74) |
| --- | --- | --- | --- | --- | --- |
| Mo-pa: | [liaŋ] | → | [lo-tiaŋ] | 'two' | (Chao 1931: 338) |
| Mai-ka: | [xuei] | → | [xuai-kuei] | 'return' | (Chao 1931: 324) |

In Na-ma, based on the Chengdu dialect, the prenuclear [u] seems to belong to the onset, in that [t] and [u] are replaced together by [n] in the first syllable. In Mo-pa, based on the Kunshan dialect, the prenuclear [i] seems to belong to the rhyme, in that [i] and [aŋ] are replaced together by [o] in the first syllable, and [iaŋ] stays together in the second syllable. In Mai-ka, based on SC, the prenuclear [u] seems to belong to both the onset and the rhyme, in that in the first syllable it stays with the onset [x], and in the second syllable it stays with the rhyme [ei].

One can account for the different behaviours of the prenuclear G by making two assumptions. The first is that the prenuclear G can be an independent segment; the second assumption is that different Chinese dialects and/or Fanqie games can have different syllable structures, especially with regard to the position of the prenuclear G (see Yip 1982 and Bao 1990*b*). Alternatively, one can maintain a stronger claim, namely, in all Chinese languages, including language games, the prenuclear G is in the onset. I will argue that such an analysis is both possible and in some ways superior to the previous account. A central assumption in the present analysis is that replaced features can be reattached to a new host, provided that they are not in conflict with those in the latter and that the resulting segment is well formed. Similar processes have been called 'structure preservation' in traditional phonology. Let us call the process 'feature recycling' and state it in (36).

(36)   Feature Recycling
    (*a*) Features in a floating sound (i.e. replaced) may be reattached (i.e. recycled) to a non-floating segment, without changing the existing features in the latter.
    (*b*) Feature recycling observes the phonotactics of the language in question.
    (*c*) Feature recycling is local.

Feature recycling observes the general constraint in feature theory that each feature of an articulator can occur only once in a segment. For example, if a non-floating segment is [+round], it cannot receive [−round] from a floating segment. The purpose of (36c), which is similar to the constraint against line crossing in autosegmental phonology, is to prevent long-distance recycling, such as reattaching a feature from a replaced coda to the onset across the nuclear vowel. Let us now reconsider the three Fanqie languages in turn.

4.6.1. Na-ma

Na-ma is based on Chengdu (N. Liu 1944), a sister dialect of SC. Its rules can be stated in (37); examples are shown in (38).

(37)   (*a*) Reduplicate the syllable.
    (*b*) Replace the first onset with [n].

(38)   (*a*) [ie]   →   [ne-ie]   (*[nie-ie])   'grandfather'
    (*b*) [liaŋ]   →   [naŋ-liaŋ]   (*[niaŋ-liaŋ])   'goodness'

(c) [tuei] → [nei-tuei] (*[nuei-tuei]) 'correct'
(d) [kuai] → [nai-kuai] (*[nuai-kuai]) 'strange'
(e) [ɕɥe] → [ne-ɕɥe] (*[nɥe-ɕɥe]) 'snow'
(f) [tɕɥan] → [nan- tɕɥan] (*[nɥan- tɕɥan]) 'curl'

In all cases, the prenuclear G is replaced with the onset. The question is why feature recycling does not take place here. For example, in (38c), if [tu-] is a single sound, and if feature recycling applies, the result should be (39), where the floating sound is shown in parentheses.

(39) Inp]ut Copy Replace Recycle
[tʷei] → [tʷei-tʷei] → [n(tʷ)ei-tʷei] → *[nʷei-tʷei]

The [+round] ([ʷ]) of the replaced onset [tʷ] should be able to reattach to the new onset [n], giving [nʷ], which is a good sound in Chengdu but not what is found in the game. There are two possible explanations; in the first place, feature recycling does not happen in Na-ma; and secondly, feature recycling is an automatic process, but Na-ma has an additional rule to simplify the first onset. There are two reasons to choose the second explanation. First, since feature recycling takes place in both Mai-ka and Mo-pa (see below), it is a stronger position to assume that it is a general process. Secondly, there is evidence of onset simplification in Mo-pa (see below). Let us then revise the rules for Na-ma in (40).

(40) *Na-ma rules*

    (a) Reduplicate the syllable.
    (b) Replace the first onset with [n].
    (c) Simplify the first onset (i.e. delete the secondary articulator).

Since feature recycling is assumed to be automatic, it is not included in the rules.

4.6.2. Mai-ka

Mai-ka is based on SC (Chao 1931). The problem of interest here is to explain why the prenuclear G survives both the onset replacement and the rhyme replacement. Its rules can be stated in (41).

(41) *Mai-ka rules*

    (a) Reduplicate the syllable.
    (b) Replace the first rhyme with [ai].
    (c) Replace the second onset with [k].

All the three rules are regular Fanqie rules (reduplication, onset change, and rhyme change). The analysis of [xʷei] 'return' is shown in (42).

(42) Input   Copy   Replace   Recycle
      [xʷei] → [xʷei-xʷei] → [xʷai(ei)-k(xʷ)ei] → [xʷai-kʷei]

It can be seen that [ei] cannot be recycled without changing the features in the existing vowels [ai]. On the other hand, since [k] does not have [+round], it can pick up the feature from [xʷ], giving [kʷ].

4.6.3. **Mo-pa**

Mo-pa is based on Kunshan (Chao 1931), which is a Wu dialect. It can be analysed by the rules in (43).

(43) *Mo-pa rules*
      (*a*) Reduplicate the syllable.
      (*b*) Replace the first rhyme with [o].
      (*c*) Switch the value of [stop] of the second onset, and
             [α stop] → [−α voice].
      (*d*) Simplify the first onset (i.e. delete the secondary articulator).

The first three rules are again regular Fanqie rules (reduplication, onset change, and rhyme change). Rule (43*c*) is rather complex, but for our purpose it suffices to know that [l] changes to [t] in the second onset. The last rule is similar to that in Na-ma, and will be further justified shortly. The analysis of [lʲaŋ] 'two' is shown in (44).

(44) Input   Copy   Change   Recycle   Simplify onset
      [lʲaŋ] → [lʲaŋ-lʲaŋ] → [lʲo(aŋ)-tʲaŋ] → [lʲo-tʲaŋ] → [lo-tʲaŋ]

Let us see what can be recycled. The first syllable produces floating [aŋ]. [ŋ] cannot be recycled, since Mo-pa does not have [oŋ] (Chao 1931: 335–9); [a] cannot be recycled either, since [a] is [+low] and [o] is [−low]. So nothing in [aŋ] is recyclable. In the second syllable, the onset is modified, not replaced. So there is no floating item to recycle. The result [lʲo-tʲaŋ] further undergoes onset simplification, by which the secondary articulator of the first onset is deleted, giving the final output [lo-tʲaŋ].

In previous analyses of Mo-pa and similar Fanqie languages such as La-pi (based on Taiwanese), the prenuclear G is assumed to be in the rhyme (Chao 1931; P. Li 1985; Bao 1990*b*). Their approach gives a simpler analysis of the prenuclear G in words like [lʲaŋ] 'two'. Take Bao's (1990*b*: 346) analysis for example, shown in (45) and (46).

(45) *Mo-pa rules*

    (*a*) Reduplicate the syllable.

    (*b*) Replace the first rhyme (including the prenuclear G) with [o].

    (*c*) Switch the value of [stop] of the second onset, and [α stop] → [−α voice].

(46) Input   Copy   Rhyme change   Onset change
     [liaŋ] → [liaŋ-liaŋ] → [lo-liaŋ] →   [lo-tiaŋ]

Bao's analysis is simpler in two ways; there is no assumption of feature recycling and there is no assumption of onset simplification. On the other hand, Bao's analysis assumes that Mo-pa (and its source Kunshan) has a different syllabic structure from languages like SC and Chengdu. In contrast, the present analysis assumes that the prenuclear G is in the onset in all Chinese languages, including Fanqie languages. A crucial difference between the two approaches lies in whether there is onset simplification and whether the prenuclear G in Kunshan is in the rhyme.

To choose between the two theories, one needs to find a case where they make different predictions. The case is found in the GV syllable. In the present analysis, the prenuclear G is in the onset, and since it is a simple onset, onset simplification does not apply, and G should appear in the first output syllable. In Bao's analysis, G is in the rhyme, and so it should be replaced by V (in this case [o]) in the first syllable. Moreover, in the present analysis, G (being an onset) should switch [stop] and [voice] in the second syllable, while in Bao's analysis, G (being in the rhyme) should not be changed in the second syllable. The two analyses are compared in (47), using [iɔ] 'want' as an example.

(47)

	G in onset	G in rhyme
Input:	[jɔ]	[iɔ]
Reduplicate:	[jɔ-jɔ]	[iɔ-iɔ]
Change rhyme:	[jo(ɔ)-jɔ]	[o-iɔ]
Change onset:	[jo(ɔ)-tɕɔ]	−
Feature recycling:	−	−
Simplify onset:	−	−
Output:	[jo-tɕɔ]	[o-iɔ]

(48) [iɔ] → [io-tɕɔ] 'want' (Chao 1931: 336)

In the present analysis, the floating [ɔ] in the first syllable cannot be recycled. In addition, since [j] is the onset, it should change to [tɕ] in the second syllable after switching [stop] and [voice]. In Bao's analysis, [i] is in the rhyme, and so it should be replaced in the first syllable and remains unchanged in the second. As the actual example in (48) shows, the present analysis makes the correct prediction.

4.6.4. Summary

I have shown that language games are consistent with the present analysis of the SC syllable. Alternative analyses that assume different syllable structures do not offer a better solution.

4.7. FINAL vs. NON-FINAL POSITIONS

In the preceding discussion I proposed that SC has only two syllables types, the heavy (C)VX and the light (C)V. In a heavy syllable, the rhyme has just two slots. One would expect then that all heavy syllables have similar durations, and so do all light syllables. This seems to be the case in controlled environments, such as read speech in a carrier sentence (Howie 1976; M. Lin and Yan 1988). However, it is also well known that syllables in a pre-pause position can be longer than those in non-final positions. For example, Woo (1969) has shown that in Standard Chinese syllables with the third tone (T3) have an extra tone feature H in pre-pause positions, and their average rhyme duration is about 50 per cent longer than that of non-final syllables. Woo suggests that a final T3 syllable has three slots in its rhyme. The difference between final and non-final T3 syllables can be represented in (49), illustrated by the word [ma3] 'horse'.

(49) Non-final   Final

      L   LH
      ∧   ∧|
    maa   maaa

Indeed, some linguists, such as Chao (1933: 132), point out that the full final T3 sounds like two syllables. Therefore, a lengthened pre-pause syllable can be analysed in (50).

(50) CVX.V
     || | |
    ma a. a

In this analysis, there is a heavy syllable CVX and a light syllable V. Both agree with the proposed syllable types.

4.8. CASUAL SPEECH AND VOWEL-LESS SYLLABLES

In casual speech, some sounds can be deleted or changed, and this can create new syllable types that do not occur in careful speech (see Chapter 13 for more discussion). For example, in careful speech no syllable in SC has the rhyme [Vm], where V is a vowel, but in casual speech such rhymes can be found. An example is shown in (51).

(51)   wo mən → wom
        I   plural
        'we'

In careful speech, 'we' has two syllables [woo.mən], but in casual speech the two syllables often merge into one [wom]. Similarly, devoicing of non-low vowels and syllabic consonants often happens for syllables that have an aspirated onset (including voiceless fricatives) and a low tone. As a result, many voiceless syllables can be created. Some examples are shown in (52), where vowel length is not shown. When a sound is devoiced, the tone cannot be heard, which is indicated by Ø.

(52)

		HL-L		HL-Ø	
[ʋ] → [f]		[təu-fʋ]	→	[tou-ff]	'tofu'
		HL-L		HL-Ø	
[z] → [s]		[ʂaŋ-tsʰz]	→	[ʂaŋ-tsʰs]	'last time'
		HL-L		HL-Ø	
[z̩] → [ʂ]		[li-ʂz̩]	→	[li-ʂʂ]	'history'
		L-LH		Ø-LH	
[ɣ] → [x]		[kʰɣ-nəŋ]	→	[kʰx-nəŋ]	'possible'
		HL-L		HL-Ø	
[i] → [ç]		[i-tɕʰi]	→	[i-tɕʰç]	'together'
		L-HL		Ø-HL	
[i] → [ç]		[tɕʰi-tʷuŋ]	→	[tɕʰç-tʷuŋ]	'start'
		H-L		H-Ø	
[y] → [çʷ]		[tʂəŋ-tɕʰʷy]	→	[tʂəŋ-tɕʰʷçʷ]	'strive for'
		L-H		Ø-H	
[y] → [çʷ]		[çʷy-tʷo]	→	[çʷçʷ-tʷo]	'many'
		L-HL		Ø-HL	
[u] → [xʷ]		[ʂʷu-tɕa]	→	[ʂʷxʷ-tɕa]	'summer vacation'

	H-L		H-Ø		
[u] → [xʷ]	[çin-kʰʷu]	→	[çin-kʰʷxʷ]		'working hard'
	L-HL		Ø-HL		
[u] → [xʷ]	[tʰʷu-tʲi]	→	[tʰʷxʷ-tʲi]		'land'

Devoicing can happen to syllables in any position (initial, medial, or final). Devoiced [z̧, i, ɤ, u, y] sound like [ş, ç, x, xʷ, çʷ], respectively. The devoiced full syllables have similar durations as the originals (all of which should be CVX, although rhyme length is not always indicated in the above transcription), and therefore they still sound like separate syllables. Such voiceless or vowel-less syllables are not unique to Chinese; similar cases have been reported in other languages, such as Japanese and Berber.

4.9. OTHER VIEWS ON THE CHINESE SYLLABLE

Some researchers have previously conceived the idea of a fixed syllable structure. For example, Chao (1968: 18–23) divides the SC syllable into four components, 'initial', 'medial', 'vowel', and 'ending', and suggests that syllables without an overt initial have the 'zero initial', syllables without an overt medial have the 'zero medial', and syllables without an overt ending have the 'zero ending'. Similarly, Yip (1982: 647) states that 'I take it that morphemes in Chinese consist of an invariant monosyllabic skeleton.' However, there are several weaknesses in their proposals. First, their proposals were not made explicit. For example, Yip allows some slots in the syllabic skeleton to be unfilled (p. 647), which weakens the claim of a fixed skeleton since one can always propose a large skeleton and derive shorter structures by leaving some slots unfilled. Secondly, both Chao and Yip consider the prenuclear glide to have an independent position, whereas I have argued that there is no evidence for such a position. Thirdly, Chao and Yip did not propose a structural difference between full and weak syllables. Finally, while Chao and Yip believe that the onset is obligatory, a view shared by Duanmu (1990, 2000), I have come to think that it is probably optional.

   Cheung (1986) proposes that Cantonese has a fixed syllable structure OV(Cd) (Onset, Vowel, and optional Coda), which is similar to the CVX I propose. However, there remain some differences. In the first place, Cheung assumes that V must be filled by a vowel. For example, the syllabic nasal [m] 'not' is analysed as [mi:m] underlyingly (p. 150), even though there is no vowel phonetically. Secondly, in the present analysis C has no mora and V and

X have one mora each. In Cheung's analysis OV(Cd) share two moras in one of three ways, such as half a mora for O, one for V, and half for Cd (p. 146). Thirdly, in Cheung's analysis the zero onset corresponds to a real phoneme—the velar nasal (p. 37), whereas in the present analysis the zero onset is not a phoneme. Cheung (p. 175) suggests that the syllable is the basic unit of phonological analysis whereas syllable constituents (e.g. onset, nucleus, coda, and tone), phonemes, and distinctive features are secondary properties that serve to classify syllables—this view is not unusual (see Ladefoged 2001 for a recent statement). In the present analysis, a syllable is made of phonemes, and a phoneme is made of distinctive features (articulatory gestures). Thus, phonemes and features are also basic phonological units.

Chung (1996) also argues for a fixed syllable template in Chinese, which he calls CVX. However, he allows considerable variations for the template. For example, the prenuclear G can be linked to C, or to V, or to both C and V at the same time. It is thus hard to interpret the notion of a sound or its duration. For example, when a glide and a vowel are both linked to V, such as [ia], is it one sound or two? In the feature theory I propose, [ia] cannot be represented as one sound (see Chapter 2). Similarly, when a glide is linked to both C and V, which Chung believes to be the case in SC, is it a long sound? There is no evidence that the G is long. But if it is not long, what do the CVX slots mean? In the present analysis, each slot represents a time unit. In addition, G is always linked to the onset slot, and every representation of a sound follows the principles of feature theory.

Yet another view has been proposed by Goh (2000), which is similar to that of Lowenstamm (1996, 1999). On this view, the only possible syllable is CV, where V is a short vowel and either C or V can be empty. Some examples in SC are shown in (53), from Goh (2000: 242–5).

(53)	Traditional	CV only	Gloss
	[kan]	[ka.nØ]	'dry'
	[kuu]	[ku.Øu]	'drum'
	[kau]	[ka.Øu]	'tall'

The word [kan] shows that the coda consonant in the traditional analysis is an onset of a vowelless syllable in the CV analysis. The words [kuu] and [kau] show that the second half of a long vowel or diphthong in the traditional analysis is the nucleus of an onsetless syllable in the CV analysis. In other words, every full syllable in Chinese is disyllabic. A similar analysis for English is offered in Lowenstamm (1999: 154), shown in (54). For each word, Lowenstamm also assumes an additional empty CV at the left edge, which I have omitted.

(54)   Word   Traditional   CV only
       kit   [kɪt]   [kɪ.tØ]
       brick   [brɪk]   [bØ.rɪ.kØ]
       it   [ɪt]   [Øɪ.tØ]

A notable property of the CV analysis is the abstractness of the empty
element, which can have no phonetic correlates. For example, there is no
phonetic evidence for the empty onset in the Chinese word for 'drum' or
'tall', nor is there phonetic evidence for the empty vowel after [b] in the
English word *brick*. On might argue that the final [t] looks like an onset
if it is released, as in [kʰɪtʰ] *kit*. However, very often the pronunciation is
[kʰɪt⁻] or [kʰɪʔ] instead, where the final [t] is unreleased or realized as a
glottal stop, yet the CV analysis still considers it to be in the onset. In contrast, in the analysis I propose, the relation between phonetics and phonology is more direct. For example, a long vowel or consonant occupies two
timing slots, and an empty timing slot must correspond to either a pause or
the lengthening of the preceding syllable (Chapter 6).

4.10. HOMOPHONE DENSITY, FREQUENCY, AND SYLLABLE LOSS

According to a text corpus of over 45 million Chinese character tokens
(Da 1998), there are more than 6,000 different Chinese characters, most
of which are monosyllabic words. This means that each SC syllable
represents about 15 words excluding tones, or five words including tones.
The homophone load is not distributed evenly, as Figure 4.1 shows, cal-
culated by myself.

    The top 15 SC syllables are shown in (55), in phonetic symbols,
where the number of words a syllable represents (ignoring tones) is
shown in parentheses. They cover a total of 1,028 words, or a sixth of the
vocabulary.

(55)   Top 15 most frequent syllables in terms of homophone density
       [i] (106), [tɕi] (93), [y] (90), [fu] (73), [tʂz̩] (72), [li] (71), [tɕʰi] (66),
       [ɥan] (64), [ɕi] (64), [tɕan] (61), [ʂz̩] (58), [u] (55), [wəi] (53), [tɕy] (51),
       [pi] (51)

Phonologists often believe that some syllables are more 'natural' or less
'marked' than others. 'Natural' or 'unmarked' syllables are usually thought
to be those that children learn first or those that are most common in the

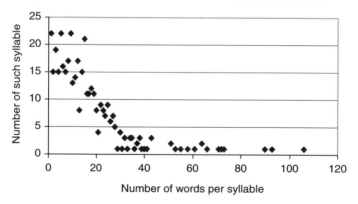

Figure 4.1 Homophone density in SC (ignoring tones), based on the analysis of 6,000 characters listed in Da (1998). Most syllables represent fewer than 20 words each, but the syllable [i] represents more than 100 words

world's languages, such as [ba], [ma], and [ta]. One might expect that the most frequent syllables in SC are the most 'natural' or 'unmarked'. However, many of those in (55) do not seem to be what are commonly thought to be unmarked syllables.

Compared with English, the average homophone density of five words per syllable in SC (including tonal distinctions) is quite high. According to the CELEX lexicon (Baayen *et al.* 1993), English has 52,447 basic words (lexical items not including regular inflections), of which 6,760 are mono-syllables. Among the monosyllables, there are 4,333 different spellings and 4,227 different primary pronunciations. This means that among the monosyllables, the average homophone density is 1.4, which is less than a third of that in SC.

Since Chinese has so many homophones, one might expect Chinese speakers to pronounce their syllables very carefully and to maintain the already small syllable inventory. Surprisingly, neither seems to be the case. For example, in a natural speech corpus of Chinese (Duanmu *et al.* 1998), about a third of all syllables are unstressed and reduced. In addition, while Middle Chinese (about AD 600) had over 3,000 syllables (including tonal distinctions), modern SC has just over 1,300. Thus, over a period of 1,500 years, Chinese lost more than half of its syllables. Moreover, the syllable inventory of modern Chinese continues to shrink. For example, SC no longer uses [p, t, k] or [m] in syllable final position, although some dialects still do. Shanghai has lost all diphthongs, and its tonal inventory has reduced to just two. In all likelihood, SC is moving in the direction of further reduction. For example, SC does not make use of such contrasts as [wi] vs. [wəi], or [ji] vs. [i], which English does (consider *we* vs. *way*, and *yeast* vs. *east*). In addition, about 200 of the 1,300 syllables in SC are now rarely used. From a functional point of view, what is happening in Chinese is quite counter-intuitive and mysterious: why is it that the high homophone density has not prevented syllable loss in SC or at least slowed it down? I suggest that there are two parts to the answer. In the first place, most lexical ambiguities are clarified by context. For example, although *sun* and *son* are homophones in English, there is hardly any context in which they would cause ambiguity. Therefore, homophone density rarely impedes how people speak. Secondly, paradoxically, high homophone density may in fact speed up syllable loss. Studies on frequency effects show that frequent words are more likely to undergo reduction than infrequent words (Bybee 2001). Because Chinese has fewer syllables than English, Chinese syllables are used more frequently, and so they are more likely to undergo reduction and loss of contrasts.

4.11. SUMMARY

In traditional analyses, both full (tone-bearing) and weak (toneless) syllables have variable structures, ranging from a minimum of C or V to a maximum of CGVX. I have proposed instead that there are two syllable types in Chinese: all full syllables are heavy (C)VX and all weak syllables are light (C)V. The onset C is optional; it can be absent, or filled by C, or by G, or by C^G (a merger of C and G). The rhyme VX or V can sometimes be filled by consonants. As far as I can see, the only argument for the traditional analysis is phonemic economy. However, the present analysis accounts for more phonetic and phonological facts at no cost to phonemic economy.

Words and Compounds

5.1. INTRODUCTION

This chapter deals with the notion of 'word' in Chinese, in particular the notion of 'compound', which is grammatically like a word. The issue may seem outside of phonology, but there are two reasons to include it here. In the first place, some phonological rules are sensitive to whether an expression is a word (compound) or a phrase. Consider the examples in (1) from Shanghai.

(1) Phrase   Compound

    LH   LH   LH   LH   L   H

    [tsʰo ve]   [tsʰo ve] → [tsʰo ve]

    fry   rice   fry   rice

    'to fry rice'   'fried rice'

Both [tsʰo] and [ve] have a rising tone, represented as LH (see Chapter 10 for the representation of tone). When they form a phrase, they keep their rising tones, but when they form a compound, the first word is L (low), the second, H (high). A phonological analysis of such problems requires knowing the distinction between a compound and a phrase. As will be seen in Chapter 6, the analysis of stress involves the notion of word and compound, and stress in turn provides the key to the analysis of the word length problem (Chapter 7), the word-order problem (Chapter 8), and tone (Chapters 10 and 11). The second reason why we include words is that there is considerable disagreement among Chinese linguists on what a word is. It would be useful, therefore, to offer a clear position on this issue.

In languages like English, 'word' is a familiar linguistic term, although it is by no means easy to define. In Chinese the corresponding term is absent; in its place is the term *zi* 'character'—a monosyllabic written graph that in most cases is also a morpheme. According to Lü (1990: 367, n. 3), the first Chinese scholar to discuss *ci* 'word', in contrast to *zi* 'character', was Shizhao Zhang (1907). Prompted by the desire to establish an alphabetic writing system, many scholars became interested in defining the notion 'word'. This is because SC has only around 1,300 syllables including tone, and an alphabetical system that is based on syllables (i.e. written with a space between syllables) will have too many homophones. If the system is based on words and compounds, then many ambiguities can be avoided. However, defining the word has proved unexpectedly hard, mainly because Chinese has little overt inflection. Besides, testing criteria often conflicted with each other. The difficulty made some scholars doubt that it is possible to define 'word' in Chinese. For example, Chao (1968: 136) says, 'Not every language has a kind of unit which behaves in most (not to speak all) respects as does the unit called "word"... It is therefore a matter of fiat and not a question of fact whether to apply the word "word" to a type of sub-unit in the Chinese sentence.' Similarly, Lü (1981: 45) says, 'The reason why one cannot find a satisfactory definition for the Chinese "word" is that there is nothing as such in the first place. As a matter of fact, one does not need the notion "word" in order to discuss Chinese grammar.' H. Wang (1999: 273) reiterates the same position and says that 'there is no clear distinction between words and phrases in Chinese.'

However, the distinction between words and phrases is important for both morphology and phonology. Without knowing what a word is, one cannot seriously talk about morphology or syntax. Similarly, many phonological facts cannot be properly understood unless we know what a word or compound is.

The definition of 'word' in fact involves two problems. The first is to distinguish a word from a morpheme, the second, to distinguish a word from a phrase. I have little to say about the first and focus on the second instead.

I use 'word' to refer to both simple words and compounds, and 'phrase' when talking about either a phrase or a clause in the ordinary sense. For example, *da de shu* 'big DE tree' will simply be called a phrase, whether one analyses it as 'a big tree' or 'a tree that is big' (see Sproat and Shih 1991 for the latter position). Similarly, for a word that contains two or more morphemes, such as *gao-xing* 'high-mood (glad)', I will simply call it a compound, even though one of them may not be free, such as *xing* 'mood' (see Chapter 7 for why some monosyllabic words are not free). I will also assume that a word can be made of words, departing from Z. Lu's (1964) position that a word can only be made of morphemes. Finally, for lack of space, I will not discuss all kinds of compounds, but will focus on nominal compounds, which constitute the majority of all compounds.

I start with a review of previous testing criteria for wordhood in Chinese and the conflicts among them. Then I discuss which criteria should be abandoned, which modified, and which adopted. Unlike Chao (1968) and Lü (1981), I conclude that wordhood in Chinese is definable. In particular, a modifier–noun [M N] nominal without the particle *de* is a compound, so are its derivatives [M [M N]], [[M N] N], [[M N][M N]], etc., as proposed by Fan (1958), B. Lu (1990), and Dai (1992).

5.2. PREVIOUS CRITERIA FOR WORDHOOD

In this section I review eleven previous criteria that have been proposed for testing wordhood in Chinese.

5.2.1. The Lexical Integrity Hypothesis

Huang (1984: 64) suggests that most differences between a word and a phrase in Chinese can be attributed to the Lexical Integrity Hypothesis (LIH), which 'is the single most important hypothesis underlying much work on Chinese compounds.' Similarly, Dai (1992: 80) suggests that 'the LIH is a theoretical universal, slight variants of which underlie most current linguistic theories.' Following Jackendoff (1972) and Selkirk (1984), Huang (1984: 60) states the Lexical Integrity Hypothesis in (2).

(2)   *The Lexical Integrity Hypothesis*
       No phrase-level rule may affect a proper subpart of a word.

Intuitively, the Lexical Integrity Hypothesis is obvious. For phrasal rules, words are the minimal units whose internal structures are not accessible. In practice, however, it is not always easy to decide which rules are phrasal, and different test criteria may give conflicting results. In what follows, therefore, I will review various test criteria separately.

5.2.2. Conjunction Reduction

Huang (1984) suggests that in both Chinese and English, Conjunction Reduction can be applied to coordinated phrases but not to coordinated words. For example, consider (3)–(5), transcribed in Pinyin (the latter two are taken from Huang 1984: 61).

(3)   (a) [jiu de shu] he [xin de shu]   (b) [jiu de he xin de] shu
         old DE book and new DE book   old DE and new DE book
         'old books and new books'   'old and new books'

(4)   (a) [huo-che] he [qi-che]   (b) *[huo he   qi] che
         fire-car   and gas-car   fire and gas car
         'train and automobile'   'train and automobile'

(5)   (a) [New York] and [New Orleans]
      (b) *New [York and Orleans]

Because (3a) is a conjunction of two phrases, Conjunction Reduction
can apply to delete the first *shu* 'book', giving (3b). In contrast, (4a) is a
conjunction of two compounds, so Conjunction Reduction cannot apply, as
shown by the ill-formed (4b). The same is true in English. Example (5a) is a
conjunction of two proper names, which behave like compounds, therefore
Conjunction Reduction cannot apply, as shown by the ill-formed (5b).

As Huang suggests, Conjunction Reduction is a phrase-level rule. By
the Lexical Integrity Hypothesis, Conjunction Reduction cannot apply to
coordinated words. In other words, the Conjunction Reduction effect is a
reflex of the Lexical Integrity Hypothesis.

The Conjunction Reduction effect has been observed before. For example, Fan (1958) suggests that there are two kinds of nominals in Chinese,
shown in (6), where M is a modifier, N a noun, and *de* a particle.

(6)   (a) [M *de* N]
      (b) [M N]

Fan observes that these nominals behave differently. Among the differences, Conjunction Reduction can apply to (6a) but not to (6b), as seen in
(3)–(5). Further examples are shown in (7) and (8).

(7)   (a) [xin   de   yi-fu]   he [xin   de   xie]
         new   DE   clothes and new   DE   shoe
         'new clothes and new shoes'

      (b) xin de [yi-fu   he   xie]
         new DE clothes and shoe
         'new [clothes and shoes]'

(8)   (a) [yang   mao]   he [yang   rou]
         sheep wool   and sheep   meat
         'sheep wool and sheep meat'

      (b) *yang [mao   he   rou]
         sheep wool and meat
         'sheep [wool and meat]'

Since (7a) is a conjunction of two [M *de* N] nominals, Conjunction Reduction can apply to give (7b). In contrast, (8a) is a conjunction of two [M N] nominals, so Conjunction Reduction cannot apply to give the intended (8b).

By Conjunction Reduction, all [M *de* N] nominals are phrases, and all [M N] nominals are words. In addition, the Conjunction Reduction criterion can apply iteratively, so that [M [M N]], [[M N] N], [[M N][M N]], etc., are also words. For example, not only is *xin shu* 'new book' a compound, but [*xiao* [*xin shu*]] 'small new book' and [[*chang mao*] [*xiao gou*]] 'long-haired small dog' are also compounds. Dai (1992: ch. 3) cites some interesting compounds that seem to pose a problem for Conjunction Reduction, such as *television and VCR table* (p. 65) and *anti- and pro-democracy* (p. 123), which contain compound-internal conjunction. I return to them later in this chapter.

5.2.3. Freedom of Parts

The Freedom-of-Parts criterion, termed after Chao (1968: 361), says that if one or both parts of an expression are 'bound', it is a word. A bound form is one that cannot be used alone. A form that can be used alone is free. Thus, in English, affixes such as *un-* (as in *unlike*) and *-er* (as in *farmer*) are bound. However, forms like *a*, *the*, and *from* are rarely used alone but are still considered free words. In Chinese, forms like *jin* 'gold' are often thought to be bound, since one would usually say *jin-zi* (where *zi* is a meaningless syllable) instead of *jin* alone. In contrast, forms like *ji* 'chicken' are free, since one can say *ji* alone. It should be noted that although *jin* 'gold' cannot be used alone, it is not an affix either; I will return to this issue in Chapter 7.

Freedom of Parts has been proposed in earlier works such as Z. Lu (1964) and Cen (1956). By this criterion, *jin-zi* 'gold' and *gao-xing* 'high-mood (glad)' are words: in the former neither part is free, and in the latter the second part is not free. Huang (1984: 63) suggests that Freedom of Parts is related to the Lexical Integrity Hypothesis, presumably because a phrase consists of words, and all words are free. If an expression contains a bound form, then it cannot be a phrase.

Lü (1979: 21) points out that Freedom of Parts can lead to wrong results, a problem also noted by Z. Lu (1964). For example, the Chinese question marker *ma* is a bound form, but it makes no sense to consider a whole question sentence to be a word only because *ma* is attached to it. In addition, the reverse of Freedom of Parts does not hold, that is, one cannot assume that if all parts of an expression are free, then the expression is a phrase. In English, for example, both *black* and *bird* are free, yet *blackbird* is a compound. Similarly, consider the Chinese examples in (9).

(9) (*a*) Free–free   (*b*) Bound–free
        ji dan   ya dan
        'chicken egg'   'duck egg'

It happens that *ji* 'chicken' is a free form, but *ya* 'duck' usually must be used with a meaningless syllable *zi*. As Lü points out, if the reverse of Freedom of Parts is true, one arrives at the rather odd conclusion that *ji dan* 'chicken egg' is a phrase but *ya dan* 'duck egg' is a word.

It is generally true, however, that if one part of an expression is bound, and if the other part is not a phrase, then the expression is a word. But if both parts are free, we must use other criteria.

5.2.4. Semantic Composition

Chao (1968: 363) proposes that if the parts of an expression are free, we should check whether the meaning is compositional—in other words, we should check whether the meaning of the whole is directly deducible from the meanings of the parts. If the meaning is not compositional then the expression is usually a word. If the meaning is compositional, then the expression is usually a phrase. Let us call this criterion Semantic Composition. For illustration, consider (10), taken from Chao (1968: 363).

(10)   da   yi
         big garment
         'overcoat' (*'big garment')

Since the meaning of (10) is not a composition of its parts, (10) is a compound. Consider also (11) and (12).

(11) (*a*) da   che   (*b*) huang   jiu
             big car   yellow wine
             'cart'   '(yellow) rice-wine'

(12) (*a*) da   shu   (*b*) bai   zhi
             big tree   white   paper
             'big tree'   'white paper'

The meanings of (11*a*, *b*) are not compositional, so they are words. The meanings of (12*a*, *b*) are compositional, so they are phrases. Since the meaning of a compound need not be compositional, an [A N] (Adjective Noun)

compound can take an additional A whose meaning may otherwise contradict that of the original A. This is shown in (13).

(13) (a) *bai   de   hei   de   ban
          white   DE   black DE   board
          'white black board'

      (b) bai   de   hei-ban
          white   DE   black-board
          'white blackboard'

      (c) bai   hei-ban
          white   black-board
          'white blackboard'

In (13a), *hei de ban* 'black board' is a phrase, so it cannot take the additional adjective *bai* 'white', which contradicts the original adjective *hei*
'black'. In contrast, in (13b, c) *hei-ban* 'blackboard' is a compound,
so adding the additional *bai* 'white' (with or without the particle *de*) is
possible, even though *bai* 'white' contradicts *hei* 'black'. Huang (1984:
61) suggests that rules for semantic interpretation are phrasal rules which
cannot see the internal semantics of a word. Therefore Semantic Composition
follows from the Lexical Integrity Hypothesis.

The Semantic Composition test has limitations. To begin with, as noted
by Chao (1968: 364) and Huang (1984: 63), the meaning of an idiomatic
expression is not compositional, yet many idioms are phrases. For example, neither *kick the bucket* nor *let the cat out of the bag* is a compound.
Secondly, even when idioms are excluded, and when Semantic Composition is used together with Freedom of Parts, *ji dan* 'chicken egg' will still
be deemed a phrase while *ya dan* 'duck egg' will be deemed a word, which
is a rather odd conclusion. Third, in English expressions such as *apple pie*
and *weekend*, both words are free and the meaning is compositional, yet
they are still compounds. Thus, Semantic Composition does not seem to
play much of a role. Finally, the results of Semantic Composition conflict
with those of Conjunction Reduction; the latter considers both *ji dan* and
ya dan as well as (11a, b) and (12a, b) to be compounds.

5.2.5. Syllable count

Lü (1979: 21–2) suggests that in deciding whether an expression is a
word or a phrase, one should consider the length of the expression. As
Lü puts it (1979: 21), 'The word in the mind of the average speaker is
a sound–meaning unit that is not too long and not too complicated, about

the size of a word in the dictionary entry.' Specifically, Lü suggests that disyllabic [M N] nominals should be treated as words, while quadrisyllabic or longer nominals should be treated as phrases. In this analysis, *ji dan* 'chicken egg', *ya dan* 'duck egg', (11*a*, *b*), and (12*a*, *b*) are all compounds. On the other hand, all the expressions in (14) are phrases.

(14) (*a*) ren-zao   xian-wei
            man-make   fiber
            'man-made fiber'

     (*b*) xiu-zhen   ci-dian
            pocket   dictionary
            'pocket dictionary'

     (*c*) luo-xuan   tui-jin-qi
            snail-turn   push-advance-instrument
            'screw propeller'

     (*d*) Beijing   shi-fan   da-xue
            Beijing   normal   university
            'Beijing Normal University'

     (e)   lian-he   guo   jiao-yu   ke-xue   wen-hua   zu-zhi
            united   nation   education   science   culture   organization
            'United Nations Educational, Scientific, and Cultural Organization'

It will be noted that in each of (14*a*–*c*), the first immediate component is not a free form. In (14*d*, *e*), the expressions are proper names. For Chao (1968), all the expressions are compounds: for Lü, however, they are too long to be compounds.

Z. Lu (1964: 22–7) proposed a different version of Syllable Count. For him, whether an [N N] (Noun–Noun) nominal is a word or a phrase depends on the length of each noun. In particular, [1 1], [1 2], [1 3], [2 1], and [3 1] (where the digits indicate the number of syllables in each N) are words regardless of other criteria, while [2 2] could be a word or a phrase depending on other criteria.

Syllable Count has two problems; it is in conflict with other criteria, such as Freedom of Parts, and it is arbitrary in nature. There is no explanation why the upper limit for compounds is set at three (or four) syllables, especially in view of the fact that even single morphemes can exceed that length, such as *jiekesiluofake* 'Czechoslovakia', which has six syllables.

5.2.6. Insertion

The Insertion test (also called the 'expansion' test) was proposed by L. Wang (1944: 16). Z. Lu (1964) considers it to be the most important test for wordhood. The Insertion test says that if an expression allows an item to be inserted between its parts, then it is a phrase; otherwise it is a word. For nominals, the typical item to be inserted is the particle *de*, by which [M N] becomes [M *de* N]. In fact, according to Z. Lu (1964: 21), *de*-insertion is the only workable test for [M N] nominals. For illustration, consider two cases from H. Zhang (1992: 33), shown in (15) and (16).

(15) (*a*) bai   zhi   (*b*) bai   de zhi
        white paper   white DE paper
        'white paper'   'white paper'

(16) (*a*) xin   zhi   (*b*) *xin de   zhi
        letter paper   letter DE   paper
        'letter paper'   'letter paper'

In (15*a*) *de*-insertion is possible, but in (16*a*) it is not (for the intended meaning). Therefore, H. Zhang considers *bai zhi* 'white paper' to be a phrase and *xin zhi* 'letter paper' a compound.

Z. Lu (1964: 8) points out that for the Insertion test to work, it is necessary that the inserted material not change the structure of the original expression. To what extent two expressions have the same structure is not made explicit, but a few illustrations are given. For example, Z. Lu considers pairs like (15*a, b*) to have the same structure, both being [modifier noun], and the particle *de* apparently having no significance. On the other hand, the expressions in (17), from Z. Lu (1964: 8), do not have the same structures.

(17) (*a*) yang   rou
        sheep meat
        'mutton'

     (*b*) yang   de   shen-shang   you   rou
          sheep DE   body   have meat
          'The sheep's body has meat.'

Although (17*a*) can be expanded into (17*b*), the original structure has changed from a nominal in (17*a*) to a sentence in (17*b*). Therefore (17) is not a genuine case of insertion.

A further restriction on the Insertion test is that the inserted material should not change the meaning of the original expression (see Z. Lu 1964: 32 and Chao 1968: 362). For example, consider the data in (18).

(18) (*a*) you   zui   (*b*) you   de   zui
        oil   mouth   oil   DE   mouth
        'glib talker'   'greasy mouth' (*'glib talker')

Although *de* can be inserted into (18*a*) to give (18*b*), the meaning has clearly changed. Therefore we should consider (18*a*) to have failed the Insertion test. Let us now state the two conditions on the Insertion test in (19).

(19)   *Conditions on the Insertion test*
    (*a*) The resulting expression should have the same structure as the original.
    (*b*) The resulting expression should have the same meaning as the original.

Proponents of *de*-insertion assume that it is possible, at least in some cases, that *de*-insertion will not change either the meaning or the structure of the original expression. But the assumption is not shared by others, since significant semantic and structural differences between [M N] and [M *de* N] have been documented (see below).

Z. Lu (1964: 8) notes a further problem with the Insertion test. Sometimes the results of *de*-insertion conflict with each other depending on whether the host expression occurs alone or in a larger structure. Consider (20) and (21) (from Z. Lu 1964: 8).

(20)   (*a*) yang   rou   (*b*) yang   de   rou
          sheep   meat   sheep   DE   meat
          'mutton'   'sheep's meat (mutton)'

(21)   (*a*) mai   yi-jin   yang   rou
          buy   one-jin   sheep   meat
          'to buy a jin of mutton'   (a *jin* is 500 grams)

    (*b*) ??mai   yi-jin   yang   de   rou
          buy   one-jin   sheep   DE   meat
          'to buy a jin of sheep's meat (mutton)'

In (20*a*, *b*), both expressions are good (although one may argue about whether the meanings are quite the same). In (21), however, *de*-insertion makes (21*b*) odd. Examples (20) and (21) show that passing *de*-insertion in one environment does not guarantee passing it in another. In view of this problem, H. Zhang (1992: 52) proposes the condition in (22).

(22)   *Condition on* de-*insertion*
    An [M N] nominal is a phrase iff it can be changed into [M de N] in the accusative position.

In other words, the proper place to apply *de*-insertion is a situation like (21), but not one like (20). According to (22), then, *yang rou* 'mutton' fails the *de*-insertion test, so it is a compound. Similarly, both *ji dan* 'chicken egg' and *ya dan* 'duck egg' are compounds. On the other hand, *xin shu* 'new book' is a phrase, as shown in (23) (H. Zhang 1992: 52).

(23) (*a*) wo   mai-le   yi-ben   xin   shu
         I   bought   one-copy   new   book
         'I bought a new book.'

     (*b*) wo   mai-le   yi-ben   xin   de   shu
         I   bought   one-copy   new   DE   book
         'I bought a new book.'

For H. Zhang, the meanings of (23*a*, *b*) are identical, so *xin shu* 'new book' passes the *de*-insertion test and is a phrase. Similarly, *da shu* 'big tree', *bai zhi* 'white paper', *hei mao* 'black cat', etc. are considered phrases.

But why is the accusative position, and the accusative position alone, selected for *de*-insertion? Zhang offers no explanation, but it is probably because it is hardest to apply *de*-insertion there. In any case, some problems remain. For example, it is not easy to tell whether pairs like (20*a*, *b*) or (23*a*, *b*) have the same meaning. For example, D. Zhu (1980) argues that *xin shu* and *xin de shu* have different meanings, as do [M N] and [M *de* N] in general. Similarly, according to Sproat and Shih (1991), *xin shu* means 'new book' but *xin de shu* means '(a) book which is new'. Moreover, the Insertion test is in conflict with Conjunction Reduction, as shown in (24) and (25).

(24) xin   shu   he   jiu   shu
      new   book   and   old   book
      'new book and old book'

(25) *[xin   he   jiu]   shu
      new   and   old   book
      'new and old books'

Since (24) cannot be reduced to (25), Conjunction Reduction regards both *xin shu* and *jiu shu* as compounds. Hence, Conjunction Reduction and the *de*-insertion provide conflicting results.

There is another problem with the *de*-insertion test. For Lu and Zhang, both *da shu* 'big tree' and *da de shu* 'big tree' are phrases, and the presence or absence of *de* has no effect. But consider (26) and (27).

(26) *da   [tie   de   shi-zi]
      big   iron   DE   lion
      'big iron lion'

(27) da   de   [tie   de   shi-zi]
      big   DE   iron   DE   lion
      'big iron lion'

If *da shu* 'big tree' is a phrase, *da [tie de shi-zi]* 'big iron lion' should also be a phrase. Yet (26) is bad. For it to be good, *de* must be added, as shown in (27). This effect has been observed before (Fan 1958; Chao 1968: 288; Sproat and Shih 1991; Dai 1992). For proponents of *de*-insertion there is no explanation why (26) is bad. For others the reason is simple: [M *de* N] and [M N] are different structures. [M *de* N] is a phrase and [M N] a compound. Even if there is no apparent semantic difference, *de*-insertion changes the structure of an [M N] nominal. In particular, in (26), [*tie de shi-zi*] is a phrase, but it occurs inside a compound structure [A N], giving a bad expression.

A further problem with the Insertion test is that even if insertion applies, a compound need not become a phrase. For example, in English both *evening class* and *evening chemistry class* are compounds (Halle and Vergnaud 1987), even though the latter is an expansion of the former. Thus, one cannot assume that a compound can not be expanded.

In summary, the Insertion test can at best be used in a limited way. If the Insertion test cannot apply to an expression, then the expression is probably a word. If the test does apply, nothing can be inferred.

5.2.7. Exocentric Structure

This test is suggested by Chao (1968: 362). An expression is endocentric if its category is related to the category of one of its parts. For example, *drink milk*, a verb phrase, is related to its part *drink*, which is a verb. An expression is exocentric (i.e. not endocentric) if its category is not directly related to the category of any of its parts. Examples (28) to (31) are instances of exocentric expressions.

(28)   NV → N
      huo   shao
      fire   burn
      'baked wheaten cake'

(29)   VN → N
      tian   fang
      fill   room
      'second wife (to a widower)'

(30)   VV → N
      kai   guan
      open   close
      'switch'

(31)   NV → A
      shou-ti   (shi)
      hand-carry   (style)
      'portable (style)'

Example (28) is a noun, so is its component *huo*, but the two nouns are unrelated. Example (29) is a noun, so is its second component, but the two nouns are again unrelated. Example (30) is a noun, but its components are verbs. In (31), *shou-ti* is made of a noun and a verb, but the combination serves as an adjective.

According to Chao, if an expression is exocentric, it is a compound. Let us call it the Exocentric Structure criterion, according to which (28) to (31) are all compounds. Huang (1984: 63) attributes the Exocentric Structure criterion to the Lexical Integrity Hypothesis, because well-formed phrases are typically endocentric. In order for an exocentric expression to appear, it must be converted to a compound so that its internal structure is no longer visible to phrasal rules. I am not aware of counter-examples for this criterion.

5.2.8. Adverbial modification

Fan (1958: 214) notes that [A *de* N] may take an adverb (typically an adverb of degree) that modifies A, but [A N] cannot. In other words, [[Adv A] *de* N] is good, as shown in (32), but [[Adv A] N] is bad, as shown in (33).

(32) (*a*) xin   de   shu
         new   DE   book
         'new book'

      (*b*) [hen xin]/[geng xin]/[zui xin]/[zheme xin] de shu
         [very new]/[more new]/[most new]/[such new] DE book
         '[very new]/[newer]/[newest]/[such new] books'

(33) (*a*) xin   shu
         new   book
         'new   book'

      (*b*) *[hen xin]/*[geng xin]/*[zui xin]/*[zheme xin] shu
         [very new]/[more new]/[most new]/[such new] book
         '[very new]/[newer]/[newest]/[such new] books'

Let us call this test Adverbial Modification. Dai (1992: 108) suggests that the badness of (33b) is due to the Lexical Integrity Hypothesis, in that A in [A N] is protected by Lexical Integrity and is not accessible to an external modifier. For example, *xin shu* '[new book]' is a compound, so *hen* cannot get inside it to give *hen xin shu* '[[very new] book]'. However, it is unclear why Dai considers *hen* to be added after *xin shu* is formed, instead of *hen xin* combining first before *shu* is added. Perhaps M in [M N] should be a single word? But this is not true either. Example (34) shows that M can expand into [A N] or [N N].

(34)   [N N]   →   [[A N] N] / [[N N] N]
        bu shou-tao   [lan bu]   shou-tao/[mian bu]   shou-tao
        cloth glove   blue cloth glove/cotton   cloth glove
        'cloth glove'   'blue-cloth glove'/'cotton-cloth glove'

Why then cannot M be expanded in (33)? One possibility is that the [adverb adjective] structure is a phrase, and because it is a phrase, it cannot occur inside a compound. A few exceptions can be found, such as *zui gao ji* '[[most high] level] (highest level)', but as Fan (1958: 214) points out, they are rare and unproductive. In contrast, [A N] and [N N] in (34) are compounds, so they can readily occur inside a compound. Another possible reason for the badness of [[Adv A] N] is that [A N] is not a productive compound structure (see below).

5.2.9. XP substitution

Fan (1958: 214) notes that N in [M *de* N] can be replaced by [X N], where X is a [Numeral-Classifier N] unit or a [Demonstrative N] unit, but N in [M N] cannot. Since there is little doubt that both [Numeral-Classifier N] and [Demonstrative N] are phrases (denoted as XPs in syntax), I will call this process XP Substitution. The schematic forms of XP Substitution are given in (35) and two examples are shown in (36) and (37).

(35)   (*a*) [M *de* N] →   [M *de* XP]
        (*b*) [M N]   ↛   *[M XP]

(36)   [M de XP]
        (*a*) xin   *de* [san   ben   shu]
               new) DE   three   copy   book
              'three books that are new'

        (*b*) xin   de   [nei   ben   shu]
               new   DE   that   copy   book
              'that book which is new'

(37)   *[M XP]
        (*a*) *xin   [san   ben   shu]
               new   three   copy   book

        (*b*) *xin   [nei   ben   shu]
               new   that   copy   book

Sproat and Shih (1991) and Dai (1992) have observed similar effects. For example, consider (38) and (39), where only intended meanings are shown (other meanings may be available but are irrelevant to the present discussion).

(38) (a) [[M *de* N] *de* N]
      [xin-xian   de   dou-sha]   de   yue-bing
      fresh   DE   bean-paste   DE   moon-cake
      'mooncake with fresh bean-paste filling'

      (b) [M *de* [M *de* N]]
      xiao   de   [xin   de   shu]
      small   DE   new   DE   book
      'small new book'

(39) (a) *[[M *de* N] N]
      *[xin-xian   de   dou-sha]   yue-bing
      fresh   DE   bean-paste   moon-cake
      'mooncake with fresh bean-paste filling'

      (b) *[M [M *de* N]]
      *xiao   [xin   de   shu]
      small   new   DE   book
      'small new book'

The examples in (38) show that both M and N in [M *de* N] can be replaced by a *de*-phrase. On the other hand, the examples in (39) show that neither M nor N in [M N] can be replaced by a *de*-phrase.

The contrast between [M *de* N] and [M N] under XP Substitution is compatible with the assumption that [M N] is a compound and [M *de* N] is a phrase. Since a phrase cannot occur inside a compound, the badness of (37) and (39) is expected. If [M *de* N] and [M N] have the same structure, as proponents of *de*-insertion assume, then the contrast between (36) and (37) and between (38) and (39) is unexpected.

5.2.10. **Productivity**

It is reasonable to assume that phrasal rules are productive. For example, if a language has the rule NP → [A N], by which an adjective and a noun can make a noun phrase, one expects most [A N] combinations to be possible. On the other hand, if most [A N] combinations are not possible, one would assume that [A N] is not a phrase.

In English, [A N] is productive. In Chinese, many adjectives, such as *da* 'big', *xiao* 'small', *xin* 'new', *jiu* 'old', *bai* 'white', *hong* 'red', *chang* 'long', and *duan* 'short', are quite productive in that they can form [A N] with many nouns. If all [A N] structures are compounds in Chinese, as proposed by Fan (1958) and Dai (1992), then the definition seems too loose. Why, for example, are all the expressions in (40) compounds in Chinese, while their structures, their meanings, and their English translations seem phrasal?

(40) (*a*) gui   dong-xi   (*b*) bao   zhi
           expensive article   thin   paper
           'expensive article'   'thin paper'

      (*c*) cong-ming hai-zi   (*d*) hua-ji   dian-ying
           clever   child   funny   movie
           'clever child'   'funny movie'

      (*e*) huang   zhi-fu   (*f*) shen   shui
           yellow   uniform   deep   water
           'yellow uniform'   'deep water'

      (*g*) duan   xiu-zi   (*h*) bai   zhi
           short   sleeve   white   paper
           'short sleeve'   'white paper'

However, the picture in (40) is deceptive. As D. Zhu (1980) points out, Chinese [A N] is not fully productive but has many gaps. For example, all the expressions in (41) are unnatural, even though they are parallel in structure to those in (40) and their English translations are perfectly well-formed (from D. Zhu 1980: 9–10; judgements are Zhu's).

(41) (*a*) *gui   shou-juar   (*b*) *bao   hui-chen
            expensive   handkerchief   thin   dust
            'expensive handkerchief'   'thin dust'

      (*c*) *cong-ming   dong-wu   (*d*) *hua-ji   ren
            clever   animal   funny   person
            'clever animal'   'funny person'

      (*e*) *huang   qi-chuan   (*f*) *shen   shu
            yellow   steam-boat   deep   book
            'yellow steam-boat'   'difficult book'

      (*g*) *duan   chen-mo   (*h*) *bai   shou
            short   silence   white   hand
            'short silence'   'white hand'

One may wonder if there are constraints on the collocation between the adjectives and nouns in (41). The answer is no. The examples in (41) will become good if *de* is added (although as Zhu points out, expressions with

a monosyllabic adjective can be made more colloquial by reduplicating
the adjective as well), as shown in (42).

(42) (*a*) gui   de   shou-juar   (*b*) bao   de   hui-chen
          expensive   DE   handkerchief   thin   DE   dust
          'expensive handkerchief'   'thin dust'

       (*c*) cong-ming de   dong-wu   (*d*) hua-ji de   ren
          clever   DE   animal   funny   DE   person
          'clever animal'   'funny person'

       (*e*) huang   de   qi-chuan   (*f*) shen de   shu
          yellow   DE   steam-boat   deep   DE   book
          'yellow steam-boat'   'difficult book'

       (*g*) duan   de   chen-mo   (*h*) bai   de   shou
          short   DE   silence   white   DE   hand
          'short silence'   'white hand'

Examples like the above indicate that while [A *de* N] is fully productive in
Chinese, [A N] is not. The gaps in (41) are not exceptions but the norm. To
appreciate how defective [A N] is, consider (43) and (44).

(43) (*a*) gao   shan   (*b*) gao   lou
          tall   mountain   tall   building
          'tall mountain'   'tall building'

(44) (*a*) *gao   shu   (*b*) *gao   ren
          tall   tree   tall   person
          'tall tree'   'tall person'

In (43), *gao* 'tall' appears productive. But (44*a*, *b*), perfectly normal from
an English point of view, are simply bad. One might suspect that the lack
of 'tall tree' and 'tall person' might be due to semantic blocking. In particular, *gao ren* has the special meaning 'highly skilled master', and perhaps
that is why it is not used for the literal meaning of 'tall person'. Similarly,
there is an expression *da shu* 'big tree', which can mean 'tall tree', and
perhaps that is why we do not need the expression *gao shu* 'tall tree' to
express the same meaning. However, there is an expression *da ren*, which
can be used for both its literal meaning 'big person' and a specialized
meaning 'sir' or 'your honour'. This shows that blocking may not be the
real reason for the lack of *gao ren* 'tall person' or *gao shu* 'tall tree'.

Alternatively, one may suspect that, since English has two words for
height, *high* (which goes with *standard*, *speed*, and *mountain*) and *tall*
(which goes with *building*, *tree*, and *person*), perhaps there is another Chinese
word for height which can go with *shu* 'tree' and *ren* 'person'. But there

is not. To express 'tall tree' and 'tall person' in Chinese, *gao* must be followed by *de*, as shown in (45).

(45) (*a*) gao   de   shu   (*b*) gao   de   ren
           tall   DE   tree   tall   DE   person
           'tall tree'   'tall person'

In other words, there is no way to express simple ideas like 'tall tree' and 'tall person' in Chinese with an [A N] structure. If [A N] is productive in Chinese, such gaps cannot be explained.

In conclusion, evidence from productivity supports the view that [M *de* N] is a phrase and [M N] is a word.

5.2.11. **Intuition**

A number of researchers have assumed that Chinese speakers, or educated linguists at least, have intuitions about what a word is, and that the predictions of one's theory should agree with these intuitions. For example, Lü (1979: 21–2) says that in the mind of the average speaker a 'word' is something that is 'not too long', and he proposes an upper limit of four syllables, beyond which an expression should be viewed as a phrase regardless of other criteria.

However, it is doubtful whether Chinese speakers have clear intuitions for what a word is. It is relevant to note that the notion 'word' was absent in Chinese linguistics until it was introduced in the twentieth century. The fact that there is still no consensus on the definition of the word in Chinese shows that people's intuitions do not always agree. Thus, unless intuition can be demonstrated, it should not be used as an argument for or against other criteria.

5.2.12. **Summary**

I have reviewed ten tests for wordhood in Chinese, focusing on [M N] nominals. The results are summarized in (46).

(46)

Test	[M N]	[M de N]
Conjunction Reduction	word	phrase
Freedom of Parts	both	phrase
Semantic Composition	both	phrase
Syllable Count	both	phrase
Insertion	both	phrase
Exocentric Structure	??	phrase

Adverbial Modification	word	phrase
XP Substitution	word	phrase
Productivity	word	phrase
Intuition	??	phrase

By these tests [M *de* N] is always a phrase. For [M N], results differ. Four tests (Conjunction Reduction, Adverbial Modification, XP Substitution, and Productivity) consider all [M N]s to be words. The Intuition test gives no definite answer, since people's intuitions do not always agree. The Exocentric Structure test considers exocentric [M N]s to be words but says nothing about other [M N]s. The remaining four tests (Freedom of Parts, Semantic Composition, Syllable Count, and Insertion) consider some [M N]s to be words and some to be phrases; however, they differ on which [M N]s are words and which phrases.

5.3. THE PRESENT ANALYSIS

In this section I discuss which criteria should be rejected, which adopted with limitations, and which adopted without reservations.

5.3.1. Tests to be rejected

I suggest that Syllable Count, Insertion, and Intuition be rejected. Consider Intuition first. There are two reasons for rejecting it: as noted by Z. Lu (1964), people's intuitions do not always agree, especially with [M N] nominals; and, when intuitions do agree, one can usually interpret them in concrete terms. For example, all people agree that *you zui* 'oil mouth (glib talker)' and *tian fang* 'fill room (second wife to a widower)' are compounds. The former follows from Semantic Composition, the latter from Exocentric Structure. It is therefore better to refer directly to the conditions that underlie intuition.

Next, consider Syllable Count. The main problem is that it is arbitrary. Why, for example, should the threshold for phrases be set at four syllables, instead of three or five? And why is there no such condition in other languages?

Finally, consider Insertion. As discussed above, the Insertion test crucially requires two conditions, repeated in (47).

(47) *Conditions on the Insertion test*
    (*a*) The resulting expression should have the same structure as the original.
    (*b*) The resulting expression should have the same meaning as the original.

But the first condition is unlikely to be met in *de*-insertion. This is because any nominal with *de* would be a phrase, whereas a nominal without it could be a word. Besides, [M N] and [M *de* N] show different syntactic behaviour so they cannot have the same structure. The second condition is also hard to apply, because it is often hard to tell when two expressions have the same meaning. For example, does 'a big tree' have the same meaning as 'a tree that is big'? The semantic judgement required here is very subtle. The same is true in Chinese. For some, such as D. Zhu (1980), [M N] and [M *de* N] never have exactly the same meanings. For others, [M N] and [M *de* N] can have the same meanings. But even if 'a big tree' and 'a tree that is big' have the same meaning, it does not follow that they have the same structure. Therefore, there is no reason to assume that pairs like *da shu* 'big tree' and *da de shu* 'big DE tree' have the same structure just because they have similar meanings.

A further reason to reject Intuition, Syllable Count, and Insertion is that they are in conflict not only with each other but also with other criteria (see section 5.2). As we will see below, once these three criteria are rejected, all the remaining criteria give converging results.

5.3.2. Tests to be adopted with limitations

Now consider Freedom of Parts, Semantic Composition, and Exocentric Structure. These tests assume that phrases should have regular syntactic and semantic behaviour: they should be made of free parts, be semantically compositional, and be structurally endocentric. If an expression fails any of these tests, it is not a phrase. All researchers agree on this issue. But what if an expression passes these tests? Obviously, we cannot say that it must be a phrase, unless we assume that no compound is made of free parts, is semantically compositional, and is structurally endocentric. But the assumption cannot be maintained, because many compounds have regular syntactic and semantic behaviours. An example is shown in (48).

(48)   apple pie

The English compound is made of two free parts, with a compositional meaning, and with an endocentric structure. The example shows that when an expression passes Freedom of Parts, Semantic Composition, and Exocentric Structure, it can still be a compound. In other words, Freedom of Parts, Semantic Composition, and Exocentric Structure can detect compounds that have peculiar syntactic and semantic properties, but they say nothing about expressions with regular syntactic and semantic properties.

5.3.3. **Tests to be adopted**

Let us now consider the remaining four criteria, Conjunction Reduction, Adverbial Modification, XP Substitution, and Productivity. They are based on the assumptions that Conjunction Reduction applies to phrases but not to compounds (but see some counter-examples below), that at least one part of a phrase should be an XP and so is replaceable by an XP (including an adverbial), and that phrasal constructions are productive. As discussed in section 5.2, these criteria offer the same conclusion that in Chinese all [M *de* N]s are phrases and all [M N]s are words.

It is interesting to note a difference between [A N] in English and that in Chinese. The English [A N] can be either a compound (e.g. *black market*) or a phrase (e.g. *black dogs*), but the Chinese [A N] can only be a compound. The difference is clearly shown by productivity. The English [A N] is productive, where A readily accepts an adverbial, as shown in (49).

(49)   difficult discussions
          very/more/most difficult discussions

In contrast, the Chinese [A N] is unproductive for many adjectives (e.g. **jian-ku tao-lun* 'difficult discussions', **kuan-da jian* 'large room'). For some adjectives, such as *da* 'big' and *xiao* 'small', [A N] seems to be productive, but A still cannot take an adverbial, as shown in (50).

(50)   da gou   * [hen da]/*[geng da]/*[zui da] gou
          big dog   [very big]/[more big]/[most big] dog
          'big dog'   '[very big]/[bigger]/[biggest] dog'

However, A can take an adverbial if *de* is present, as shown in (51).

(51)   [hen da]/[geng da]/[zui da] de gou
          [very big]/[more big]/[most big] DE dog
          '[very big]/[bigger]/[biggest] dog'

If the Chinese [A N] is the same as the English [A N], such facts are hard to explain.

Paul (2005) argues that some Chinese [M N]s are phrases. She offers two arguments. First, with regard to syntactic restrictions on Chinese [M N]s, Paul argues that English [M N]s also have syntactic restrictions; for example, she cites some cases from Bolinger (1967) such as *the then president* vs. **the now president*, and *a nearby building* vs. **a nearby bus*). However, as can be seen in the examples I discussed, the restrictions on the Chinese [M N] are extensive and systematic (especially with regard to Conjunction Reduction, Adverbial Modification, XP Substitution, and Productivity), whereas those on the English [M N] seem to be sporadic. To equate the Chinese [M N] with the English [M N] would leave some significant differences unaccounted for. Paul's second argument is more interesting. She argues that some syntactic structures seem to show that [M N] can be a phrase in Chinese. Consider the example in (52).

(52) Bu   mai   mutou   zhuozi,   mai   tie   de   Ø
      not   buy   wood   table   buy   iron   DE   Ø
      'Don't buy a wood table; buy an iron one.'

Paul argues that the empty noun Ø in the second clause refers to 'table' in the first clause. If *mutou zhuozi* 'wood table' is a compound, its internal structure should be invisible (protected by Lexical Integrity), and the empty noun can only refer to 'wood table' as a whole instead of 'table' alone. However, it is not clear whether structures like (52) are a good test for compounds. Consider a parallel example in English, shown in (53).

(53)   I don't like meat pies; I like the one without meat.

By all standards, *meat pie* is a compound. Still, the anaphor *one* in (53) can refer to *pie*, instead of *meat pie* as a whole. This shows that structures like (52) and (53) are not good tests for compounds, and there is no compelling evidence for treating [M N] as phrases in Chinese.

5.3.4. **Summary**

I have offered arguments for rejecting Syllable Count, Insertion, and Intuition as tests for wordhood in Chinese. Once this is done, the remaining criteria provide converging results. In particular, all [M N] nominals, as well as their iterative derivatives, such as [M [M N]] and [[M N] N], are compounds.

The lack of [M N] phrases in Chinese may seem unusual, but there is a possible explanation. Assume that the main difference between a phrase and a compound is that a phrase has inflection or a function word (such as *'s* and *of* in English or *de* in Chinese) but a compound does not. For example, *bird's house* and *birds' house* are phrases, but *bird house* is a compound. Since the Chinese [M N] lacks inflection or a function word, it cannot be a phrase. Instead, Chinese nominal phrases are expressed by [M *de* N], as are nominals with a relative clause.

5.4. COMPOUND INTERNAL CONJUNCTION

As discussed above, Conjunction Reduction should apply to phrases but not to compounds. However, there are some apparent counter-examples. First, consider the examples in (54), which have an internal conjunction, yet they are usually treated as compounds.

(54)   (*a*) meat-and-potato eater (Dai 1992: 112, citing Bates 1988: 228)
         (*b*) television and VCR table (Dai 1992: 65)

I suggest that (54*a*) does not come from Conjunction Reduction, since *meat-and-potato eaters* does not mean *meat eaters and potato eaters*. Example (54*b*) does not come from Conjunction Reduction either, since *television and VCR tables* does not mean *television tables and VCR tables*. If so, one can still maintain the claim that Conjunction Reduction does not apply to compounds, and the conclusion that [M N] is a word and [M *de* N] a phrase remains unaffected. Next, consider (55), cited in Cen (1956: 13), where the plural marker *men* is a bound form.

(55)   xue-sheng   he   lao-shi   men
         student   and   teacher   PL
         'students and teachers'

Unlike (54), (55) seems to come from *xue-sheng men he lao-shi men* via Conjunction Reduction (by deleting the first *men*). However, it is also possible that *men* is attached to the phrase 'student and teacher' directly. The reason is that some bound forms can attach to a phrase. For example, the question marker *ma* is a bound form and it attaches to a sentence. If so, (55) need not have come from Conjunction Reduction, nor is (55) necessarily a compound. Finally, consider the example in (56), cited in Dai (1992: 123).

(56)   pro- and anti-democracy

If (56) means the same as *pro-democracy and anti-democracy*, it must have undergone Conjunction Reduction. Now if (56) is a compound, it violates the assumption that Conjunction Reduction applies to phrases only. A possible solution is that *pro-* and *anti-* are used here not as prefixes but as prepositions, so that (56) is similar to (57).

(57)   for and against democracy

If so, (56) can be treated as a phrase, as (57) is. Thus, (56) does not contradict the claim that Conjunction Reduction applies to phrases but not to compounds.

If expressions like [[*meat and potato*] *eaters*] are compounds and if the internal conjunction is a phrase, then a compound can sometimes contain a phrase. A similar example is [[*American history*] *teacher*], which is usually considered to be a compound, yet the internal constituent *American history* is a phrase. Now if compounds can contain phrases, then phrases should be able to contain phrases all the more. The fact that Chinese [M N] in general cannot contain phrases, as shown by Conjunction Reduction and XP Substitution, suggests that [M N] is a compound and not a phrase.

5.5. [M *DE* N] INSIDE [M N]

It was suggested under Adverbial Modification and XP Substitution that [M *de* N] cannot occur inside [M N]. However, Chao (1968: 288) notes an apparent exception, shown in (58), which has two possible readings.

(58) zheng   de   cao-mei   gao
      whole   DE   strawberry   cake

    (*a*) 'strawberry cake which is whole'
    (*b*) 'strawberry cake with whole strawberries'

The reading (58*a*) is expected, because its structure is [A *de* [N N]], where a compound [N N] occurs inside a phrase. However, (58*b*) is unexpected, because its structure seems to be [[A *de* N] N], where a phrase [A *de* N] occurs inside a compound. Chao offers an explanation for the use of (58*b*). Speakers may prefer to keep the compound *cao-mei gao* 'strawberry cake' together, but in the 'expected' structure for (58*b*), *cao-mei gao* is split by *de*, as shown in (59).

(59) [zheng   cao-mei]   de   gao
       whole   strawberry   DE   cake
      'cake with whole strawberries'

Now, to keep *cao-mei gao* together, one can repeat the word *cao-mei*, as in (60).

(60) [zheng   cao-mei]   de   [cao-mei   gao]
       whole   strawberry   DE   strawberry   cake
      'strawberry cake with whole strawberries'

However, (60) is rather wordy. If we omit the first *cao-mei*, the result is (58*b*). In other words, the intended structure of (58*b*) is not [[A *de* N] N] but [[A Ø] *de* [N N]], where Ø is the omitted *cao-mei*. If so, it is still true that [M *de* N] cannot occur inside [M N].

5.6. LOCATIVES

A Chinese nominal can be followed by a locative, which indicates the location in relation to the object referred to by the nominal. The locatives can be monosyllabic or disyllabic. The disyllabic form usually contains an extra syllable *mian* 'side' or *bian* 'side', as shown in (61).

(61)   Monosyllabic   Disyllabic

qian	qian-mian	'front(-side)'
hou	hou-mian	'back(-side)'
li	li-mian	'in(-side)'
wai	wai-mian	'out(-side)'

Some linguists consider Chinese locatives to be postpositions; others see them as nominals (see McCawley 1992: 228–31). The two give different interpretations to a locative construction, exemplified in (62).

(62)   beizi   li
       cup   in(-side)

   (*a*) 'inside the cup'
   (*b*) 'the inside of the cup'

The main argument for the postposition view, shown in (62*a*), is that the monosyllabic locative is a bound form, which, like a preposition or postposition, cannot be used alone but must attach to a nominal. However, it will be argued in Chapter 7 that there is a phonological reason why a monosyllabic locative cannot be used alone. Thus, there is no need to consider a locative to be a postposition just because it is not free. In contrast, there are several reasons to consider a locative to be a nominal. To begin with, the disyllabic form is in all respects a noun. Consider the examples in (63) and (64).

(63)   Qian-mian   you   hua   yuan.
       Front-side have   flower garden
       'The front has a garden.'

(64)   Wuzi   de   qian-mian   you   hua   yuan.
       House   DE   front-side have   flower garden
       'The front of the house has a garden.'

In (63) the locative can serve as the subject of a sentence. In (64) the locative can occur after *de*, a position that requires a nominal.

Now if locatives are nominals, there is the question of whether a locative construction is a compound or a phrase. There are two cases. The locative (L) can combine directly with a noun (N), or they can combine with the particle *de* in between. The simplest assumption, therefore, is that [N L] is a compound and [N *de* L] is a phrase. However, examples like (65), offered by Chen (2000), and (66), offered by B. Lu (p.c.), pose a problem.

(65) [wo   de   xuexiao]   li
      I   DE   school   in(-side)
      'the inside of my school'

(66) [wo   mai   de   [na   ben   shu]]   li
      I   buy   DE   that   copy   book   in(-side)
      'the inside of the book that I bought'

In (65), the locative is attached to [M *de* N], which is an XP. In (66), the locative is attached to a classifier phrase with a relative clause, which is also an XP. The examples suggest that a locative can directly attach to either a word or an XP, and consequently, the result can be either a word or an XP.

5.7. *DE*-OMISSION

In our discussion, the presence or absence of *de* in a Chinese nominal is crucial. However, there is evidence that *de* may occasionally be omitted. Consider (67) (from A. Hashimoto 1969: 88).

(67) Wo   de   shi   ji   fan.
      Wo   shi   ji   fan
      I   DE   be   chicken   rice
      'Mine is chicken rice.'

The sentence in (67) can be said with or without *de*. With *de* the meaning is 'Mine (my order for the meal) is chicken rice'. Without *de* the meaning can be the same, although it can also be 'I am chicken rice'. For the two forms to have the same meaning, it is reasonable to assume that there is an underlying *de* in the second form, which is (optionally) omitted. The availability of *de*-omission can help explain some problematic cases, to be seen below.

5.8. PSEUDO-COMPOUNDS AND PSEUDO-WORDS

Many Chinese words can occur either as a monosyllable or as a disyllable. The disyllable is a compound in structure but semantically the same as one of its components. I will call such words pseudo-compounds. Some examples are shown in (68), where the redundant part in the pseudo-compound is italicized. In some cases, such as *qian-cai* 'money-wealth', either part can be dropped, but only one is shown.

(68) Pseudo-compounds   Literal meaning   Gloss

li-bie	leave-depart	'to depart'
fu-fan	repeat-return	'to return'
yun-*cai*	cloud-colour	'cloud'
jin-jia	metal-armour	'armour'
mei-*tan*	coal-charcoal	'coal'
shi-*jian*	time-interval	'time'
shang-dian	business-store	'store'
jin-qian	gold-money	'money'
qian-cai	money-wealth	'wealth'
cai-*chan*	wealth-product	'wealth'
xue-xiao	study-school	'school'
jia-*li*	home-inside	'home'
guo-*jia*	country-home	'country'
shu-*zi*	number-character	'number'
er-*zi*	son-child	'child'
su-*du*	speed-measure	'speed'
xie-*hui*	association-society	'association'

Some of the compounds are semantically repetitive, such as *li-bie* 'leave-depart', *jin-jia* 'metal-armour', and *mei-tan* 'coal-charcoal', and the redundant word can be either the first or the second. A. Cheng and Yu (1979) suggest that in such compounds the word order is usually determined by historical tones and syllable types, whereby the historical level tone precedes the historical rise, which in turn precedes the historical fall, which in turn precedes the historically 'checked syllables', those that end in a stop consonant. Y. Zhang (1980) observes that many disyllabic compounds can have either word order, with no difference in meaning. For example, *li-qi* 'force-air' and *qi-li* 'air-force' both mean 'strength'. If these are true compounds, the word-order variation is hard to explain. If these are pseudo-compounds, the word-order variation is expected, because the disyllable is created only for its length and not for its internal structure.

Pseudo-compounds are quite easy to find in Chinese. To see how often they occur, I examined one news article and eight modern folk poems. The news article was taken from the June 2, 2005 issue of *Beijing Ribao* 'Beijing Daily'; it is about the Chinese government's decision to give pandas to Taiwan and has a total of 1,693 syllables. The poems were collected using an online search; they refer to social issues and have a total of 54 lines and 365 syllables. The texts were segmented by hand into words, and the percentages of pseudo-compounds in disyllabic nominals were counted. The results are shown in (69), where NN refers to disyllabic nominal compounds.

(69)

	Poems	News token	News type
All NN	65	337	135
Pseudo NN	32	128	39
% of pseudo NN	49%	38%	29%

In the poems, 49 per cent of the disyllabic nominals were pseudo-compounds. In the news article, with repeated tokens, 38 per cent of the disyllabic nominals were pseudo-compounds, and without repeated tokens 29 per cent of the disyllabic nominals were pseudo-compounds. If these data are representative, 30 to 50 per cent of all compounds in Chinese are pseudo-compounds. Considering the rarity of pseudo-compounds in English, the rate in Chinese is strikingly high.

It is commonly thought that the creation of pseudo-compounds is triggered by homophone density. In particular, most Chinese words are monosyllabic, yet Chinese has a very small syllable inventory; as a result, many words sound alike. To avoid ambiguity, disyllabic pseudo-compounds were created. However, I will argue in Chapter 7 that pseudo-compounds are created not for ambiguity avoidance but for metrical requirements.

Besides creating pseudo-compounds, Chinese also has the opposite process, in which disyllabic (or longer) words are shortened to monosyllables through truncation. Some examples are shown in (70).

(70)   Monosyllabic pseudo-words created by truncation

Disyllabic	Monosyllabic	
zhong-xue	zhong	
middle-school	middle	'middle school'
da-xue	da	
big-school	big	'university'
fei-ji	ji	
fly-machine	machine	'airplane'
lun-chuan	lun	
wheel-boat	wheel	'(powered) ship'
dian-shi	dian	
electricity-vision	electricity	'TV'

Helan	He	
Holland		'Holland'
Yinggelan	Ying	
England		'England'

While the monosyllables created by truncation may seem ambiguous by themselves, they are not when used in combination, such as those in (71).

(71) san zhong
      three middle   'The Third Middle School'

      shi da
      teacher big   'teachers college'

      ji zhang
      machine head   'airplane pilot'

      ke lun
      guest wheel   'passenger ship'

      cai dian
      color electricity 'color TV'

      He fang
      Holland side   'the Holland side'

      Ying Fa
      England France   'England and France'

However, the truncated monosyllables are rarely used alone (for the intended meaning), but usually in combination with other words. For this reason, they can be called pseudo-words.

5.9. [A N] AND FOOT SHELTER

[N N] compounds are quite easy to find, but [A N] compounds are less productive. Compare the data in (72) and (73).

(72) [N N]
      jingji/gongzuo/xuexi wenti
      'economics/work/study problem'

(73) [A N]
      ?kunnan/?jiandan/?qiguai wenti
      'difficult/simple/strange problem'

Those in (73) will be perfect if *de* is added, as shown in (74).

(74)   [A de N]
       kunnan/jiandan/qiguai de wenti
       'difficult/simple/strange problem'

The marginal status of [A N] suggests a constraint against it, which I state in (75).

(75)   *[A N]:
       [A N] cannot form a compound.

Cases like those in (73), should they occur, are probably phrases, which may have *de* underlyingly but in which *de*-omission has taken place. There is an apparent problem for (75) though. While perfect [2 2] of [A N] is not common, [1 1] of [A N] is more productive. Consider the examples in (76), which parallel those in (74).

(76)   nan/?*jian/guai ti
       'difficult/simple/strange problem'

Two of the cases are now perfect. Adding *de* does not improve the bad case, as shown in (77).

(77)   nan/?*jian/guai de ti
       'difficult/simple/strange problem'

The fact that [1 1] can be exempt from *[A N] requires an explanation. I suggest that there is a special provision that allows [A N], stated in (78).

(78)   *Foot Shelter*
       A foot or potential foot can be treated as a word whose internal morpho-syntactic structure can be ignored.

A disyllabic unit with initial stress is a foot (SS). A disyllabic unit with final stress is S(SØ), which I call a potential foot because when it occurs in non-initial positions, where the empty beat is unavailable, it will become (SS). In other words, Foot Shelter can apply to any disyllabic unit. Therefore, [1 1] can be treated as a word and its internal structure ignored (though collocational conditions may still exist, which account for the lack of ?*jian ti 'simple question' or *gao shu 'tall tree'). Foot Shelter also explains two further facts, namely, [1 1] compounds can tolerate various unusual structures discussed under Exocentric Structure above, and [A N] cannot be changed to [[Adv A] N], as discussed under Adverbial Modification, above. For example, while [xiao gou] 'small dog' is good, *[[hen xiao] gou] 'very small dog' is bad. The reason is that [xiao gou] is disyllabic and can be protected by Foot Shelter.

In contrast, [[*hen xiao*] *gou*] is too long, where [*hen xiao*] forms a foot and *gou* can form a foot with an empty beat, so the expression is not protected by Foot Shelter and *[A N] is violated.

Z. Xu (2005) proposes that *[A N] and Foot Shelter can be replaced by *[A(σσ) N], which prohibits a disyllabic adjective from combining with a noun. Z. Xu's proposal achieves similar results but has two shortcomings. First, the constraint is in principle not limited to disyllabic adjectives: any adjective longer than one syllable is disallowed (although long adjectives are rare in Chinese). Secondly, in the present analysis, Foot Shelter predicts that most syntactically idiosyncratic expressions are disyllabic, such as the exocentric compounds *tian fang* 'fill house (second wife to a widower)' and *cha shao* 'fork burn (a kind of roasted meat)'. In contrast, *[A(σσ) N] does not predict this fact.

5.10. [PRONOUN N]

Personal pronouns like *wo* 'I' and *ni* 'you' usually cannot occur directly before a noun but must be followed by the particle *de*, as shown in (79) and (80).

(79) *wo shu   *wo shou   *ni shu   *ni shou
      I   book   I   hand   you book   you hand
      'my book'   'my hand'   'your book'   'your hand'

(80) wo de shu   wo de shou   ni de shu   ni de shou
      I   DE book   I   DE hand   you DE book   you DE hand
      'my book'   'my hand'   'your book'   'your hand'

Such facts can be explained if pronouns are XPs, so that they cannot occur inside a compound [Pronoun N] but must occur in a phrase [Pronoun *de* N]. However, there are some exceptions, as seen in (81).

(81) wo ba   wo xiao   ni ba   ni xiao
      I   dad   I   school   you dad   you school
      'my dad'   'my school'   'your dad'   'your school'

Such cases cannot be explained by *de*-omission, since adding *de* will make them worse, as shown in (82).

(82) ?*wo de ba   *wo de   xiao
      I   DE dad   I   DE   school
      'my dad'   'my school'

Instead, (81) can be explained by Foot Shelter: a disyllabic unit can be treated as a single word, and so its internal syntax is ignored. The examples in (83) seem to be of a different kind.

(83)   wo (de) baba   women (de) xuexiao
      I   (DE) dad   we   (DE) school
      'my dad'   'our school'

Here the expressions are good with or without *de*. The simplest analysis is to say that they involve optional *de*-omission.

5.11. SUMMARY

I have argued that there is good evidence for a distinction between compounds and phrases in Chinese. In particular, [M *de* N] is a phrase but [M N] is a compound. Similarly, [M [M N]], [[M N] N], [[M N][M N]], etc., are compounds, as argued by Fan (1958), B. Lu (1990), and Dai (1992). Under this analysis, Chinese words and compounds cover a broader range of structures than has been recognized in most other works, such as Z. Lu (1964), Chao (1968), and Lü (1979). Moreover, a preliminary study by myself shows that about 80 per cent of words form compounds in modern Chinese texts, whereas just about 20 per cent do so in English texts. The difference is strikingly large. In Chapter 7 I will discuss the reasons for the frequent use of compounds and pseudo-compounds in Chinese.

6

Stress

6.1. JUDGEMENT ON STRESS

In some languages, such as English, it is often easy to tell which syllables have stress. In other languages, such as Chinese, it is a lot harder to do so. For example, Chao (1968: 38) notes the difficulty in obtaining agreement from SC speakers on the relative stress among full syllables. Similarly, Selkirk and Shen (1990: 315) report that native speakers of Shanghai Chinese have no judgement on stress. Moreover, Hyman (1977) classifies Chinese as a language without stress.

It is possible that the realization of stress can vary in different languages, as some linguists assume (e.g. Beckman 1986; Hayes 1995). For example, it is possible that stress in English is realized phonetically, so that it is easy to perceive, while stress in Chinese is realized abstractly, making it hard to perceive. However, I will argue that stress is in fact realized in the same way in English and Chinese.

Interestingly, it is not always easy to judge stress in English, nor is it always hard to judge stress in Chinese. When a full syllable occurs with a light syllable in SC, such as *maa-ma* 'mother', it is easy to tell that the full syllable has stress and the light syllable does not. In fact, some minimally contrastive pairs are available in SC. Two are shown in (1).

(1) HL-HL   vs.   HL-Ø
     [taa ii]   [taa i]
      big idea   big idea
     'main idea'   'careless'

     HL-LH   vs.   HL-Ø
     [taa jee]   [taa je]
      big grandpa   big grandpa
     'spoiled man'   'uncle (who is older than father)'

In 'main idea' and 'spoiled man', the syllables are full–full, and it is not easy to tell which has more stress. In 'careless' and 'uncle', the syllables are full–light, and it is easy to determine that the first syllable has more stress. Apart from the fact that full syllables have lexical tones and light syllables do not, full syllables are louder and have greater duration and amplitude than light syllables. For example, the rhyme duration of full syllables is on the order of 200 ms, whereas that of light syllables is on the order of 100 ms. In addition, light syllables show considerable reduction in the rhyme (M. Lin and Yan 1980). In this regard, all full syllables are phonetically stressed and all light syllables are phonetically unstressed. One might argue that it is not the lack of stress, but the lack of tone, that characterizes light syllables. However, this view has three shortcomings: it must explain why toneless syllables are phonetically short and have a reduced vowel; when a light syllable sometimes gets tone, as when it occurs after Tone 3 (see Chapter 10), it remains short; and stress must be assumed for Chinese anyway (to be discussed later).

In English, judgement for stress is clear in words like *panda*, *Japan*, *Chicago*, and *pancake*, where the stressed vowel is underlined. However, opinions differ in other cases, such as those in (2).

(2)   English examples where stress judgement is less obvious

   Red Cross
   real deal

According to Kenyon and Knott (1944) and Jones (1950), in expressions like *Red Cross* and *real deal* the two words have equal stress. However, according to Chomsky and Halle (1968), the second word has more stress than the first one. Such examples are similar to full–full disyllables in Chinese, in that some linguists think they have equal stress, whereas others think the second syllable has slightly more stress (Chao 1968).

We have seen then that in both English and Chinese, stress judgement is sometimes clear and sometimes unclear—the question is why. The answer lies in the phonetic cues for stress. According to Fry (1958), the most important phonetic cues for stress are F0 contour and duration (intensity was found to be the least important). In addition, we also know that rhyme reduction occurs in unstressed syllables. Now consider various cases of stress judgement with regard to these cues. First, consider heavy–light disyllables, shown in (3) and (4).

(3)   English heavy–light: stress is clear

	Pe-	*ter*	'Peter'
Length	long	short	
Reduction	no	yes	
Tone	yes	no	

(4) SC heavy–light: stress is clear

	[maa-	mə]	'mom'
Length	long	short	
Reduction	no	yes	
Tone	yes	no	

In English, the heavy syllable is longer, has an unreduced vowel, and a tone (which is called 'pitch accent' in intonational phonology; Pierrehumbert 1980). In contrast, the weak syllable is short, has a reduced vowel, and no pitch accent. Similarly, in Chinese, the heavy syllable is longer, has an unreduced vowel, and a lexical tone, whereas the weak syllable is short, has a reduced vowel, and no lexical tone (M. Lin and Yan 1988). Thus, in both languages the difference between the two syllables is clear. Next consider heavy–heavy disyllables, shown in (5)–(7).

(5) English heavy–heavy: stress is clear

	meat	*ball*
Length	long	long
Reduction	no	no
Tone	yes	no

(6) English heavy–heavy: stress is less clear

	Red	*Cross*
Length	long	long
Reduction	no	no
Tone	yes	yes

(7) SC heavy–heavy: stress is less clear

	[zɐu	wan]	'meat ball'
Length	long	long	
Reduction	no	no	
Tone	yes	yes	

In (5), both syllables are long and have unreduced vowels. However, the first syllable also has a pitch accent, whereas the second does not. Thus, the stress difference is still clear. In (6), both syllables are long and have unreduced vowels. In addition, both have a pitch accent. Thus, the stress difference is less obvious. The SC case in (7) is similar to that of (6), where both syllables have lexical tones, and so the stress difference is less clear.

If the manifestation of stress is the same in English and Chinese, as we have seen, why is stress judgement so much easier in English overall?

The main reason, I suggest, is that (*a*) Chinese is a tone language but English is not and (*b*) most Chinese words are monosyllabic but most English words are polysyllabic. Thus, in Chinese there are far more chances of getting case (7) than case (4). For example, according to W. Li (1981: 37), there are some 30,000 disyllabic compounds (or pseudo-compounds) in a large dictionary of SC, and just about 2,000 are clearly heavy–light (the rest are either heavy–heavy or optionally heavy–heavy). In contrast, in English just about 13 per cent of the words are monosyllabic (based on a basic lexicon of 52,447 words, Baayen *et al*. 1993), and so most cases are like (3) (one pitch accent in a polysyllabic word), and cases like (6) are far less common (heavy–heavy with two pitch accents).

6.2. STRESS AND SYLLABIC WEIGHT

The weight of a syllable refers to whether the syllable has one or two moras. A mora is essentially a segment slot in the rhyme (see Chapter 4). Syllables like [maa], [mai], [man], and [mat] have two moras and are called heavy. Syllables like [ma] and [a] have one mora and are called light. In many languages heavy syllables attract stress, which Prince (1990) attributes to the principle stated in (8).

(8)   *The Weight-to-Stress Principle*
      If a syllable is heavy, then it is stressed.

There are some exceptions to the Weight-to-Stress Principle. For example, in words like *campus*, the second syllable seems to be heavy CVC but is unstressed. Similarly, in words like *McDonald* and *exchange*, the first syllable seems to be heavy CVC but is again unstressed. In order to maintain the Weight-to-Stress Principle, some refinements are needed, such as assuming extrametricality for the final and initial syllable, or assuming that the final C at a word or morpheme boundary need not be syllabified with the preceding V.

Assuming that the Weight-to-Stress Principle is essentially correct, one may wonder whether the reverse is also true, namely, if a syllable is stressed, then it is heavy. An apparent problem comes from words like *city*. If we assume that a syllable must have an onset, the syllabification is *ci.ty* (Halle and Vergnaud 1987; Hayes 1995; and others). If so, the first syllable is light, yet it carries stress, but if we assume that syllabification is sensitive to stress, then *city* can be syllabified as *cit.y*, where the first syllable is heavy (Prokosch 1939; Bailey 1978; Selkirk 1982; Blevins 1995;

Hammond 1999; and others). If the second analysis is correct, then all stressed syllables are heavy, and a simple generalization can be made with regard to weight and stress, namely, a syllable is heavy if and only if it is stressed.

6.3. STRESS AND FEET

The theory of stress is called metrical phonology (M. Liberman 1975; Prince 1980; Halle and Vergnaud 1987; Hayes 1995; Halle and Idsardi 1995; Halle 1998). A fundamental property of stress and rhythm is the alternation between strong and weak beats. Each alternation constitutes a basic unit called foot. A typical foot is represented in (9), where the parentheses indicate its boundaries, each x inside the boundaries denotes a beat, and the x on Line 1 indicates the strong beat. The strong beat is also called the stress or the head.

(9)   A left-headed foot (trochee)

       Line 1   x   Head (stress)
       Line 0   (x x)   Boundaries and beats

In this representation, stress is part of a foot, and the presence of stress implies the presence of a foot and vice versa. It is therefore not correct to discuss one without the other. In the analysis of Halle and Vergnaud (1987), there can be many lines in the metrical representation. An example with three lines is shown in (10).

(10)   Line 2   x
        Line 1   (x   x)
        Line 0   (x x)   (x x)

Each x on line 1 is the head of a foot on Line 0. The x marks on Line 1 in turn form another foot, whose head is the x on Line 2. There are, therefore, three feet, or metrical constituents, in (10). In common practice, however, the term 'foot' refers to metrical constituents on Line 0 only. In addition, it is not clear whether metrical constituents above the syllabic foot are needed. I return to this shortly.

   Some researchers propose that only one side of the foot boundaries needs to be marked (Idsardi 1992; Halle and Idsardi 1995). In addition, some researchers believe that feet can be built over every three beats (Halle and Vergnaud 1987; Burzio 1994). Since such issues do not seem to be relevant for Chinese, I do not discuss them here.

6.4. PITCH ACCENT, DOWNSTEP, UPSTEP, AND LEVELS OF STRESS

To see how many levels of stress are needed, consider the analysis of the English word *compensation* by Halle and Vergnaud (1987), shown in (11), where S represents a syllable.

```
(11)   Line 2          x
       Line 1  (x      x  )
       Line 0  (S S)  (S S)
               compensation
```

The syllables serve as the beats on Line 0 and form two feet, of which the second has more stress, indicated by an x on Line 2. The representation shows three degrees of stress: the third syllable has main stress, the first syllable has secondary stress, and the second and the final syllables have no stress.

According to Chomsky and Halle (1968), M. Liberman (1975), Halle and Vergnaud (1987), and others, the number of stress levels is in principle unlimited. In practice, however, speakers could only judge a limited number of stress levels. For this reason, Gussenhoven (1991) argues that there should be just two degrees of stress—a syllable is either stressed or not. Judgement beyond two degrees should be represented in other ways. For example, his analysis of *compensation* is shown in (12), where S represents a syllable.

```
(12)          H
        x     x
       (S S)  (S S)
       compensation
```

In this word, the first and third syllables are stressed, the second and fourth are not. The third syllable seems to have more stress than the first not because it actually does but because it has a pitch accent H, which usually falls on the last foot of a word in English.

Next, consider the analysis of *panda* and *alpine* by Gussenhoven (1991) and Halle and Vergnaud (1987), shown in (13).

```
(13)   Both    Gussenhoven    Halle and Vergnaud

                               x
        x       x             (x    x )
       (S S)   (S S)          (S)  (S)
       panda   alpine         alpine
```

Both analyses agree that *panda* has one stress and that the first syllable of *alpine* has stress. For Halle and Vergnaud (1987) the second syllable of *alpine* also has stress (secondary stress), but for Gussenhoven
(1991) it does not. Instead, Gussenhoven argues that the perceived
secondary stress on the second syllable of *alpine* is due to the fact that
it has a full vowel, and the perceived lack of stress on the second syllable of *panda* is due to the fact that it has a reduced vowel. There is
therefore no need to represent the difference twice, once in the vowel
and once in stress.

Another case of interest comes from the SC examples in (14). Each
expression forms two syllabic feet. Hoa (1983: 102) suggests that in the
phrase the second foot has more stress, but in the compound the first foot
has more stress. I agree with her judgement.

(14)   Downstep (↓) and upstep (↑):

       Phrase   Compound

       x   x   x   x
      (S S) (S S)   (S S) (S S)
      HL-↓HL ↑H-L↓H   HL-↓HL ↓H-L↓H
      chuang-zao tian-cai chuang-zao tian-cai
      create genius   create genius
      'to create genius'   'creative genius'

If we do not have an additional stress level above the syllabic foot, how
do we distinguish the phrasal prosody from the compound prosody? In my
judgement the difference lies in downstep, whereby a high tone H is realized at a reduced pitch level, and upstep (or pitch reset), whereby a high
tone is realized at the normal high pitch level. In both cases, downstep
occurs on the second and fourth syllables, indicated by the down arrow.
However, the third syllable shows upstep in the phrase, indicated by the up
arrow, but downstep in the compound.

In the following discussion, I will follow Gussenhoven and assume that
the number of stress levels is limited. However, I will argue that we need
to represent three degrees of stress instead of just two.

6.5. FOOT BINARITY AND THE EMPTY BEAT

Since rhythm is the alternation between strong and weak beats, a typical
foot requires two beats. In metrical phonology this has been called the
Foot Binarity requirement. An apparent exception is monosyllabic words.

For example, English has many monosyllabic words, such as *cat, bee, yes,* and *John.* Since they have stress, they must form a foot. Some researchers assume that such a foot is a unary foot, with only one beat (e.g. Halle and Vergnaud 1987). Others argue that such a foot still has two beats. On the latter view, an empty beat is assumed (also called zero beat, silent beat, empty syllable, or zero syllable)—a beat that does not correspond to an overt syllable. The two analyses are compared in (15), where Ø indicates an empty beat.

(15)   Unary foot   Binary foot

     x   x
    (S)   (SØ)
    cat   cat

Many people have argued for the empty beat (e.g. Abercrombie 1967; M. Liberman 1975; Selkirk 1984; Giegerich 1985; Hogg and McCully 1987; Burzio 1994; Harris 1994). Abercrombie (1967: 35–6) gives an excellent example which shows that a syllable need not be audible. He points out that the English expression *thank you* is often pronounced as ['kju], where the first syllable *than(k)* is acoustically silent. But there is still muscular action during the silent syllable, which resembles the production of a stressed syllable. Similarly, as far as duration is concerned, a stressed monosyllable can count as two beats in verse, which supports the view that it is followed by an empty beat. An example is shown in (16).

(16)   (Ding Ø) (dong Ø) (bell Ø)
      (Kit-ty's) (in the) (well Ø)

Here each line has three feet. On the first line each foot consists of a monosyllable and an empty beat. On the second line the first two feet consist of two syllables each, the third foot consists of a monosyllable and an empty beat. The empty beat need not be realized as silence, but can be filled by lengthening the preceding syllable. Thus, the first two feet on the first line can be read as a prolonged *ding* and a prolonged *dong*, without pauses.

   Some linguists use the empty element in more abstract and liberal ways. For example, Burzio (1994) allows an empty beat to occur both initially and finally, as shown in (17).

(17)   x   x   x   x
    (Ø S) (S Ø)   (Ø S) (S S)
     sardine   bandanna

Similarly, Lowenstamm (1996) assumes that the only possible syllable is CV. Words that are not made of sequences of CVs contain empty Cs and Vs. Three examples are shown in (18).

(18) CVCV   CVCVCV   CVCVCVCV
      Øɪ.tØ   bØ.ɾɪ.kØ   tɛ.kØ.sØ.tØ
      it   brick   text

Goh (2000) applies the theory of Lowenstamm (1996) to Chinese and offers the analysis in (19), in which every Chinese syllable is disyllabic.

(19)   CVCV   CVCV   CVCV
      Analysis   ku.Øu   ka.nØ   ka.Øu
      Phonetic   kuu   kan   kau
                  'drum'   'dry'   'tall'

In what follows I also assume the empty beat, but only in a phonetically concrete way. In particular, I assume that the empty beat can occur in phrase-final positions, where it is realized either as a pause or as the lengthening of the preceding syllable, in agreement with the phonetic facts (Klatt 1975, 1976 for English; M. Lin, Yan, and Sun 1984, J. Yan and Lin 1988, Yang 1992, Y. Xu and Wang 2005 for Chinese). On the other hand, I avoid assuming empty elements that do not have phonetic correlates. Thus, the empty beat is not available phrase-medially or compound-medially; this agrees with the fact that when a word is read in a carrier frame, the lengthening effect disappears (L. Feng 1985; J. Wang and Wang 1993). Nor is the empty beat available in word-initial positions. The present position faces an apparent challenge in the analysis of words like *sardine*, *pancake*, and *electricity*. In *sardine* and *pancake*, if both syllables have stress, there is the question of how to ensure Foot Binarity for the first foot. In *electricity*, if the second and the third syllables both have stress, there is also the question of how to ensure Foot Binarity and left-headedness for the first foot. I return to them below.

6.6. FOOT STRUCTURE AND THE DUAL TROCHEE

Some linguists believe that languages can vary in foot structure. For example, the beats can be syllables or moras, and the head can be on the first beat (left-headed or trochee) or the second beat (right-headed or iamb) (McCawley 1978; Halle and Vergnaud 1987; Kager 1993; Hayes 1995). The two variations give four possible foot types, shown in (20).

(20)   Beats are syllables   Beats are moras

	Beats are syllables	Beats are moras
Stress on left	Syllabic trochee	Moraic trochee
Stress on right	Syllabic iamb	Moraic iamb

If the beats are moras, then stress is sensitive to syllable weight because every heavy syllable has two beats, and so every heavy syllable can form a foot and have stress. If the beats are syllables and if the language does not count moras, then stress ought not be sensitive to syllable weight.

There are three problems with the above typology. In the first place, clear cases of moraic and syllabic iambs are rare, and some linguists argue that they either do not exist or can be analysed in terms of trochees (e.g. Hayes 1995 and van de Vijver 1998). Secondly, it is not always easy to tell the foot type of a language. Consider the English word in (21).

(21)   Syllabic iamb   Syllabic trochee   Moraic trochee (m = mora)

x	x	x
(S S)	S (S Ø)	m . (mm)
today	today	today

Superficially, *today* seems to be a syllabic iamb. However, according to Giegerich (1985), Burzio (1994), and others, *today* contains a free syllable plus a syllabic trochee with an empty beat; according to Mester (1994) and Hayes (1995) it contains a free mora plus a moraic trochee. The example shows that even for well-studied languages it is not easy to decide what the proper analysis is. The third problem with the foot typology is the tacit assumption that a given language can count moras or syllables but not both. However, in many languages stress is sensitive to both. For example, as Kager (1992) argues, in what seem to be syllable-counting languages, such as Estonian (Prince 1980) and English, stressed monosyllables must be heavy; this suggests that such languages also count moras, so that a word has at least two moraic beats. On the other hand, all mora-counting languages obey the syllable integrity constraint by which the two moras of a heavy syllable cannot be split into two feet; this means that stress is sensitive to syllables even in mora-counting languages.

In what follows I will ignore iambic feet. In addition, I assume that stress is sensitive to both moras and syllables (Duanmu 1999a; Kim 2000), in that a language can have both moraic feet and syllabic feet. Moreover, I take it that a foot must have (at least) two beats. Finally, I assume that stressed syllables must be heavy. This analysis predicts two good disyllabic structures, shown in (22), and two bad ones, shown in (23). Since the foot contains both the moraic trochee and the syllabic trochee, it will be called the Dual Trochee.

(22)   The Dual Trochee

```
      x                    x
   (S      S  )         (S      S)         Syllabic foot
   (m m).(m m)          (m m).m            Moraic foot
      x      x             x
   heavy–heavy          heavy–light
   (HH)                 (HL)              Shorthand
```

(23)   Bad foot structures

```
      x                    x
   (S  S)               (S  S  )          Syllabic foot
   m.m                  m.(m m)           Moraic foot
                            x
   light–light    light–heavy
```

Since a heavy syllable forms a moraic foot, it always has some stress. The proposal is similar to that of Duanmu (1999a), although the latter did not explain the reason for the bad feet in (23) clearly. In the present analysis, the light–light and light–heavy patterns are bad because stress falls on a light syllable. There is also some evidence from Japanese for the Dual Trochee. In particular, although Japanese is widely thought to count moras and have moraic feet (McCawley 1968; Poser 1990), Kubozono (2003) has shown that it also makes use of a disyllabic unit that is HH or HL, with the accent on the first syllable. In the present analysis, the HH and HL in Japanese are Dual Trochees.

The proposed foot types can be abbreviated as (HH) and (HL), where H is a heavy syllable, which always forms a moraic foot and has stress, and L is a light syllable and has no stress. Let us now examine some apparent problems in English, such as the words in (24).

(24)   H(HØ)   (HH)   LH(HL)L

```
          x                  x                        x
   S    (S    Ø)       (S      S  )    S  S   (S      S) S
   (mm).(mm).Ø         (mm).(mm)       m.(mm).(mm).m.m
      x    x              x    x          x      x
   sardine             alpine            electricity
```

In previous analyses, *sardine* is a problem because the first syllable has stress but is not in a binary foot. In the present analysis, the first syllable of *sardine* is a bimoraic foot. In previous analyses, *alpine* is also a problem because the first syllable has stress but cannot form a binary foot with the second syllable, because the latter has stress and so has its own foot. In the present analysis, the two syllables of *alpine* form a syllabic foot. The second syllable has stress because it is a moraic foot. Finally, in *electricity*, the second syllable need not be in a syllabic foot because its stress comes from it being a moraic foot.

6.7. WORD STRESS

A main difference between English and Chinese is that in English a light syllable can occur in any position of a word. For example, in *banana*, a light syllable occurs in the first and third positions, and in *America*, a light syllable occurs in the first, third, and fourth positions. In contrast, a light syllable in Chinese does not occur word initially. As a result, there are fewer word-stress patterns in Chinese than in English. The reason Chinese does not have unstressed initial syllables seems to be that in non-final positions all disyllabic words have initial stress, even though some such words have final stress in isolation. For example, in SC *xin-zang* 'heart' has final stress in isolation but initial stress in *xin-zang bing* 'heart disease'.

Let us consider monosyllables first. In English, a monosyllable can be stressed, as in *cat*, or unstressed, as in *the*. The same is true in Chinese. Indeed, there are minimal pairs that are distinguished by stress alone. Consider the pair in (25) from SC.

(25)   Stressed (heavy)   Unstressed (light)
       LH   Ø
       [tʂau]   [tʂə]
       'contact'   'be doing'

The words are written with the same character. The vowel difference is due to reduction in the unstressed word. If 'be doing' is read with stress, it would become [tʂau] and carry the tone LH.

Next consider disyllabic words, including commonly used compounds and pseudo-compounds (see Chapter 5). As noted by W. Li (1981) and Hoa (1983), there is some variation among speakers. For example, *mian-hua* 'cotton-flower (cotton)' can be heard as heavy–heavy or heavy–light from news readers in SC. Nevertheless, Hoa (1983) reports three general patterns based on her own speech and a dozen other Beijing speakers:

1-0 (heavy–light), 1-2 (heavy–heavy where the first syllable has more stress), and 2-1 (heavy–heavy where the second syllable has more stress). They are exemplified and analysed in (26). The top line shows the foot structure in shorthand. Below it is the full foot structure. Hoa's stress notation is shown immediately above the phonetic transcription, and tones are shown below the transcription.

(26) (HL)   (HH)   H(HØ)

    x   x   x
  (S   S)   (S   S)   S (S   Ø)
  (mm).m   (mm).(mm)   (mm).(mm).Ø
    x   x   x   x   x
  1-0   1-2   2-1

  [paa.pa]   [tɕii.xʷaa]   [sʷuu.ʂɤɤ]
  HL-Ø   HL-HL   HL-HL
  'dad'   'plan'   'dorm'

Word stress in Chinese is unpredictable and some minimal pairs can be found that are distinguished by stress, such as those in (27).

(27) H-LH   vs.   H-Ø
    [pau-xan]   [pau-xã]
    'include'   'forgiving'

Some linguists, such as Chao (1968), only distinguish two stress patterns for disyllabic words, heavy–light (HL) and heavy–heavy H(HØ). However, Hoa's proposal seems to be more accurate, which is also shared by Z. Yin (1982) and S. Xu (1982). Xu offers a rough count of the three patterns in a total of 20,000 commonly used disyllabic words and compounds; the result is shown in (28).

(28) Pattern   Count   %
    (HL)   1,500   7.5%
    (HH)   4,500   22.5%
    H(HØ)   14,000   70.0%
    All   20,000   100.0%

Clearly, H(HØ) is the dominant pattern in SC. This is similar to the case in Southern Min (Wright 1983; Yue-Hashimoto 1987), but different from the case in Shanghai or Chengdu. In the latter two dialects all disyllabic words are (HL) or (HH). It is worth noting that in non-final positions—when followed by another word in a compound—only (HL) and (HH) are used in SC. I return to this in section 6.9.

Duanmu (2000, 2005) assumes just two foot structures for disyllabic words, (HL) and (HH), both of which have initial stress. The perceived final stress in Hoa's 2-1 is attributed to final lengthening. A major reason is that 2-1 changes to initial stress (either 1-2 or 2-3) when another word follows. For example, xin-zang 'heart' is 2-1 but xin-zang bing 'heart disease' is 2-3-1. However, to distinguish three stress patterns in isolated disyllabic words, we still need three representations: (HL) for 1-0, (HH) for 1-2, and (HH+) for 2-1, where H+ is a lengthened heavy syllable. In addition, one must explain why the final H lengthens in 2-1 but not in 1-2. Therefore, it is better to recognize final stress directly as a third stress pattern.

In compounds of three syllables or longer, the stress pattern is affected by the internal syntax, to be discussed in section 6.9. Simple words of three syllables or longer are either foreign names or number digits. For words made of full syllables, Chao (1968) assumes that in all cases the stress pattern is 2-x-1, where 1 is stronger than 2 and x is one or more syllables weaker than 2. Other analyses assume that in such words disyllabic feet are formed from left to right (Shih 1986; S. Feng 1998a; Chen 2000; Duanmu 2000). Hoa (1983: ch. V) offers the most detailed judgement, shown in (29), where 1 is stronger than 2, 2 is stronger than 3, and x is weaker than 3 but is still a full syllable. The examples are transcribed in Pinyin. Hoa (1983: 187) also offers x-2-x-1 as an optional pattern for some quadrisyllabic words, but the examples all have a low tone on the first syllable, and so the pattern is not included here.

(29)   Simple words made of full syllables

Length	Hoa's pattern	Example	Gloss
2 syllables	2-1	Yuedan	Jordan
3 syllables	2-x-1	Makesi	Marx
4 syllables	2-x-x-1	Heluxiaofu	Khrushchev
5 syllables	2-x-3-x-1	Laikeyaweike	Reykjavik
6 syllables	2-x-3-x-x-1	7-3-6-5-4-2	7-3-6-5-4-2
	3-x-2-x-x-1	7-3-6-5-4-2	7-3-6-5-4-2
	2-x-x-3-x-1	7-3-6-5-4-2	7-3-6-5-4-2
7 syllables	3-x-2-x-3-x-1	Gelannuoliye'ersi	Granolliers
	2-x-3-x-3-x-1	Gelannuoliye'ersi	Granolliers
	2-x-x-3-x-x-1	Gelannuoliye'ersi	Granolliers

It is interesting to note that even for the same words alternative patterns are possible, as shown by the six- and seven-syllable examples.

This is probably because long words are rather rare in SC and speakers are not quite sure what foot structure to use. In any case, a few generalizations can be observed. First, a foot is usually formed from the left; secondly, the final syllable usually forms another foot (with the empty beat); thirdly, binary feet are formed for other syllables, with some flexibility, as long as there is no stress clash (two adjacent stresses) or two free syllables in succession. Ignoring the distinction between 2 and 3, which is rather subtle and often optional, the foot structures of the patterns are shown in (30), where I replace Hoa's digits with S for strong and W for weak.

(30)

Length	Hoa's pattern	Foot structure
2 syllables	WS	H(HØ)
3 syllables	SWS	(HH)(HØ)
4 syllables	SWWS	(HH)H(HØ)
5 syllables	SWSWS	(HH)(HH)(HØ)
6 syllables	SWSWWS	(HH)(HH)H(HØ)
	SWWSWS	(HH)H(HH)(HØ)
7 syllables	SWSWSWS	(HH)(HH)(HH)(HØ)
	SWWSWWS	(HH)H(HH)H(HØ)

The final syllable may sound stronger probably because it is longer, owing to the empty beat, although the first syllable in fact has greater amplitude and higher F0 peak (M. Lin *et al.* 1984; J. Yan and Lin 1988; Yang 1992; Y. Xu and Wang 2005). Therefore, no additional stress is needed in the representation. Also, the stress on the final syllable will be lost when the word is followed by another in a compound (owing to the lack of the empty beat), to be discussed under phrasal stress.

6.8. THE INFORMATION-STRESS PRINCIPLE

Most literature on stress deals with word stress. It is less obvious whether all languages have phrasal stress (including compound stress), and if they do, whether they all have the same rule for phrasal stress. I will argue that the answer is yes, because all languages observe a principle that I call the Information-Stress Principle.

Let us begin with contrastive stress, which all languages seem to have. An example in Chinese is shown in (31), where contrastive stress is shown in uppercase. Phonetically, syllables with contrastive stress in SC have a greater pitch range than those that do not (J. Shen 1985).

(31)   Wo   xing   HUANG,   bu   xing   WANG.
       I   name   HUANG   not   name   WANG
       'I (am) named HUANG, not named WANG.'

I assume that in all languages contrasted words have extra stress and that no language does it the other way round. But why is it so? Apparently, contrasted words carry more information of interest and we give more stress to words that have more information and less stress to words that have less information. This may seem like common sense, but I will show that it explains many well-known stress effects. So let me state the principle explicitly in (32).

(32)   *The Information-Stress Principle*
       A word or phrase that carries more information than its neighbour(s) should be stressed.

The Information-Stress Principle explains two well-known facts right away. First, pronouns usually do not carry stress, because pronouns are used for entities that are either obvious or have already been mentioned, so they do not carry much information. Second, as noted by Hayes (1995: 373) and others, phrasal stress is often quite flexible. In the present analysis, it is because the information load of a word is not fixed but dependent on the context, including the speaker and the listener.

Next consider how information load is determined. Following Information Theory (Shannon 1948), the information load of a form is defined by its probability of occurrence, which is given in (33).

(33)   *Information load*
       The more predictable a form is, the less information it carries.

Consider a simple phrase [Art N] (article–noun), such as *the car*, shown in (34).

(34)   *(John is in)*   *the*   *car*
       Category: Article   Noun
       Choices: 2   thousands
       Information: low   high

In English, there are only two choices for an article before a singular noun, *the* or *a*. Each has a probability of 1/2 in this environment. In contrast, English has thousands of nouns and each has a very small probability of occurring after an article. Therefore, in this structure the article carries far less information than the noun. Not surprisingly, if we omit the article, there is not much loss of information, but if we omit the noun, the information

loss is more serious. Similarly, consider the difference between prepositions and verbs. Suppose that a language has six prepositions and 1,000
verbs (and suppose that we can determine the category of a word through
syntactic context). Their information load is analysed in (35).

(35) Category   P   V
      Number of words   6   1,000
      Probability of each word   1/6   1/1,000
      Information of each word   low   high

The information load of an average verb far exceeds that of an average preposition. This explains a well-known stress difference between
functional (or closed-class) words and lexical (or open-class) words.
A functional word is usually unstressed because its information load is low.
In contrast, the information load of a lexical word is high, so it is usually
stressed.

The Information-Stress Principle can also explain a well-known correlation between frequency and reduction, namely, frequent words tend to
undergo stress loss and vowel reduction more often than infrequent words
(Bybee 2001). An example is shown in (36).

(36)   Infrequent   Frequent
      Predictability   low   high
      Information   high   low
      Stress   more   less
      Example   importation   information
                           [oɚ]   [ɚ]

The second syllable is unstressed and reduced in *information* but not
in *importation*, because *information* is a frequent word while *importation* is not. In the present analysis, a frequent word has less information
so it tends to have less stress and more likely to undergo reduction.
Another word of interest is *trombone*, whose first vowel is [ɒ] for
most people but [ə] for trombonists. This is because *trombone* is an
infrequent word for most people but a frequent one for trombonists
(Fidelholtz 1975).

The frequency effect is relevant for the discussion of phrasal stress. In
particular, in an infrequent compound like [N1 N2], phrasal stress should
go to the nonhead N1 because it contains more information (see below).
However, in a frequent or commonly used compound, N1 need not contain
more information, and so the compound may be treated like a word and
follow the pattern of word stress.

6.9. PHRASAL STRESS

Duanmu (1990, 2000) proposes a general rule for assigning compound
and phrasal stress, Nonhead Stress, shown in (37).

(37) *Nonhead Stress*
      In the syntactic structure [X XP] (or [XP X]), where X is the syntactic
      head and XP the syntactic nonhead, XP should be stressed.

In the present analysis, Nonhead Stress is a consequence of the Information-Stress Principle. The reason is shown in (38).

(38) Deriving Nonhead Stress from the Information-Stress Principle

	[X	XP]
Syntax	head	nonhead
Choices	fewer	more
Predictability	high	low
Information	low	high
Stress	less	more

In standard X-bar syntax, the head X is an element at the word (or affix)
level, the nonhead XP, an element at the phrase level. Since there are more
possible phrases than possible words (or affixes), the occurrence of a nonhead (phrase) is less predictable than the occurrence of a head (word or
affix). Therefore, the information load of XP is far greater than that of X.
By the Information-Stress Principle, therefore, the default phrasal stress
should go to XP.

The analysis of compound stress is similar. A compound [N1 N2] is
parallel to a phrase [XP X], where N1 is the counterpart of XP and N2 that
of X. Therefore, N1 should receive phrasal stress.

Y. Yuan (1999) proposes that there is a general relation between information and word order in Chinese: a word that has less information should
come before a word that has more information. It can be seen that Yuan's
proposal is compatible with verb–object phrases but not with [N N] compounds.

6.9.1. **Phrasal stress in English**

The above proposal offers fairly good results for English. In (39) I compare the predictions with those of Chomsky and Halle (1968). For clarity
syntactic heads are underlined. Also, following Gussenhoven (1991), relative stress among stressed elements is not represented.

(39) | Syntax | Nonhead Stress | Chomsky and Halle |
|---|---|---|
| [V̱ N] | buy CARS | (same) |
| [P̱ N] | in SCHOOL | (same) |
| [N Ṉ] | WRIST-watch | (same) |
| [N [N Ṉ]] | GOLD WRIST-watch | (same) |
| [[N Ṉ] N] | WRIST-watch store | WRIST-watch STORE |
| [N [V̱ N]] | COWS eat GRASS | (same) |
| [N [A [V̱ N]] | COWS OFTEN eat GRASS | (same) |
| [Ḏ N] | the CAR | (same) |
| [N's̱ N] | JOHN 's FRIEND | John's FRIEND |
| [A (F̱) N] | RED (F) CARS | red CARS |

In the first seven cases, the syntactic heads are as traditionally understood. In [D N] the syntactic head is D, following Abney (1987). In [N's N] the syntactic head is the possessive {s}, following Pollock (1989). The noun phrase [A N] is [A (F) N], where the syntactic head is the inflectional element {F}. This follows from the view that noun phrases are headed by a functional element, not always present in English but required in some other languages (Ritter 1991; Cinque 1993). For example, the Chinese counterpart to an English [A N] phrase is [A *de* N], where the head *de* is a functional element (Dai 1992, Duanmu 2000).

In most cases the analyses predict similar results. Where they differ, the Nonhead Stress analysis seems to be more accurate. For example, in [N's N] and [A N], both words have stress in the Nonhead Stress analysis, in agreement with the traditional judgement (Kenyon and Knott 1944; Jones 1950). Similarly, as Hayes (1995: 373–82) argues, in structures like [[N N] N] and [[[N N] N] N], no stress should be assigned after the main stress (here the first N). Finally, the present analysis agrees with the observation that verbs are less likely to be stressed than nouns (Ladd 1980: 90–2). This is because (*a*) verbs often occur as syntactic heads, which do not receive Nonhead Stress, and (*b*) there are usually more nouns than verbs in a language, and so an average noun carries more information than an average verb. For example, in the 3,600 commonly used words in Chinese (ZWGW 1959), there are about 900 verbs and twice as many nouns. Similarly, my calculation shows that the ratio between nouns and verbs in the CELEX lexicon of English (Baayen *et al.* 1993) is 3:1.

The idea that there might be a universal rule for compound and phrasal stress has been proposed in different forms by Cinque (1993) and Zubizarreta (1998). According to them, the degree of stress is related to the depth of a syntactic tree: the deeper a branch, the more stress it has. Since a syntactic head generally does not branch, and the syntactic nonhead is a phrase, which can always branch, the syntactic nonhead is generally deeper and has more stress than the syntactic head. Thus, their theories predict similar stress patterns as Nonhead Stress. However, since they do not relate phrasal stress to information load, they need additional assumptions to account for other stress facts, such as the lack of stress on pronouns and the fact that emphasis or contrastive stress can fall on any syntactic position.

6.9.2. Phrasal stress in Chinese

We have seen in English that in a compound [N1 N2] phrasal stress goes to N1 and in a phrase [V N] it goes to N. The same is true in Chinese. For example, Hoa (1983: 102) gives the examples in (40), transcribed in Pinyin. Above the transcription is Hoa's stress judgement, where 1 is stronger than 2, and then the foot structure in the present analysis.

(40) Phrase   Compound
      H(HØ)   (HH)
      2-1   1-2
      guai4 ren2   guai4 ren2
      blame person   strange person
      'blame others'   'strange person'

Hoa's stress judgement for the phrase is 2-1, the metrical structure of which is H(HØ). Her judgement for the compound is 1-2, the metrical structure of which is (HH). Both patterns agree with Nonhead Stress. The stress difference between a phrase and a compound may also provide an answer to another problem in SC. Chao (1968: 27) observes that Tone 3 Sandhi, which changes T3-T3 to T2-T3 (see Chapter 11), can neutralize the difference in many disyllabic pairs, such as *zhao3 huo3* → *zhao2 huo3* 'seek fire' and *zhao2 huo3* 'catch fire', which sounds the same. However, Chao (1968: 55) notices that *you3 jing3* → *you2 jing3* 'have well' remains different from *you2 jing3* 'oil well', even though Tone 3 Sandhi has applied. Chao offers several ways to represent the difference, but none of which seems satisfactory. In the end, Chao decides to represent the difference in terms of syntactic boundaries: 'oil well' is a compound and has no internal boundary, and 'have well' is a phrase and does have an internal boundary. However, it remains unclear how syntactic boundaries affect pronunciation; if the present analysis is correct, the difference lies in stress: 'oil well' is a compound and has initial stress (HH), whereas 'have well' is a phrase and has final stress H(HØ).

Another pair of examples from Hoa is shown in (41), where 1 is stronger than 2 and 2 is stronger than x.

(41) Phrase   Compound
      (HH)↑(HH)   (HH)↓(HH)
      2-x-1-x   1-x-2-x
      chuang4-zao4 tian1-cai2   chuang4-zao4 tian1-cai2
      create genius   create genius
      'to create genius'   'creative genius'

If there is no additional stress level above the syllabic foot, there are two questions for the present analysis. First, Is Nonhead Stress still observed? And secondly, How do we distinguish the two cases? The answer to the first question is 'yes'. Nonhead Stress does not require the syntactic nonhead to have more stress than the syntactic head; it only requires the syntactic nonhead to have stress, which is the case. For the second question, the answer lies in downstep and upstep, as discussed earlier. In the compound the second foot undergoes downstep, indicated by the down arrow. In contrast, in the phrase the object undergoes upstep or pitch reset and starts at a higher level, indicated by the up arrow.

Although the compounds in (40) and (41) follow Nonhead Stress, many disyllabic compounds do not seem to. For example, in the survey of 20,000 disyllabic words by S. Xu (1982), most of which being compounds, 70 per cent have final stress. Some examples are shown in (42).

(42) H(HØ)   H(HØ)   H(HØ)   H(HØ)
      2-1   2-1   2-1   2-1
      huo3 che1   qi4 che1   huo4 che1   gong1 ji1
      fire car   gas car   cargo car   male chicken
      'train'   'car'   'truck'   'rooster'

Why does Nonhead Stress not apply to such compounds? The reason seems to lie in frequency. When a disyllabic compound is frequently used, such as those surveyed by Xu, they are treated as words and follow the pattern of word stress, which can be (HL), (HH), or H(HØ). In contrast, when a compound is not frequently used, such as those in (39) and (40), they follow Nonhead Stress. The most telling examples can be seen in (43) and (44), from Hoa (1983: 110).

(43) Frequent   Infrequent   Infrequent
      H(HØ)   (HH)   (HH)
      2-1   1-2   1-2
      Huang2 He2   Liao2 He2   Huai2 He2
      'Yellow River'   'Liao River'   'Huai River'

(44) Frequent   Infrequent   Infrequent
      H(HØ)   (HH)   (HH)
      2-1   1-2   1-2
      Xiang1 Shan1   Huang2 Shan1   Tian1 Shan1
      'Fragrant Mountain' 'Yellow Mountain'   'Heaven Mountain'

Both 'Yellow River' (the cradle of the Chinese people) and 'Fragrant Mountain' (a place in Beijing) are frequent expressions, and so they have the stress pattern WS or H(HØ). In contrast, other river names and mountain names are less frequent, and so they follow Nonhead Stress and have the stress pattern SW or (HH). In summary, while Nonhead Stress is not always observed, all stress patterns follow from the interaction between the Information-Stress Principle and the frequency of occurrence.

Let us now consider trisyllabic compounds. According to Hoa (1983), if we ignore light syllables, a common pattern is 2-x-1, regardless of the internal syntax. Consider the examples in (45) and (46).

(45) (HH)(HØ)   cf. H(HØ)
      2-x-1   2-1
      xin1-zang4 bing4   xin1-zang4
      'heart disease'   'heart'

(46) (HH)(HØ)   cf. H(HØ)
      2-x-1   2-1
      da4 gong1-ji1   gong1-ji1
      'big rooster'   'rooster'

The word *xin1-zang4* 'heart' is H(HØ) in isolation. However, it is not H(HØ) but (HH) when followed by 'disease', because the empty beat is not available compound-medially. It is fine for *bing4* 'disease' to form (HØ), because the empty beat is available for it. Thus, the result is (HH)(HØ). The word *gong1-ji1* 'rooster' is H(HØ) in isolation. In the compound, the free H *gong1* can form a foot with *da4*. So the result is again (HH)(HØ). As discussed earlier, (HH)(HØ) is the proper interpretation of 2-x-1: the final syllable may seem stronger because it is longer than the first, owing to the empty beat.

Hoa (1983: 103–8) also notes that compounds like (45) need not always be 2-x-1 but can also be 1-x-2. In the present analysis, it is because the third syllable need not be stressed and lengthened, because it is not a syntactic nonhead. Some examples are shown in (47), where 1-x-2 is interpreted as (HH)H.

(47) (HH)H   (HH)H   (HH)H
      1-x-2   1-x-2   1-x-2
      tuo3-yuan2 xing2   ke1-xue2 jia1   Sai4-na4 he2
      'oval shape'   'science expert'   'Seine River'

In the trisyllabic compounds so far, the nonhead is stressed, in agreement with Nonhead Stress, but some trisyllabic compounds seem to
violate Nonhead Stress. Three examples are shown in (48), where the third
syllable is light. Hoa (1983: 229) marks them as 2-1-0. In the present analysis, they are interpreted as H(HL).

(48) H(HL)   H(HL)   H(HL)
      2-1-0   2-1-0   2-1-0
      lao3 gan4-bu0   jin1 jie4-zi0   xiao3 mi4-shu0
      'old carder'   'gold ring'   'little secretary'

In these cases, the first word, which is the syntactic nonhead, remains without
phrasal stress. Why does Nonhead Stress fail here? I suggest that it is again
because such compounds are frequent expressions and so the syntactic nonhead
does not carry much information. In particular, 'old carder' is like an official title,
rather than a true compound. Similarly, 'gold ring' is a common expression for
'ring', where 'gold' is rather redundant. The expression 'little secretary' is used
to imply that the job of a secretary is insignificant, and therefore 'little' is rather
redundant, too. It is interesting to compare the compounds in (48) with those
in (49), which look similar in structure but have a different stress pattern. Hoa
(1983) does not give such examples but would probably mark them as 1-2-0.

(49) (HHL)   (HHL)   (HHL)
      1-2-0   1-2-0   1-2-0
      xin1 gan4-bu0   hong2 jie4-zi0   zheng4 mi4-shu0
      'new carder'   'red ring'   'head secretary'

The compounds in (49) are infrequent (or less frequent) expressions, and
phrasal stress applies regularly and does go to the first word, in agreement
with Nonhead Stress.

   Next, consider compounds made of two disyllabic words without light syllables. Hoa (1983) offers a few patterns, shown in (50)–(52). The judgement
on (50) also agrees with Luo and J. Wang (1981: 146) for similar examples.

(50) Second word is 1-2

      (HH)(HH)
      1-x-2-x
      chuang4-zao4 tian1-cai2
      'creative genius'

(51)   First word is 1-2; second word is 2-1

       (HH)H(HØ)
       2-x-x-1
       ke1-xue2 hui4-yi4
       'science meeting'

(52)   Both words are 2-1

       (HH)H(HØ), or ?H(HH)(HØ)
       2-x-x-1 or ?x-2-x-1
       ren2-zao4 wei4-xing1
       'man-made satellite'

Apart from x-2-x-1 in (52), which seems to be marginal, the generalization seems to be that the first word is (HH), owing to the lack of the empty beat, and the second word keeps its original stress location. The pattern x-2-x-1 in (52) is metrically fine; the preference for 2-x-x-1 over x-2-x-1 suggests that, if there is an option, it is better to build separate feet for separate words, rather than building a foot across two words.

Finally, consider a compound made of a monosyllable and a trisyllable, shown in (53), which has the stress pattern SWWS (ignoring relative stress between the Ss).

(53)   (HH)H(HØ)   Compare: (HH)(HØ)
       SWWS   SWS
       da4 xi1-hong2-shi4   xi1-hong2-shi4
       'big tomato'   'tomato'

According to Nonhead Stress, da4 'big' should be stressed. For this stress to form a foot, the original stress on the second syllable, xi1, must be deleted, and the result is SWWS. It is worth noting that in (53) the first word is monosyllabic, so the first foot has to cross a word boundary.

Hoa (1983) discusses a wealth of other stress patterns in other syntactic structures, but for lack of space they are not discussed here. It suffices to say that three requirements seem to govern all the patterns: Nonhead Stress, Foot Binarity, and the availability of the empty beat in final position only.

6.10. STRESS EFFECTS IN CHINESE

Besides being compatible with the phonetic judgement of stress, the proposed analysis can also account for a number of phonological effects in Chinese. First, consider the difference between full (heavy) and weak (light) syllables: full syllables have stress and light syllables do not. The difference follows if SC counts moras. Since each full syllable has two moras, it forms a moraic foot and has stress. Since a light syllable has just one mora, it cannot form a moraic foot and will remain unstressed. Another consideration is the fact that a disyllabic word can be HH or HL but not LH. The reason again seems to be related to stress. While words and frequent compounds can be H(HØ) in isolation, they are generally (HH) when followed by another word, where the initial syllable has stress. For infrequent compounds, Nonhead Stress goes to the first syllable. Thus, the first syllable often has to carry stress and cannot be light. The proposed foot structure can also help account for the well-known Tone 3 Sandhi in SC (also called Third-Tone Sandhi), to be discussed in Chapter 11. Another well-known sandhi process in SC is that the second tone LH can reduce to H when it occurs between A and B, where A is a full syllable whose tone is either H or LH and B a full syllable with any tone (to be discussed in Chapter 10). In general, reduction occurs in a position that lacks stress. In the present analysis a trisyllabic word is usually SWS, where the second syllable has no phrasal stress. It is natural, therefore, that this is in the position that tonal reduction occurs.

Disyllabic minimal-word requirement (Chapter 5) is another issue. In the present analysis, the disyllabic requirement follows from the fact that a stressed word is at least one syllabic foot, which needs two syllables in non-final positions. If Chinese has no metrical structure, it is not clear why a minimal word must be disyllabic.

Next consider restrictions on word length. Many Chinese words have two forms, one disyllabic and one monosyllabic, with little semantic or syntactic distinction between them. Some examples are shown in (54).

(54) suan   da-suan   'garlic'
     zhong   zhong-zhi   'to plant'
     mei   mei-tan   'coal'
     dian   shang-dian   'store'

It has been proposed that the reason for this apparent redundancy is that modern Chinese has lost many syllabic contrasts, giving too many monosyllabic homophones. As a result, disyllabic forms are created to avoid ambiguities (see Chapter 7). However, the choice between the two forms of a word is not always free. Consider the examples in (55) and (56).

(55)   [Verb   Object]

        (a) zhong-zhi   da-suan

    (*b*) *zhong-zhi   suan
    (*c*) zhong   da-suan
    (*d*) zhong   suan
          plant   garlic   'to plant garlic'

(56)   [Modifier   Noun]
    (*a*)   mei-tan   shang-dian
    (*b*)   mei-tan   dian
    (*c*) *mei   shang-dian
    (*d*)   mei   dian
          coal   store   'coal store'

In [V O] (Verb–Object), [2 1] (disyllabic monosyllabic) is bad, but in [M N] (Modifier–Noun), [1 2] is bad. In general, [2 1] is bad for [V O] and [1 2] is bad for [M N]. This asymmetry was noted by Lü (1963) but has remained a mystery. In particular, if the disyllabic form is created to avoid ambiguity, why should (55*b*) and (56*c*) be bad? In the present analysis, the proper choice of word length is determined by stress. Briefly, by Nonhead Stress, M has main stress in [M N], O in [V O]. Since stress should fall on a disyllabic unit, [1 2] is usually bad for [M N] and [2 1] is usually bad for [V O]. The details will be given in Chapter 7.

    Restrictions on word order are an issue, too. Word order in Chinese compounds is variable under some restrictions: consider the examples in (57) and (58).

(57) qie cai dao   (*cai qie dao)
     cut vegetable knife
     'knife for cutting vegetables'

(58) pingguo jiagong dao   (*jiagong pingguo dao)
     apple process knife
     'knife for processing apples'

Both compounds are made up of a verb (V), an object of the verb (O), and a noun (N). However, the word order must be [V O N] in (57) but [O V N] in (58). The reason for the difference is that V and O are monosyllabic in (57) but disyllabic in (58). However, the relation between word length and word order is difficult to explain unless we consider metrical structure, to be discussed in Chapter 8.

    Finally, the analysis of stress helps the analysis of poetic rhythm. In particular, it is not obvious what the relation is between the syntax of a line and its rhythm. For example, consider the lines in (59).

(59)   [[Fenghuang Shan] [you [bai fenghuang]]]
       Phoenix Mountain have white phoenix
       'The Phoenix Mountain has a white phoenix.'
       [[Fenghuang Shan] [gang [you fenghuang]]]
       Phoenix Mountain just have phoenix
       'The Phoenix Mountain has just had a phoenix.'

The lines look similar syntactically, but they do not have the same rhythm. Why is that? What rhythm does each line have and how is it determined? Such questions will be discussed in Chapter 12, where I will show that phrasal stress plays a key role.

6.11. OTHER VIEWS OF STRESS AND FOOT IN CHINESE

As Chao (1968: 38) observes, Chinese speakers often find it hard to judge stress. Naturally, some linguists believe that Chinese has no stress (Gao and Shi 1963; Hyman 1977; Selkirk and Shen 1990). When a full syllable occurs with a light syllable, the full syllable does seem to have more stress, but there is also a difference in tone: the full syllable has a lexical tone but the light syllable does not. Thus, the difference between the two can be attributed to tone, instead of stress. However, this view has several shortcomings. To begin with, it must explain why toneless syllables are phonetically short and have a reduced vowel. In addition, it cannot account for subtle stress differences among full syllables, such as H(HØ) vs. (HH), or other patterns provided by Hoa (1983). Finally, every language uses contrastive stress, including Chinese, so stress must be assumed for Chinese anyway.

While acknowledging that stress judgement can be difficult in SC, Chao (1968) proposes that there is a general pattern: in a string of full syllables, the last has most stress, the first has slightly less stress, and the intermediate ones have the least stress. Some examples are shown in (60), where M means medium stress, W means weak stress (i.e. weaker than what is on other full syllables, but as a full syllable it is still stronger than what is on a light syllable), and S means strong stress. This has been called the MWS theory.

(60)   The MWS theory (Chao 1968: 35)

Length	Pattern	Example	Gloss
2 syllables	M-S	hao ren	'good person'
3 syllables	M-W-S	Shanhaiguan	'Shanhaiguan'
4 syllables	M-W-W-S	dong nan xi bei	'east, south, west, and north'

The main criticism for the MWS theory is that it is too simple. For example, it does not account for the difference between H(HØ) and (HH) in disyllabic words, or the difference between SWWS and SWSW in quadrisyllabic words, or the effect of internal syntax on stress.

Hoa (1983) offers perhaps the most detailed phonological study of stress patterns in SC. In fact, my analysis has been significantly revised because of her work. There remain some important differences though. Hoa uses a numeric representation of stress, following M. Liberman and Prince (1977), which in principle allows an infinite number of stress levels. In contrast, I only assume three levels of stress. Another difference is that Hoa does not assume feet, whereas I do. And finally, Hoa uses a rule to reverse the stress of a word when it is not final. For example, *Beijing* 'Peking' is WS in isolation but reverses to SW in *Beijing hua* 'Peking dialect' SW-S and *Beijing Daxue* 'Peking University' SW-WS. In Hoa's analysis the rule is arbitrary. In the present analysis, it is due to the fact that a foot must be binary and an empty beat is available compound-finally but not compound-medially.

Shih (1986, 1997) and Chen (2000) both assume a foot formation process in SC. However, feet are formed without regard to stress. For example, a foot can be (SW), (WS), (SWS), (WSW), etc. Their feet are supposed to help account for the Third Tone Sandhi in SC, but I will argue in Chapter 11 that the sandhi process can be accounted for with regular metrical feet that are (SW).

H. Wang (2004) proposes that feet are formed differently in English and Chinese. In English, syllables form feet according to stress. However, in Chinese, syllables form feet according to their syntactic 'closeness', a view shared by B. Lu (1989). Syllables that are syntactically close belong to the same foot, and syllables that are not syntactically close belong to different feet. This analysis faces some questions. First, all disyllabic words should form one foot. However, disyllabic words can be SW or WS (S. Xu 1982; Hoa 1983). This means that either the proposed feet are insensitive to stress, or some other explanations are needed. Second, it is not obvious how feet should be formed in polysyllabic words or flat structures (such as a string of digits), which do not have internal syntax. Finally, the analysis overlooks some important similarities between English and Chinese, especially with regard to phrasal stress.

S. Feng (1998a, 2004) proposes that Chinese has directional foot formation that is sensitive to syntax. In polysyllabic words, compounds, and flat structures, foot formation is left-to-right, whereas in phrases foot formation is right-to-left. Like Shih (1986, 1997), Chen (2000), and H. Wang

(2004), S. Feng (2004) does not think that stress plays a role in foot formation in Chinese. For example, in his analysis every disyllabic unit forms a
foot, whether it is a word or a phase, and whether it is SW or WS. Therefore, his analysis faces the same questions as those of Shih (1986, 1997),
Chen (2000), and H. Wang (2004).

In Duanmu (2000) I proposed that all Chinese words have initial stress.
In particular, I suggested that SW is the only stress pattern for disyllabic
words. However, the analysis cannot account for the fact that SC has
both SW and WS words, as reported in S. Xu (1982) and Hoa (1983). In
addition, to account for poetic rhythm, one must assume final stress for
line-final disyllabic words, to be discussed in Chapter 12.

6.12. SUMMARY

The two most important ideas in this chapter are (*a*) the Dual Trochee foot
structure and (*b*) the Information-Stress Principle. I have shown how they
lead to an analysis of word and phrasal stress in SC, which agrees well
with the stress judgements in previous studies, in particular Hoa (1983).

The understanding of stress in SC provides the key to the analysis
of several other problems in SC, in particular the word-length problem
(see Chapter 7), the word-order problem (discussed in Chapter 8), the
tone-sandhi problem (see Chapter 11), and poetic rhythm (the topic of
Chapter 12).

The Word-Length Problem

7.1. INTRODUCTION

The word-length problem in Chinese refers to the fact that though the same expression can be composed of different numbers of syllables, there are restrictions on word-length combinations. The problem is illustrated in (1), transcribed in Pinyin. The number of syllables in each parallel sentence is given in parentheses.

(1) The word-length problem

Gloss	S1	S2	S3	*S4
come	qian-lai	lai	lai	qian-lai
visit	fang-wen	fang	fang-wen	fang
DE	de	de	de	de
important	zun-gui	gui	zun-gui	gui
guest	ke-ren	ke	ke-ren	ke-ren
tomorrow	ming-tian	ming	ming	ming-tian
evening	wan-shang	wan	wan	wan
reach	dao-da	dao	dao	dao-da
Beijing	Beijing	Jing	Beijing	Jing
	(17)	(9)	(13)	(13)

'The important guest who is coming to visit arrives in Beijing tomorrow evening.'

The sentences show an interesting property of Chinese that is not found in English: many monosyllabic words can alternate with a synonymous disyllabic word, often a pseudo-compound. For example, in S1 all words except the particle *de* are disyllabic, whereas in S2 every word is monosyllabic. More surprisingly, however, is the fact that word length choices are not always free. For example, S1, S2, and S3 are all good, but S4 is bad, even though it has the same number of syllables as S3. A similar example is shown in (2).

(2) | Gloss | S1 | S2 | S3 | *S4 |
| --- | --- | --- | --- | --- |
| house | zhu-fang | fang | zhu-fang | fang |
| price | jia-ge | jia | jia | jia-ge |
| unexpectedly | jing-ran | jing | jing-ran | jing |
| like | jiu-xiang | xiang | xiang | jiu-xiang |
| ride | zuo-le | zuo | zuo-le | zuo-le |
| elevator | dian-ti, | dian-ti, | dian-ti, | dian-ti, |
| more | yue | yue | yue | yue |
| rise | sheng | sheng | sheng | sheng |
| more | yue | yue | yue | yue |
| high | gao | gao | gao | gao |
| | (16) | (11) | (14) | (14) |

'Unexpectedly, housing prices are like riding an elevator, rising higher and higher.'

Despite the variation in word length, S1, S2, and S3 are again all good. However, S4 is bad, even though it has the same number of syllables as S3.

The above examples pose problems for two popular views about Chinese. The first is that most Chinese words are monosyllabic. For example, Karlgren (1949: p. iii) considers Chinese to be 'the most typical example of a mono-syllabic and isolating tongue'. Similarly, Jespersen (1922: 369) says, 'Each [Chinese] word consists of one syllable, neither more nor less.' This view fails to note the extensive use of disyllabic words, or the restrictions on word-length choices. The second popular view is that Chinese developed disyllabic words in order to compensate for its small syllable inventory. Otherwise, too many ambiguities will arise. This view is intuitively plausible but rarely given any proof. In addition, it cannot explain why word-length choices are not always free.

In this chapter I address three questions; How extensive are disyllabic words used in Chinese? Why are there so many disyllabic words in Chinese if there is already a corresponding monosyllabic set? And, what are the restrictions on word-length choices? I will argue that the variation in word length is governed by stress. In particular, the need for a disyllabic word in stressed positions can stretch a monosyllable to a disyllable through compounding. Similarly, the need for shorter words in unstressed positions can shorten a disyllable to a monosyllable through truncation.

7.2. ABUNDANCE OF DISYLLABIC WORDS IN CHINESE

To count disyllabic words, we must know what a word is. Traditional Chinese dictionaries contain only characters (monosyllabic morphemes), and the notion 'word' did not occur in Chinese linguistics until the twentieth century. By the 1950s, some initial consensus was reached on the definition of word in Chinese (although disagreements still remain, especially with trisyllabic and longer expressions, see Chapter 5). In 1959, the first systematic study on Chinese words, entitled *Putonghua San Qian Chang Yong Ci Biao* '3,000 Commonly Used Words in Standard Chinese', was completed by Zhongguo Wenzi Gaige Weiyuanhui Yanjiu Tuiguang Chu 'Chinese Language Reform Committee Research and Popularization Office', hereafter ZWGW (1959). The study involved about forty scholars over nearly three years, and the word list was checked for statistical accuracy with a selection of modern written texts that totalled 130,000 characters. Modern written Chinese is often called *baihuawen* 'plain speech writing (vernacular writing)', which represents the language as people use it today.

For the first time, ZWGW (1959) offers clear evidence that monosyllabic words constitute only a small part of modern Chinese usage. ZWGW (1959) lists a total of 3,624 words, which represent about 80 per cent of all occurrences of words in modern SC. Of the list, monosyllabic words comprise just 29 per cent. This is shown in (3).

(3)   Commonly used words in modern SC (ZWGW 1959)

Category	Total	Monosyllabic	% monosyllabic
Noun	1,690	262	16
Verb	925	380	41
Adjective	451	140	31
Adverb	194	41	21
Others	364	223	60
All	3,624	1,046	29

Of all the words, the majority are disyllabic (and occasionally trisyllabic). Since proper names have generally been excluded, the disyllabic (or trisyllabic) words are mostly compounds. A similar result is found by K. He and Li (1987), who compiled a frequency list of 3,000 most common Chinese words, based on a modern SC text corpus of 1,070,000 character tokens. Their result is shown in (4).

(4)
Length	1 syllable	2 syllables	3 syllables	4 syllables	All
Count	809	2,094	89	8	3,000
%	27.0	69.8	3.0	0.3	100.0

Once again, monosyllabic words make up just 27 per cent of the total, disyllabic words dominating the vocabulary. One might notice that ZWGW (1959) and K. He and Li (1987) gave only a small number of trisyllabic words, fewer still quadrisyllabic words, and none that has more than four syllables. The reason is probably that long compounds are not frequent enough to make the list.

Most new words introduced in the past century are disyllabic. For example, consider the two kinds of verbs in (5), taken from ZWGW (1959).

(5)

	Total	% monosyllabic
(a) Bodily and daily activities	280	73
(b) Political and legislative activities	135	3

There are 280 verbs that refer to bodily or daily activities, which obviously belong to the native vocabulary. Of them, 73 per cent are monosyllabic. In fact, the other 27 per cent 'disyllabic verbs' contain some verb–object structures that in some ways behave like a phrase. Some examples are shown in (6).

(6) wo   shou   li   fa   ban   jia
hold hand   cut hair   move house
'to shake hands'   'to have haircut'   'to move house'

sao   di   shua ya   xi   lian
sweep floor   brush teeth   wash face
'to sweep the floor'   'to brush teeth'   'to wash face'

If such items are excluded, then monosyllabic verbs in (5a) will rise to about 85 per cent. In contrast, there are 135 verbs that refer to politics and legislature activities, most of which were introduced in the past century. Of them, only three are monosyllabic. Further evidence for the lack of monosyllabic words in the new vocabulary can be seen in Z. Li and Bai (1987) and Yu (1993), which record new words, including some phrases, such as *wu gaizi* 'hold down the lid (hide problems)'. Their results are summarized in (7). In both studies, there is a total lack of monosyllabic words in the new vocabulary.

(7)

	Year introduced	Total terms	% monosyllabic
Z. Li and Bai (1987)	mostly since 1949	982	0
Yu (1993)	1992	448	0

7.3. THE DUAL VOCABULARY

Interestingly, most disyllabic words in Chinese also alternate with monosyllables. Indeed, many disyllables are just alternative forms of monosyllabic words. Consider the examples in (8).

(8)   Dual vocabulary based on compounding

	Disyllabic	Monosyllabic	
(a)	mei-tan coal-charcoal	mei coal	'coal'
(b)	shang-dian business-store	dian store	'store'
(c)	da-suan big-garlic	suan garlic	'garlic'
(d)	zhong-zhi plant-colonize	zhong plant	'to plant'
(e)	gong-ji attack-hit	gong attack	'to attack'
(f)	er-duo ear-petal	er ear	'ear'

In these words, the extra syllable in the disyllabic form is semantically redundant. For example, in (8a) *mei-tan* does not mean 'coal and charcoal' but just 'coal'. Similarly, in (8c) *da* does not add the meaning 'big', and even small garlic is called *da suan*. For this reason, such disyllables are not real compounds but pseudo-compounds.

Sproat and Shih (1996: 58) suggest that in some monosyllabic–disyllabic pairs, such as *yi–mayi* 'ant', there are morphological and semantic distinctions. Morphologically, the monosyllable is a root, which cannot be used alone, but a disyllable is a word. Semantically, the monosyllable denotes a type whereas the disyllable denotes a canonical instance of the type. However, most monosyllabic–disyllabic pairs cannot be explained this way. For example, both *cai* 'vegetable' and *shucai* 'vegetable' are words, since one can say *mai cai* or *mai shucai* for 'buy vegetables'. Similarly, *mei* 'coal' and *meitan* 'coal' are both words, and there is no apparent semantic distinction between *mei dian* 'coal store' and *meitan dian* 'coal store'.

The presence of two synonymous forms, one monosyllabic and one disyllabic, creates an unusual dual vocabulary. It is not clear how many Chinese words have dual forms, since a quantitative study is lacking. My own intuition is that most Chinese words do, because most of the time, when I randomly think of a monosyllabic word, I can also think of a disyllabic word that has a similar meaning. This property is not found in polysyllabic languages such as English and French and seems to be unique to Chinese. It is possible that this property also exists in other monosyllabic languages such as Vietnamese, although I have not seen such reports.

The dual vocabulary is not created just by stretching monosyllabic words through compounding though. The opposite process is just as active, in which disyllabic (or longer) words are shortened to monosyllables through truncation. Some examples are shown in (9).

(9) Dual vocabulary based on truncation

Disyllabic → Monosyllabic

(a) zhong-xue   zhong
    middle-school   middle   'middle school'

(b) da-xue   da
    big school   big   'university'

(c) fei-ji   ji
    fly-machine   machine   'airplane'

(d) lun-chuan   lun
    wheel-boat   wheel   '(powered) ship'

(e) dian-shi   dian
    electricity-vision   electricity   'TV'

(f) Helan   He
    Holland   'Holland'

(g) Yinggelan   Ying
    England   'England'

While the truncated monosyllables may seem ambiguous by themselves, they are not when used in combination, such as those in (10).

(10) (a) san zhong
          three middle   'The Third Middle School'

      (b) shi da
          teacher big   'teachers college'

      (c) ji zhang
          machine head   'airplane pilot'

      (d) ke lun
          guest wheel   'passenger ship'

      (e) cai dian
          color electricity   'color TV'

      (f) He fang
          Holland side   'the Holland side'

      (g) Ying Fa
          England France   'England and France'

The truncated monosyllables were called pseudo-words in Chapter 5 because they are mostly used in combination with another word and are rarely used alone (for the intended meaning).

It is unclear whether the dual vocabulary has existed in Chinese all along. Dobson (1959: 6) suggests that compounds in Late Archaic Chinese (LAC, fourth and third centuries BC) were never higher than 3 per cent, far below the percentage in modern SC (see above). Similarly, S. Feng (1998b: 219) suggests that by the Han Dynasty (AD 100), Chinese had less than 3 per cent compounds. If so, most words in classical Chinese must be monosyllabic, there cannot be a large dual vocabulary. However, the definition of compounds used by Dobson and S. Feng is rather narrow: the only expressions they regard as compound are those whose meanings are specialized (that is, using the Semantic Composition test in Chapter 5). For example, expressions like *you deng* 'oil lamp' and *shui jing* 'water well' are treated not as compounds but as phrases because the meaning is transparent. As a result, their estimates of disyllabic words and compounds in classical Chinese must be too low.

There is also another difficulty. Because of the scarcity of writing materials, historical Chinese texts may not reflect the spoken language, but, rather, a highly condensed writing style. For example, no linguist would assume that the language of the oracle bones (between 1400 BC and 1100 BC) represented the spoken language. In addition, because of the reverence for ancient texts, the original writing style may have influenced the entire literary tradition. As Karlgren (1949: 57) observes, 'in the written language of the pre-Christian era right down to our own day, people have continued to use the original short and concise word material.' This tradition dominated until the twentieth century, when *baihuawen* 'plain-speech writing' finally replaced it.

Nevertheless, Guo (1938) observes that classical Chinese also had words with flexible length. Some examples are shown in (11), transcribed in Pinyin.

(11)   Flexible word length in classical Chinese (Guo 1938)

Type	Disyllabic	Monosyllabic	Gloss
Reduplication	ai-ai	ai	'sad'
Merger	nai-he	ne	'helpless'
Truncation	you-yu	yu	'hesitate'
Truncation (name)	Guan-Zhong	Guan	'Guan-Zhong'
	Yan-Ying	Ying	'Yan-Ying'
Addition (name)	a-Wu	Wu	'Wu'
Repetition	xu-ju	xu, ju	
	save-gather	save, gather	'save'

Opposites	yi-tong	yi, tong	
	different-same	different, same	'difference'
	huan-ji	huan, ji	
	slow-urgent	slow, urgent	'urgency'

Such data show that a dual vocabulary must have existed in the past, too, although the exact extent remains unknown.

The presence of the dual vocabulary makes it hard or meaningless to answer a seemingly simple question, namely, are most Chinese words monosyllabic or disyllabic? We might be able to answer this etymologically if for each word in the dual vocabulary we can tell whether the monosyllable or the disyllable is the original. For example, we might decide that all pseudo-compounds are derived and their corresponding monosyllables are the original (e.g. *mei* 'coal' is the original and *mei-tan* is derived). Similarly, we might decide that all truncated monosyllabic words are derived and their corresponding disyllables (or polysyllables) are the original (e.g. *zhong xue* 'middle school' is the original and *zhong* is derived). However, such information is not always provided in the dictionary, and speakers may not always be sure of it. What we can say is that nearly all syllables in Chinese are words, although most of them can also appear as disyllables. Also, in a modern text or in speech, most words used are disyllabic, although most of them also have a monosyllabic form.

7.4. AMBIGUITY AVOIDANCE?

Many people believe that disyllabic words are created in Chinese in order to avoid ambiguity (Guo 1938; L. Wang 1944; Karlgren 1949; Lü 1963; C. Li and Thompson 1981; and many others). Two typical statements of this view are given in (12) and (13).

(12) Lü (1963: 21), 'Why is there a strong tendency for disyllabic words in modern Chinese? The large number of homophones should be an important factor. Because of sound change, many characters that used to sound different historically have now become homophones, and the creation of disyllabic forms is a compensating measure.'

(13) C. Li and Thompson (1981: 14), 'The threat of too many homophonous syllables has forced the (Chinese) language to increase dramatically the proportion of polysyllabic words, principally by means of the compounding process . . .'

The decrease of syllable inventory in modern Chinese is quite dramatic. For example, Middle Chinese (about AD 600) had over 3,000 syllables (including tonal contrasts), but modern SC has just over 1,300. Thus, in the past one thousand years or so Chinese lost more than half of its syllables. This has created a large number of homophones. For example, modern SC has about 7,000 characters (excluding 2,000 rare ones), most of which are monosyllabic morphemes (see Guojia Yuyan Wenzi Gongzuo Weiyuan-hui 1989). This gives an average of 5.4 homophonous morphemes per syllable. In addition, because the distribution is not even, some syllables represent more morphemes than others. For example, [i4] ([i] with the fourth tone) represents 63 common morphemes, or over 90 morphemes if rare words are included.

Given the large number of homophonous morphemes, many of which are independent words, it is not hard to imagine situations in which ambiguity arises and disyllabic expressions are used to avoid it. For example, in SC 'crow' and 'duck' are separate morphemes (written with different characters), but they are both pronounced as [ja1]. If one wants to say the former without ambiguity, one can use [u-ja] '(black) crow'. For the ambiguity-avoidance approach, this is how disyllabic words are created.

Although the ambiguity-based argument seems plausible, there are several problems. To begin with, most homophones can be disambiguated by context. For example, it is rare that the English homophones *sun* and *son*, or *bear* and *bare*, cause ambiguity in actual speech. In addition, when ambiguities do arise, a speaker can resort to a variety of ways to clarify them. It is unlikely, therefore, that the entire speech community would come to decide on a single way of disambiguating each of the many homophones. For example, *pen* and *pin* are homophones in some English dialects. Suppose ambiguity arises in 5 per cent of the contexts. In these 5 per cent of cases, one can clarify the ambiguity by saying *ink pen*, *fountain pen*, *ball pen*, *pen to write with*, etc. It is unlikely that one of these options will be chosen and established as the only usage. More likely, no compound will be established, because most of the time there is no ambiguity.

Secondly, there is evidence that many words remain monosyllabic even though they have many chances of causing ambiguities. For example, in SC 'he', 'she', and 'it' are different words (written with different characters), but they are all pronounced as [tʰa1]. Since they are high-frequency words, their chances of causing ambiguities are high. However, all three remain monosyllabic. Similarly, most native verbs have remained mono-syllabic, as seen in (5). This fact is not expected by ambiguity avoidance.

The third problem, as Lü (1963) points out, is that most of the increase in disyllabic words took place in the past 100 years or so, during which period there has been little change in the phonology of Chinese. This fact is another puzzle for ambiguity avoidance.

Fourth, many proponents of ambiguity avoidance, such as Karlgren (1949) and Dobson (1959), assume that classical Chinese mostly consisted of monosyllabic words. However, when Chinese characters were created, which was before the oldest written records (around 1400 BC), Chinese already had numerous homophones. This is evidenced by the fact that over 80 per cent of Chinese characters are partly phonetic. For example, the character for 'to shampoo' is made of a semantic part and a phonetic part. The semantic part is the character for 'water'; the phonetic part is the character for 'wood', because 'to shampoo' and 'wood' had the same pronunciation. Since more than 80 per cent of the characters were created this way, at least 80 per cent of all characters (or words) sounded similar or identical to another character. In other words, there must have been many homophones from the beginning. Why, then, did people not create disyllabic words to avoid ambiguity then? The answer, as suggested by Guo (1938), must be that classical written texts did not reflect the spoken language, in part because of the scarcity of writing materials, and in part because characters offer more distinctions than speech. And even so, many disyllabic words can still be found in classical texts, as Guo documents extensively, not because of homophone avoidance, but because of rhythmic considerations (see below). In any case, there is no solid evidence that classical spoken Chinese mostly consisted of monosyllabic words.

Fifth, ambiguity avoidance does not explain why the need to avoid ambiguity has not prevented the loss of syllabic contrasts. Indeed, it begs the question of why Chinese started as a monosyllabic language in the first place.

Sixth, there are restrictions on the use of disyllabic words, as seen in (1) and (2). Further examples are shown in the [N N] pattern in (14) and the [V O] pattern in (15), where 1 indicates a monosyllable, 2 a disyllable.

(14)   [N   N]
    [2 2]   mei-tan   shang-dian
    [2 1]   mei-tan   dian
  *[1 2]   mei   shang-dian
    [1 1]   mei   dian
              'coal   store'

Other examples:

ji-shu gong-ren, ji-shu gong, *ji gong-ren, ji gong 'skilled worker'

shou-biao gong-chang, shou-biao chang, *biao gong-chang, biao chang
    'watch factory'
yi-yao shang-pin, yi-yao pin, *yao shang-pin, yao pin 'medical goods'

(15)   [V   O   ]
    [2 2]   cheng-zuo   fei-ji
    *[2 1]   cheng-zuo   ji
    [1 2]   cheng   fei-ji
    ?[1 1]   cheng   ji
              '(to) ride   airplane'

Other examples:

xue-xi hui-hua, *xue-xi hua, xue hui-hua, ?xue hua 'study painting'
gou-mai liang-shi, *gou-mai liang, mai liang-shi, ?mai liang 'buy grains'
shou-ge mai-zi, *shou-ge mai, ge mai-zi, ?ge mai 'cut wheat'
zhong-zhi da-suan, *zhong-zhi suan, zhong da-suan, zhong suan 'plant
    garlic'

When both words have a monosyllabic form and a disyllabic form, there
are four possible combinations: [2 2], [2 1], [1 2], and [1 1]. But while
three of them are good in [N N], [1 2] is bad. Similarly, of the four combinations of [V O], three are good (or marginal, indicated by a question
mark), and one is bad. Moreover, the bad pattern in [N N] is the opposite
of that in [V O]. As noted by Lü (1963), this contrast is quite general: in
[N N], [1 2] is usually bad, and in [V O], [2 1] is—native intuition on such
cases is quite sharp. However, the ambiguity-avoidance approach offers
no account for such facts. (For fixed-length words, their combinations can
differ from these in (14) and (15); I return to them below.)

Seventh, the ambiguity-avoidance approach predicts a correlation
between the number of homophones and the number of disyllabic words.
The more homophones there are, the more likely disyllabic words would
be created. However, no evidence for such a correlation has been shown.
For example, Lü (1963: 21) suggests that, because Cantonese has more
syllables than SC (about 1,800 in Cantonese vs. about 1,300 in SC), there
should be fewer disyllabic words in Cantonese than in SC. A similar claim
is made by Chao (1973), citing some data in S. W. Williams (1889), who
translated a classic passage of about 219 words into several dialects. However, the data is inconclusive. For example, although Cantonese indeed
has fewer disyllabic words than Beijing Mandarin (presumably because
Cantonese has a larger syllable inventory), the Hankow dialect has fewer
disyllabic words than Beijing Mandarin, even though Hankow has a smaller
syllable inventory than Beijing Mandarin. Thus, there is no evidence for

the correlation between the size of syllable inventory and the amount of disyllabic words. On the other hand, though the SC words in (16) have no homophones, they still have disyllabic forms.

(16) hou3/hou3-jiao4   chong3/chong3-ai4
      yell/yell-call   spoil/spoil-love
      'to yell'   'to spoil (by loving too much)'

Similarly, the syllable *bao2* represents only two words, the noun 'hail' and the adjective 'thin'. Since they hardly occur in the same environment, there is little chance they would be confused. Nevertheless, 'hail' has a disyllabic form, shown in (17).

(17) bao2/bing1-bao2
      hail/ice-hail
      'hail'

Such examples show that there must be other reasons why disyllabic words were created.

Finally, the ambiguity-avoidance approach may have a problem explaining the creation of monosyllabic words through truncation, such as *lun chuan* 'wheel boat (powered ship)' → *lun*. If there are already too many monosyllabic homophones, why does Chinese keep adding more through truncation? The fact that truncation frequently happens shows that most of the time there is no ambiguity.

7.5. OTHER VIEWS ON THE USE OF DISYLLABIC WORDS

There are a few other views on the creation of disyllabic words in Chinese. For convenience, I call them (*a*) the speech-tempo approach, (*b*) the grammatical approach, (*c*) the rhythm approach, (*d*) the morphologization approach, and (*e*) the stress-length approach. These approaches are not all proposed by different people. For example, Guo (1938) suggests that both (*a*) and ambiguity avoidance play a role, Lü (1963) suggests that both (*a*) and (*b*) are involved, and L. Li (1990) suggests that both (*b*) and (*c*) play a role.

7.5.1. The speech-tempo approach

Guo (1938) suggests that word-length variation in Chinese is motivated by the tempo of speech. When the tempo is high, one uses monosyllabic words, and when it is low, one uses disyllabic words.

The main problem with Guo's proposal is that it does not specify at which points the tempo can be high and at which points it can be low. As a result, there is no explanation for the restrictions on word length—for example, why in [N N] both nouns can be spoken slowly, giving [2 2], or both spoken quickly, giving [1 1], or the first slowly and the second quickly, giving [2 1], but not the first quickly and the second slowly. Nor is there any explanation for the asymmetry between [N N] and [V O].

7.5.2. The grammatical approach

The grammatical approach attempts to explain the use of a disyllabic word in terms of grammatical or semantic considerations. For example, L. Li (1990) offers a number of interesting examples. Consider (18) and (19) first (judgement was Li's).

(18)   mai/*mai-zang   le   si   mao
       bury   ASP   dead   cat
       'buried a dead cat'

(19)   *mai/mai-zang   le   jiu   shehui
       bury   ASP   old   society
       'buried the old society'

Although both *mai* and *mai-zang* mean 'to bury', there is a subtle semantic difference, namely, *mai* means to bury something concrete, while *mai-zang* means to bury something abstract. Therefore, *mai-zang* cannot be used with 'cat', and *mai* cannot be used with 'old society'. Next, consider (20) and (21).

(20)   mai/gou-mai   le   yi   dun   zhi
       buy   ASP   one   ton   paper
       'bought a ton of paper'

(21)   mai/*gou-mai   le   yi   zhang   zhi
       buy   ASP   one   sheet   paper
       'bought a sheet of paper'

While both *mai* and *gou-mai* mean 'to buy', the latter has the additional meaning of '(to buy) in large quantities'. Therefore, *gou-mai* cannot be used with 'a sheet of paper'.

The examples in (18)–(21) show that some monosyllabic–disyllabic pairs are not completely synonymous. However, other monosyllabic–disyllabic pairs cannot be accounted for this way. Li is aware of it and suggests that in some cases there is a grammatical difference between the members of a monosyllabic–disyllabic pair. Consider (22) and (23).

(22) Huai   ren   pian/qi-pian   le   wo-men
     bad   person   cheat   ASP   us
     'The bad person cheated us.'

(23) huai   ren   de   *pian/qi-pian
     bad   person 's   cheat
     'bad person's cheating'

In (22) both *pian* and *qi-pian* mean 'to cheat'. Unlike previous cases, there is no apparent semantic difference between the forms here. However, in (23) one must use *qi-pian* and not *pian*. The reason, Li suggests, is that the disyllabic form is preferred in a nominal position. A further example is shown in (24).

(24) di-ren   de   gong-ji/*gong
     enemy   's   attack
     'enemy's attack'

Although both *gong* and *gong-ji* mean 'to attack', in the nominal position in (24), only the disyllabic *gong-ji* can be used.

F. Liu (1992) reiterates Li's proposal that monosyllabic verbs cannot be used as a nominal. Consider (25) and (26), adapted from Liu.

(25) zhong-zhi/zhong   shu-cai
     plant   vegetable
     'to plant vegetables'

(26) zhong-zhi/*zhong   fang-fa
     plant   method
     '(the) planting method'

In (25) both *zhong-zhi* and *zhong* mean 'to plant'. However, in (26) only *zhong-zhi* can be used. For Liu, this is because the modifier in (26) is a nominal, which requires a disyllabic form.

The grammatical approach has both theoretical and empirical problems. Theoretically, why should a nominal verb require, or prefer, a disyllabic form? There is no explanation. Empirically, there is no evidence that a nominalized verb must be disyllabic. Consider (27).

(27) (*a*) ta   si   le   (*b*) ta de si
          he   die   ASP   he 's die
          'He died.'   'his death'

The word *si* is a verb in 'he dies' and a nominal in 'his death', but it is monosyllabic in both cases. This is generally true for verbs that do not have a disyllabic form. Even for verbs that have a disyllabic form, the disyllabic form cannot always be used in a nominal position. This is shown in (28), which is identical to (24) except that (28) has an extra modifier *meng* 'fierce'.

(28)   di-ren   de   meng   gong/*gong-ji
        enemy   's   fierce   attack
        'enemy's fierce attack'

While 'attack' must be disyllabic in (24), it cannot be disyllabic in (28), even though it is a nominal in both cases. The difference is unexpected if a nominalized verb must be disyllabic. Finally, consider (29), which is identical to (26), except that 'method' is a monosyllabic, *fa*, in (29) but a disyllabic, *fang-fa*, in (26).

(29)   zhong-zhi/zhong   fa
        plant   method
        '(the) planting method'

Unlike in (26), where 'plant(ing)' must be disyllabic, in (29) it can be either monosyllabic or disyllabic. Now, if 'plant(ing)' is a nominal, as assumed by Liu, and if a nominal verb must be disyllabic, it is unexplained why 'plant(ing)' can be monosyllabic in (29).

7.5.3. The rhythm approach

Many linguists have noticed a rhythmic preference for [1 1] or [2 2] in Chinese, including L. Li (1990) and F. Liu (1992). However, this approach has two problems; it does not specify what rhythm is and it does not explain the restrictions on word-length choices. In particular, since neither [1 2] nor [2 1] satisfies the ideal rhythm [1 1] or [2 2], one would expect both [1 2] and [2 1] to be bad. However, while [1 2] is bad for [N N], [2 1] is good. Moreover, in [V O], the reverse happens: [2 1] is bad and [1 2] is good. The asymmetry between [N N] and [V O] remains a mystery for the rhythmic approach.

7.5.4. The morphologization approach

Dai (1990: 20) suggests that Chinese is undergoing a process in which 'a syntactic coordinate phrase (A, B) first becomes a compound (A-B), then one of its components is morphologized to a bound form (A-B or A-B), and finally the other one is, too (A-B)'. A bound form is one that cannot be used alone; according to Dai, it is either a root or an affix. Because what used to be free words are now bound roots or affixes, the process is called 'morphologization'. As a result, many morphemes cannot occur alone any more, which gives rise to disyllabic words in Chinese.

Most of Dai's examples are verbs. But as discussed above, the majority of old verbs remain monosyllabic, the majority of disyllabic verbs being new compounds. It is not obvious, therefore, to what extent morphologization explains the increase of disyllabic verbs.

Dai (1990: 35) suggests that morphologization also affects Chinese nominals. For example, in *lao-hu* 'old tiger (tiger)', both parts are bound. Dai suggests that *lao*, which is semantically empty here, is a prefix and *hu* is a bound root, which must occur with an affix. There are several problems with this analysis. The first is that *lao* is not needed by disyllabic nouns. A real affix should be added regardless of word length. One might point out that some English morphemes are also sensitive to word length (Z. Xu 2005), such as the comparative *-er* and the superlative *-est*, which do not go with words longer than two syllables. However, for words longer than two syllables, *-er* and *-est* are realized as *more* and *most*, which means that the affixes are still needed. Secondly, an affix usually plays either a semantic or a grammatical role. For example, *un-* in the English word *unlike* means 'not', and *-ness* in the English word *quickness* changes an adjective to a noun. In contrast, *lao* plays no such role in *lao-hu*. The third problem is that a bound root usually requires a prefix or a suffix, but *hu* can occur with any syllable, on either side, even if it is not an affix. For example, *meng-hu* 'fierce tiger' and *hu-shan* 'tiger mountain' are both good, where neither *meng* 'fierce' nor *shan* 'mountain' is an affix. In summary, most disyllabic words cannot be explained by morphologization. In addition, morphologization offers no explanation for restrictions on word length choices.

7.5.5. The stress-length approach

Duanmu and Lu (1990) argue that word-length choices in Chinese are related to stress. Their proposal is summarized in (30).

(30) In a two-word construction, the word with more stress should not be shorter than the word with less stress.

Let us call it the stress-length approach. This approach can explain the word-length difference between [N N] and [V O]. Assuming Nonhead

Stress (see Chapter 6), in [N1 N2], N1 has more stress, therefore N1 should not be shorter than N2. In [1 2], N1 is shorter than N2, so it is bad. In [2 2], [2 1], and [1 1], N1 is not shorter than N2, so they are all good. Similarly, in [V O], O has more stress, so [2 1] is bad and the others are good.

The stress-length approach leaves several questions unaddressed; it does not discuss the details of foot structure; it does not explain why the less-stressed word is not shorter in [2 2]; it does not explain why the more-stressed word is not longer in [1 1]; and it does not explain some finer differences between [N N] and [V O]. For example, while [1 1] is always good for [N N], it is sometimes marginal for [V O], such as *mai liang* 'buy grain' and *cheng ji* 'ride airplane'.

7.6. STRESS, FOOT, AND WORD-LENGTH CHOICES

Word-length variation in Chinese is governed by stress. In particular, I propose the requirements in (31) and (32), where Anti-Allomorphy is a term borrowed from Burzio (1994), although the definition is different. In the present definition, an allomorph is a variation of a word, and Anti-Allomorphy requires a word not to change its shape when it has phrasal stress.

(31)   *Stress Length*
       Phrasal stress should be carried by a syllabic foot.

(32)   *Anti-Allomorphy*
       A stressed word should keep the same phonological shape. (If a word has a disyllabic shape, it should be used when the word has phrasal stress.)

Stress Length can be satisfied either by two syllables (SS) or by one syllable (SØ), where Ø is an empty beat (see Chapter 6). However, Anti-Allomorphy requires that if a word has a disyllabic form, it should be used when the word carries phrasal stress. The reason is that a disyllabic word is always (SS) in stressed non-final positions. Therefore, it should be disyllabic in stressed final positions, too, whether it is (SS) or S(SØ).

Let us consider how the requirements apply to the patterns of [N N] and [V O], as seen in (14) and (15), where both words have flexible length. Cases where one or both words lack flexible length will be discussed in a later section, along with other special cases. Let us begin with [N N] compounds, where [2 2], [2 1], and [1 1] are good and [1 2] is bad. Unlike Duanmu (2000), who assumes that all SC words have initial stress, I follow S. Xu (1982) and Hoa (1983) and assume that a disyllabic word can have either initial stress (SS) or final stress S(SØ), where S is a syllable and Ø is an empty beat. In addition, a disyllabic word is always (SS) in non-final positions. Given these considerations, the analysis of [N N] compounds is shown in (33), where a hyphen indicates a word boundary.

(33) Second noun is (SS) or (SØ)

[2 2]	[2 1]	[1 1]	*[1 2]
x x	x x	x	x x
(SS)-(SS)	(SS)-(SØ)	(S-S)	(S)-(SS)

Second noun is S(SØ)

[2-2]	*[1-2]
x x	x x
(SS)-S(SØ)	(S)-S(SØ)

In [N N], the first noun has phrasal stress (Chapter 6), and according to Stress Length, the first noun should be a foot, which is true in [2 2] and [2 1]. In [1 1], the two syllables can be treated as a single word under Foot Shelter (Chapter 5); so there is no problem either. This leaves the two cases of [1-2], where the first foot is not binary, which violates foot structure (Chapter 6). One might wonder whether (S)-S(SØ) can be restructured to (S-S)(SØ), which is metrically fine. The avoidance of (S-S)(SØ) is probably due to syntactic or perceptual reasons: because of Foot Shelter, (S-S)(SØ) is likely to be perceived as [2 1].

Now consider [V O] phrases, where [2 2] and [1 2] are generally good, [1 1] somewhat marginal, and [2 1] generally bad. The metrical structure is shown in (34). In the present analysis, the object has phrasal stress (Chapter 6). The verb has no phrasal stress but can have word stress if it is disyllabic.

(34) Object is (SS) or (SØ)

[2 2]	*?[2 1]	?[1 1]	[1 2]
x x	x x	x	x
(SS)-(SS)	(SS)-(SØ)	S-(SØ)	S-(SS)

Object is S(SØ)

[2 2]	[1 2]
x x	x
(SS)-S(SØ)	S-S(SØ)

In all cases the object contains a binary foot, so Stress Length is satisfied. This explains why [2 2] and [1 2] are good. As for [2 1] and [1 1], there is a violation of Anti-Allomorphy, because the object has a disyllabic form, which should be used. This explains why [2 1] is bad. But why is [1 1] not as bad? The reason, I suggest, is Foot Shelter: because [1 1] is disyllabic, it can be treated as a word—a VO compound. This compound is unrelated to the disyllabic object so there is no violation of Anti-Allomorphy.

Let us now consider other examples discussed earlier. First, consider compounds where the first word is a (nominal) verb, repeated in (35).

(35)   zhong-zhi   fang-fa
        zhong-zhi   fa
        *zhong   fang-fa
        zhong   fa
        plant   method
        '(the) planting method'

According to L. Li (1990) and F. Liu (1992), a nominal verb should be disyllabic. However, their proposal cannot explain why [1 1] is good. In the present analysis, the explanation for the length patterns is the same as for other [N N] compounds, where [1 2] is bad but others are good. Therefore, there is no need to assume that a change in word category must be accompanied by a change in word length, or vice versa. Next consider (36).

(36)   huai ren   de *pian/qi-pian
        bad   person 's cheat
        'bad person's cheating'

In current syntactic theory, *de* is the head of [X *de* Y] and X and Y are the nonheads, therefore both X 'bad person' and Y 'cheat' receive phrasal stress (via Nonhead Stress). And because 'cheat' has a disyllabic form, it is required by the Anti-Allomorphy requirement. The same analysis applies to (24). Now consider (37).

(37)   x   x
        (ta   de)   (si Ø)
        he   's   die
        'his death'

This structure is again [X *de* Y], so phrasal stress falls on *ta* and *si*. The former can form a foot with *de,* the latter, one with an empty beat. Now, because *si* 'die' does not have a synonymous disyllabic form (there is a disyllabic word *si-wang*, which is not quite synonymous with *si*), the Anti-Allomorphy requirement is not violated, and (37) is still usable.

Sproat and Shih (1996: 66) notice a similar example: *hong de mayi* 'red ant' is good but *hong de yi* 'red ant' is bad, even though *mayi* and *yi* seem to be synonymous. They suggest that *mayi* is a word and *yi* is a *root* and that *de* must be followed by a word. However, their analysis cannot explain why (36a) in which *pian* is a word, is bad. In my analysis, what follows *de* has phrasal stress and a disyllabic word is preferred. Therefore the disyllabic *mayi* is better than the monosyllabic *yi*.

As a final example, consider another problem. Lü (1963: 13) observes that when a noun is used as a classifier (or measure word), a monosyllable is better, but when it is not used as a classifier, a disyllabic form is better. For example, in (38a) *bei* is better than *bei-zi*, but in (38b) *bei-zi* is better than *bei*.

(38) (a) yi   bei/?bei-zi niu-nai   (b) yi   ge   ?bei/bei-zi
         one cup   milk   one CLASS. cup
         'a cup of milk'   'a cup'

In my analysis these are classifier phrases in which the classifier is the syntactic head. In (38a) 'cup' is the head, and in (38b), *ge* is. The metrical structure of (38a) is shown in (39), where phrasal stress falls on 'one' and 'milk'.

(39) (a) x   x   (b) x   x   x
          (yi bei) (niu-nai)   (yi) (bei-zi) (niu-nai)
          one cup milk   one cup milk

If *bei* is used, it has no stress and can form a foot with *yi*, and so the structure has no problem. If *bei-zi* is used, it forms a foot by itself, and so *yi* cannot form a binary foot. Thus, (39a) is better. Next consider the analysis of (38b), shown in (40).

(40) (a) x   x   (b) x   x
          (yi ge) (bei-zi)   (yi ge) (bei Ø)
          one Class. Cup   one Class. cup

Here 'cup' has phrasal stress and a disyllabic form, and so by Anti-Allomorphy the disyllabic form is preferred.

7.7. THE MINIMAL WORD AND NAME USAGE

The analysis just discussed can account for another property in Chinese, which is a strong tendency to avoid using a monosyllabic word alone. Consider the examples in (41)–(45).

(41) Lao Li   Xiao Li   *Li
      'Old Li'   'Little Li' 'Li'

(42) Wuxi   Shanghai   *Sha (Sha Shi)
      'Wuxi'   'Shanghai'   'Sha (Sha City)'

(43)   Riben   Helan   *Fa (Fa Guo)
       'Japan'   'Holland'   'France (France Country)'

(44)   *lao* hu   *lao* shu   zhuo *zi*   xue *xi*
       '(old) tiger' '(old) rat'   'table (son)' 'study (practice)'

(45)   shu cai   mei tan   hui hua   zhong zhi
       'vegetable' 'coal'   'to paint' 'to plant'

If the name of a person, city, or country is monosyllabic, a semantically redundant syllable ('old', 'little', 'city', 'country') is added, as shown in (41)–(43). In (44), a semantically empty morpheme (italicized and in parentheses) is added to a monosyllabic word. In (45), each disyllabic word consists of two semantically repetitive morphemes.

It is well known cross-linguistically that a word has to be of a certain minimal size; this has been called the 'minimal word' (McCarthy and Prince 1986). It is not as obvious what motivates the minimal-word effect. In particular, according to McCarthy and Prince (1986), a minimal word is a foot which contains at least two moras. But since a full Chinese syllable already has two moras, why is another syllable needed? Duanmu (2000) proposes that the minimal expression has phrasal stress, which requires a syllabic foot; a disyllabic word is required because it is a syllabic foot. However, as discussed in Chapter 6, in pre-pause positions a monosyllable can form a syllabic foot with an empty beat. If so, there is no need to use another syllable. Also, a disyllabic word in SC can have either initial stress or final stress (Chao 1968; S. Xu 1982; Hoa 1983; and others), as shown in (46).

(46)   Final stress   Initial stress   monosyllable
           x   x   x
        S (SØ)   (SS)   (SØ)
        shu cai   Fa Guo   yu
        'vegetable'   'France'   'fish'

In 'vegetable', *cai* is a foot with an empty beat, and *shu* is outside the foot. If so, why is *shu* needed? Indeed, there are some words, such as *yu* 'fish', that do not need another syllable. Therefore, the disyllabic requirement still seems to be a mystery.

In the present analysis, the minimal-word effect is the result of Anti-Allomorphy, which requires a stressed word to keep its original shape. When a word is used in isolation, it has stress. Therefore, the disyllabic form should be used if the word has one.

The minimal-word effect can also explain how people address others in Chinese. As in English, when addressing people formally, the complete names should be used, along with a proper title. However, when addressing people informally, the default choices depend on the length of the family name and the given name. There are four common cases, shown in (47), where F is a monosyllabic family name, FF a disyllabic family name, G a monosyllabic given name, GG a disyllabic given name, and X pseudotitle, which can be *Lao* 'Old' if the addressee is older than you, or *Xiao* 'Little' if the addressee is younger than you, or simply *a* in some dialects, such as Shanghai or Southern Min. The full name comes before the given name in Chinese.

(47) Informal ways of addressing people in Chinese

Full names	Example	Address	Example
FG	Wang Li	FG	Wang Li
		XF	Lao Wang, Xiao Wang
FGG	Deng Xiaoping	GG	Xiaoping
		XF	Lao Deng, Xiao Deng
FFG	Duanmu San	FF	Duanmu
		*XFF	*Lao Duanmu, *Xiao Duanmu
		?XF	?Lao Duan, ?Xiao Duan
		?FG	?Mu San
FFGG	Ouyang Jueya	FF	Ouyang
		GG	Jueya
		*XFF	*Lao Ouyang, *Xiao Ouyang
		*XF	*Lao Ou, *Xiao Ou

The examples show that overall it is not so important whether the family name (e.g. *Ouyang*), or the given name (e.g. *Xiaoping*), or both (e.g. *Wang Li*) are used. Rather, it is important that the address contains two syllables. The trisyllabic form XFF is too long. It is also interesting to compare FFG and FFGG. For FFG, XF and FG are sometimes used, often by people who are not aware that the family name is disyllabic. In contrast, in FFGG, there is no ambiguity that the family name is FF, and so XF is rarely used.

7.8. NON-METRICAL FACTORS

In section 7.2 we have seen that most newly introduced words are disyllabic. In fact, most of them come from borrowings after the Opium War. By some estimates (e.g. B. Wang 1998: 71), 70 per cent of modern Chinese terms, mostly compounds, in the humanities and social sciences are borrowed from Japanese alone.

After the Opium War, many Chinese students went abroad to study modern knowledge, and they introduced a large amount of new vocabulary into Chinese. People who studied in the west introduced new terms directly from English. People who studied in Japan contributed new terms from Japanese, which itself had borrowed them from English. The second way soon won over, because when Japanese borrowed a term from English, it often created a compound out of Chinese characters that it had borrowed from China before. As a result, many Japanese borrowings from English look like Chinese compounds—if Chinese had borrowed them directly from English, it would probably have created them the same way. An example is shown in (48).

(48)   dian   hua
       electricity voice
       'telephone'

Japanese had borrowed the characters *dian* 'electricity' and *hua* 'voice' from Chinese before. When Japanese borrowed the English word *telephone*, it created a compound *dian hua*, which is a good translation of the original with a transparent meaning for anyone who knows Chinese characters.

Disyllabic (or longer) words that are directly introduced into Chinese often belong to one of the three cases in (49).

(49)   Origins of disyllabic (or longer) words
       (*a*) The source is a disyllabic (or polysyllabic) name
              zhi-jia-ge   'Chicago'
       (*b*) The source word is made of two morphemes
              dian-shi   'electricity vision (television)'
       (*c*) The word is a description of the original object
              lun chuan   'wheel boat (powered ship)'
              tian dian   'sweet snack (dessert)'

In fact, most loan words from Japanese are a case of (49*b*). It is hard to imagine how cases like those in (49) can be introduced with a monosyllabic word. For example, if a disyllabic name is changed to a monosyllabic loan word, it will sound too removed from the original. Similarly, every existing monosyllabic word already has a specific referent, and using it to refer to a new object will be confusing. For example, Chinese has a native word *chuan* for a boat or a non-motorized ship. If a steamboat is also called *chuan*, the listener cannot tell whether the referent is a traditional Chinese ship or a steamboat. In other words, expressions like those in (49) must be introduced as (at least) disyllabic words in any language.

Sometimes new characters are created to accommodate new words. For example, most new chemical elements are named by creating a new character, which usually consists of two parts. One part is phonetic, representing the sound of the syllable. The other part is categorical, with either the symbol for 'gas', denoting a gas, or the symbol for 'gold', denoting a metal, or the symbol for 'stone', denoting a non-metal solid. However, this method is rarely used elsewhere. Besides, there is a reason why chemical elements are introduced as monosyllables. By convention, chemical elements are abbreviated as one or two letters in formulas and the periodic table. It will be very cumbersome to read the name of a formula by pronouncing the full names of the elements.

Sometimes when a foreign word is introduced as a disyllabic word, yet another morpheme is still added. An example is shown in (50).

(50) ji-pu che
      'Jeep car'

The addition of *che* 'car' is clearly not due to the possibility of ambiguity, since *ji-pu* has no homophone in Chinese. However, for a person who does not know what a Jeep is, the extra morpheme *che* provides a helpful clue. Similarly, consider (51).

(51) pi jiu
      'pi wine (beer)'

For beer, a new Chinese character *pi* has been created. There is, therefore, no ambiguity with other words in writing. In speech, there is hardly any ambiguity either, since although there are twenty or so words that sound the same as *pi* (with the same tone), none of them refers to a beverage. Nevertheless, *jiu* 'wine (alcoholic drink)' is often added to *pi*. There are two reasons; for someone who does not know what beer is, *jiu* offers a clue that it is an alcoholic beverage, and *pi jiu* can serve as a disyllabic foot when metrical structure needs it.

The above discussion shows that while non-metrical considerations are involved in creating disyllabic words in modern Chinese, they have little to do with ambiguity avoidance or the size of syllable inventory. In particular, for the cases in (49), any language would have created disyllabic or longer words, whether its syllable inventory is large or small.

Despite the fact that most new words were introduced as polysyllabic, many soon acquire a monosyllabic form through truncation and join in the dual vocabulary, as a result of metrical forces on word length choices. Some examples are shown in (52).

(52) | Polysyllabic | Monosyllabic | Example |
|---|---|---|
| dian-shi | dian | cai dian |
| electricity vision | electricity | color electricity |
| 'TV' | | 'color TV' |
| zhi-jia-ge | zhi | zhi da |
| 'Chicago' | | 'Chicago University' |
| lun chuan | lun | you lun |
| wheel boat | wheel | tour wheel |
| 'powered ship' | | 'cruise ship' |

As discussed earlier, the truncated monosyllables are not used alone. But when they are used in combination with another word, they carry the full meaning of the untruncated words.

7.9. MONOSYLLABLES IN DIFFERENT WORD CATEGORIES

ZWGW (1959) divides 3,624 commonly used Chinese words into eleven categories. The percentages of monosyllabic words in them vary sharply, as shown in (53).

(53) Percentages of monosyllabic words by word category

Category	Total	Monosyllabic	% monosyllabic
Noun	1,690	262	16
Verb	925	380	41
Adjective	451	140	31
Adverb	194	41	21
Classifier	112	106	95
Numeral	68	33	49
Pronoun	46	11	24
Preposition	47	32	68
Conjunction	45	7	16
Aspect	21	20	95
Exclamation	25	14	56
All	3,624	1,046	29

Classifiers and aspect markers show the highest percentages of monosyllables, at 95 per cent each. In contrast, nouns show only 16 per cent. Among content words there is also considerable variation. For example, there are only 16 per cent of monosyllables in nouns, but 41 per cent in verbs. The variation calls for an explanation.

I propose that the percentage of monosyllables in a word category is related to whether the category usually functions as a syntactic head or nonhead. In the present analysis, syntactic nonheads have stress, syntactic heads need not (see Chapter 6). Therefore, syntactic nonheads usually need to be disyllabic, whereas syntactic heads need not. An initial comparison between the present predictions and the actual data is shown in (54).

(54)   Relation between word length and syntactic function

   (a) Syntactic nonheads: stressed and low percentages of monosyllables

      Noun   16%
      Adjective   31%
      Adverb   21%

   (b) Syntactic heads: no phrasal stress and high percentages of monosyllables

      Classifier   95%
      Preposition   68%
      Aspect   95%

   (c) Unaccounted for

      Verb   41%
      Numeral   49%
      Pronoun   24%
      Conjunction   16%
      Exclamation   56%

Nouns usually occur as the object or the subject, adjectives as modifiers of nouns, and adverbs are typically used as modifiers of verbs. So the three categories are often used as nonheads. We see in (54a) that they indeed show the lowest percentages of monosyllables. Next consider heads. In current syntactic theory, classifiers are heads of classifier phrases, prepositions are heads of preposition phrases, and aspect markers are heads of aspect or inflectional phrases. We see in (54b) that these three categories indeed have the highest percentages of monosyllables.

Still unaccounted for are the five categories in (54c). Since the syntactic status of exclamations is unclear, I will not discuss them. In the pronoun category, ZWGW (1959) includes not only regular pronouns such as *wo* 'I' and *ni* 'you', but also demonstratives (*zhe ge* 'this one', *na yang* 'that way'), question words (*na ge* 'which one', *duo-shao* 'how many'), and other words, such as *bie ren* 'other people' and *da-jia* 'everybody'. Obviously, this is not a homogeneous category, and I do not discuss it further. The numeral category also contains some arbitrary items. For example, besides the numbers 1 to 10, it also includes 11 to 20, and then the tens (30, 40, …, 100), but no other numbers in between. Thus, nothing specific can be said about this category. Finally, the category 'conjunction' is also questionable. It contains a few true conjunctions, such as *he* 'and' and *er* 'but', but also other items which might better be called adverbials, such as *tong-shi* 'at the same time', *jin-guan* 'even though', *jia-ru* 'suppose', *bi-ru* 'for example', and *zhi-yao* 'as long as'. If such items are not syntactic heads, then their high disyllabic rate is expected.

Let us now consider the last category, the verb. In my analysis, verbs usually occur as the head of a verb phrase, and only occasionally as a nominalized subject or object, which are nonheads. Therefore, verbs should mostly be monosyllabic, though that seems not to be the case. However, there are two kinds of vocabulary, the native (or old) vocabulary and the new vocabulary. ZWGW (1959) divides most word categories into smaller groups. Some groups contain both old and new vocabulary. For example, the noun group 'household items' contains old words such as *zhuo-zi* 'table' and *chuang* 'bed', and new words such as *fei-zao* 'soap' and *ya-gao* 'toothpaste'. Some groups contain mostly old vocabulary, such as the noun groups 'plants', 'animals', and 'body parts', or the verb groups 'arm and hand movements', 'leg and foot movements', and 'daily activities'. Some groups contain mostly new vocabulary, such as the noun group 'political, legal, and economic terms' and the verb group 'political, legislative, and social activities' (see Z. Liu *et al.* 1984). The data in (55)–(57) show a comparison between old and new vocabulary in nouns and verbs.

(55)   Percentage of monosyllabic words in old and new verbs

    (*a*) Old verbs (bodily and daily activities)

        Total   % monosyllabic
        280   73

    (*b*) New verbs (political and legislative activities)

        Total   % monosyllabic
        135   2

(56)   Percentage of monosyllabic words in old and new nouns

    (*a*) Old nouns (time, animals, plants, natural foods, body parts, kinship terms)

        Total   % monosyllabic
        453   17

    (*b*) New nouns (political, legal, and economic terms)

        Total   % monosyllabic
        106   5

(57)   Comparison between verbs and nouns (% of monosyllables)

	Old	New
Verbs	73%	2%
Nouns	17%	5%

The data show that in the new vocabulary both verbs and nouns are mostly disyllabic, and that in the old vocabulary most verbs are monosyllabic while nouns are usually disyllabic. In the present analysis, the results are expected. For non-metrical reasons, new words are mostly disyllabic or longer. For metrical reasons, nouns are mostly disyllabic because they mostly occur in nonhead positions, and verbs are mostly monosyllabic because they mostly occur in head positions.

In summary, my analysis explains variations in the percentage of monosyllables across different word categories, an issue that has not been accounted for in other approaches.

7.10. FIXED-LENGTH WORDS

We have seen earlier that, for words with flexible length, [1 2] is bad for [N N], [2 1] for [V O]. However, fixed-length words can behave differently. First, consider the examples in (58), where *lü* 'aluminum' has no disyllabic form.

(58)   [V   O]
        sheng-chan   lü
        chan   lü
        produce   aluminum
        'to process aluminum'

The question here is why [2 1] is good. In the present analysis, the object can form a binary foot with the empty beat, which satisfies Stress Length. In addition, because *lü* 'aluminum' has no disyllabic form, it does not violate Anti-Allomorphy, so [2 1] is good.

Turning to [1 2] of [N N], shown in (59), we see that *xi* 'department' does not have a disyllabic form and *zhu-ren* 'head' does not have a monosyllabic form.

(59)   [N   N]
        xi   zhu-ren
        department   head
        'department chair'

The metrical analysis is shown in (60), where a hyphen indicates a word boundary.

(60) [1 2] of [N N]

$$
\begin{array}{ccc}
x & x & x \\
(S\text{-}S)\,(S\varnothing) & \text{or} & (S\text{-}S)\,S
\end{array}
$$

Here the first two syllables form a foot; the third may or may not, because the latter need not be stressed. The availability of (60) can account for other [N N] compounds that are [1 2], such as *shi zhengfu* 'city government', *pi dayi* 'leather coat', *jin xianglian* 'gold necklace', *shui longtou* 'water tap', *dian bingxiang* 'electric refrigerator', *zhi laohu* 'paper tiger', *men bashou* 'door handle', and *he qianting* 'nuclear submarine', as pointed out by an anonymous reviewer. However, such compounds should not obscure the fact that when both words have flexible length, [1 2] is the disfavoured length pattern for [N N].

Not all usage is explained by metrical requirements alone though. For example, we have seen earlier that *maizang jiu shehui* 'bury old society' is good but *maizang si mao* 'bury dead cat' is not (L. Li 1990), because *maizang* usually requires an abstract object. Similarly, the [V O] example in (61) does not quite fit metrical predictions.

(61) | ?[2 2] | da-sao | shang-dian |
|---|---|---|
| ?[1 2] | sao | shang-dian |
| *[2 1] | da-sao | dian |
| ??[1 1] | sao | dian |
| | 'sweep | store' |

Metrically, [2 1] is bad for [V O] if the object has a disyllabic form, and [2 2] and [1 2] should be good. So why are [2 2] and [1 2] marginal here? The reason seems to be that *shang-dian* 'store' usually refers to the function of a store—a place to buy things—rather than the physical aspect of a store, a place that can be cleaned. Similarly, [1 1] should be good if it can be treated as a compound word. But since 'sweep store' is not a natural expression, its compound status is also marginal.

7.11. [A N] COMPOUNDS

We saw in Chapter 5 that it is easier to make [N N] compounds than [A N] compounds. In particular, [2 2], [2 1], and [1 1] are always good for [N N] but not always for [A N], as can be seen in (62)–(64).

(62)   [A N] with [2 2]

    ?kun-nan wen-ti   'difficult problem'
    ?mei-li feng-jing   'beautiful scenery'
    ?qian-xu xue-sheng 'modest students'

(63)   [A N] with [2 1]

    ?*mei-li jing   'beautiful scenery'
    ?*kun-nan ti   'difficult problem'

(64)   [A N] with [1 1]

    ?*gao shu   'tall tree'
    ?*duan he   'short river'
    ?*nan shu   'difficult book'
    ?*chang hu   'long lake'

For this reason, I proposed in Chapter 5 that [A N] is a bad compound, repeated in (65).

(65)   *[A N]
    [A N] cannot form a compound.

However, many [A N] with [1 1] do occur. Some examples are shown in (66).

(66)   [A N] with [1 1]

    gao shan   'tall mountain'
    duan ku   'short pants'
    nan ti   'difficult problem'
    chang zhuo   'long table'
    hao ren   'good person'

To account for such cases, I proposed Foot Shelter in Chapter 5, repeated in (67).

(67)   *Foot Shelter*
    A foot or potential foot can be treated as a word, whose internal morpho-syntactic structure can be ignored.

Foot Shelter allows disyllabic units to be used as words, regardless of their internal syntax. However, Foot Shelter does not guarantee that every [1 1] is good or will be used in the language. For example, those in (64) are not used in SC, although they probably could be.

    There is an apparent exception to *[A N] and Foot Shelter. In particular, there are some [2 2] compounds that are [A N] but good, such as *zhongda* *sunshi* 'heavy loss', *zhongyao zhishi* 'important instruction', *chenfu guan-nian* 'stale mentality', *cuotuo suiyue* 'wasted years', *fengliu caizi* 'scholar with celebrity and talent', *zuigao sudu* 'top speed', *fenhong yanse* 'pink color', etc. There are two possible ways to explain them. First, in some cases the first word is probably a noun, such as *zuigao* 'top', *fenhong* 'pink', and *fengliu* 'talent and celebrity'. Secondly, some of them may have undergone *de*-omission (see Chapter 5). For example, *zhongyao zhi-shi* 'important instruction' is probably *zhongyao de zhishi* underlyingly, and *chenfu guannian* 'stale mentality' is probably *chenfu de guannian* underlyingly.

A more difficult problem is that although some adjectives are not productive, such as those in (64), others seem to be fully productive. Consider those in (68), which can occur not only with monosyllabic nouns but also with disyllabic nouns.

(68)   xiao/da/lao/hao/huai ren   'small/big/old/good/bad person'
        xiao/da/lao/hao/huai shu   'small/big/old/good/bad tree'
        xiao/da/lao/hao/huai fang-zi   'small/big/old/good/bad house'
        xiao/da/lao/hao/huai xue-sheng   'small/big/old/good/bad student'

It is not obvious how to account for the differences among adjectives. S. Feng (1997: 19) suggests that some monosyllabic adjectives, such as *xiao* 'small' and *da* 'big', are prefixes, which can freely attach to a noun. However, there is no independent evidence for this. In addition, such adjectives can be modified by an adverb (*hen* 'very', *xiangdang* 'quite') which shows that they are words. Moreover, there is no explanation why the difference between a prefix and an adjective should depend on syllable count. For example, why should *mei-li* 'beautiful' be an adjective and *mei* 'beautiful' be a prefix? In a different proposal, S. Feng (1998a: 45) suggests that compounds do not allow [1 2] but phrases do; [A N] allows [1 2] because it is a phrase. However, there are questions for this proposal, too. The first question is, Why do compounds and phrases prefer different word-length patterns? In my analysis it is due to a difference in phrasal stress; in Feng's analysis, which is not based on stress, the reason remains unclear. Another question is, If [A N] is a phrase, why is it less productive than [N N], which is a compound? One would expect the opposite, namely, that phrases are more productive than compounds.

Overall, therefore, it does not seem better to treat [A N] as a productive form. My analysis does have the problem of explaining the productive monosyllables (*da* 'big', *xiao* 'small', *hong* 'red', *huang* 'yellow', etc.). It would be good if such words are nouns. It is easier to say that *hong* 'red' and *huang* 'yellow' are nouns, harder to argue that *da* 'big' and *xiao* 'small' are nouns. On the other hand, perhaps *xiao* is like a nominal prefix 'mini-' and *da* is like a nominal prefix 'mega-'. If so, the pattern is really simple: [N N] is in general good, [A N] bad, with some exceptions.

It is important to note that, apart from some [2 2] expressions that probably involve *de*-omission, the A in [A N] compounds that do occur is always monosyllabic. This means that A is never a foot by itself. In particular, [1 1] can be treated as a word, and [1 2] has two foot structures in SC, shown in (69), where a hyphen indicates a word boundary.

(69) [A N] with [1 2]

x	x x
S-(SS)	(S-S) (SØ)
xiao tuzi	xiao maolü
'little rabbit'	'little donkey'

In neither case does A form a foot by itself, which shows that in such forms it is not treated as a real independent word, which in turn shows that [A N] is not a productive structure.

The inability for A to form a foot explains the lack of ambiguity in some cases. Consider the example in (70).

(70)

S(SØ)	(S-S)(SØ)	S-S(SØ) or (S-S)(SØ)
[hong hua]	*[[da hong] hua]	[da [hong hua]]
red flower	big red flower	big red flower
'red flower'	'bright-red flower'	'big red flower'

Syntactically, 'big red flower' has two interpretations, either [1 2] or [2 1]. In practice, however, only [1 2] is available. In [2 1], the disyllabic adjective forms a foot and the noun forms another. As a result, *[A N] is violated, which explains why it is not available. In [1 2], main stress seems to remain on the noun 'flower', although the first two syllables may form another foot. In either case, neither *da* nor *hong* forms a foot by itself. Therefore, [1 2] is useable probably because it is treated as a trisyllabic word.

7.12. SUMMARY

I have shown that Chinese has a large dual vocabulary where each word has a monosyllabic form and a disyllabic (or polysyllabic) form. The dual vocabulary is not motivated by ambiguity avoidance. Instead, it is motivated in part by metrical needs, according to which a word with phrasal stress should be disyllabic. As a result, many disyllabic pseudo-compounds are created for monosyllabic words. Truncation is another process in the creation of the dual vocabulary in which polysyllables are truncated to monosyllabic pseudo-words, which are used to generate other compounds.

I have also offered a stress-based analysis of word-length choices. The analysis explains various length patterns in different syntactic structures, the percentages of monosyllabic words in different word categories, and the fact that many monosyllabic words cannot be used alone.

It would be interesting to know whether other 'monosyllabic' languages— those in which most syllables are words—also have a dual vocabulary. The answer will be left for future research.

The Word-Order Problem

8.1. INTRODUCTION

This chapter discusses word-order variation in two types of Chinese compound. I call the first [V–O N] compounds, the second, [X Y N] compounds. [V–O N] compounds are exemplified in (1).

(1) Phrase   Compound

　　[[V O] N]   [V O N]
　　qie   cai   de   dao   qie   cai   dao
　　cut   vegetable   DE   knife   cut   vegetable   knife
　　'knife that cuts vegetables'   'vegetable-cutting knife'

　　[[V O] N]   [O V N]
　　jiagong   luobo   de   dao   luobo   jiagong   dao
　　process   turnip DE   knife   turnip   process   knife
　　'knife that processes turnip'   'turnip-processing knife'

The column on the left shows nominal phrases with a relative clause that contains a verb (V) and an object (O). The particle *de* can be considered as a relativizer, the equivalent of *that* in English. The column on the right shows the corresponding compounds. The phrase column has one word order, [V O N], but the compound column can be either [V O N] or [O V N]. The compound word order depends on the word length of the constituents. For example, when V and O are both monosyllabic, [V O N] is the only possible order, but when V and O are both disyllabic, [O V N] is the only possible order.

Now consider [X Y N] compounds, exemplified with two dictionary titles in (2) and (3), where X and Y are modifiers of N.

(2) Daxing   Hanyu   Cidian   *Hanyu   Daxing   Cidian
　　large-scale Chinese   dictionary   Chinese   large-scale dictionary
　　'A Large Chinese Dictionary'   'A Large Chinese Dictionary'

(3)   ??Da   Hanyu   Cidian   Hanyu   Da   Cidian
      large   Chinese dictionary   Chinese large   dictionary
      'A Large Chinese Dictionary'   'A Large Chinese Dictionary'

In (2), 'large' must precede 'Chinese', but in (3) the reverse order is preferred. The difference again depends on word length: in (2) 'large' is disyllabic, but in (3) it is monosyllabic. Judgements on such word orders are quite sharp, but the explanation has not been previously understood.

The above data raise a number of questions. For example, why does word order vary in Chinese compounds? Why is it constant in the English counterparts? What is the full range of word-order patterns in Chinese compounds? What is the syntactic bracketing of the compounds? Does word order vary in English compounds? This chapter intends to address these questions.

Besides the two kinds of word-order variation, there is also a third case, which involves word-order variation in a disyllabic compound, such as *li-qi* vs. *qi-li* 'strength' (Y. Zhang 1980). This case was discussed under pseudo-compounds in Chapter 5 and is not repeated here.

In section 8.2 I discuss [X Y N] compounds, turning to [V–O N] compounds in section 8.3. Section 8.4 deals with [V–O N] compounds in English, and some further issues are discussed in sections 8.4–7.

8.2. [X Y N] COMPOUNDS

In [X Y N] compounds, X and Y are modifiers of N. I assume that syntactic structures are strictly binary branching (see Kayne 1994) and the basic bracketing structure of [X Y N] compounds is [X [Y N]]. The ordering of the modifiers in English is restricted by their meanings. For example, a partial hierarchy of modifier ordering is Size > Shape > Colour > Provenance, where '>' stands for 'precedes' (see Quirk *et al.* 1972). In addition, Sproat and Shih (1991) have argued that the same hierarchy holds for all languages. If we consider both monosyllabic words (X, Y, and N) and disyllabic words (XX, YY, and NN), there are eight cases. Six have a fixed word order, which is the same as in English, shown in (4). Two have an alternative word order, shown in parentheses, given in (5).

(4)   [X [Y N]]   da mu chuan 'big wood boat'
                       bu shou tao 'cloth hand glove'
      [X [Y NN]]   xiao hong denglong 'small red lantern'
      [XX [Y N]]   xuesheng shi tang 'student dining hall'

[XX [Y NN]]   zhongguo mian dayi 'Chinese cotton coat'
[XX [YY N]]   Shanghai Huoche Zhan 'Shanghai Train Station'
[XX [YY NN]]   daxing hanyu cidian 'large-scale Chinese dictionary'

(5) [X [YY N]]   Dong Changan Jie 'East Changan Road'
    ([YY [X N]])   Sichuan Bei Lu
                  Sichuan North Road
                  'North Sichuan Road'
    [X [YY NN]]   Xin Ying–Han Cidian 'New English–Chinese dictionary'
    ([YY [X NN]])   Hanyu Da Cidian
                  Chinese large dictionary
                  'Large Chinese Dictionary'

The bracketing in (4) and (5) is based on constituent analysis and semantics. For example, 'big wood boat' is not [[X Y] N] but [X [Y N]], because the former means 'boat made of big wood', which is not the intended meaning. Similarly, 'Chinese large dictionary' is not [[YY X] N] but [YY [X NN]], because 'Chinese large' is not a possible constituent but 'large dictionary' is. Also, whether a modifier is X or Y is determined by semantics. For example, 'Sichuan North Road', an actual street in Shanghai, is not part of 'North Road' but part of 'Sichuan Road'. Therefore, the analysis is not [XX [Y N]] but [YY [X N]], because the latter corresponds to the original meaning [X [YY N]] 'North Sichuan Road'.

The typical foot boundaries of [X Y N] compounds are shown in (6), largely based on stress judgement, such as Hoa (1983). Some of the foot boundaries differ from those in Duanmu (2000), which was not always based on stress judgement.

(6) [X [Y N]]   (X Y)(NØ)
    [X [Y NN]]   (X Y)(NN), (X Y)N(NØ)
    [XX [Y N]]   (XX)(Y N), (XX)Y(NØ)
    [XX [Y NN]]   (XX)(Y N)(NØ)
    [XX [YY N]]   (XX)(YY)(NØ)
    [XX [YY NN]]   (XX)(YY)(NN), (XX)(YY)N(NØ)
    [X [YY N]]   (X Y)Y (NØ)
    ([YY [X N]])   (YY)(X N), (YY)X(NØ)
    [X [YY NN]]   (X Y)Y (NN), (X Y)Y N(NØ)
    ([YY [X NN]])   (YY)(X N)(NØ)

In Chapter 6 we discussed the foot analysis of disyllabic and trisyllabic words, so here we focus on the first two or three syllables. In the first two cases, XY forms a foot, in the next four cases, XX does. Therefore, there is no need to change the position of X or XX. This leaves the two cases that have alternative word orders, which both start with XYY, reminiscent of the problem with [1 2] for [N N] compounds (Chapter 6). In [X [YY N]], YY forms a foot; X cannot, unless the stress on YY is deleted. If YY is fronted, it can form a foot and XN can form another, which is metrically fine. Similarly, in [X [YY NN]], YY forms a foot—X cannot unless the stress on YY is deleted. If YY is fronted, it can form a foot and XNN can be footed as a trisyllabic word.

The analysis shows that although stress deletion (from YY in [X [YY N]] and [X [YY NN]]) and YY-fronting can improve metrical structure, they both have a cost. YY-fronting violates the default word order, so if the original foot structure is good, YY-fronting is not used (e.g. [YY XX NN] is bad, even though it has good metrical structure). Stress deletion also seems to have a cost; if it does not, YY-fronting (which has a cost) would not be an alternative.

B. Lu (1989) proposes a different analysis. He suggests that Chinese has a preference to avoid 'big-belly' structures, in which a long word occurs in the middle of short words. Instead, Chinese favours small-belly structures, in which long words occur at the beginning and the end of an expression and short words occur in the middle. It is true that both [X [YY N]] and [X [YY NN]] are big-belly structures, [YY [X N]] and [YY [X NN]], small-belly structures. However, Lu cannot explain why [1 2] of [N N] is bad, which is not big belly. In the present analysis, [1 2] has the same problem as [X [YY N]] and [X [YY NN]]: in both cases, the first word has phrasal stress, but it is monosyllabic and followed by another foot, so it cannot form a foot by itself without some structural change.

Lu (pers. comm.) offers an interesting case for the belly-shape analysis. Consider the examples in (7) and (8) (the judgement is Lu's; '?*' stands for marginal or unacceptable).

(7) (a)   [gaoceng [shuini jianzhu]]
            'multi-story concrete building'
     (b) ?*[shuini [gaoceng jianzhu]]
            'concrete multi-story building'

(8) (a)   [gaoceng [[gangjin shuini] jianzhu]]
            'multi-story steel-grid concrete building'
     (b)   [[gangjin shuini] [gaoceng jianzhu]]
            'steel-grid concrete multi-story building'

The structure in (7) does not have a big belly, so it should use the default word order, in which the shape 'multi-story' comes before the material 'concrete'. The structure in (8) has a big belly, 'steel-grid concrete (reinforced concrete)', so the long word can be fronted.

The examples raise a question for my analysis, namely, since every word in (8) is disyllabic and can form a foot, what motivates the word-order change? I suggest that (8*b*) does not derive from (8*a*) but from (9).

(9) [[gangjin   shuini]   de   [gaoceng   jianzhu]]
    steel-grid concrete   DE   multi-story   building
    'multi-story building of steel-grid concrete'

This structure contains an underlying *de* and can change to (8*b*) via *de*-omission (Chapter 5). If this suggestion is correct, (8) is not a compelling example against the present analysis.

8.3. [V–O N] COMPOUNDS

I describe the data first. Then I present the analysis.

8.3.1. **The data**

For ease of exposition, I use V, M, O, and N for monosyllabic length (where M is a modifier of O) and VV, MM, OO, and NN for disyllabic length. Thus, in [V O N] the verb, the object, and the head noun are all monosyllabic. In [M O VV NN] the object noun and its modifier are monosyllabic, the verb and the head noun, disyllabic. The compound patterns are given in (10) and (11), along with their corresponding phrasal forms. Some disyllabic words can be further split into two morphemes; for example, *gongju* 'tool' is literally 'work-tool'. However, the decomposition has little consequence and will be ignored (alternative patterns are given in parentheses).

(10)   Compounds with a monosyllabic verb

    Phrase   Compound

  (*a*) [[V O] N]   [[V O] N]
      qie cai   de dao   qie cai   dao
      cut vegetable DE knife   cut vegetable knife
      'knife that cuts vegetables' 'vegetable-cutting knife'

  (*b*) [[V O] NN]   [[V O] NN]
      qie cai   de gongju   qie cai   gongju
      cut vegetable DE tool   cut vegetable tool
      'tool that cuts vegetables' 'vegetable-cutting tool'

(c) [[V OO] N]

qie luobo de dao
cut turnip DE knife
'knife that cuts turnips'

?[[V OO] N]
(?[OO [V N]])
qie luobo dao
cut turnip knife
'turnip-cutting knife'

(d) [[V OO] NN]

qie luobo de gongju
cut turnip DE tool
'tool that cuts turnips'

?[[V OO] NN]
(?[OO [V NN]])
qie luobo gongju
cut turnip tool
'turnip-cutting tool'

(e) [[V [M O]] N]

qie bai   cai   de dao
cut white vegetable DE knife
'knife that cuts cabbage'

?[[V [M O]] N]
(?[[M O][V N]])
qie bai   cai   dao
cut white vegetable knife
'cabbage-cutting knife'

(f) [[V [M O]] NN]

qie bai   cai   de gongju
cut white vegetable DE tool
'tool that cuts cabbage'

?[[V [M O]] NN]
(?[[M O][V NN]])
qie bai   cai   gongju
cut white vegetable tool
'cabbage-cutting tool'

(g) [[V [M OO]] N]

qie bai   luobo de dao
cut white turnip DE knife
'knife that cuts white turnips'

?[[V [M OO]] N]
(?[[M OO]][V N]])
qie bai   luobo dao
cut white turnip knife
'white turnip-cutting knife'

(h) [[V [M OO]] NN]

qie bai   luobo de gongju
cut white turnip DE tool
'tool that cuts white turnips'

?[[V [M OO]] NN]
(?[[M OO]][V NN]])
qie bai   luobo gongju
cut white turnip tool
'white turnip-cutting tool'

(i) [[V [MM O]] N]

xue luobo pi   de dao
peel turnip skin DE knife
'knife that peels turnip skin'

[MM [[V O] N]]
(?[[MM O][V N]] or
?[[V [MM O]] N])
luobo xue pi   dao
turnip peel skin knife
'turnip skin-peeling knife'

(j) [[V [MM O]] NN]

xue luobo pi   de gongju
peel turnip skin DE tool
'tool that peels turnip skin'

[MM [[V O] NN]]
(?[[MM O][V NN]] or
?[[V [MM O]] NN])
luobo xue pi   gongju
turnip peel skin tool
'turnip skin-peeling tool'

(k) [[V [MM OO]] N]

xi   pingguo zhongzi de gang
wash apple   seed   DE pot
'pot that washes apple seeds'

?[[V [MM OO]] N]
(?[[MM OO][V N]])

xi   pingguo zhongzi gang
wash apple   seed   pot
'apple seed-washing pot'

(l) [[V [MM OO]] NN]

xi   pingguo zhongzi de gongju
wash apple   seed   DE tool
'tool that washes apple seeds'

?[[V [MM OO]] NN]
(?[[MM OO][V NN]])

xi   pingguo zhongzi gongju
wash apple   seed   tool
'apple seed-washing tool'

(11)   Compounds with a disyllabic verb

Phrase

Compound

(a) [[VV O] N]
jiagong cai   de dao
process vegetable DE knife
'knife that processes vegetables'

?[O [VV N]]
cai   jiagong dao
vegetable process knife
'vegetable-processing knife'

(b) [[VV O] NN]
jiagong cai   de gongju
process vegetable DE tool
'tool that processes vegetables'

?[O [VV NN]]
cai   jiagong gongju
vegetable process tool
'vegetable-processing tool'

(c) [[VV OO] N]
jiagong luobo de dao
process turnip DE knife
'knife that processes turnips'

[OO [VV N]]
luobo jiagong dao
turnip process knife
'turnip-processing knife'

(d) [[VV OO] NN]
jiagong luobo de gongju
process turnip DE tool
'tool that processes turnips'

[OO [VV NN]]
luobo jiagong gongju
turnip process tool
'turnip-processing tool'

(e) [[VV [M O]] N]
jiagong bai   cai   de dao
process white vegetable DE knife
'knife that processes cabbage'

[[M O][VV N]]
bai   cai   jiagong dao
white vegetable process knife
'cabbage-processing knife'

(f) [[VV [M O]] NN]
jiagong bai   cai   de gongju
process white vegetable DE tool
'tool that processes cabbage'

[[M O][VV NN]]
bai   cai   jiagong gongju
white vegetable process tool
'cabbage-processing tool'

(g) [[VV [M OO]] N]
jiagong bai   luobo de dao
process white turnip DE knife
'knife that processes white turnips'

[[M OO][VV N]]
bai   luobo jiagong dao
white turnip process knife
'white turnip-processing knife'

(*h*) [[VV [M OO]] NN]   [[M OO][VV NN]]
    jiagong bai   luobo de gongju   bai   luobo jiagong gongju
    process white turnip DE tool   white turnip process tool
    'tool that processes white turnips'   'white turnip-processing tool'

(*i*) [[VV [MM O]] N]   [[MM O][VV N]]
    jiagong luobo pi   de dao   luobo pi   jiagong dao
    process turnip skin DE knife   turnip skin process knife
    'knife that processes turnip skin'   'turnip skin-processing knife'

(*j*) [[VV [MM O]] NN]   [[MM O][VV NN]]
    jiagong luobo pi   de gongju   luobo pi   jiagong   gongju
    process turnip skin DE tool   turnip skin process   tool
    'tool that processes turnip skin'   'turnip skin-processing tool'

(*k*) [[VV [MM OO]] N]   [[MM OO][VV N]]
    jiagong pingguo zhongzi de dao   pingguo zhongzi jiagong dao
    process apple   seed   DE knife   apple   seed   process knife
    'knife that processes apple seeds'   'apple seed-processing knife'

(*l*) [[VV [MM OO]] NN]   [[MM OO][VV NN]]
    jiagong pingguo zhongzi de gongju   pingguo zhongzi jiagong gongju
    process apple   seed   DE tool   apple   seed   process tool
    'tool that processes apple seeds'   'apple seed-processing tool'

Several comments are in order. First, totally bad forms are not listed. For example, (10*a*) cannot be [O V N], [V N O], or [N V O]. Forms with a question mark can be good or bad depending on a given expression; for example, [[V OO] NN] is marginal for *qie luobo gongju* 'cut turnip tool (turnip-cutting tool)', but there is an existing expression *dong naojin yeye* 'move brain grandpa (the Wise Grandpa)', a columnist in a children's newspaper who answers science questions. Similarly, [OO [V N]] is marginal for *luobo qie dao* 'turnip cut knife (turnip-cutting knife)', and bad for *malu sao ji* 'street sweep machine (street-sweeping machine)', yet it is good for *shitou diao che* 'stone lift car (stone-lifting machine)'. Many length combinations have no perfect word order, such as (10*c–h*) and (11*a–b*); in such cases, speakers can use a phrase instead. Examples (10*a*) and (10*b*) have no alternative patterns, (10*i*) and (10*j*) have two, and the rest in (10) have one. Most alternative patterns involve a constituent [V N] or [V NN], to which I will return. The cases in (11) have no alternative patterns.

Secondly, one may wonder whether [V–O N] compounds are related to [V–O N] phrases, or whether they are created independently. For example, is [OO [VV N]] in (11*c*) derived from the phrase [[VV OO] N] by fronting OO, or is it the result of adding OO directly to an independent compound [VV N]? I will assume the former and give the argument in section 8.5.

Thirdly, when a compound word order differs from that of the phrase, the compound has two meanings. For example, (11*c*) can mean either 'a processing knife made of turnip' (despite its unlikelihood in real life) or 'a knife for processing turnip', shown in (12).

(12) (*a*) [MM$_j$ [[VV Ø$_i$] N]]
        luobo   jiagong   dao
        turnip   process   knife
        'processing knife made of turnip'

   (*b*) [OO$_i$ [[VV Ø$_i$] N]]
        luobo   jiagong   dao
        turnip   process   knife
        'knife for processing turnip'

Following a standard assumption in syntax (e.g. Chomsky 1981; Kayne 1994), a transitive verb always has an object position, which can be filled by an overt word or an empty element. In (12*a*) *luobo* 'turnip' is the modifier (MM) of [[VV Ø] N] and is unrelated to the empty object (Ø) of the verb, shown by different indexes. In (12*b*) *luobo* is co-indexed with the empty object of the verb. The meaning of (12*b*) is the same as the phrase, but that of (12*a*) is not. Compounds that have the same word order as the phrase, such as (10*a*), are not ambiguous. For each compound in (10) and (11), only the meaning that corresponds to the phrasal meaning is given.

The fourth point to note is that the bracketing of the phrases is not controversial. The bracketing of a compound is based on standard constituent analysis. For example, in (10*c*), [OO V N] is not [[OO V] N] but [OO [V N]] because [OO V] cannot be a good constituent independently but [V N] can. In addition, I assume structural consistency, so that corresponding structures have the same constituent brackets. For example, because [OO V N] in (10*c*) is not [[OO V] N] but [OO [V N]], we assume that [OO VV N] in (11*c*) is not [[OO VV] N] but [OO [VV N]], even though both [OO VV] and [VV N] are good.

Finally, the compound word order is primarily determined by syllable count, not by semantics or syntax. For example, (10*a*) and (10*c*) are syntactically identical, yet (10*a*) has just one word order, which is well formed, whereas (10*c*) has two word orders, neither of which is always good. The difference between (10*a*) and (10*c*) is solely due to the fact that O is monosyllabic in (10*a*) but disyllabic in (10*c*). Similarly, the word-order difference between (10*a*) and (11*a*) is solely due to the fact that V is monosyllabic in (10*a*) but disyllabic in (11*a*).

8.3.2. **The analysis**

The analysis I offer here is considerably more simple than that in Duanmu (1997, 2000), where I assumed phonologically triggered syntactic movement and multiple levels of stress, and I assumed that main stress in a compound must fall on the first syllable. As R. Zhou (2005) argued, that analysis is too complicated.

I now assume that a foot must be binary and that phrasal stress goes to the syntactic nonhead—these two assumptions seem to be non-controversial (Chapter 6). The essence of the proposal is given in (13) and (14).

(13)   [verb object] is a phrase.

(14)   (*a*)   *Internal Phrase: a compound should not contain an internal phrase.
       (*b*)   Foot Shelter (see Chapter 5).
       (*c*)   *[V N]/*[V NN]: a foot cannot cross a clause boundary.

Both (13) and (14*a*) are self-evident and will not be further justified here. They rule against compounds that contain the verb–object word order, such as [[VV OO] N] and [[VV O] N], except those protected by Foot Shelter, in particular the disyllabic VO, as in [[V O] N]. The main effect of (14*c*) is to rule out disyllabic [V N] and trisyllabic [V NN] and other compounds that contain them. The reason for the unacceptability of *[V N] and *[V NN] is probably that the foot structure is (V N) or (V N)(NØ), where the foot (V N) crosses a clause boundary. Let us now consider how the analysis accounts for the data. First, consider (10), analysed in (15).

(15)   Compounds with a monosyllabic verb

	Structure	Comments
(*a*)	[[V O] N]	[V O] protected by Foot Shelter
(*b*)	[[V O] NN]	[V O] protected by Foot Shelter
(*c*)	?[[V OO] N]	*Internal Phrase [V OO]
	?[OO [V N]]	*[V N]
(*d*)	?[[V OO] NN]	*Internal Phrase [V OO]
	?[OO [V NN]]	*[V NN]
(*e*)	?[[V [M O]] N]	*Internal Phrase [V [M O]]
	?[[M O][V N]]	*[V N]
(*f*)	?[[V [M O]] NN]	*Internal Phrase [V [M O]]
	?[[M O][V NN]]	*[V NN]
(*g*)	?[[V [M OO]] N]	*Internal Phrase [V [M OO]]
	?[[[M OO]][V N]]	*[V N]

(h) ?[[V [M OO]] NN]   *Internal Phrase [V [M OO]]
     ?[[M OO]][V NN]]   *[V NN]

(i) ?[[V [MM O]] N]   *Internal Phrase [V [MM O]]
     [MM [[V O] N]]   [V O] protected by Foot Shelter
     ?[[MM O][V N]]   *[V N]

(j) ?[[V [MM O]] NN]   *Internal Phrase [V [MM O]]
     [MM [[V O] NN]]   [V O] protected by Foot Shelter
     ?[[MM O][V NN]]   *[V NN]

(k) ?[[V [MM OO]] N]   *Internal Phrase [V [MM OO]]
     ?[[MM OO][V N]]   *[V N]

(l) ?[[V [MM OO]] NN]   *Internal Phrase [V [MM OO]]
     ?[[MM OO][V NN]]   *[V NN]

It can be seen that all the questionable forms violate either *[V N]/*[V NN] or *Internal Phrase, and the four good forms are all protected by Foot Shelter for the [V O] portion. The questionable forms can be used in some special cases, to be discussed later. Let us now take a closer look at the metrical structure of the four good forms, shown in (16).

(16)   Syntax   Foot structure

       [[V O] N]   (SS)(SØ)
       [[V O] NN]   (SS)(SS), (SS)S(SØ)
       [MM [[V O] N]]   (SS)(SS)(SØ),
       [MM [[V O] NN]]   (SS)(SS)(SS), (SS)(SS)S(SØ)

As discussed in Chapter 6, a disyllabic non-final unit can form (SS), a final N can form a foot with an empty beat, and a final NN can form either (SS) or S(SØ). Thus, all the structures are metrically good. Now consider the analysis of compounds with a disyllabic verb, shown in (17).

(17)   Compounds with a disyllabic verb

       Phrase   Compound

(a) *[[VV O] N]   *Internal Phrase [VV O]
     ?[O [VV N]]   Foot Binarity

(b) *[[VV O] NN]   *Internal Phrase [VV O]
     ?[O [VV NN]]   Foot Binarity

(c) ?[[VV OO] N]   *Internal Phrase [VV OO]
     [OO [VV N]]

(d) ?[[VV OO] NN]   *Internal Phrase [VV OO]
     [OO [VV NN]]

(e) ?[[VV [M O]] N]   *Internal Phrase [VV [M O]]
    [[M O][VV N]]

(f) ?[[VV [M O]] NN]   *Internal Phrase [VV [M O]]
    [[M O][VV NN]]

(g) ?[[VV [M OO]] N]   *Internal Phrase [VV [M OO]]
    [[M OO][VV N]]

(h) ?[[VV [M OO]] NN]   *Internal Phrase [VV [M OO]]
    [[M OO][VV NN]]

(i) ?[[VV [MM O]] N]   *Internal Phrase [VV [MM O]]
    [[MM O][VV N]]

(j) ?[[VV [MM O]] NN]   *Internal Phrase [VV [MM O]]
    [[MM O][VV NN]]

(k) ?[[VV [MM OO]] N]   *Internal Phrase [VV [MM OO]]
    [[MM OO][VV N]]

(l) ?[[VV [MM OO]] NN]   *Internal Phrase [VV [MM OO]]
    [[MM OO][VV NN]]

Two forms start with [VV O], which are completely bad, probably not
only because they violate *Internal Phrase, but the O has phrasal stress
and cannot form a binary foot; in particular, the O cannot form a foot
with the following N, because such a foot would cross a clause boundary.
Two of the questionable forms start with a monosyllabic O followed by a
disyllabic VV, in which case the O (which has phrasal stress) cannot form
a binary foot, unless a structural change is made to delete the stress from
the following VV. The same issue exists for those that start with [M OO],
to be discussed shortly. The other questionable forms all violate *Internal Phrase. Again, the questionable forms can sometimes be used, which
we return to later. Let us now consider the metrical structure of the good
forms, shown in (18).

(18) Syntax   Foot structure
      [OO [VV N]]   (SS)(SS)(SØ)
      [OO [VV NN]]   (SS)(SS)(SS), (SS)(SS)S(SØ)
      [[M O][VV N]]   (SS)(SS)(SØ)
      [[M O][VV NN]]   (SS)(SS)(SS), (SS)(SS)S(SØ)
      [[M OO][VV N]]   (SS)S(SS)(SØ)
      [[M OO][VV NN]]   (SS)S(SS)(SS), (SS)S(SS)S(SØ)
      [[MM O][VV N]]   (SS)S(SS)(SØ)
      [[MM O][VV NN]]   (SS)S(SS)(SS), (SS)S(SS)S(SØ)
      [[MM OO][VV N]]   (SS)(SS)(SS)(SØ)
      [[MM OO][VV NN]]   (SS)(SS)(SS)(SS), (SS)(SS)(SS)S(SØ)

Again, a disyllabic non-final unit can form (SS), a final N can form a foot with an empty beat, and a final NN can form either (SS) or S(SØ). In addition, in [MM O], O is a syntactic head and need not be stressed. Finally, in those that have [M OO], the [M OO] must be an existing, well-formed compound, whose foot structure is (SS)(SØ) in final positions and (SS)S in non-final positions (Chapter 6). Thus, all the structures are metrically good.

8.4. [V–O N] COMPOUNDS IN ENGLISH

We see in (10) and (11) that, although the Chinese compounds varied in word order, their English counterparts are consistently [(M) O V N]. The question is why. In fact, the present analysis already provides an answer. The English verb has the ending -ing, so it is at least disyllabic. Thus, the English counterparts are like the Chinese compounds in (11), where the order is also consistently [(M) O V N]. It is interesting that there are a few cases where the English verb is monosyllabic, without the ending -ing, and in such cases the word order [V–O N] can occur, as the present analysis predicts. Some examples are given in (19).

(19)   breakneck speed
        makeshift plan
        killjoy person/attitude
        spoilsport person/attitude

Such English examples correspond to the Chinese [V O N] and [V O NN] compounds in (10a) and (10b), in which the object is not fronted.

My analysis also offers a better analysis of English compounds like *truck driver* than that offered by Lieber (1983). According to Lieber, the argument structure of *truck driver* suggests that the bracketing is [[*truck drive*] -*er*]. However, it is unclear why the word order in the inner unit is [O V] instead of [V O]. In addition, as Booij (1988) points out, the analysis of [[*truck drive*] -*er*] predicts that [*truck drive*] is a possible compound, which is not the case. In the present analysis, *truck driver* is like a [V–O N] compound; its underlying structure is shown in (20), where -*er* is co-indexed with the empty subject of the verb.

(20)   [[Ø$_i$ [drive truck]] -er$_i$]

However, (20) is ill-formed because -*er* needs to be attached to a verb. On the other hand, the structure (21a) is good, which is phonologically equivalent to (21b).

(21) (a) [truck$_j$ [[Ø$_i$ [drive Ø$_j$]] -er$_i$]]
      (b) [truck [drive -er]]

Here, *truck* is the modifier of the 'compound' [*drive -er*] and is co-indexed with the empty object of *drive*. In addition, *-er* can attach to the verb, so the structure is good. The analysis in (21) accounts for the apparent bracketing paradox that [drive truck] forms a closer unit syntactically, in that order, whereas [*drive -er*] forms a closer unit phonologically.

8.5. MOVEMENT OR NOT?

When the word order of a compound differs from that of the corresponding phrase, we need to ask how the two expressions are related. For example, consider the pair in (22). The empty subject of the verb should also be co-indexed with N, which is not shown.

(22) Phrase   Compound

      [[VV OO] N]]   [OO$_i$ [[VV Ø$_i$] N]]
      jiagong luobo de dao   luobo jiagong dao
      process turnip DE knife   turnip process knife
      'knife that processes turnips' 'turnip-processing knife'

It seems that the compound is derived from the phrase by moving the object OO to the front—such movement is familiar in syntax. For example, Chomsky (1994) discusses three kinds of movement: head movement, XP movement by substitution, and XP movement by adjunction. In the first, a head moves to join another head; in the second, an XP moves to an empty XP position; and in the third, an XP is raised and adjoined to an XP node. The third case fits the analysis in (22) in two ways: an XP is a syntactic nonhead—which the object OO is—and the OO is adjoined to the original compound, which can be seen as an XP node (a maximal projection).

  However, it is not necessary to assume movement literally. Instead, we can assume that, as a regular compounding process, a noun NN can be added to [VV N], which is independently good. The added NN may or may not be co-indexed with the empty object of the verb. The two cases are shown in (23).

(23) (a) Not co-indexed   (b) Co-indexed (= [OO$_i$ [[VV Ø$_i$] N]])

          [NN$_j$ [[VV Ø$_i$] N]]   [NN$_i$ [[VV Ø$_i$] N]]
          luobo jiagong dao   luobo jiagong dao
          turnip process knife   turnip process knife
          'processing knife made of turnip'   'turnip-processing knife'

In (23a) 'turnip' is not the object of 'process', owing to lack of co-indexing. In (23b) 'turnip' is interpreted as the object of 'process'. The ambiguity is available not because there is literal movement in (23b) but because there are two ways to index the NN. It is also possible to interpret movement abstractly, so that it is another term for co-indexing in any structure.

A similar analysis can be used to account for word order variation in [X Y N] compounds. For example, I have argued that 'Sichuan North Road' is related to 'North Sichuan Road', because it is part of 'Sichuan Road' and not part of 'North Road'. The relation between the two word orders is shown in (24).

(24)   (a) [X [YY N]]   (b) [YY$_i$ [X [Ø$_i$ N]]]

      Bei Sichuan Lu   Sichuan Bei Lu

      North Sichuan Road   Sichuan North Road

      'North Sichuan Road'   'North Sichuan Road'

It is reasonable to assume that 'Road' always implies a name (i.e. 'what Road'). In (24a) the name position is filled by 'Sichuan'; in (24b) it is empty but co-indexed with 'Sichuan'. Thus, the two structures are related by the co-indexing relation.

8.6. [V N] COMPOUNDS

In section 8.3 I proposed that [V N] and [V NN] are usually bad, where N or NN is the logical subject of the verb. However, the reason for the lack of [V N] and [V NN] is not so obvious. It does not seem to be due to syntax, since [VV N] and [VV NN] are both quite productive. This is shown in (25).

(25)   [VV NN]   yunshu   jiqi

      [VV N]   yunshu   ji

      [V NN]   *yun   jiqi

      [V N]   *yun   ji

               transport   machine

           'machine for transportation'

Because [VV NN] and [VV N] are good, we cannot rule out all verb–noun compounds. Metrical consideration is not sufficient either. For example, one might notice that since the verb (or nominal verb) is the syntactic nonhead, it has phrasal stress (Chapter 6), and so it should be disyllabic. This seems to explain why [VV NN] and [VV N] are good and why [V NN] is bad. However, [V N] is disyllabic and ought to be protected by Foot Shelter (Chapter 6).

Why then is [V N] bad? Let us take a closer look at the syntactic and metrical structure, shown in (26), where the inner clause is indicated by curly brackets.

(26)   (SS)   (SS)
    [{Ø$_i$ [VV Ø$_j$]} NN$_i$]
            (SS)   (SØ)
    [{Ø$_i$ [VV Ø$_j$]} N$_i$]
            (S   S)(SØ)
    *[{Ø$_i$ [V Ø$_j$]} NN$_i$]
            (S   S)
    *[{Ø$_i$ [V Ø$_j$]} N$_i$]

Following syntactic theory, I assume that a transitive verb always projects a subject position and an object position. In (26) the empty subject is co-indexed with the noun, and the structure is similar to a nominal with a relative clause. In the two bad forms, there is a foot that crosses a clause boundary, which I suspect is the reason why they are bad.

Although [V N] and [V NN] compounds are generally rare, some do occur in Chinese. Some examples are shown in (27).

(27)   [V N]   tuo che   'pull car'
                 diao che   'lift car'
                 ti dao   'clip knife (clippers)'
                 jian dao   'cut knife (scissors)'

       [V NN]   kang xueqing   'oppose serum (anti-serum)'

I was only able to find one example of [V NN], thanks to Jerry Packard. The availability of the compounds in (27) allows other compounds that contain them, such as those in (28).

(28)   [OO [V N]]   shitou   diao   che
                           stone   lift   car
                           'machine for lifting stone'

       [[M OO][V N]]   mu   fangzi diao   che
                           wood   house   lift   car
                           'machine for lifting wood house'

       [[MM O][V N]]   shuini   ban   diao   che
                           cement   board   lift   car
                           'machine for lifting cement board'

       [[MM OO][V N]]   jingmi   yiqi   diao   che
                           precision instrument   lift   car
                           'machine for lifting precision instrument'

[OO [V NN]]	ganmao	kang	xueqing
	cold	oppose	serum
	'antiserum for cold'		

[[M OO][V NN]]	fei	jiehe	kan	xueqing
	lung	tuberculosis	oppose	serum
	'antiserum for pulmonary tuberculosis'			

[[MM O][V NN]]	jiehe	bing	kan	xueqing
	tuberculosis	disease	oppose	serum
	'antiserum for tuberculosis disease'			

[[MM OO][V NN]]	liuxing	ganmao	kan	xueqing
	spreading	cold	oppose	serum
	'antiserum for flu'			

However, the presence of the examples in (27) and (28) should not overshadow the fact that in most cases [V N] and [V NN] compounds are bad, so are compounds that contain them.

As in Chinese, [V N] and [V NN] compounds are quite rare in English. Some exceptions are found though, such as those in (29).

(29)   [V N] compounds in English

hit man   'man who hits (someone)'
watchman   'man who watches (something)'
tow-truck   'truck that tows (cars)'
tow-boat   'boat that tows (ships)'

Again, the presence of such examples should not obscure the fact that [V N] and [V NN] compounds are in general unproductive in English. For example, those in (30) seem to parallel those in (29) but are all bad.

(30)   *help-man   'man who helps (someone)'
       *see-man   'man who sees (something)'
       *move-truck 'truck that moves (cars)'
       *move-boat   'boat that moves (ships)'

It is possible that the V in (29) is in fact a noun, and the cases in (29) are in fact [N N] compounds. If so, there is more reason to believe that [V N] is bad. It is also relevant to note that I found only one case of [V NN] in Chinese and no case of [V NN] in English. It is possible that in the Chinese [V NN] *kang xueqing* 'antiserum', the V is not used as a verb but a prefix, translated from its English source 'anti-'. If so, there is no [V NN] but just [V N], which is the exact length for Foot Shelter.

8.7. COMPOUNDS WITH INTERNAL VO PHRASES

We saw in (10) and (11) that many compounds are questionable because they violate *Internal Phrase, in other words, they contain an internal VO phrase. It has been noted that some compounds seem to contain a VO phrase (Y. He 2004; D. Shi 2003; R. Zhou 2005). First consider the cases in (31), which contain [VV OO+], where OO+ is disyllabic or longer.

(31) Compounds with internal [VV OO+]

[[VV NN] N]	caozuo	diannao	zhe
	operate	computer	person
	'person who operates computer'		
[[VV NN] N]	zhizhao	yaoyan	zhe
	create	rumor	person
	'person who creates rumor'		
[[VV NN] N]	guaipian	ertong	fan
	swindle	child	criminal
	'criminal who swindles children'		
[[VV NN] N]	qinfan	yinsi	an
	breach	privacy	case
	'privacy-breaching case'		
[[VV NN] N]	zousi	duping	zui
	smuggle	drug	crime
	'crime of smuggling drugs'		
[[VV [NN NN]] N]	xielou	guojia	jimi	zui
	leak	state	secret	crime
	'crime to leak state secrets'			
[[VV [NN [NN N]]] N]	chufan	xingfa	diliu	tiao	zhe
	break	law	sixth	clause	person
	'person who broke clause six of the law'				
[[VV [[Neg AA] NN]]] N]	shoushou	bu	zhengdang liyi	zhe
	accept	not	proper	benefit person
	'person who accepts improper benefit'			

The compound 'breach privacy case' is not a real [V–O N] compound, because the logical subject of the verb is not 'case' but the person who commits the case. However, the rest seem to be [V–O N] compounds. As Y. He (2004) and R. Zhou (2005) observe, all the compounds can use the [OO+ VV N] word order. In addition, such compounds seem to be limited to certain head nouns, in particular *zhe* 'the person who '...', *zui* 'crime', and *fan* 'criminal'. Still, the examples in (31) seem to be quite acceptable. So how do we explain the fact that they contain a VO phrase?

One might question whether the cases in (31) are true compounds and whether the internal VO is a true phrase. However, cross-linguistically, compound-internal phrases are not uncommon. Some examples in English are shown in (32).

(32) Phrasal compounds in English
    TV-and-VCR table
    meat-and-potato eater
    over-the-fence gossip
    over-the-counter drug
    nobody-cares attitude
    take-it-or-leave-it offer

Wiese (1996) calls such compounds 'phrasal compounds'. According to him, the internal phrase is not a true phrase but a 'quotation'—an extra-linguistic symbol inserted into a compound. As an argument, Wiese shows that the 'quotation' can be a phrase, a non-language sound, or a piece of another language. If Wiese is right, as it seems to me, then the VO phrases in (31) are also 'quotations'.

R. Zhou (2005) also cites some interesting compounds that contain [V OO+], which are shown in (33).

(33) Compounds with internal [V OO+]

[[V NN] N]	chou	youyan	ji
	suck	smoke	machine
	'kitchen ventilator'		

[[V NN] N]	qu	si-pi	qian
	remove	dead-skin	tweezers
	'tweezers for removing dead-skin'		

[[V NN] N]	jiang	xue-ya	yao
	lower	blood-pressure	medicine
	'medicine for lowering blood-pressure'		

[[V NN] N]	ling	huzhao	tiao
	receive	passport	slip
	'slip for picking up passport'		

[[V NN] NN]	kang	bingdu	jiaonang
	oppose	virus	gel
	'anti-virus gel'		

[[V NNN] NN]	fan	faxisi	xuanyan
	oppose	Fascist	declaration
	'anti-Fascist declaration'		

[[V [NN NN]] NN]	fang	laji	youjian	chengxu
	prevent	trash	mail	program
	'program for preventing trash mail'			

Some of the examples are not real [V–O N] compounds. For example, in 'receive passport slip', 'slip' is not the logical subject of 'receive'. Similarly, in 'oppose Fascist declaration', it is hard to say whether 'declaration' is the logical subject of 'oppose' or whether the person who wrote it is. Nevertheless, all the examples in (33) seem to be compounds and contain [V OO+]. As with the previous set of examples, they can be accounted for by the 'quotation' analysis of Wiese (1996).

As far as foot structure is concerned, all the above examples are good. In particular, in the [V OO+] or [VV OO+] part, phrasal stress goes to OO+. Since OO+ is disyllabic or longer, there is no problem carrying the phrasal stress, and there is no need for the empty beat. The final N or NN can use the empty beat if needed, so there is no problem for their foot structure either.

Finally, consider another set of compounds cited in R. Zhou (2005) which contain an internal [O V], shown in (34). It is important to note that the structure is not [O [V N]], to which I return shortly.

(34)   Compounds with internal [O V]

[[O V] N]	yu	gua	qi
	rain	scrape	machine
	'screen wiper'		

[[O V] N]	ke	yun	zhan
	guest	transport	station
	'passenger transportation station'		

[[O V] N]	hou	shi	jing
	rear	view	mirror
	'rear view mirror'		

A couple of remarks are needed. First, [[O V] N] compounds are rare and unproductive. Secondly, in 'rear view mirror', 'view' is probably not V but N, and the compound is probably not [[O V] N] but [[A N] N]. However, the first two examples seem to be [[O V] N] compounds. Thirdly, the first two compounds can both use the word order [[V O] N]. The question is: if [[V O] N] is already good, why is [[O V] N] also possible?

The question is a problem only if we assume that [[O V] N] is derived from [[V O] N] via movement, as proposed in Duanmu (2000). In the present analysis, there is no derivation (see section 8.5). Two compounds may seem related if they have similar co-indexing relations, but each compound is independently made in the regular compounding process. Now in the case of [[O V] N], [O V] is independently made. The details are shown in (35).

(35) (S   S)   (SØ)
      [[O$_j$ [Ø$_i$ [V Ø$_j$]]] N$_i$]

The O is co-indexed with the empty object, which is why the compound is related to [[V O] N]. Metrically, the first foot crosses a clause boundary, which is why such compounds are rare. Also, [O V] is disyllabic, which is probably why it can be protected by Foot Shelter.

The compounds in (34) are not [O [V N]] but [[O V] N]. The reason is that [V N] is not independently good in the given cases, but [O V] is. The lack of [O [V N]] has a metrical explanation: [V N] is bad because the foot would cross a clause boundary, as discussed earlier. In addition, [O [V N]] is bad because O has phrasal stress but cannot form a binary foot, unless additional structural change is made to remove stress from V and create a foot (O V).

8.8. SUMMARY

I have described some word order variations in [X Y N] compounds, where X and Y are modifiers of N, and [V–O N] compounds, where O is the object of V and N is the logical subject. I have also offered an analysis that makes a few simple assumptions: a foot should be binary; a compound should not contain an internal phrase; and [V N] and [V NN] are bad compounds probably because a foot cannot cross a clause boundary—the analysis seems to apply to both Chinese and English. There are occasional cases where compound internal phrases are found which can be explained as 'quotations' (Wiese 1996). There are also occasional cases where a [V N] compound is used, which seems to happen to disyllabic units only and which are probably protected by Foot Shelter.

9

The [ɚ] Suffix

9.1. INTRODUCTION

A main characteristic of the Beijing dialect is the use of the [ɚ] suffix, which is spelled as -er or -r and sometimes transcribed as [r]. The suffix merges with the syllable it attaches to; two examples are shown in (1).

(1) Unsuffixed   Suffixed
     [xʷaa]   [xʷaɚ]   'flower'
     [pʰan]   [pʰaɚ]   'plate'

Historically, the [ɚ] suffix is related to the word [ɚ] 'son', which can also mean 'smallness'. For this reason the suffix has been called the diminutive suffix. However, [ɚ] can also be added to adjectives (e.g. *gao-gaor-de* [kau-kaɚ-də] 'rather tall') and some verbs (e.g. *wanr* [waɚ] 'to play'), which undergo the same merger process. Many Chinese dialects do not use it as much, and some (such as Shanghai) do not use it at all. Besides, the suffix does not always add a meaning of smallness, but is often a stylistic feature rather than a grammatical one. When people who are not from Beijing speak SC, they often do not use the [ɚ] suffix, which causes no problem in communication. The analysis of [ɚ]-coloured syllables is rather complicated and this chapter examines it in some detail.

9.2. BASIC FACTS

Syllables with the [ɚ] suffix can be full (stressed) or weak (unstressed). According to Jia (1992), there are two types of rhyme when [ɚ]-suffixed syllables are weak: [ɤ̃r] for syllables whose original coda was [ŋ], [ər] for others. If a weak syllable has only one rhyme slot (see Chapter 4), the two rhymes ought to be [ɤ̃] and [ɚ] instead. In what follows I focus on [ɚ]-suffixed full syllables. There is some variation among speakers. I will first discuss the most common style, based on the studies of L. Wang and He (1985) and T. Lin and Shen (1995). Variations are discussed in section 9.5.

Standard Chinese has 19 rhymes (without prenuclear glides), including two syllabic consonants [z, ʐ̩] (Chapters 2 and 3). They are shown in (2), transcribed in phonetic symbols.

(2) z   ʐ̩   i   u   y   a   ɤ   e   o
     ai əi au əu in ən an əŋ aŋ uŋ

When the [ɚ] suffix is added, some rhymes are merged. Two analyses are shown in (3). The transcription of unsuffixed rhymes is based on the discussion in Chapter 3. The transcription of L. Wang and He (1985: 48) is their own, while the transcription of Chao (1968: 46–52) is an interpretation of the spelling system he used; sample words will be given later.

(3)

Unsuffixed	Chao (1968)	L. Wang and N. He (1985)
z, ʐ̩, əi, ən	ər	ər
a, ai, an	ar	ar
o	or	or
u	ur	ur
ɤ	ɤr	ɤr
au	aur	aur
əu	əur	our
əŋ	ə̃r	ə̃r
aŋ	ãr	ãr
uŋ	ũr	ũr
e	ɛr	ɛr
i, in	iər	iər
y	yər	yər

Following Chapter 3, there is no need to distinguish between [əu] vs. [ou], [e] vs. [ɛ], or [a] vs. [ɑ]. Thus, (3) can be summarized in (4).

(4)

Unsuffixed (19 rhymes)	Suffixed (11 rhymes)
z, ʐ̩, əi, ən	ər
a, ai, an	ar
o	or
u	ur
ɤ	ɤr
au	aur
əu	əur
əŋ	ə̃r

aŋ	ãr
uŋ	ũr
e	er
(i, in	iər)
(y	yər)

The last two lines are in parentheses because the rhyme in the suffixed form is [ər] (prenuclear glides are not in the rhyme), which is the same as that of the first line. Thus, the nineteen unsuffixed rhymes are reduced to eleven suffixed ones. The issues that need to be addressed are listed in (5).

(5)   (a) Why is [ə] added for some forms (e.g. [in]) but not for others (e.g. [uŋ])?
      (b) Why are final [i] and [n] deleted but final [u] not?
      (c) Why is the nasality of [ŋ] preserved but that of [n] is not?
      (d) How can suffixed rhymes like [aur] and [əur] fit into the CVX syllable structure discussed in Chapter 4, which has only two rhyme slots?

The discussion that follows assumes that sounds are made of features. Feature theory is introduced in Chapter 2.

9.3. PREVIOUS ANALYSES

There have been many studies on the [ɚ] suffix. Some focus on the description or transcription (e.g. Chao 1927, 1968; S. Xu 1980; L. Wang and He 1985), others, on rule-based analyses (e.g. C. Cheng 1973; Y. Lin 1989; Y. Yin 1989; Duanmu 1990; J. Wang 1993). I will review three of them, Y. Lin (1989), Duanmu (1990), and J. Wang (1993), as they offer a good illustration of the variety of proposals made and the kind of problems involved.

9.3.1. Y. Lin (1989)

Lin transcribes the suffix as [r], which is treated as a sound. It is merged with the host syllable in four steps, rephrased in (6) and illustrated in (7), where replaced sounds are shown in parentheses (Lin 1989: 112). Since Lin considers [uŋ] to be [wəŋ], there is no rhyme [uŋ].

(6)   (a) Replace the coda of the host syllable with [r] (or add [r] to the coda if the syllable lacks a coda).
      (b) Reattach the replaced coda to the nucleus, if the coda is [+back].
      (c) Delete unattached sounds.
      (d) Add [ə] between a front high vowel and [r].

(7)

Input	Replace	Reattach	Delete	Add [ə]	Surface
o	or	–	–	–	or
u	ur	–	–	–	ur
ɤ	ɤr	–	–	–	ɤr
e	er	–	–	–	er
a	ar	–	–	–	ar
au	a(u)r	aᵘr	–	–	aᵘr
əu	ə(u)r	əᵘr	–	–	əᵘr
əŋ	ə(ŋ)r	əᵑr	–	–	ə̃r
aŋ	a(ŋ)r	aᵑr	–	–	ãr
əi	ə(i)r	–	ər	–	ər
ən	ə(n)r	–	ər	–	ər
an	a(n)r	–	ar	–	ar
ai	a(i)r	–	ar	–	ar
i	ir	–	–	iər	iər
y	yr	–	–	yər	yər
in	i(n)r	–	ir	iər	iər

For the two syllabic consonants [z] and [ʐ], Lin assumes that they are spread from the onset consonant when the syllable lacks a vowel. Ordering [r]-suffixation before consonant spreading, along with an [ə]-insertion rule, Lin gets [ər] as the suffixed form for syllabic consonants.

Lin's analysis has several problems: the reattachment rule, which links [u] and [ŋ] to the nucleus but disregards [i] and [n], is stipulative; and [ə]-insertion is not fully motivated. Lin refers to a remark by Chao (1968: 46) that [i, y] and [r] have contradictory articulatory features. The tongue is flat in [i] and [y] but retroflexed in [r]. Therefore, [ə] is added to separate them. However, while it is true that contradictory features cannot occur in the same sound, there is no reason why they cannot occur in separate sounds. For example, SC has [ai], in which [a] is [+low] and [i] is [−low]. The third problem is that the reattachment rule creates the so-called short diphthongs in the nucleus, such as [aᵘ] and [əᵘ]. A short diphthong is made of two vowels that are linked to one timing slot. The existence of short diphthongs is controversial in feature theory because they allow two feature values in a single sound. For example, [aᵘ] is [-high, +high] and [−round, +round]. If a sound can take two feature values, we predict far more potential sounds than have been found in the world's languages (see Duanmu 1994). The final problem is that the reattachment of the velar nasal is not fully explained. For example, [aŋ] should become [aᵑr] after the velar nasal is reattached to the nucleus, but Lin transcribes the result as [ãr]. This suggests that only the feature [+nasal] is reattached and the velar closure is not. But if so, why is [+nasal] in [n] not reattached as well?

9.3.2. Duanmu (1990)

The analysis of Duanmu (1990) is summarized in (8) and illustrated in (9). The retroflex feature of the coda can spread to the nuclear vowel, which is not shown; the reattached nasal feature can spread to the coda [r], which is not shown either.

(8) (*a*) Replace the coda of the syllable with [r].
     (*b*) Reattach any compatible features.
     (*c*) Unattached features do not surface.

(9) | Input | Replace | Reattach | Surface |
     |-------|---------|----------|---------|
     | a | ar | – | ar |
     | i | ir | – | ir |
     | au | a(u)r | ar^w | ar^w |
     | aŋ | a(ŋ)r | ãr | ãr |
     | an | a(n)r | – | ar |
     | ai | a(i)r | – | ar |

Duanmu's analysis avoids some problems in Y. Lin (1989). First, the fact that the coda [i] is discarded is because [i] is not retroflex but [r] is; the fact that the [+round] feature of [u] is preserved is because [r] is unspecified for [round] and so can accept it. Second, there is no [ə] insertion between [i] and [r]. Third, there is no short diphthong. For example, in [au] → [ar^w], the coda [r^w] is a single sound, a rounded [r] (see Chapter 2 for the representation of complex sounds). Fourth, in [aŋ] → [ãr], the velar closure is not reattached, because [ŋ] is [+stop] but [r] is [−stop] (Duanmu 1990 uses the feature [continuant]; I have replaced it with [stop]).

There are two problems in Duanmu's analysis: as noted by Duanmu (1990: 55), it is not clear why [+nasal] can be saved out of [ŋ] but not out of [n]; and in most analyses the suffixed form of [i] is [iər], instead of [ir], which needs to be explained.

9.3.3. J. Wang (1993)

In Wang's analysis the retroflex suffix is not a sound but a single feature [−anterior], under the articulator Coronal (Wang actually uses [posterior] for [−anterior] because she does not use binary features). This feature is directly added to the rhyme of the host syllable. There are three cases. In the first, the sound in the host rhyme does not contain Coronal, and the suffix feature is simply added. This case covers eight rhymes, shown in (10), where the absorbed [−ant] makes the original sounds retroflexed, indicated by J. Wang with a under dot.

(10) Direct addition of [–ant] for eight rhymes without Coronal

Unsuffixed	Suffixed
a	a̠
ɤ	ɤ̠
o	o̠
u	u̠
au	a̠u
əu	ə̠u
aŋ	a̠ŋ
əŋ	ə̠ŋ
(uŋ	u̠ŋ)

The rhyme [uŋ] is shown in parentheses because Wang considers it to be a variant of [əŋ]. If [uŋ] is a separate rhyme, as the present analysis assumes (see Chapter 3), it should act as shown.

The second case involves five rhymes that contain a Coronal articulator and a non-high nuclear vowel (for Wang the front vowel [e] also has a Coronal articulator). In this case the Coronal articulator of the suffix will replace that of the host sound. The result is that the coda sound changes to [r] (after certain features are filled by default rules), and the nuclear vowel changes to non-front, as shown in (11).

(11) Feature change in five rhymes with Coronal and a non-high vowel

Unsuffixed	Suffixed
e	ə̠
əi	ə̠r
ən	ə̠r
ai	a̠r
an	a̠r

The third case involves four rhymes that contain a Coronal articulator and no non-high vowel. In this case the Coronal of the suffix will again replace that of the host sound. In addition, the nucleus will become mid. This is shown in (12).

(12) Feature change in four rhymes with Coronal and no non-high vowel

Unsuffixed	Suffixed
z	ə̠r
r (ʐ̩)	ə̠r
i	iə̠r
y	yə̠r
(in	iə̠r)

The rhyme [r] is [z̩] in my analysis. The rhyme [in] is shown in parentheses because Wang analyses it as [iən], which belongs to [ən] of the second case. If [in] is a separate rhyme, as the present analysis assumes (Chapter 3), it should act as shown.

As Wang suggests, there is a difference between her analysis and previous ones, in which the suffix is a full sound that replaces the original coda, after which certain compatible features are reincorporated into the syllable. In J. Wang's analysis, the suffix is not a sound but a feature, so it is added directly, and only incompatible features are replaced by it. No feature is recycled after it is replaced.

Wang's analysis also has some problems. First, she distinguishes the suffixed forms of [a] and [an], which L. Wang and He (1985) do not. Secondly, she does not distinguish the suffixed forms of [ie] and [i], which Wang and He do. Thirdly, the loss of the coda [n] and the preservation of the coda [ŋ] is still unclear. According to Wang, the Coronal of [n] is not retroflex, so it is replaced by the Coronal of the [r] suffix. But since Wang's analysis is based on features, she must explain why the nasal feature of [n] is also lost. Wang suggests that 'Beijing Mandarin does not allow a retroflex nasal in its sound system', yet we do find a retroflex nasal in the coda of the suffixed forms [aɳ] (from [aŋ]) and [əɳ] (from [əŋ]). Finally, it is unclear why schwa is added in her third case, such as [i] → [iɚr]. She suggests that there is a constraint against *[+hi]–[+hi] (an OCP constraint). The rhyme [i] first changes to [ir], where [i] is the prenuclear glide and [r] is the rhyme. Because [ir] violates *[+hi]–[+hi] (assuming that [r] is [+hi]), it is changed to [iɚr]. But why does [ir] not change to [iə] instead? Similarly, since [sz̩] 'silk' also changes to [sɚr] (instead of [sr]), J. Wang must assume that [s] is [+hi]. If so, [t] is probably also [+hi]. But then why does [ti] 'brother' not violate *[+hi]–[+hi]?

9.4. THE PRESENT ANALYSIS

In my analysis the suffix is [ɚ], which I specify as Coronal-[+retroflex], similar to the proposal of J. Wang (1993). It differs from [z̩], which is Coronal-[+retroflex, +fricative]. It is clear that the retroflex suffix must be realized and incompatible features in the original coda must be replaced. I assume that [n] and the high front vowels [i, y] are specified for Coronal-[−retroflex] and are incompatible with [ɚ], whereas [ŋ] and other vowels are unspecified for Coronal and are compatible with [ɚ]. I propose the analysis in (13)–(15).

(13) Add [ɚ]: Add [ɚ] to the coda position. If a sound is incompatible with it, the sound is replaced. Otherwise [ɚ] is added onto the sound.

(a) V → Vɚ	(b) VX → Vɚ	(c) VX → VXʳ
NC → NC	NC → NC	NC → NC
V ||	|| ||	|| |\
V V ɚ	VX V ɚ	VX VXɚ

(14) Rhyme-Harmony: rhyme sounds cannot differ in [retroflex].

(15) Mid: The default height of the nucleus is mid.

The rule in (13) applies to the coda and states which sounds are replaced and which preserved; I follow J. Wang (1993) in assuming that once a sound (or feature) is replaced, it cannot be reattached. The constraint in (14) is an extension of the Rhyme-Harmony constraints discussed in Chapter 3; it affects the nucleus once [ɚ] is added to the coda. In particular, if the nucleus is [i] or [y] or a syllabic consonant [z] or [ʐ], the sound would be pushed into the onset by the [ɚ] in the coda. The analysis of the 19 rhymes is shown in (16), where [j, ɥ] are prenuclear glides and [ʳ] the [+retroflex] feature on a given sound. For illustration, the requirements are shown in three steps, although they all hold on the surface form. Since [ɚ] is added to full syllables, all rhymes are in fact long (see Chapter 4), which is not always indicated. In the first five cases, sounds in parentheses are those pushed into the onset.

(16)

Unsuffixed	Add [ɚ]	Harmony	Mid	Surface	Example
z	zɚ	(z)ɚ	(z)əɚ	(z)əɚ	tsz/tsəɚ 'character'
ʐ	ʐɚ	(ʐ)ɚ	(ʐ)əɚ	(ʐ)əɚ	tʂʐ/tʂəɚ 'twig'
i	iɚ	(j)ɚ	(j)əɚ	(j)əɚ	tɕi/tɕəɚ 'chicken'
in	iɚ	(j)ɚ	(j)əɚ	(j)əɚ	tɕin/tɕəɚ 'today'
y	yɚ	(ɥ)ɚ	(ɥ)əɚ	(ɥ)əɚ	y/ɥəɚ 'fish'
əi	əɚ	–	–	əɚ	pəi/pəɚ 'tablet'
ən	əɚ	–	–	əɚ	kən/kəɚ 'root'
u	uɚ	–	–	uɚ	hu/huɚ 'lake'
o	oɚ	–	–	oɚ	wo/woɚ 'nest'
e	eɚ	–	–	eɚ	ɥe/ɥeɚ 'moon'
ɤ	ɤɚ	–	–	ɤɚ	kɤ/kɤɚ 'song'
a	aɚ	–	–	aɚ	pa/paɚ 'handle'
ai	aɚ	–	–	aɚ	pʰai/pʰaɚ 'plaque'
an	aɚ	–	–	aɚ	pʰan/pʰaɚ 'dish'
au	auʳ	–	–	auʳ	tau/tauʳ 'knife'
əu	əuʳ	–	–	əuʳ	kəu/kəuʳ 'hook'

əŋ	əŋʳ	–	–	əŋʳ	təŋ/təŋʳ 'lamp'
aŋ	aŋʳ	–	–	aŋʳ	kaŋ/kaŋʳ 'jar'
uŋ	uŋʳ	–	–	uŋʳ	kʰuŋ/kʰuŋʳ 'free time'

Several comments are in order. First, although the output rhyme for [əi, ən] is the same as that for [i, in, yn], [əi, ən] are not preceded by [i] or [y] (or their glide forms). Therefore, there is no neutralization between the two sets of syllables. Second, most nuclear vowels are probably [+retroflex] in the suffixed form. For example, [əɚ] is often realized as a monophthong mid vowel [ɚ:], and [aŋʳ] is in fact [ã̃ʳ] (or [ɑ̃ʳ:]). For simplicity the retroflexion and nasality of the nuclear vowel is not shown. Third, the difference between [əɚ] and [ɤɚ] is probably that the former is realized as a monophthong [ɚ] while the latter remains a diphthong. It is also possible that the vowel [ɤ], which does not contrast with the high vowel [ɯ] in SC, has created a prenuclear glide [ɰ]. Therefore, the contrast between [əɚ] and [ɤɚ] is [ɚ:] and [ɰɚ:]. Other output forms are mostly self-apparent.

I have explained why [ɚ] is added to some codas (as [ʳ]) but replaces others. We can see how all the suffixed forms agree with the CVX syllable structure (see Chapter 4). Let us consider some other questions:

(17)   (a) Why is there no [ə] insertion in [uɚ] and [aɚ]?
      (b) Why is there no [ə]-insertion in the unsuffixed syllabic consonants [z̩] and [z̩]?
      (c) Why are [əŋʳ, aŋʳ, uŋʳ] written as [ə̃r, ãr, ũr] in some other studies?

As to (17a), the insertion of [ə] follows from the requirement that the default height of the nucleus is mid. This applies only to a nucleus that is unspecified for height. Since [u] and [a] are specified for height, no change is made. In contrast, [ɚ] is unspecified for height, so it will become mid in the nuclear position. This is shown in (18), where R means [+retroflex], M means [−high, −low] (mid), N is the nucleus, and C the coda.

(18)   Default mid for the nucleus ([ə]-insertion)

$$[ɚ] \quad \rightarrow \quad [əɚ]$$

NC   NC
∨   ∧
R   M R

Next consider why there is no [ə]-insertion in the unsuffixed syllabic consonants [z̩] and [z̩]. A reasonable suggestion is that when [z̩, z̩] occur in the onset, they are [+fricative], which by definition have considerable constriction in the vocal tract. In contrast, the feature mid (or [–high]) requires the mouth to be open. Thus, [fricative] is incompatible with mid. This is illustrated in (19).

(19)   Incompatibility of consonants with mid

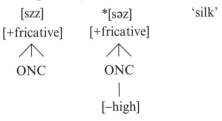

Next consider why many studies transcribe [əŋ^r, aŋ^r, uŋ^r] as [ə̃r, ãr, ũr] (see section 9.2). According to Y. Xu (1986) and J. Wang (1993), oral closure is not required for nasal codas in SC. This means that they are not [+stop] but [–stop]. If so, [ŋ^r] is similar to [ə̃˞]. And given the fact that vowels are nasalized before a nasal coda, what I write as [əŋ^r, aŋ^r, uŋ^r] are similar to [ə̃ə̃˞, ã ə̃˞, ũ ə̃˞] or what others write as [ə̃r, ãr, ũr].

To summarize, the 19 rhymes in SC can reduce to 11 after the [ə˞] suffix, as shown in (20).

(20)   Unsuffixed (19 rhymes)   Suffixed (11 rhymes)

z, r, əi, ən, i, in, yn	əə˞ (or [ə˞ː])
u	uə˞
o	oə˞
e	eə˞
ɤ	ɤə˞ (or [ɣə˞ː])
a, ai, an	aə˞
au	au^r
əu	əu^r
əŋ	əŋ^r
aŋ	aŋ^r
uŋ	uŋ^r

Some of the rhymes may be further distinguished and some may be merged; to be discussed next.

9.5. VARIATIONS

L. Wang and He (1985) discuss some alternative pronunciations of suffixed rhymes, summarized in (21) and illustrated in (22). The alternatives do not necessarily come from one particular style. Prenuclear glides are

written as vowels. The suffixed rhymes in Wang and He's analysis are
transcribed according to the present analysis. In [tɕe], (22c), the prenuclear glide is realized on the palatal onset. The alternative in (21f) is in
parentheses because its validity is in doubt (see below).

(21)   Variations in the [ɚ] suffix

	Unsuffixed	Wang and He	Alternative
(a)	uən/uo	uɚ ≠ uoɚ	uɚ = uɚ
(b)	ɤ/ən	ɤɚ ≠ əɚ	əɚ = əɚ
(c)	i/ie	iɚ ≠ ieɚ	iɚ = iɚ
(d)	a/an	aɚ = aɚ	aɚ (central) ≠ æɚ (front)
(e)	əi/ən	əɚ = əɚ	eɚ ≠ əɚ
(f)	y/yin	yɚ = yɚ	(yɚ ≠ yɚ)

(22)   Examples

	Unsuffixed	Wang and He	Alternative
(a)	kuəi/kuo 'ghost'/'fruit'	kuɚ ≠ kuoɚ	kuɚ = kuɚ
(b)	kɤ/kən 'song'/'root'	kɤɚ ≠ kəɚ	kəɚ = kəɚ
(c)	tɕi/tɕe 'chicken'/'street'	tɕɚ ≠ tɕeɚ	tɕɚ = tɕɚ
(d)	pa/pan 'handle'/'petal'	paɚ = paɚ	paɚ ≠ pæɚ
(e)	kuəi/kuən 'ghost'/'roll'	kuɚ = kuɚ	kueɚ ≠ kuɚ
(f)	y/yin 'fish'/'cloud'	yɚ = yɚ	(yɚ ≠ yɚ)

For (22a–c), Chao (1968) suggests that the contrast is disappearing among
young speakers, but a survey of 50 young Beijing speakers by Wang and
He shows that the three pairs are still distinct. S. Li (1986) even suggests
that young Beijing speakers make more distinctions than old speakers, but
L. Wang and H. Wang (1991) disagree. In (23d–e), some studies suggest
that there is a contrast in each pair, but in Wang and He's perception study
there is little contrast. A survey of 449 speakers in 1982–4 by T. Lin and
Shen (1995) largely confirms Wang and He's result.

Let us focus on how the variation can be represented. For (22a–c), the
alternative pronunciation seems to replace the entire rhyme with [ɚ], and
as a result the mid vowel loses [back] and [round] features. For (22d),
we can account for the difference in the nuclear vowel by saying that it

is front in [an] or [æn], owing to the influence of the coda [n]. The alternative in (22e) can be explained if those speakers pronounce [kuəi] as [kuei], where [−back] has spread from [i] to the nuclear vowel. As a result, the suffixed rhymes could be [eɚ] vs. [əɚ]. Another possibility for (22e) is that the unsuffixed forms are [kʷəi] and [kʷn̩] and the suffixed ones are [kʷəɚ] (mid vowel) and [kʷɚ] (high vowel). The alternative in (22f) is more problematic. If [yɚ] is the rhyme, it violates Rhyme-Harmony. If [yɚ] becomes [yəɚ], the contrast between the pair cannot be maintained. In fact, the validity of (22f) is in doubt. Wang and He (1985: 33) point out that the only reference to a contrast between [yɚ] and [yəɚ] is Chao (1979: 34), which is a Chinese translation of Chao (1968). However, Chao (1968) does not make the distinction, it is likely, therefore, that [yɚ] is an error in the translation.

9.6. INTERACTION BETWEEN TONE AND THE [ɚ] SUFFIX

Chao (1968: 51) observes that the [ɚ] suffix interacts with tone for some rhymes. For example, the suffixed forms of [i] and [ie] are distinct with T1 and T2, but non-distinct with T3 and T4, as exemplified in (23).

(23) (a) Distinct in T2
           Unsuffixed   i/ie   'aunt'/'grandpa'
           Suffixed   iəɚ ≠ ieɚ
      (b) Not distinct in T4
           Unsuffixed   i/ie   'meaning'/'leaf'
           Suffixed   iəɚ = iəɚ

Wang and He observe the same effect, which also applies to the pairs [ie]–[in], [y]–[ye], and [ye]–[yin]. The reason for the interaction remains unclear.

9.7. THE [ɚ] SUFFIX IN OTHER MANDARIN DIALECTS

Many dialects in the Mandarin family, of which Beijing is a member, have the diminutive suffix. In some dialects, such as Jiyuan and Yanggu, the process is quite complicated; in others the process is simple (see Y. Lin 1989, 1993 and Duanmu 1990 for more discussion). Here I illustrate the diminutive suffix in Chengdu, which is simpler than that in Beijing.

The diminutive suffix in Chengdu is also [ɚ]. However, it replaces the entire rhyme of the host syllable except its tone, as shown in (24) (tones omitted).

(24)

Unsuffixed	Suffixed	Gloss
kən	kɚ	'root'
kəu	kɚ	'ditch'
pʲan	pʲɚ	'side'
pan	pɚ	'class'
pau	pɚ	'pocket'
kʷan	kʷɚ	'hall'
kan	kɚ	'stem'
ja	jɚ	'bud'
wan	wɚ	'bowl'
ɥan	ɥɚ	'yard'

Prenuclear glides are not replaced by [ɚ], which is expected, since they are in the onset (see Chapter 4).

9.8. SUMMARY

Following J. Wang (1993), I assume that the diminutive suffix [ɚ] is specified only for the feature Coronal-[+retroflex]. Its merger with the host syllable follows the requirements in (13)–(15). If the sounds in the host rhyme are incompatible with [+retroflex], they will be replaced or pushed into the onset, otherwise [ɚ] is added to the coda or merged with the sound already there.

10

Tone: Basic Properties

10.1. TONE AND TONAL TRANSCRIPTION

In producing voiced sounds, the vocal cords will vibrate to open and close the airflow in quick succession. The rate of the vibration is called the fundamental frequency, or F0. Pitch is the perceived height of F0; a higher F0 will be heard as a higher pitch. However, F0 does not correspond to pitch proportionally. For example, when the F0 value doubles, the pitch is not twice as high. Having said this, we will not be concerned with the difference between F0 and pitch. All languages use pitch for various linguistic purposes such as intonation. When pitch is used to distinguish words, it is called tone.

SC is a typical tone language in that the pitch contour over a syllable can distinguish word meanings. On full syllables there are four tones, which I refer to by T1 through T4 in (1), where vowel length is ignored.

(1) T1   T2   T3   T4

    ma   ma   ma   ma
    'mother' 'hemp'   'horse'   'scold'

The tones in SC have been transcribed in various ways. Five systems are shown in (2).

(2)   T1   T2   T3   T4

    (*a*) ma1   ma2   ma3   ma4
    (*b*) ma˧   ma˧˥   ma˩˩˦   ma˥˩
    (*c*) ma55   ma35   ma214   ma51
    (*d*) mā   má   mǎ   mà
    (*e*) mha   mar   maa   mah
        'mother' 'hemp'   'horse'   'scold'

System (2*a*) numbers the four tones from 1 to 4, which is convenient typographically. System (2*b*) shows what is known as Chao letters, first introduced by Chao (1930) and later adopted by the International Phonetic Association. The system is visually intuitive. The vertical bar on the right indicates the pitch range, the contour line on the left indicates pitch movement relative to the pitch range. Thus, T1 is a high level tone, T2 is a rising tone, T3 is a dip-rise, and T4 is a fall. System (2c), which is a numeric translation of (2b), can be called Chao digits, where 5 represents the highest pitch and 1 the lowest. Each tone is represented by a starting pitch and a final pitch, and optionally a mid pitch. For example, [55] starts high and ends high, so it is a high level. Tone [214] starts fairly low, moves to the lowest, and ends fairly high, so it is a dip-rise. System (2d) is a simplified version of (2b) and is commonly used in Pinyin. System (2e) shows the National Romanization system (see Chao 1968: 29 for a description). It does not use separate diacritics for tone but encodes tone by spelling syllables differently. It has two merits: it uses Roman letters only, and it forces the learner, especially those who are not Chinese speakers, to remember tone as an integral part of the syllable instead of something extra that can be stripped away, as in the other systems. However, (2e) is less intuitive and can confuse those who do not know the encoding rules.

While the transcription systems in (2) offer practical convenience, they have various weaknesses. For example, (2a) and (2e) give no indication of the pitch values of the tones. Although Chao letters (or their variants) do indicate pitch values, they have other shortcomings. First, Chao letters are intrinsically vague. In particular, the choice of five levels is not based on phonological principles, as Chao acknowledges, but on a balance between phonetic details and phonological distinctions. In addition, as Chao remarks, a distinction of one degree (e.g. between [44] and [55], between [24] and [35], or between [12] and [13]) is usually not significant, but that of two degrees usually is. Such lack of precision is well known to those who work on Chinese tones, and it is common that two transcriptions of the same dialect do not give the same digits for the same tones. For example, in nonfinal positions, T3 in SC is transcribed as [21] in Chao (1968) but [11] in Chao (1931) and L. Wang (1979). Similarly, for the Shanghai tone named 'Yang Ru', some transcribe it as [2] and some transcribe it as [13]. Such flexibility causes problems when one attempts to convert Chao digits into a level tone system such as that of Yip (1980), in which tonal primitives are upper and lower registers and H and L in each register (see below). For example, [2] could be L or H in the lower register, and [13] must be LH in the lower register. But if a tone is [2] in one transcription and [13] in another, how should one interpret it? Similarly, in the lower register, [11] is clearly L, and [31] is probably HL, but what is [21]? It could be interpreted as HL (Bao 1990*a*: 105–11 for Wenzhou) or L (Yip 1980: 280 for T3 in SC). Such ambiguities have caused much confusion in the literature.

A second problem with Chao letters lies in their dubious status between a phonetic system and a phonemic one. For example, in transcribing Old Shanghai, T. Shen (1981: 132) says (Yin Ping, Yin Qu, etc. are names of the tones; underlining indicates a short tone):

> The real value of Yin Ping is 52; this paper marks it as 53. The real value of Yin Qu is 33 or 24; this paper marks it as 35. The real value of Yang Qu is 113 or 13; this paper marks it as 13. The real value of Yin Qu is a short tone 5 or 4; this paper marks it as a short tone 55. The real value of Yang Ru is a short tone 23; this paper marks it as a short tone 13.

Similarly, in his transcription of Lhasa tones, T. Hu (1980: 25) says: 'In the marking system with five levels, [the Lhasa high level tone] is 44. For visual clarity, it is written as 55.' The practice of modifying tone letters is extremely common. It is, to some extent, justified. If [44] does not contrast with [55] in a language, why not write it as [55]? Besides, if there is no [55], it is likely that sometimes people will pronounce [44] as [55]. But the issue is not so simple. Take SC tones, for example. In nonfinal positions, Chao (1968) writes them as [55], [35], [21], and [51]. But why does Chao not write them as [55], [15], [11], and [51], since there are no [15] and [11] in SC? One may suspect that [35] and [15] probably contrast in other Chinese languages, but in fact they never do (Bao 1990*a*: 123). Similarly, to my knowledge, [21] and [11] never contrast. On the other hand, [33] and [24] do contrast in Gao'an (S. Yan 1981), but that did not prevent T. Shen (1981: 132) from writing [33] as [24] in Old Shanghai (see above). It appears, then, that people can modify the phonetic values in their transcriptions as they please. In addition, many people do not indicate whether they have or have not modified their transcriptions. When one reads Chao letters, therefore, one cannot be sure what the exact pitch values are, except that they are somewhere around the given digits. Sometimes this vagueness does not matter. But sometimes it does. For example, [24] is close to both [35] and [13]. Now [35] is an upper register tone, but [13] is a lower register one. If one wants to interpret [24], which direction should one choose? We saw above that Shen has changed [24] to [35] yet [24] to [13]. Such changes have serious consequences for phonological interpretation.

A third problem with Chao digits is that they are based on phonetic or perceptual terms. However, there is some evidence that phonological features are based on articulation (see, for example, A. Liberman and Mattingly 1985 from the viewpoint of the motor theory, and Halle 1995 from the viewpoint of feature theory).

A fourth problem with Chao digits is that they cannot explain the relations among tones. For example, if a language has [55], [33], [22], and [11], there is often a relation between [55] and [22], but not between [22] and [33]. Chao digits cannot explain why [22] may relate to the more distant [55] and not to the closer [33]. In contrast, in a register system, such as Yip (1980), the relation can be captured (see below).

We should add that Chao letters were designed more than seventy years ago and were probably meant to be an aid to the field linguist. Naturally, one should not expect them to translate readily into phonological features of the present day.

10.2. PHONETIC CORRELATES OF TONE

Tone has both articulatory and acoustic correlates. There are many studies on the articulatory characteristics of tone. In an earlier attempt, Halle and Stevens (1971) suggest that tone is controlled by a single articulatory mechanism—the tension of the vocal cords. They further suggest that there are three states of vocal cord tension, stiff, slack, and neither stiff nor slack. The three states give rise to three tone levels, high, mid, and low.

Zemlin (1981) surveyed previous works on articulatory pitch control and identified two major mechanisms: the cricothyroid and vocalis muscles. The former mechanism controls the elongation and the thickness of the vocal cords; the latter, the 'isometric tension' of the vocal cords. However, Zemlin does not discuss how many states each mechanism can assume, or how many combined states there are between the two mechanisms.

The primary acoustic correlate of tone is fundamental frequency (F0), which probably corresponds to the cricothyroid mechanism. In some languages, there is also a second dimension, which has been called 'murmur' or 'breathiness', which probably corresponds to the vocalis mechanism. The second dimension often correlates with broader formant width and flatter spectral envelope. Murmur and F0 interact closely, such that murmured tones usually have lower F0 contours and non-murmured tones usually have higher ones; a good example is Shanghai (B. Xu *et al.* 1988). In SC, murmur does not play a systematic role, nor is voice contrastive in consonants (sonorants are voiced, obstruents are unvoiced; see Chapter 2).

Nevertheless, while T1, T2, and T4 in SC are not murmured, T3 is; it sounds very similar to [23] (or [113]) in Shanghai.

The F0 contour of a tone can be affected by many factors. Native speakers are often unaware of such effects. For example, a sonorant syllable onset can give an unstable F0 contour that departs from the expected curve. Consonant voicing, aspiration, vowel height, the position of the syllable, stress, and rate of speech can also affect F0. Voiced obstruents tend to lower the initial F0. Aspirated obstruents tend to raise the initial F0. For the same tone, high vowels often give a higher F0 contour than low vowels. Also, for the same tone, the F0 contour is somewhat higher when a syllable occurs at the beginning of an intonation group than when it occurs towards the end. Lack of stress can lead to loss of underlying tone. In addition, the F0 contour of an unstressed syllable often depends on the tone of the preceding syllable. Finally, a syllable usually has higher amplitude when it occurs with a higher tone than a lower tone.

10.3. TONAL FEATURES: PITCH AND REGISTER

A phonological representation of tone must address four questions: How many components does tone have? How many degrees of contrast are there in each component? How should contour tones be represented? And, what is the tone-bearing unit? I address these questions next.

10.3.1. Pitch and register

As discussed above, there are two major articulatory mechanisms for tone, the cricothyroid movement and the vocalis movement. In addition, there are two major acoustic correlates of tone, F0 and murmur. Phonologically, pitch and murmur are independent properties. Murmur is related to consonant voicing, but pitch need not be. For example, in all Chinese dialects that have a voicing contrast in obstruents, murmur invariably co-occurs with a voiced onset consonant. In contrast, the pitch contour of a tone cannot always be predicted from consonant voicing. For example, in Shanghai, although a monosyllable with a voiced onset can have only a rising tone, a monosyllable with a voiceless onset can have either a rising tone or a falling tone.

A murmured vowel usually has lower pitch contours than a non-murmured vowel. In other words, there is a generalization that voiced onset consonants tend to co-occur with murmured vowels, which in turn tend to have lower pitch, and voiceless onset consonants tend to co-occur with non-murmured vowels, which in turn have higher pitch. The generalization has been called 'voiceless–high and voiced–low'. The same effect has been observed in African languages, such as Zulu, where voiced obstruents can depress the pitch of a neighbouring vowel and give it a murmured quality (see Laughren 1984).

In Chinese dialects that have lost voicing contrast in obstruents, the relation between voicing and murmur can be blurred. For example, both T1 and T2 in SC come from the historical tone called *Ping*. Onset voicing later caused a split, whereby syllables with voiceless onsets became the present T1 and syllables with voiced onsets became the present T2. At the time of the split, T2 was probably murmured, but it is not today. Similarly, the SC T3 is murmured, even though SC has no voiced obstruents (see Chapter 2). Moreover, Yue-Hashimoto (1986) surveyed 997 Chinese dialects and found 340 cases where a tone with historically voiceless onsets has a lower pitch contour than a tone with historically voiced onsets. However, all the 340 cases come from dialects that have lost voicing contrast. In dialects that have not, voiceless–high and voiced–low is always true. This suggests that violations of voiceless–high and voiced–low are due to subsequent change.

The above discussion suggests the analysis in (3), which combines articulatory, acoustic, and phonological properties of tone.

(3)   Two components of tone

	Pitch	Register
Acoustic	F0	murmur (and F0)
Articulatory	cricothyroid (vocal-cord thickness)	vocalis (vocal-cord tension)

Let us call the two phonological components Pitch (in contrast to pitch, which is the perceived F0) and Register. Articulatorily, Pitch is related to cricothyroid movement, which affects the thickness of the vocal cords, Register is related to the vocalic movement, which affects the tension of the vocal cords (Zemlin 1981). A change in the thickness of the vocal cords affects F0 in the acoustic dimension. A change in the tension of the vocal cords primarily affects murmur in the acoustic dimension. However, since lax vocal cords vibrate slower than tense vocal cords, a change in the tension of the vocal cords also lowers F0 as a secondary acoustic effect.

10.3.2. Levels of contrast

In Asian languages, three or four contrastive tone levels are quite common. Five contrastive levels have been reported (Chang 1953; F. Shi, L. Shi, and

Liao 1987), but the facts are sketchy. As far as clear evidence is concerned, four contrastive levels are sufficient. This suggests two contrasts in Register—stiff(non-murmured)andslackvocalcords(murmured)—andtwo contrasts in Pitch—thin vocal cords (high pitch, or H) and thick vocal cords (low pitch, or L). The four combinations are shown in (4); (5) shows their relative pitch height.

(4) Register   Pitch

    stiff   thin   (non-murmured H)
    stiff   thick (non-murmured L)
    slack   thin   (murmured H)
    slack   thick (murmured L)

(5) Predicted relative F0 levels ('>' means 'has higher F0 than')

    non-murmured H > non-murmured L > murmured L
    non-murmured H > murmured H > murmured L
    non-murmured L can overlap with murmured H

The model predicts that for the same vocal cord tension (Register), thinner vocal cords give higher F0, and that for the same vocal cord thickness (Pitch), stiffer vocal cords give higher F0. Stiff and thin vocal cords give even higher F0 than slack and thick vocal cords. On the other hand, there is no specific prediction as to whether slack and thin vocal cords will give higher or lower F0 than stiff and thick vocal cords.

The model can also account for the interaction between consonant voicing on the one hand and vowel murmur and lower pitch on the other, following an idea from Halle and Stevens (1971). Since obstruents have great constriction in the vocal tract, the transglottal pressure is low, and the stiffness of the vocal cords can prevent vocal cord vibration, giving voicelessness. In vowels, there is not much constriction in the vocal tract and the transglottal pressure is high. Whether the vocal cords are stiff or slack, they can still vibrate. However, the vibration of slack vocal cords leads to murmur in the vowel. Thus, the same articulatory action, vocal-cord tension, can give different acoustic effects: voicing in obstruents and murmur and lower pitch in vowels. What gives rise to voiceless–high and voiced–low, therefore, can be seen as the spreading of [stiff (vocal cords)] or [slack (vocal cords)] from the consonant to the vowel.

The model above is similar to that of Yip (1980), rephrased in (6) and (7). Her [+upper], [−upper], [+raised] and [−raised] correspond, respectively, to stiff, slack, thin, and thick in (4).

(6)   Tonal model of Yip (1980)

Register	Pitch	F0 level
+upper	+raised (H)	I (high)
+upper	−raised (L)	II (mid high)
−upper	+raised (H)	III (mid low)
−upper	−raised (L)	IV (low)

(7)   Predicted relative F0 levels ('>' means 'has higher F0 than')
      I > II > III > IV

A major difference between the two models is that, in my model, Register primarily corresponds to murmur, whereas in Yip's model both Register and Pitch correspond to F0. In other words, Yip's model does not assume that [−upper] Register tones are murmured. The difference has three consequences. First, in Yip's model all tones are distinguished by F0 alone along a single scale I > II > III > IV. Specifically, II must have higher F0 than III. In contrast, in the present model II and III can overlap in F0. Evidence supports the present analysis. For example, Shanghai has two rising tones, which B. Xu *et al.* (1988) transcribe as [34] and [23]. [34] is not murmured and [23] is. In Yip's analysis, [34] is II–I, [23] is IV–III, where the beginning of [34] (II) should be higher than the end of [23] (III); however, both these points are transcribed with the same F0 level [3]. In fact, in the transcription of B. Xu, Tang, and Qian (1981), the two rising tones are [24] and [13], where the low point of non-murmured [24] is lower than the high point of murmured [13]. In the present analysis, the overlap between II and III is expected.

Second, in Yip's model there is a heavier burden on the speaker and the listener, who has to handle four distinct levels of pitch. The task is rather daunting in view of the fact that both pitch height and pitch range can vary from speaker to speaker, as a result of which tone levels must be interpreted in relative terms. In the present analysis, the task for the speaker and the listener is much easier. They only need to distinguish between murmur and non-murmur on the one hand, and between higher and lower pitch on the other.

Finally, Yip's model cannot account for the interaction between consonants and vowels, voiceless–high and voiced–low. In my model, the interaction is a matter of feature spreading.

Let us now consider the structural relation between Register and Pitch. Two proposals have been made. First, Register and Pitch are in a sister relation (Yip 1980; Bao 1990*a*, 1999; Duanmu 1990), as shown in (8), where TBU is the tone-bearing unit (see below); Secondly, Register dominates Pitch (Yip 1989), as shown in (9).

(8)   TBU

Pitch Register

(9)   TBU

Register

Pitch

The evidence for (9) is not compelling. In addition, in articulator-based theory of phonological features (e.g. Sagey 1986; Ladefoged and Halle 1988; Halle 1995, 2005), features can be dominated by articulators but not by other features. If so, (8) is a better model. Since Register plays little role in SC, the difference between (8) and (9) will not be elaborated on further.

10.4. CONTOUR TONES AND THE TONE-BEARING UNIT

A level tone is one whose pitch stays level through the syllable. A contour tone is one whose pitch changes over the syllable. An important insight offered by Woo (1969) is that all contour tones are combinations of level tones. For example, a rise is a combination of L (low) and H (high), and a fall is a combination of H and L. This view has since been widely adopted.

Let us assume that on a given syllable, HH is the same as a long [H:] and LL is the same as a long [L:]. Ignoring Register, my model has two levels of tone, H and L, which can combine to give four contour tones, shown in (10).

(10)   Level tones   Simple contours   Complex contours
     high low   rise fall   rise–fall fall–rise
     H   L   LH   HL   LHL   HLH

Contour tones made of more than three level tones are not found in Chinese dialects. In fact, contour tones made of three level tones (complex contour tones) are not common and are found only in pre-pause positions.

In Chinese dialects, the Register of a syllable comes from the (historical) voicing of the onset. As a result, each syllable has just one Register value, either murmured or not. In principle, therefore, there are four possible simple tones in the present model, two murmured and two not. Similarly, there are four possible simple contour tones, and four possible complex contour tones.

Now consider the tone-bearing unit (TBU). There are different views of what the TBU is. Five proposals are shown in (11), where S is the syllable node, O is the onset node, R is the rhyme node, and m is a mora. The SC syllable [mai] 'sell' has a falling tone, or HL.

(11)   (a) mai   (b) mai   (c) mai   (d) ma i   (e) HL
          ∨ | ∖   ∨ | | | | |
          S   O R   m m   mm   ma i
          ∧   ∧ | | | | | |
          HL   HL   H L   H L   mm

In (11a) the two tones are carried by the syllable node; this view is similar to that of W. Wang (1967: 95) and Chao (1968: 19, 25). In (11b) the two tones are carried by the rhyme node, while the onset carries no tone; this view is similar to that of Kratochvil (1970: 515) and Howie (1976: 218). In (11c) and (11d) each tone is carried by a mora. The difference is that in (11c) the first mora includes the onset consonant (Hyman 1985) while in (11d) it does not (Hayes 1989a). In (11e) each segment in the rhyme has a mora, yet tones are not linked to moras but to the rhyme segments; this view is similar to that of Woo (1969) and Duanmu (1990).

Example (11a) represents the traditional view that tone is a suprasegmental property that belongs to units larger than segments. However, phonetic studies show that the F0 contour on the onset consonant is irregular, and that the expected contour does not start until the rhyme starts (Kratochvil 1970; Howie 1976; Y. Xu 1999). In this regard, (11b) is a better model than (11a), and (11d) and (11e) are better models than (11c). The difference between (11d) and (11e) is small and not crucial for the present discussion, therefore, they will be considered notational variants.

The real choice, then, lies between (11b) and (11e). The difference between them is that in (11b) there is no relation between the length of a syllable and the number of tones it can carry. In contrast, (11e) predicts that a short syllable can carry just one tone and a long syllable can carry two. As far as I can see, the evidence supports (11e). For example, in Chinese languages, level tones and simple contour tones are common on full syllables. This is because a full syllable is bimoraic (Chapter 4) and has two TBUs.

Complex contour tones are less common and generally occur in pre-pause positions only, where the syllable is lengthened. This is also expected, because a complex contour tone requires three moras and it is easy to lengthen a syllable before a pause but not elsewhere.

In autosegmental phonology (Leben 1973; E. Williams 1976; Goldsmith 1976; D. Pulleyblank 1986), it is often assumed that a nonfinal TBU can carry just one tone, but a final TBU can carry two (or more) tones in some languages, such as Igbo, Mende, and Tiv. However, the final vowel in such languages is lengthened (Duanmu 1994: 601–2 and references therein); therefore it is likely that the final vowel has two (or more) TBUs instead of just one.

In summary, there is no compelling evidence that the TBU is the syllable or the rhyme. Instead, there is evidence that the TBU is the moraic segment, and that each TBU can carry just one tone.

10.5. IS TONE A PROSODIC FEATURE?

Traditionally, tone has been considered a prosodic feature which belongs to a unit larger than a segment (e.g. Chao 1930; Pike 1948; Firth 1957; W. Wang 1967). There are several reasons for this view: a tone pattern usually remains constant independent of its carrier; tone can survive vowel deletion and relocate to another vowel; and tone is quite free to move or spread from one syllable to another. In contrast, segmental features are usually not so mobile.

On the other hand, there are reasons to consider tone a segmental feature. First, although a tone pattern can extend over two (or more) syllables, each moraic segment carries just one tone, H or L. In this regard, a tone feature is like a segmental feature, which ultimately resides in a segment and which cannot occur twice within a segment. Secondly, in tonogenesis, tone and consonant features interact. In particular, the feature [slack] is a voicing feature on the consonant and a Register feature on the vowel, and it can spread from the former to the latter. If we treat a feature consistently, we ought to consider [slack] to be a segmental feature in both cases. Thirdly, tone is not unique in surviving segment deletion. Features like [nasal], [back], and [round] are also able to survive segment deletion. Finally, regarding the mobility of tone, we note that tone is not unique in spreading. Vowel features like [back] and [round] and consonant features like [nasal] and [retroflex] have all been found to spread. In feature theory, every feature lies on an independent tier. A feature F can spread when there is nothing in its way, in other words, when there is no specification of F in the intervening segments. Tone is mobile only because unstressed syllables are unspecified for tone, and tone only spreads to unstressed syllables (see the Tone–Stress Principle below). It is worth noting that in tone spreading it is usually the Pitch feature that spreads, and not the Register feature. This follows if Register is the same as voicing, which is usually specified for consonants. Since most syllables have a consonant, Register rarely spreads out of a syllable.

If the above reasoning is correct, tone features are not fundamentally different from segmental features, such as [nasal], [round], and [back]. In the phonemic tradition, tone has also been called a phoneme. The reason seems to be that lexical tones are contrastive and they did not appear to be part of the segments. In my view, tones reside on segments and tone features are essentially similar to other segmental features. There is therefore no motivation to call tones phonemes, as there is no motivation to call [nasal] or [round] a phoneme.

10.6. TONES IN STANDARD CHINESE

10.6.1. Tones on full syllables

On full SC syllables, there are four tones, represented in (12), which are similar in duration in nonfinal positions, on the order of 200 milliseconds (ms).

(12)   SC tones on nonfinal full syllables

T1	T2	T3	T4	
55	35	21	51	Chao digits
H	LH	L	HL	Pitch features
∧	| |	∧	| |	
mm	mm	mm	mm	TBUs
∨	∨	∨	∨	
−mur	−mur	+mur	−mur	Register features

T3 is murmured, the other three are not. But since T3 is L and other tones are not, murmur is not distinctive in SC. The representations of T1, T2, and T4 are not controversial, but representation of T3 requires some comment. The pitch of a nonfinal T3 is mostly low level, with a slight dip at the beginning. Although Chao (1968: 27) writes it as [21], other studies, such as Chao (1931) and L. Wang (1979), write it as [211] or [11]. Since there is no evidence that the initial dip is relevant phonologically, the nonfinal T3 is represented as a murmured L.

On monosyllables, T1, T2, and T4 do not change their values, but T3 is often [214] or [114] (Taiwanese speakers of SC often still use L for a monosyllabic T3 instead of [214]; see Chapter 13). In addition, [214] is considerably longer than other tones. For this reason, some researchers consider [214] to have three moras (Woo 1969; Shih 1997). Following their proposal, tones on monosyllables can be represented in (13).

(13) SC tones on full monosyllabes

T1	T2	T3	T4
55	35	214	51
H	LH	L H	HL
∧	| |	↖ |	| |
mm	mm	mmm	mm
∨	∨	∨↙	∨
−mur	−mur	+mur	−mur

Both T2 and T3 are rising tones on monosyllables, but they have four differences: T2 rises right away, but T3 does not rise till after halfway; T2 occurs with a higher pitch than T3; T2 is not murmured but T3 is; and T2 is shorter than T3.

Since T1, T2, and T4 basically remain the same, their underlying forms are H, LH, and HL, respectively (all non-murmured). For T3, there is the question of whether it is underlyingly [21] or [214]. The two options are shown in (14), where (H) is a floating H.

(14) Milliken (1989)   Duanmu (1999a)

L (H)	L
∧	∧
mm	mm

Milliken (1989) suggests that T3 is L followed by a floating H. The floating H is realized in the [214] and [35] forms, as well as on the weak syllable after a T3. The advantage of this analysis is that it accounts for the appearance of H in three separate cases. However, Duanmu (1999a) argues that T3 is just L (see also Yip 1980). The H in [214] and on the weak syllable after a T3 comes from a polarity requirement that L should be followed by H in a disyllabic foot. In both approaches, T3 would occur with a H. The difference lies in where the H comes from. The choice between the two is rather subtle and need not concern us here (see Duanmu 1999a).

The representation of T4 also requires a comment. Since T4 is in the upper Register ([−murmur]), its values should strictly speaking be [53], instead of [51] (Yip 1980). Indeed, Chao (1968: 28–9) points out that when T4 is followed by another T4, the sequence is [53 51], instead of [51 51]. It is likely that [51] is used only before T3 or before a pause or a toneless syllable, and [53] is a better pitch label for T4 overall.

10.6.2. Variation of T3

Among the four tones, T3 shows most variation. It was noted above that T3 is [21] in nonfinal positions and [214] on a monosyllable. Let us now consider T3 in final positions (but not a monosyllable). Chao (1968: 27) implies that the final T3 is always [214]. However, in natural speech a final T3 need not be [214], but is often [21]. For example, I once surveyed six native SC speakers in 1998 (four of them being Chinese language teachers) and asked them to read at normal speed 16 expressions that contain a final T3, written in characters. The expressions are shown in (15), where [M N] is a modifier–noun compound. The results are given in (16).

(15)   (a) [V O] phrases in isolation

	T1 T3	T2 T3	T3 T3	T4 T3
	tiao ma	qi ma	yang ma	fang ma
	'pick horse'	'ride horse'	'raise horse'	'graze horse'

(b) [M N] compounds in isolation

	T1 T3	T2 T3	T3 T3	T4 T3
	hei ma	bai ma	hao ma	kuai ma
	'black horse'	'white horse'	'good horse'	'fast horse'

(c) [V O] phrases in a sentence

	T1	T4	T1/T2/T3/T4	T3
	ta	zai	tiao/qi/yang/fang	ma
	he	is	pick/ride/raise/graze	horse

'He is picking/riding/raising/grazing horses.'

(d) [M N] compounds in a sentence

	T1	T4	T1/T2/T3/T4	T3
	ta	yao	hei/bai/hao/kuai	ma
	he	want	black/white/good/fast	horse

'He wants a black/white/good/fast horse.'

(16)   Expression   Speakers using [21]   Speakers using [214]

      [V O] in isolation   5   1
      [M N] in isolation   6   0
      [V O] in a sentence   6   0
      [M N] in a sentence   6   0

Five of the six speakers pronounced all the 16 final T3s with [21]. One speaker, who once took an entrance exam at the Beijing Broadcasting Institute and was apparently very careful in her pronunciation, used [214] for the four final T3s in (15a) but [21] for the other twelve cases. All the speakers agree that a final [214] carries some emphasis, especially with the [M N] expressions in (15b) and (15d). The data in (17) illustrates the same point.

(17)   Contrast between [M N] and [V O] for final T3

    (a) [M N]   (b) [V O]

       51   21 (?214)   51   214 or 21
       sai   ma   sai   ma
       race   horse   race   horse
       'a race horse'   'to race horses'

In [M N], the final T3 can be [21] but not [214] (unless it is emphasized). In [V O], the final T3 can be [21] or [214]. This means that the value of a final T3 is sensitive to syntax. In general, a final T3 need not be [214], and it is harder to use [214] in a compound than in a [V O] phrase. The difference between [M N] and [V O] has been observed by Hoa (1983: 100), who reports that [M N] has initial stress but [V O] has final stress. In the present analysis (Chapter 6), the difference follows from phrasal stress. In [M N] phrasal stress goes to M and in [V O] phrasal stress goes to O. I will return to this issue shortly.

   A well-known rule of T3 is T3 Sandhi (T3S), by which a T3 followed by another T3 changes to T2. When many T3s occur together, the effect of T3S can be quite complicated. This will be discussed in Chapter 11.

10.6.3. Variation of T2

Chao (1968: 27–8) describes a change concerning T2. In a trisyllabic expression, if (a) the first syllable is T1 or T2, (b) the middle syllable is T2, and (c) the final syllable is not weak, then the middle T2 can change to T1 in conversational speed. Chao's examples are quoted in (18).

(18)   T2 → T1 in trisyllabic expressions

T1-T2-T1	→	T1-T1-T1	xi yang shen	'(occidental) ginseng'
T1-T2-T2	→	T1-T1-T2	san nian ji	'third-year grade'
T1-T2-T3	→	T1-T1-T3	cong you bing	'onion oil cake'
T1-T2-T4	→	T1-T1-T4	Dong Heyar	'East Riverside'
T1-T3-T3	→	T1-T1-T3	fen shui ling	'watershed'
T2-T2-T1	→	T2-T1-T1	shei neng fei	'Who can fly?'
T2-T2-T2	→	T2-T1-T2	hai mei wan	'not yet finished'
T2-T2-T3	→	T2-T1-T3	you zha gui	'fried hollow doughnut'
T2-T2-T4	→	T2-T1-T4	Longfu Shi	'Longfu Temple'
T2-T3-T3	→	T2-T1-T3	han shu biao	'thermometer'
T3-T3-T3	→	T2-T1-T3	hao ji zhong	'quite a few kinds'

A T2 that comes from T3 (by T3S) is treated the same as a real T2. Thus, by T3S, T1-T3-T3 first becomes T1-T2-T3, which then changes to T1-T1-T3. T2-T3-T3 first becomes T2-T2-T3 and then changes to T2-T1-T3. T3-T3-T3 first becomes T2-T2-T3 and then changes to T2-T1-T3.

Since T2 is LH, and since the first syllable in the environment ends in H, the change in T2 appears to be a case of assimilation, whereby HLH → HHH. But there is the question of why the third syllable is needed when its tone is not relevant anyway. The answer seems to lie in stress. The foot structure of a typical trisyllabic expression in SC is (SS)(SØ), where the second syllable has least stress (Chapter 6). In contrast, the foot structure of a typical disyllabic expression in SC is S(SØ), where the second syllable has main stress. In this regard, the T2 sandhi seems to be a case of tonal simplification, which occurs when T2 lacks stress. However, there remains the question of why other medial syllables do not undergo simplification. For example, a medial T4 (HL) does not simplify to H or L.

According to Luo and Wang (1981: 133), for T2 Sandhi to occur, the first syllable need not be T1 and T2 but can also be T3 and T4. The case with an initial T3 is rather limited. In particular, when the first syllable is T3, the second must also be T3, so that the first T3 will change to T2 by T3 Sandhi (see the last example in (18)). When the first syllable is T4, there is only one example, *gong4-chan3 dang3* 'communist party', where T3 Sandhi first applies to the last two syllables and changes the underlying HL-L-L to HL-LH-L, which then changes to HL-H-L. The change from HL-LH to HL-H in the first two syllables seems to be another case of simplification, although a slightly different one from those when the initial syllable is T1 (i.e. H-LH → H-H) or T2 (i.e. LH-LH → LH-H). It remains to be seen whether there are more examples with initial T4. It is worth noting that *gong4-chan3 dang3* 'communist party' is a high-frequency expression in

SC and is more likely to undergo change (Bybee 2001). My own sense is that T2 Sandhi is not a productive or required rule. Instead, it is likely to be conditioned by the speed of speech (Shih 2005) and frequency of the expression.

10.6.4. Tone on weak syllables

According to Chao (1968: 36), the tone of a weak syllable depends on the tone of the preceding syllable. This is shown in (19), where T0 is a weak syllable, whose pitch is represented by one Chao digit, because the syllable is short.

(19)   T1   T0   55   2
       fei   le   →   fei   le   'fly ASP (flew)'
       T2   35   3
       lai   le   →   lai   le   'come ASP (came)'
       T3   21   4
       mai   le   →   mai   le   'buy ASP (bought)'
       T4   51   1
       mai   le   →   mai   le   'sell ASP (sold)'

As Chao observes, the weak syllable is high after T3 and (relatively) low after other tones.

There are two possible analyses of the underlying tone on weak syllables: (*a*) weak syllables have L, and (*b*) they are toneless—the low pitch is a phonetic reflection of the lack of tone. There are three arguments for the second analysis. First, if a weak syllable is L, it ought to have a low pitch consistently, as T3 does (except under T3S). However, (19) shows that its pitch is not stable but influenced by the preceding tone. Secondly, if a weak syllable is L, we must explain why it is H after T3. In particular, if T3 is L, the change in T3-T0 may appear to be a case of dissimilation, namely, L-L → L-H. However, there is the question of why T3-T3 changes to T2-T3, i.e. L-L → LH-L, instead of T3-T1, i.e. not L-L → L-H. In addition, there is the question of why T0-T0 does not become L-H, as shown in (20).

(20)   T4   T0   T0   51   1   1
       mai   guo   le → mai   guo   le   'sell ASP ASP (have sold)'

Thirdly, unstressed syllables generally lose their underlying tones. For example, in SC [tuŋ55 tʰian55] 'winter day (winter)' can be read as [tuŋ55 tʰiə̃2]. In the latter case, [tʰiə̃2] is unstressed (accompanied by rhyme reduction, see Chapter 4), and it loses its T1 and assumes a low pitch. If weak syllables cannot keep their underlying tones, how can they carry L? Moreover, since [thian] is originally H, there is the question of where the L comes from. In summary, there is no evidence that a weak syllable has L. Instead, it is more reasonable to say that it is toneless.

As observed by X. Wang (1992), when a weak syllable follows T1 or T2, it can sometimes become T4. For example, *shi-liu* 'pomegranate' was originally T2-T2, which later became T2-Ø, but now it is often T2-T4. When a weak syllable takes T4, it also returns to a full syllable by being longer and without rhyme reduction.

10.6.5. **T3S and weak syllables**

C. Cheng (1973: 45–6) notes an interesting contrast between the two expressions in (21).

(21)   T3 T3 → 35 L   T3 T3 → 21 H

xiao-jie   jie-jie
little sister   sister sister (reduplicated)
'miss'   'sister'

Underlyingly, each expression has T3-T3. At the surface level, C. Cheng considers the second syllable in both expressions to be weak, because it is not [214]. The puzzle, however, is that in the first expression, T3S occurred, because the first T3 has changed to T2. In contrast, T3S does not occur in the second expression.

If the second syllable is weak in both cases, we must explain why it triggers T3S in one case but not in the other. There are three possible solutions. The first is offered by C. Cheng, which makes use of an internal word boundary. It assumes that the second syllables are both T3 underlyingly, while there is a word boundary (#) inside *xiao-#-jie* but not inside *jie-jie*. T3S applies only across a word boundary, namely, in *xiao-#-jie* but not *jie-jie*. After T3S, a de-stressing rule applies which changes the second syllables to weak syllables. The second solution assumes reduplication and orders it after T3S. The analysis is shown in (22).

(22)   'miss'   'sister'

Underlying   T3-T3   T3
                        xiao-jie   jie
T3S   T2-T3   N/A
                        xiao-jie

Reduplication	N/A	T3-T3
		jie-jie
De-stressing	T2- T0	T3-T0
	xiao-jie	jie-jie
Surface	35-L	21-H

The key is to order reduplication after T3S, so that *jie-jie* cannot trigger T3S. Then the second syllable is de-stressed, and its tone lost. Finally, T0 is realized as [1] after T2 and [4] after T3.

Both solutions assume that the second syllables are unstressed at surface. There is no question that the second syllable in *jie-jie* is T0, since it does not trigger T3S and its pitch is like that of a weak syllable (H after T3). However, it is not obvious that the second syllable in *xiao-jie* is T0. The reason Cheng considers it to be T0 is probably due to the assumption that a final T3 ought to be [214], which the second syllable in *xiao-jie* is not. However, as discussed above, a final T3 need not be [214], especially in an [M N] compound. Since *xiao-jie* is an [M N] compound, its final T3 can be [21], or L. If so, there is no reason to consider the second syllable in *xiao-jie* to be T0. This gives the third solution, shown (23), where the second syllable is T3 in one case and T0 in the other.

(23)   T3-T3 → T2-T3   T3-T0
         xiao-jie   jie-jie
         'little sister (miss)'   'sister'

In this analysis, T3S is triggered only by T3, and not by T0. There is no need to assume special boundary markers or ordered steps of rule application.

10.6.6. **Tone and vowel height**

It is well known that high vowels are inherently higher in pitch than low vowels. It is less known whether tone can affect vowel height. In SC, a high tone can raise the vowel and a low tone can lower the vowel (see Chapter 3). Consider the examples in (24).

(24)   T1 (H)   [wii]   [juu]
                   'tiny'   'excellent'

         T3 (L)   [wəi]   [jəu]
                   'tail'   'have'

In SC there is no contrast between [wii] and [wəi]; [wii] usually occurs with a high tone and [wəi] usually occurs with a low tone. Similarly, there is no contrast between [juu] and [jəu]; [juu] usually occurs with a high tone and [jəu] usually occurs with a low tone. In Chapter 9, we also discussed that the [ə˞]-suffixed forms of [i] and [je] in SC are distinct with T1 and T2, but non-distinct with T3 and T4. It is not clear how the interaction between tone and vowel height can be analysed in terms of distinctive features.

10.6.7. Tone and length

The durational difference among T1, T2, T4 and the nonfinal T3 [21] is rather small. According to Luo and Wang (1981: 127), T2 is 7 per cent longer than T4 and T1 is 2.6 per cent longer than T4. According to Howie (1976: 20, 220), T2 is 3 per cent longer than T4, T4 is 6 per cent longer than T1, and the non-final T3 [21] is 10 per cent longer than T4. According to L. Feng (1985: 178), T1, T3, and T4 are similar in duration, and T2 is 4 per cent longer than them.

The [214] form of T3, which mostly occurs on a monosyllable and sometimes on a final syllable, is much longer than other tones. For this reason, Woo (1969) and Shih (1997) consider [214] to have three moras, in contrast to other tones, which have two moras. In fact, Chao (1933: 132) points out that a monosyllabic T3 'often breaks into two syllables', with a glottal stop appearing in between. Two examples are shown in (25).

(25)   L   L-H
        [xau]   →   [xaa-ʔu]
        'good'

        L   L-H
        [nii]   →   [nii-ʔi]
        'you'

Chao's description is shared by other linguists in an email discussion (the Chinese list, April–May 1998). If [214] is indeed two syllables, there is an explanation of why it is easier for it to occur in a disyllabic [V O] than in a disyllabic [M N]. Consider the foot structures of [V O] and [M N] in (26), where S indicates a syllable (see Chapter 6).

(26)   [V O]   [M N]

        x   x
        S (SØ)   (SS)

In [V O], phrasal stress is on O, which can form a foot with an empty beat. The empty beat can be filled by a lengthened T3. This explains why a final [214] can occur in [V O]. In contrast, [M N] forms a disyllabic foot, where no empty beat is needed, so the final T3 is L only.

10.6.8. Some special syllables

Some words in SC have special tone changes. Four well-known words are *yi* 'one', *qi* 'seven', *ba* 'eight', and *bu* 'not'. Chao (1968: 45) gives their patterns in (27), where the tones in parentheses are used by a minority of speakers.

(27)		Final	Before T4	Before T1, T2, and T3
	yi 'one'	T1	T2	T4
	qi 'seven'	T1	T1 (T2)	T1 (T4)
	ba 'eight'	T1	T1 (T2)	T1 (T4)
	bu 'not'	T4 (T1)	T2	T4

For 'seven' and 'eight', the use of T2 and T4 might still be heard from some Beijing speakers, but the dominant trend today is to use only T1 in all environments. However, the alternations in 'one' and 'not' are still used by most SC speakers. Some examples in Pinyin are given in (28).

(28) Final	Before T4	Before T1	Before T2	Before T3
55 55	35 51	51 55	51 35	51 21
jia yi	yi ge	yi tian	yi nian	yi wan
'add one'	'one unit'	'one day'	'one year'	'one bowl'
35 51	35 51	51 55	51 35	51 21
jue bu	bu yao	bu jia	bu lai	bu mai
'surely not'	'not want'	'not add'	'not come'	'not buy'

The tonal alternation just described is sensitive to syntactic structure. For example, consider the case in (29), transcribed in Pinyin, where the point of interest is the tone of *yi* 'one'.

(29)	T2-T1-T2 (*T2-T4-T2)	T2-T4-T2 (*T2-T1-T2)
	[[shi yi] nian]	[mang [yi nian]]
	ten one year	busy one year
	'eleven years'	'busy for a year'

Linearly, *yi* 'one' is between two T2s in both cases. If tonal alternation is insensitive to syntax, *yi* should have the same tone in both cases. However, in 'eleven years' *yi* must be T1, and in 'busy for a year' *yi* must be T4. The difference can be explained if tonal alternation is sensitive to syntax. In 'eleven years', *yi* is in the final position of the inner constituent [*shi yi*], so it should be T1. In 'busy for a year', *yi* is before T2 in the inner constituent [*yi nian*], so it should be T4.

The tonal alternation of *yi* is restricted to its cardinal meaning 'one' and does not extend to its ordinal meaning 'first' or 'number 1'. This is shown in (30).

(30)   Cardinal meaning 'one'

Before T1	Before T2	Before T3	Before T4
51 55	51 35	51 21	35 51
yi tian	yi nian	yi wan	yi ge
'one day'	'one year'	'one bowl'	'one unit'

Ordinal meaning 'first'/'No. 1'

Before T1	Before T2	Before T3	Before T4
55 55	55 35	55 21	55 51
yi qi	yi lou	yi zu	yi ce
'session 1'	'floor 1'	'team 1'	'volume 1'

While *yi* alternates between 51 and 35 in the cardinal meaning, it stays 55 in the ordinal meaning. The difference can be explained if the ordinal meaning is underlyingly [*di yi*] 'first', so that the above expressions are [[*di yi*] *qi/lou/zu/ce*] 'the first session/floor/team/volume'. Because *yi* is final in [*di yi*], it takes 55 as expected.

It is worth noting that *yi* 'one', *qi* 'seven', *ba* 'eight', and *bu* 'not' all belong to the historical syllable category Ru, which used to end in a stop. In many Chinese dialects Ru syllables still form a distinct category. In SC, Ru syllables no longer form an independent category but have split up among other tones. A comparison between SC and Shanghai can be seen in (31). All Ru syllables in Shanghai have laryngealized vowels, indicated by [ˀ].

(31)   Ru syllables in SC

55	35	21	51
[xəi]	[tsu]	[pəi]	[kʰɤ]
'black'	'foot'	'north'	'guest'

Ru syllables in Shanghai

55	55	55	55
[xaˀ]	[tsoˀ]	[poˀ]	[kʰaˀ]
'black'	'foot'	'north'	'guest'

The fact that Ru syllables have split up among other tones in SC may in part explain why *yi* 'one', *qi* 'seven', *ba* 'eight', and *bu* 'not' can (or did till recent past) alternate among different tonal categories. It may also explain why some other Ru syllables also have tonal alternation, such as *da* 'answer', which is T2 in *jie3-da2* 'solve-answer (explain)' and *da1-ying4* 'answer-respond (agree)'.

10.6.9. Reduplicated patterns

Some reduplicated forms in SC have special tonal patterns. For example, there is an X-Xr-*de* form, where X is a monosyllabic adjective or adverb, Xr is the [ə˞]-suffixed form of X (see Chapter 9), and *de* is an unstressed particle. The X-Xr-*de* form adds a subtle meaning to X, such as 'rather X' or 'nice and X'. Some examples are shown in (32), where *de* is probably [tə] underlyingly but [də] at surface.

(32) X   X-Xr-*de*
      T1   T1-T1-Ø
      [tɕan]   [tɕan-tɕaə˞-də]   'sharp-pointed'
      T2   T2-T1-Ø
      [ɥan]   [ɥan-ɥaə˞-də]   'round'
      T3   T3-T1-Ø
      [pʲan]   [pʲan-pʲaə˞-də]   'flat'
      T4   T4-T1-Ø
      [man]   [man-maə˞-də]   'slowly'

The X-Xr-*de* pattern can be analysed as a case of reduplication that involves a partially specified suffix template, which is given in (33) and exemplified in (34).

(33)   The suffix for the X-Xr-*de* pattern

       H
       \
       CVX-CV
       | | |
       ə˞ d ə

(34)   Illustration with [man] 'slow'

       HL   H   HL   H   HL   H
       | | \ | | \ | | \
       CVX   CVX-CV   →   CVX   CVX-CV   →   CVX   CVX-CV
       | | | | | | | | | | | | | | | | | | | |
       ma n   ə˞ d ə   ma n   manə˞ d ə   ma n   ma ə˞ də

The suffix consists of two syllables. The first is specified for the coda and the tone, but not for the onset and the nucleus. The second is a weak syllable [də]. The suffix triggers a copying of the original syllable (only segments are shown, since tone is already specified). The onset and the nucleus of the copied syllable then link to the empty slots in the suffix. The unlinked coda [n] is not realized in the pronunciation.

Besides X-Xr-*de*, there is also an X-X-Y-Yr-*de* (or X-X-Y-Y-*de*) pattern, which is related to a disyllabic X-Y adjective. For example, *re-nao* 'hot-noisy (bustling with activity)' can become *re-re-nao-naor-de*. In X-X-Y-Yr-*de* (or X-X-Y-Y-*de*), the first X carries its own tone, the second X carries a low tone, Y-Yr (or Y-Y) both carry a high tone, and *de* carries a low tone. Like X-Xr-*de*, X-X-Y-Yr-*de* (or X-X-Y-Y-*de*) can be analysed in terms of a partially specified template that triggers reduplication. Both X-Xr-*de* and X-X-Y-Yr-*de* are characteristic of the Beijing dialect. Non-Beijing speakers often use X-X-*de* and X-X-Y-Y-*de* instead, such as *yuan2-yuan2-de* 'round' and *re4-re4-nao4-nao4-de* 'bustling with activity', where all Xs and Ys carry their own tones.

In SC spoken in Taiwan (TWSC), there is a special X-X pattern that is used for kinship terms, such as *jie-jie* 'sister', *di-di* 'younger brother', *ba-ba* 'dad', and *wa-wa* 'baby'. The tone is a fixed L-LH pattern, regardless of the tone of the original X. The pattern can be analysed with a disyllabic template that is pre-specified with the tones L-LH, and the sounds of the template are filled with those of the reduplicated X-X.

10.7. TONE AND STRESS: THE TONE-STRESS PRINCIPLE

We have seen that weak syllables cannot keep their underlying tones in SC. There is evidence that the same is true in other languages. For example, some studies have shown that in African languages, stressed (accented) syllables either attract tone or are accompanied by a tone pattern (e.g. Goldsmith 1984; Hyman 1987; Kenstowicz 1987; Sietsema 1989; Kisseberth and Cassimjee 1992). In languages like English and Dutch, where pitch is used for intonation, the standard analysis is that only stressed syllables can be assigned a pitch accent (M. Liberman 1975; Pierrehumbert 1980; Beckman and Pierrehumbert 1986; Gussenhoven 1988). In Chinese dialects there are two cases. In some dialects, such as SC, there is a contrast between full (stressed) and weak (unstressed) syllables, and only full syllables bear underlying tones. In other dialects, such as Nantong and Shanghai, there is no contrast between full and weak syllables, and only those syllables that occur in stressed positions are accompanied by an underlying tone (Ao 1993; Duanmu 1993, 1999a). Such facts suggest a relation between tone and stress, which I state in (35), where pitch accent is a tonal unit that differs from a boundary tone.

(35)   *Tone-Stress Principle*
       A stressed syllable can be assigned a lexical tone or pitch accent.
       An unstressed syllable is not assigned a lexical tone or pitch accent.

The Tone-Stress Principle governs the use of lexical tones and pitch accents. It does not govern boundary tones, which can be used on unstressed syllables. Consider the case in English. According to Goldsmith (1981), in neutral speech, a stressed English syllable is accompanied by the pitch pattern MHL, where H is linked to the stressed syllable and M is used for syllables before the stressed one. If we consider M to be a default pitch for a toneless syllable before stress, we can assume H*+L%, where H* is the pitch accent and L% is a boundary tone (M. Liberman 1975; Pierrehumbert 1980; Beckman and Pierrehumbert 1986). Some examples are shown in (36), where Ø indicates lack of tone and stressed syllables are italicized.

(36)   *John*   H*L%   De-*troit*   Ø-H*L%
       Bos-ton   H*-L%   Chi-*ca*-go   Ø-H*-L%

When the stressed syllable is in final position, it carries both the pitch accent H* and the boundary tone L%, and the combination is realized as a fall. When an unstressed syllable follows the stressed one, it takes over the boundary tone.

The Tone-Stress Principle had been proposed before in Duanmu (1996), according to which every stressed syllable is accompanied by a tone pattern. The statement in (35) differs from it in that a stressed syllable can, but need not, be accompanied by a lexical tone or pitch accent. This accounts for the fact that in an English word like *compensation*, where stress falls on the first and third syllables, the third is accompanied by a pitch accent but the first need not be. Similarly, in compounds like *potato eater*, both words have stress, but only the first has a pitch accent.

Stress can affect pitch range. J. Shen (1985) notes that the pitch range of SC varies considerably in read sentences. Chu and Lü (1996) have observed the same effect in broadcast speech. For example, in *ming2 nian2* 'next year', the first word has wider pitch range than the second. Similarly, in *zhong1guo2 zu2qiu2* 'Chinese soccer', the first word has a wider pitch range than the second, and in the second word, the first syllable has a wider pitch range than the second. The facts can be accounted for if a syllable with word stress has a wider pitch range than a syllable without, and within a compound, downstep applies to each successive foot (see Chapter 6). The structure of *zhong1guo2 zu2qiu2* 'Chinese soccer' (in nonfinal position) is (SW)(SW), where the second foot has a narrower pitch range than the first owing to downstep. In addition, within each foot the first syllable has a higher pitch level than the second owing to stress.

10.8. TONE AND INTONATION

Pitch contours in non-tone languages such as English and Dutch are called intonation. Intonation differs from tone in that tone distinguishes lexical meanings, whereas intonation expresses syntactic or contextual meanings. However, ignoring their functions, we would like to ask whether tone and intonation can be represented with the same phonological features.

As discussed in the previous section, according to M. Liberman (1975), Pierrehumbert (1980), and others, intonation in English can be represented by a linear sequence of 'pitch accents' and 'boundary tones', which in effect is a sequence of H and L tones. This approach essentially treats intonation and tone as the same thing. The approach has also been applied to pitch-accent languages such as Japanese (Beckman and Pierrehumbert 1986).

In languages like Chinese, word tones are lexically determined and there is little flexibility in varying the sequence of Hs and Ls independently (I ignore tonal Register here). This raises the question of how languages like Chinese express intonational meaning, such as statement, doubt, surprise, query, command, etc.

Chao (1933) suggests that many functions of intonation in other languages are fulfilled in Chinese by the use of particles. When particles are not used, tone and intonation can be combined through two ways of 'addition'. The first is 'successive addition', where a rise or a fall is added to the end of an utterance; this is similar to a boundary H or L in English. Two examples in SC are shown in (37) and (38) (see Chao 1933: 131). Strictly speaking, the resulting syllable will be lengthened in order to carry an extra tone. For simplicity the lengthening is not shown.

(37)   Tone   Intonation

    LH   +   L   →   LHL
    nan   nan
    'difficult'   'affirmation'   'Surely difficult!'

(38) Tone   Intonation

    HL + H   →   HLH

    mai   mai

    'sell'   'question'   'Sell?'

In (37) [nan] has LH and the final intonation L carries an affirmation meaning. When the two are added, the result is a rise–fall (LHL). In (38) [mai] 'sell' has HL and the final intonation H carries a question meaning. When the two are added, the result is a fall–rise (HLH).

The second way of addition is 'simultaneous addition', where intonation is superimposed on word tones. As a result, the pitch range of an utterance is raised, lowered, expanded, or compressed. Simultaneous addition is supported by the phonetic studies of S. Shen (1989) and Y. He and Jing (1992), who found that the question intonation raises the pitch height of the entire utterance, without changing the distinctiveness of word tones.

If simultaneous addition is real, tone and intonation must involve different features. This raises a theoretical problem. First, to represent tone and intonation in Chinese, we may need two layered sequences of Hs and Ls, one for tones and one for intonation, but no other feature, such as [round], [nasal], or [voice], comes in two layers. If tone features are segmental features, as I argued above, we need to explain why only tone features can come in two layers. Secondly, since the English pitch contour can be represented by a single sequence of Hs and Ls (M. Liberman 1975; Pierrehumbert 1980), there is the question of whether the sequence reflects tone, or intonation, or both. If it reflects tone, one wonders why English has no intonation. If it reflects intonation, it means that, like tone, intonation can be represented by a sequence of Hs and Ls, but then there is the question of what relation there is between the intonational Hs and Ls and the tonal Hs and Ls. If it reflects both, then one wonders why a single sequence of Hs and Ls can represent both tone and intonation in English but just tone in Chinese.

It is necessary then to take a closer look at the evidence for simultaneous addition. It is interesting that Chao (1933) mentioned only two cases of simultaneous addition in Chinese, 'raised level of pitch' and 'lowered level of pitch' (pitch range widening and narrowing were found to be correlated to pitch raising and lowering). In Y. He and Jing (1992), six intonational meanings were designed (statement, expecting confirmation, question, simple request, command, and exclamation), but again just two cases of simultaneous addition were observed: raised or lowered. If these are the only cases of simultaneous addition (besides the neutral intonation), there is an alternative to Chao's proposal. The raised level may have an accented final boundary H, which (whether it is actually produced or not) is targeted at a higher pitch level (as any H with a main accent is) and so may have prevented downstep in the preceding syllables. Similarly, the lowered level may have an accented final boundary L, which is targeted at a lower pitch level and so may have accelerated downstep in the preceding syllables. Whether this proposal is the right account of simultaneous addition will be left open.

10.9. TONE IN SONGS

Since both tone and musical notes make use of pitch, a common question is whether tones get lost in a song. At the outset there are two possibilities: tone and musical notes are made with different articulatory mechanisms, so they can co-exist and be both present; tone and musical notes are made by the same mechanism, so they will influence each other.

There is little evidence for the first hypothesis. Instead, I believe that (the Pitch component of) tone and musical notes are made with the same articulatory mechanism and therefore they do interfere with each other. Unfortunately, I am not aware of any experimental study that demonstrates such interference (or the lack of it). Moreover, casual reflections by Chinese speakers do not seem to suggest obvious difficulties in perceiving words in songs.

One might suggest that perhaps tones can be superimposed on musical notes in some subtle ways. For example, in SC the falling tone (T4) on a high musical note might be realized as a slight fall in the high pitch range, and the falling tone on a low musical note might be realized as a slight fall in the low pitch range. The rising tone (T2) can be similarly coded. The low tone (T3) can be realized with a level pitch and a murmured voice quality and the high tone (T1) can be realized with a level pitch and normal voice quality. This suggestion is quite plausible but there is again no experimental evidence for it.

There are two other possible reasons for the apparent absence of the interference between tones and musical notes. First, in SC, tones do not seem to be crucial for understanding the meaning when words are used in context. For example, if compounds are written without space in the Pinyin alphabet, one can often read them correctly even when tones are omitted. An example is shown in (39).

(39)   You henduo Zhongguo ren buhui shuo Putonghua.
        have many China people not-can speak Putonghua
        'There are many Chinese people who cannot speak Standard Chinese.'

Another reason for the lack of difficulty in perceiving words in songs is that in some dialects, musical notes are chosen in such a way as to match tonal levels. This is especially true in Cantonese, which has four (or five level) tones. When songs are composed for Cantonese, song writers often choose higher notes for word that have higher tones and lower notes for words that have lower tones (Wong and Diehl 2002).

10.10. TONAL FREQUENCIES IN STANDARD CHINESE

SC has about 1,300 syllables, including tones. Most of them are full syllables, each of which carries one of four tones. The four tones are fairly evenly distributed, as shown in (40).

(40) Frequency of tones

Tone:	First	Second	Third	Fourth	All
Number of syllables:	337	255	316	347	1,255

We can see that there are slightly fewer second tones than other tones, but not by a lot. In principle, any full syllable in SC can carry any of the four tones. However, many syllables carry fewer than four tones. Consider the data in (41)

(41) Tonal density on syllables

Tones per syllable:	4	3	2	1	All
Number of such syllables:	178	130	59	35	402

We can see that most syllables have four or three tones each, and a small number of syllables have two or one tone each.

10.11. SUMMARY

I have discussed the representation of the tones in SC and several other tonal issues. The analysis assumes two tonal features, Register and Pitch, each with two values (Yip 1980). In addition, I follow the common analysis that contour tones in SC are made of the level tones H and L (Woo 1969; Yip 1980), and a tone-bearing unit is a segment in the rhyme (Woo 1969). Moreover, I have proposed the Tone-Stress Principle in (35), according to which only stressed syllables can be accompanied by a lexical tone or pitch accent, whereas unstressed syllables can only carry boundary tones.

Tone 3 Sandhi (T3S)

11.1. INTRODUCTION

Tone 3 Sandhi (T3S, also called Third-Tone Sandhi) is perhaps the best-known phonological process in SC. In T3S, a T3 becomes a T2 when it precedes another T3. The rule is given in (1) and exemplified in (2).

(1) T3-T3 → T2-T3   (or LL → LHL)

(2) mai3 ma3 → mai2 ma3   mai2 ma3
     buy horse   bury horse
     'to buy a horse'   'to bury a horse'

T3S can create ambiguities, because T2-T3 and T3-T3 are both realized as T2-T3 at surface. For example, although *mai3* 'buy' and *mai2* 'bury' have different tones when they are spoken alone, 'to buy a horse' and 'to bury a horse' sound the same at surface.

T3S was observed as early as the sixteenth century (Mei 1977). Some studies have asked whether the changed T3 is completely identical to T2 in SC. The perception study of W. Wang and Li (1967) shows that, as far as the listener is concerned, T2 and the changed T3 are indistinguishable.

It is tempting to think that T3S is triggered by stress. For example, Dell (2004) suggests that T3S is a case of neutralization or reduction, probably because the first syllable in a 3-3 pair lacks stress. On the other hand, Meredith (1990) and de Lacy (2002) propose that a stressed syllable tends to co-occur with a high tone. If so, one might wonder if the first syllable in a 3-3 pair has more stress. However, it is easy to show that T3S applies regardless of which syllable has more stress (Duanmu 2004). For example, in the case of *mai3 ma3* 'buy horse', one can put emphatic stress on either syllable and T3S applies the same way. Also, T2 is a full syllable, which contrasts with T1, T4, T3, and weak syllables. Thus, when T3 changes to T2, it remains a full syllable, not a weak syllable. In this regard, T3S differs from typical neutralization processes, where all contrasts in a given paradigm are lost, and the result is often none of the originally contrastive forms. For example, the flapping rule in American English neutralizes [t] and [d] and the result is [ɾ]. Similarly, when stressed vowels neutralize in American English, the result is [ə], which does not occur in a stressed syllable (I assume that the vowel in words like *cup* is [ʌ], not [ə]; see Hammond 1999). Thus, to equate T3S with neutralization is to overlook a number of important differences between them.

It is also tempting to think of T3S as a case of dissimilation (C. Cheng 1973), which disallows two identical tones in sequence. For example, if T3 is L, T3-T3 is L-L, which triggers dissimilation. Similarly, Yip (2002) attributes T3S to the Obligatory Contour Principle, which also disallows a sequence of two identical tones. However, two questions remain: Why is there no dissimilation in H-H (T1-T1)? And, why is there no dissimilation in HL-L (T4-T3), L-LH (T3-T2), or HL-LH (T4-T2), all of which contain L-L? Since there is no good answer to such questions, the reason for T3S will be left open.

The main challenge in the analysis of T3S is to explain how it applies to long strings of T3 syllables. For example, is T3S sensitive to syntactic bracketing? Is it sensitive to syntactic categories? Are there alternative patterns for a given string of T3s? In what follows I first present the basic data, then I review previous analyses, followed by the present analysis and offer some concluding remarks.

11.2. THE DATA

First, T3S can apply across any syntactic domain, whether it is a word, a compound, or a phrase. This is shown in (3), transcribed in Pinyin.

(3) Word   ma3yi3   →   2-3   'ant'
    Compound   mi3-jiu3   →   2-3   'rice-wine'
    Phrase   ni3 hao3   →   2-3   'you good (How are you?)'

Secondly, T3S can give alternative surface patterns, shown in (4). In the second expression, T2 can further change to T1 in the proper environment (see Chapter 10); for ease of exposition I do not discuss this additional change.

(4) [mai3 [hao3   jiu3]] → 3-2-3, or 2-2-3 (*2-2-2, *3-2-2, *2-3-2, *2-3-3, *3-3-2, etc.)
    buy   good   wine
    'to buy good wine'

[xiao3 [zhi3   [lao3-hu3]]] → 2-3-2-3, 3-2-2-3, 3-2-1-3, 2-2-2-3, or 2-1-1-3
small   paper   old-tiger
'small paper tiger'

Thirdly, T3S is sensitive to syntactic branching. A left-branching structure
usually has just one pattern, but a right-branching structure can have two
or more, as shown in (5).

(5)   Left-branching   Right-branching

    [[3 3] 3] → 2-2-3 only   [3 [3 3]] → 3-2-3 or 2-2-3
    [[mai hao] jiu]   [mai [hao   jiu]]
      buy good wine   buy good wine
    'finished buying wine'   'to buy good wine'

    [[[3 3] 3] 3] → 2-2-2-3 only   [3 [3 [3 3]]] → 2-3-2-3, 3-2-2-3, or 2-2-2-3
    [[[zhan-lan] guan] li]   [xiao [zhi   [lao-hu]]]
      show-see hall   inside   small paper old-tiger
    'inside of exhibition hall'   'small paper tiger'

Fourthly, T3S is optional in certain cases, such as between two binary
branches of a syntactic tree (F. Liu 1980; Kaisse 1985) (a tree is equivalent
to layered brackets). For example, T3S need not apply between *Li3* and
mai3 in (6a) for some speakers, but must apply between *zhi3* and *lao3* in
(6b).

(6)   (a)   [[Lao3 Li3] [mai3 shu1]] → 2-3-3-1 (2-2-3-1 is also acceptable)
      'Old Li buy book (Old Li buys books).'

    (b)   [xiao3 [zhi3 [lao3-ying1]]] → *2-3-3-1 (must be 3-2-3-1 or 2-2-3-1)
      'small paper old-eagle (small paper eagle)'

Fifthly, tree structure alone is insufficient for predicting the outcome of
T3S. For example, the two expressions in (7a) have the same tree structure
and input tones, but the first can become 2-3-3-1 for some speakers and the
second cannot. Similarly, each of the other pairs in (7) has the same tree
structure, but not the same surface tone patterns (only relevant patterns are
shown).

(7)   (a)   3-3-3-1 → 2-3-3-1   3-3-3-1 → *2-3-3-1
      [wo [xiang [mai shu]]]   [xiao [zhi   [lao-ying]]]
       I   want   buy book   small paper old-eagle
      'I want to buy a book.'   'small paper eagle'

    (b)   3-3-3-3 → *?3-2-2-3   3-3-3-3 → 3-2-2-3
      [wo [xiang [mai jiu]]]   [xiao [zhi   [lao-hu]]]
       I   want   buy wine   small paper old-tiger
      'I want to buy wine.'   'small paper tiger'

(c) 3-3-3-3 → 2-3-2-3
[gou [[bi ma] xiao]]
dog than horse small
'Dogs are smaller than horses.'

3-3-3-3 → *2-3-2-3
[gou [[hen hao] yang]]
dog very good raise
'Dogs are very easy to raise.'

(d) 3-3-3-4 → 2-3-3-4
[gou [[bi ma] kuai]]
dog than horse fast
'Dogs are faster than horses.'

3-3-3-4 → *2-3-3-4
[gou [[hen hao] kan]]
dog very good look-at
'Dogs are very nice to look at.'

(e) 3-3-3-3 → *2-3-2-3
[[[zhan-lan] guan] li]
show-see hall inside
'inside of exhibition hall'

3-3-3-3 → 2-3-2-3
[[[nei zhong] jiu] hao]
which kind wine good
'Which kind of wine is good?'

In the sixth place, flat structures, such as phone digits, seem to form disyllabic pairs from left to right. For example, a four-digit number ABCD seems to form [AB][CD], so that T3S need not apply to BC, as shown in (8).

(8) 3-3-3-3 → [2 3][2 3]
wu-wu-wu-wu
'five-five-five-five'

1-3-3-1 → [1 3][3 1] (1-2-3-1 is also OK)
qi-wu-wu-qi
'seven-five-five-seven'

Finally, as noted by Z. Zhang (1988), emphasis can affect T3S. For example, without emphasis, (9) can become 2-3-3-4, but with emphasis on 'buy', 2-3-3-4 cannot be used.

(9) 3-3-3-4 → 2-3-3-4
xiang mai gu-piao
want buy stock
'want to buy stocks'

3-3-3-4 → 3-2-3-4 (*2-3-3-4)
xiang MAI gu-piao
want buy stock
'want to BUY stocks'

Before I present my analysis of T3S, I review two previous ones, which I will call the tree-only analysis and the stress-insensitive foot analysis. For lack of space, other proposals are not reviewed here.

11.3. THE TREE-ONLY ANALYSIS

C. Cheng (1973) and J. Shen (1994) are two representatives of this analysis. According to C. Cheng (1973: 46–53), T3S is sensitive to both the syntactic tree and the speed of speech. When the speed is low, T3S applies to the smallest branches only. When the speed is high, T3S can apply to larger branches. An example is shown in (10) (T3S domains are underlined).

(10)   [[Lao3 Li3] [mai3 [hao3 jiu3]]] 'Old Li buys good wine'
         [[2 3] [3 [2 3]]]   Slow A (disyllabic units)
         [[2 2] [3 [2 3]]]   Slow B (one more T3S, after Slow A)
         [[2 3] [2 [2 3]]]   Medium (up to trisyllabic units)
         [[2 2] [2 [2 3]]]   Fast (entire tree)
         ([[2 1] [1 [1 3]]]   Still faster, with additional change T2 → T1)

At low speed, T3S applies to disyllabic units (the innermost brackets),
which are *Lao Li* and *hao jiu* (Slow A). At a higher speed (Slow B), T3S
may reapply to remaining T3 pairs. At medium speed, T3S can apply
to a trisyllabic unit (besides disyllabic units), which is *mai hao jiu*, all
of which except the last change to T2s. At high speed, T3S applies to
the entire tree, and all T3s except the last change to T2s. At still higher
speed, medial T2 can change to T1 by a separate rule (see Chapter 10).
Now consider (11).

(11)   [wo3 [mai3 [hao3 jiu3]]] 'I buy good wine'
         *[3 [3 [2 3]]]   Slow T3S
         [2 [3 [2 3]]]   Reapply T3S

At low speed, T3S only applies to *hao jiu*, giving *3-3-2-3, which is bad.
Cheng suggests that if there is a sequence of T3s at the beginning or the
end of an expression, the reapplication of T3S is obligatory. The result,
therefore, is 2-3-2-3. The same analysis accounts for (12).

(12)   [[zhan3-lan3] guan3] 'show-see hall (exhibition hall)'
         *[[2 3] 3]   Slow T3S
         [[2 2] 3]   Reapply T3S
         [[2 2] 3]   Fast T3S

At low speed, T3S only changes the first T3. The remaining T3s trigger
T3S again, giving 2-2-3. At high speed, the first two T3s change to T2 in
one step, and the result is the same as that of low speed. This explains why
(12) has no alternative patterns.

   Cheng's analysis has several problems. In the first place, it is unclear
why the reapplication of T3S is obligatory when there are T3s at the beginning or the end of an expression but optional when there are T3s in the
middle of an expression. Secondly, the reapplication of T3S can make
wrong predictions. Consider (13).

(13)   (a)   'show-see hall inside (inside of exhibition hall)'
             [[[zhan3-lan3] guan3] li3]
             *[[[2 3] 3] 3]   Slow T3S
             *[[[2 3] 2] 3]   Reapply T3S

(b) 'small paper old-eagle (small paper eagle)'
　　[xiao3 [zhi3 [lao3-ying1]]]
　　*[3 [3 [3 1]]]　　　　Slow T3S (no effect)
　　*[2 [3 [3 1]]]　　　　Reapply T3S

In (13a), at low speed, T3S only changes the first T3. If we reapply T3S to the last two T3s, the result is 2-3-2-3, which is still bad. In (13b), at low speed, T3S only looks at [3 1], to which it makes no change. If we reapply T3S to the first two T3s, the result is 2-3-3-1, which is still bad. A third problem with Cheng's analysis is that it cannot account for why expressions with the same tree structure and input tones can have different output tone patterns (see (7)). Finally, Cheng offers no discussion of flat structures.

In J. Shen's (1994) analysis, which is similar to Duanmu (1989), T3S is cyclic; it starts from the innermost brackets and moves on to larger and larger brackets. In addition, T3S consists of two parts, stated in (14).

(14)　(a)　T3 must change before T3.
　　　(b)　T3 can optionally change before T2 that came from T3.

The cyclic application ensures that left-branching structures have just one pattern, shown in (15a), but right-branching structures can have more, shown in (15b), where V means T2 or T3 and where an underline shows the domain of T3S at each cycle.

(15)　(a)　[[[zhan3-lan3] guan3] li3] 'show-see hall inside (inside of exhibition hall)'
　　　　　　[[[2 3] 3] 3]　　　　　Cycle 1
　　　　　　[[[2 2 3] 3] 3]　　　　Cycle 2
　　　　　　[[[2 2] 2 3] 3]　　　　Cycle 3 (final output)
　　　(b)　[xiao3 [zhi3 [lao3-hu3]]] 'small paper (old-)tiger'
　　　　　　[3 [3 [2 3]]]　　　　　Cycle 1
　　　　　　[3 [V [2 3]]]　　　　　Cycle 2
　　　　　　[V [V [2 3]]]　　　　　Cycle 3 (final output)
　　　　　　V V 2 3 = 2 3 2 3, 3 2 2 3, or 2 2 2 3

In (15b), the first cycle includes the innermost [3 3], which changes to [2 3]. The second cycle includes [3 [2 3]], where the first T3 can change to T2 or remain T3, indicated by V (variable). The final cycle includes [3 [V [2 3]]], where the first T3 must change to T2 if the following V chooses to be T3; if the following V chooses to be T2, the first T3 can be either T3 or T2. Thus, the final output V-V-2-3 translates into three patterns depending on the choices of the Vs. As a further example, consider (16).

Following Hoa (1983), Chen assumes that in a polysyllabic expression some syllables have more stress (S) than others (W), and those in (18) have the stress patterns as shown. In addition, by the foot formation rules in (17), all the expressions in (18) form one foot each. Now, such feet are not metrical feet for two reasons. First, in metrical theory each language typically chooses one foot type, either left strong (SW) or right strong (WS). However, both (SW) and (WS) are found in (18). Secondly, in metrical theory each foot can only have one S, and each S should belong to a separate foot. In (18), however, some feet have two S syllables each. For these reasons, Chen (2000) introduces a new term, the minimal rhythmic unit (MRU) to refer to the 'foot' in (18). Since the MRU is an unfamiliar term, I will call it 'stress-insensitive foot', and when there is no ambiguity, I will just call it a 'foot'.

Let us now consider how T3S is accounted for by stress-insensitive feet. Consider the example in (19), which follows the rules in (17).

(19)   'Old Li want buy good wine (Old Li wants to buy good wine)'
       [[Lao3 Li3] [xiang3 [mai3 [hao3 jiu3]]]]

n.a.	Foot for emphasis
n.a.	Foot for polysyllabic words
(3 3) 3 3 (3 3)	Compounds
n.a.	Foot at lowest branches
(3 3)(3 3)(3 3)	Left-to-right footing
n.a.	Joining
(2 3)(2 3)(2 3)	T3S (in each foot)

In (19), there is no emphasis or polysyllabic words. There are, however, two compounds, 'Old Li' and 'good wine' (see Chapter 5 on compounds), which each forms a foot. This leaves two free syllables for which a foot is built. Finally, T3S applies to each foot, giving 2-3-2-3-2-3, which is the pattern for slow speed. Next consider the cyclic effect, shown in (20).

(20)   'finished buying wine'   'to buy good wine'
       buy good wine   buy good wine
       [[mai3 hao3] jiu3]   [mai3 [hao3 jiu3]]

n.a.	n.a.	Emphasis/polysyllables
n.a.	3 (3 3)	Compounds
(3 3) 3	n.a.	Lowest footing
((3 3) 3)	(3 (3 3))	Joining
((2̲ 3̲) 3)	(3 (2̲ 3))	T3S cycle 1
((2 2̲) 3)	(3̲ (2 3))	T3S cycle 2

There is again no emphasis or polysyllabic word. After other foot formation rules, each expression forms a layered foot. In ((3 3) 3), T3S applies
twice, giving 2-2-3. In (3 (3 3)), T3S has no effect on the second cycle,
giving 3-2-3.

At high speed, T3S can apply to the entire foot in one step, turning all
but the last T3 into T2 (Shih 1997: 85, 92). This is shown in (21).

(21)   [[3 3] 3]   [3 [3 3]]

    ((3 3) 3)   (3 (3 3))   Foot structure

    ((2̲ 2̲) 3)   (2̲ (2̲ 3))   One-step T3S

The fast pattern for [[3 3] 3] is the same as its slow pattern, but that of
[3 [3 3]] is different. This explains why [[3 3] 3] has one pattern but [3 [3 3]]
has two. Next, consider different speeds for (19), shown in (22).

(22)   [[3 3] [3 [3 [3 3]]]]

    (3 3) (3 3) (3 3)   Foot structure

    (2̲ 3) (2̲ 3) (2̲ 3)   Slow (as in (19))

    (2̲ 3) (2̲ 2̲) (2̲ 3)   Medium

    (2̲ 2̲) (2̲ 2̲) (2̲ 3)   Fast

At medium speed, T3S can apply to the last two feet in one step. At fast
speed, T3S can apply to the entire sentence in one step.

Since feet are built from syntactic trees, the main challenge to the stress-
insensitive foot analysis is to explain why expressions with the same tree
structure and the same underlying tones can have different tone patterns.
Consider the pair in (23) first.

(23)   (a) 3-3-3-3 → 2-3-2-3 (*?3-2-2-3)   (b) 3-3-3-3 → 3-2-2-3 (*?2-3-2-3)

    [gou [[bi   ma] xiao]]   [gou [[hen   hao] yang]]
    dog   than horse small   dog   very good raise
    'Dogs are smaller than horses.'   'Dogs are very easy to raise.'

The neutral pattern for (23a) is 2-3-2-3 but that for (23b) is 3-2-2-3. The
analysis given so far is shown in (24).

(24)   [3 [[3 3] 3]]

    n.a.   Emphasis/polysyllables/compounds

    3 (3 3) 3   Foot at lowest branches

    n.a.   Left-to-right footing

    3 ((3 3) 3)   Joining

    (3 ((3 3) 3))   Joining

    (3 ((2̲ 3) 3))   T3S cycle 1

(3 ((2 2) 3))   T3S cycle 2
(3 ((2 2) 3))   T3S cycle 3 (no effect)

The rules for emphasis, polysyllabic words, and compounds have no effect. Next, the innermost two syllables form a foot; then the free syllables are joined into the foot; then T3S applies cyclically, giving 3-2-2-3, which is the pattern for (23*b*). To get (23*a*), Shih suggests that certain words, such as *bi* 'than' in (23*a*), are clitics, which attach to a preceding word. The cliticization process alters the syntactic tree. The analysis of (23*a*) is shown in (25), which gives the correct output.

(25)   [3 [[3 3] 3]]

    [[[3 3] 3] 3]   Cliticization
    n.a.   Emphasis/polysyllables/compounds
    (3 3) 3 3   Foot at lowest branches
    (3 3)(3 3)   Left-to-right footing
    (2 3)(2 3)   T3S

Next consider the pair in (26), which also have the same tree structure and underlying tones.

(26)   (*a*) 3-3-3-3 → 2-2-2-3 (*2-3-2-3)   (*b*) 3-3-3-3 → 2-3-2-3

    [[[zhan-lan] guan] li]   [[[nei   zhong] jiu] hao]
     show-see hall inside   which kind   wine good
    'inside of exhibition hall'   'Which kind of wine is good?'

The neutral pattern for (26*a*) is 2-2-2-3 but that for (26*b*) is 2-3-2-3. The difference is that (26*a*) contains a compound [zhan-lan guan] 'exhibition hall' but (26*b*) does not. The analysis is shown in (27).

(27)   (26*a*)   (26*b*)

    [[[3 3] 3] 3]   [[[3 3] 3] 3]

    n.a.   n.a.   Emphasis/polysyllables
    ((3 3) 3) 3   n.a.   Compound
    n.a.   (3 3) 3 3   Foot at lowest branches
    n.a.   (3 3)(3 3)   Left-to-right footing
    (((3 3) 3) 3)   n.a.   Joining
    (((2 3) 3) 3)   (2 3)(2 3)   T3S cycle 1
    (((2 2) 3) 3)   n.a.   T3S cycle 2
    (((2 2) 2) 3)   n.a.   T3S cycle 3

Because compounds undergo different foot-formations rules, the resulting foot structures are different, so are the results of T3S. It is worth noting that the clitic solution is insufficient to give (27). The reason is that clitics are usually grammatical words (tense and aspect particles, prepositions, pronouns, classifiers, etc.), but *lan* 'see' and *guan* 'hall' are lexical words (a verb and a noun), which cannot be considered clitics. Also, if we consider *li* 'inside' to be a clitic, we would get [[3 3][3 3]], which gives two feet (3 3)(3 3), which gives the incorrect (2 3)(2 3).

So far we have shown that T3S applies after all steps of foot formation are completed. It is also possible to apply T3S after each step. The result would be the same. Consider the analysis of 'inside of exhibition hall' again, shown in (28).

(28) [[[zhan3-lan3] guan3] li3] 'inside of exhibition hall'

(3 3) 3 3	Compound foot for *zhan-lan*
(2 3) 3 3	T3S
(2 3 3) 3	Compound foot for *zhan-lan guan* (joining)
(2 2 3) 3	T3S
(2 2 3 3)	Final foot (joining)
(2 2 2 3)	T3S

In this interpretation, there is no need to keep layered foot boundaries. As a further example, consider the difference in (7*a*), repeated in (29).

(29) (*a*) 3 3 3 1 → 2 3 3 1   (*b*) 3 3 3 1 → 3 2 3 1 (*2 3 3 1)

    [wo [xiang [mai shu]]]   [xiao [zhi   [lao-ying]]]
    I   want   buy book   small paper old-eagle
    'I want to buy a book.'   'small paper eagle.'

The expressions have the same underlying tones and the same bracketing structures but different surface tones. The reason again is that (29*b*) is a compound but (29*a*) contains no compound. The analysis is shown in (30).

(30) (29*a*)   (29*b*)
      [3 [3 [3 1]]]   [3 [3 [3 1]]]

n.a.	n.a.	Emphasis/polysyllables
n.a.	(3 (3 (3 1)))	Compound foot
3 3 (3 1)	n.a.	Foot at lowest branches
(3 3)(3 1)	n.s.	Left-to-right foot
(2 3)(3 1)	(3 (2 (3 1)))	T3S

The phrasal 'I want to buy a book' has two feet, which gives 2-3-3-1. The two T3s can both surface because T3S is optional across feet (2-2-3-1 is also possible, because T3S can optionally apply across the two feet). In the compound 'small paper eagle', there is only one foot, which surfaces as 3-2-3-1.

Let us now consider the effect of emphasis. Although Shih did not discuss it, the emphatic boundary cannot create a monosyllabic foot. Consider the case in (31), analysed in (32), where '!' marks the emphatic boundary.

(31)　[mai3 [HAO3 shu1]] → 2-3-1 (*3-3-1)

　　　buy GOOD book
　　　'buy GOOD books'

(32)　(a)　[3 [3 1]]　　　(b)　[3 [3 1]]

3 !(3 1)	3 !(3 1)	Emphasis
(3)!(3 1)	(3 !(3 1))	Final foot
*(3)!(3 1)	(2 !(3 1))	T3S

In (32a) the emphatic boundary creates a monosyllabic foot; since for Shih T3S is not required between two feet, 3-3-1 is expected to be acceptable. In (32b) there is no monosyllabic foot, and the expected output is 2-3-1. The pattern in (31) shows that only (32b) is correct. Similarly, the emphatic syllable cannot form a foot by itself, but must form a foot with the following syllable; for example, [!3 (3 3)] cannot become (!3)(3 3) but must be (!3 (3 3)). Now consider the analysis of (9), shown in (33).

(33)　'want to buy stocks'　　　'want to BUY stocks'
　　　[xiang3 [mai3 gu3-piao4]]　　[xiang3 [MAI3 gu3-piao4]]

n.a.	3 (!3 3 4)	Emphasis
3 3 (3 4)	3 (!3 (3 4))	Compound
(3 3)(3 4)	n.a.	Left-to-right foot
n.a.	(3 (!3 (3 4)))	Joining
(2 3)(3 4)	(3 (!2 (3 4)))	T3S

The emphatic expression forms just one foot. In contrast, the non-emphatic expression forms two feet. The difference in foot structure gives rise to different tone patterns.

To summarize, the analysis with stress-insensitive feet is more sophisticated than the tree-only analysis, but it still has several problems. It essentially attributes alternative patterns to speed of speech. However, as Shih (1997: 85) points out, for a given expression, one could easily use all the variants with the same speech rate. Also, it must assume clitics and the 'feet', or what Chen (2000) calls minimal rhythmic units, are inconsistent with metrical feet, as seen earlier. Finally, it is unclear why emphasis should create a foot boundary.

11.5. THE PRESENT ANALYSIS

The present analysis also assumes foot structure, except that the feet are metrical feet. Each metrical foot starts with a stressed syllable followed by an unstressed one. Stress is determined by the Information-Stress Principle, which covers both Nonhead Stress and emphatic stress (Chapter 6). Consider the example in (34) (0 is a toneless syllable).

(34)   Stress-insensitive feet   Metrical feet

x		x		x		x		Stress
[[Lao Li][you [jie-jie]]				[[Lao Li][you [jie-jie]]				Syntax
(3	3) (3	(	0))	(3	3)	3	(3	0)	Feet
(2	3) (2	(3	0))	(2	3)	2	(3	0)	T3S
'Old Li has sister.'				'Old Li has sister.'				

Both analyses agree on where the stressed syllables are. In the previous analysis, where stress is irrelevant (except for emphatic stress), there are two feet, which are (SW) and (WSW). In the present analysis, (WSW) is not a good metrical foot, and so both feet are (SW). Now, what is interesting is that the verb *you* must undergo T3S. In the previous analysis, it is because *you* and *jie* are in the same foot, in which T3S is obligatory. In the present analysis, *you* and *jie* are not in the same foot. How, then, can we ensure that T3S applies over *you* and *jie*? The simplest solution is to say that T3S can apply beyond the metrical foot. However, while T3S is obligatory over *you* and *jie*, it is optional over *Li* and *you*. This can be seen in a similar sentence, shown in (35).

(35)   Stress-insensitive feet   Metrical feet

x		x		x		x		Stress
[[Lao Li][you [ma-ma]]				[[Lao Li][you [ma-ma]]				Syntax
(3	3) (3	(1	0))	(3	3)	3	(1	0)	Feet
(2	3) (3	(1	0))	(2	3)	3	(1	0)	T3S
'Old Li has a mom.'				'Old Li has a mom.'				

In (35), *Li* and *you* can remain T3, which means that T3S need not apply to them. In the previous analysis, it is because *Li* and *you* are in different feet, and T3S is optional across feet. In the present analysis, *you* is a free syllable between two feet. Why, then, is T3S obligatory over *you* and the following syllable but not over *you* and the preceding syllable?

The answer seems to be that *you* is syntactically closer to the following syllable. In other words, T3S seems to be obligatory over two syllables that are syntactically adjacent. In addition, the syllables in a foot are also adjacent. Therefore, I propose the condition for T3S in (36).

(36)   *Condition on T3S*
       T3S is obligatory over two syllables that are adjacent.
       T3S is optional over two syllables that are not adjacent.
       Definition
       Two syllables are adjacent if they belong to the same immediate syntactic constituent and they do not belong to separated full feet.
       (A full foot contains two (or more) syllables.)

The effect of (36) is illustrated in (37), where parentheses indicate foot boundaries, brackets indicate syntactic boundaries, A, B, C, and D are syllables, and Ø is an empty beat.

(37)   (. . . A)B]   AB adjacent
       [A(B. . .)   AB adjacent
       (. . . A)B](CD)   AB adjacent; BC not adjacent
       (. . . A)B][C(D. . .)   AB and CD adjacent; BC not adjacent
       (AB)(CD)   BC not adjacent
       (AB)(CØ)   BC adjacent

In (. . . A)B] and [A(B. . .), AB are syntactically adjacent. In (. . . A)B](CD), BC are not adjacent, because B is adjacent to A and C is adjacent to D. Similarly, in (. . . A)B][C(D. . .), BC are not syntactically adjacent. In (AB)(CD), BC are not adjacent because they belong to separate full feet. However, in (AB)(CØ), BC are adjacent because (CØ) is not a full foot. An example of (AB)(CØ) is shown in (38).

(38)   Stress-insensitive feet   Metrical feet
           x   x   x   x   Stress
       [sheng-chan jiu]   [sheng-chan jiu]   Syntax
       ((1   3)   3)   (1   3)   (3 Ø)   Feet
       ((1   2)   3)   (1   2)   (3 Ø)   T3S
       'produce wine'   'produce wine'

Both analyses agree that the stress pattern is SWS. In the previous analysis, the expression forms one foot; in the present analysis, each stress must start a new foot. The object can form a binary foot with an empty beat, which is available in phrase-final position. Now the point of interest is that T3S must apply to *chan* and *jiu*. In the previous analysis, it is because *chan* and *jiu* are in the same foot, and T3S is obligatory within a foot. In the present analysis, it is because *jiu* is not in a disyllabic foot, and so it is still adjacent to *chan*; therefore T3S is obligatory over *chan* and *jiu*.

Having discussed the condition on T3S, let us consider the rest of the analysis. I propose the rules in (39).

(39) (*a*) Build disyllabic feet left-to-right for polysyllabic words.
      (*b*) Build feet cyclically based on phrasal stress.
      (*c*) Build disyllabic feet left-to-right for free words.
      (*d*) T3S starts from each foot and then cyclically.
      (*e*) In a T3S domain, T3 must change before T3, but can optionally change before T2 that came from T3.

The rule (39*e*) is similar to what is proposed by Duanmu (1989) and J. Shen (1994), which was discussed in section 11.3. The assignment of phrasal stress follows the Information-Stress Principle, which covers both emphatic stress and Nonhead Stress (Chapter 6); the result mostly agrees with previous judgement (Chao 1968; Hoa 1983). Free words refer to those that do not yet have metrical structure; they in fact only include monosyllables, since polysyllabic words and compounds would already have been assigned stress.

Consider first a flat structure shown in (40). Whether such a string of digits is considered a polysyllabic word or a string of unstructured words, the analysis is the same.

(40) 'five-five-five-five'
      wu-wu-wu-wu

      (3   3) (3   3)   Feet
      (2   3) (2   3)   T3S

Next, consider disyllabic expressions. According to Hoa (1983), disyllabic words and compounds can be either SW or WS. In addition, all analyses agree that in a verb–object phrase the object has more stress. However, whether stress pattern is SW or WS, the T3S result is the same. This is shown in (41), where *kour* has the [ɚ] suffix (see Chapter 9).

(41) 'miss'   'couple'   'buy wine'
      little sister   two mouth   buy wine

      x   x   x
      [xiao jie]   liang kour   [mai jiu]
      (3   3)   3 (3 Ø)   3 (3 Ø)   Foot
      (2   3)   2 (3 Ø)   2 (3 Ø)   T3S

Turning to trisyllabic expressions, there are three cases, SWS, WSW, and SWW. The first case is shown in (42), where the stress judgement is based on Chao (1968) and Hoa (1983). I also underlined the syllables that undergo T3S in each step.

(42) 'exhibition hall'   'little couple'
     show-see hall   little two-mouth

x x	x x	
[zhan-lan guan]	[xiao liang-kou]	
(3 3) (3 Ø)	(3 3) (3 Ø)	Foot
(2 3) (3 Ø)	(2 3) (3 Ø)	T3S cycle 1
(2 2) (3 Ø)	(2 2) (3 Ø)	T3S cycle 2

The two expressions undergo two cycles of T3S. On the first cycle each foot is a T3S domain, although T3S is not applicable to the foot (3 Ø). After that, T3S can apply one more time, because (3 Ø) is not a full foot. Next consider WSW, shown in (43), where, like *xiao-jie* 'miss', *lao-hu* 'tiger' also has initial stress.

(43) 'there are tigers'   'I am very well'
     have old-tiger   I very well

x	x	
[you lao-hu]	[wo [hen hao]]	
3 (3 3)	3 (3 3)	Foot
3 (2 3)	3 (2 3)	T3S cycle 1
V (2 3)	V (2 3)	T3S cycle 2

Using the notation of J. Shen (1994), V indicates an optional change when a T3 occurs before a T2 that came from T3 (see section 11.3). Thus, V-2-3 means either 2-2-3 or 3-2-3. Now consider SWW, shown in (44).

(44) 'paper tiger'
     paper old-tiger

x x	
[zhi lao-hu]	
3 (3 3)	Foot cycle 1
3 (2 3)	T3S cycle 1
(3 2 3)	Foot cycle 2
(V 2 3)	T3S cycle 2

This compound undergoes two cycles of foot formation and T3S. The first cycle looks at *lao-hu* 'tiger', which has initial stress. On the second cycle, *zhi* is assigned compound stress, which triggers the deletion of the stress on *lao*. The result is V-2-3, that is, 2-2-3 or 3-2-3.

Longer expressions can yield more alternative patterns. This is illustrated in (45).

(45) 'small paper tiger'
     small paper old-tiger

```
x    x    x
[xiao [zhi [lao-hu]]]
 3    3   (3   3)        Foot cycle 1
 3    3   (2   3)        T3S cycle 1
 3   (3   2    3)        Foot cycle 2
 3   (V   2    3)        T3S cycle 2
(3    V   2    3)        Foot cycle 3
(V    V   2    3)        T3S cycle 3
```

The compound undergoes three cycles of foot formation, as discussed above. On the first cycle of T3S, *lao* must change to T2. On the second cycle, the change of *zhi* is optional, indicated by V. On the third cycle, the change of *xiao* is conditional on the change of *zhi*. The result is V-V-2-3, which can be 2-3-2-3, 3-2-2-3, or 2-2-2-3, as discussed in section 11.3. It is worth noting that in the analysis of Shih (1997) and Chen (2000), alternative patterns are attributed to speed of speech. In the present analysis, there is no need to link alternative patterns to speed of speech. Instead, the alternative patterns come from the fact that a T3 can, but need not, change to T2 before a T2 that came from T3.

It is interesting to compare (45) with (46). They are both right-branching but have different T3S patterns. The reason is that they have different foot structures.

(46)   'want to buy good wine'
       want buy good wine

```
       <x>          x
       [xiang [mai [hao jiu]]]
        3     3   (3   3)      Foot cycle 1 (based on phrasal stress)
        3     3   (2   3)      T3S cycle 1
       (3     3)  (2   3)      Foot cycle 2 (for free words)
       (2     3)  (2   3)      T3S cycle 2
```

In (46), only *hao* received phrasal stress. This leaves two free words *xiang* and *mai*, which can form another foot, which introduced a new stress, shown as <x>. This gives 2-3-2-3 as the default pattern. The pattern 3-2-2-3, which is possible for (45), is not used for (46).

Let us now move on to why left-branching structures lack alternative patterns, shown in (47).

(47)   'inside of exhibition hall'
       show-see hall inside

```
            x
       [[[zhan-lan] guan] li]
```

(3	3)	3	3	Foot (based on phrasal stress)
(2	3)	3	3	T3S cycle 1
(2	2)	3	3	T3S cycle 2
(2	2)	2	3	T3S cycle 3

In this expression only *zhan* has phrasal stress, which leaves the last two syllables free. However, the last two syllables do not form another foot, because they are part of a compound (at least *guan* is, if *li* is a postposition) and not free words. After three cycles of T3S, we get the only output 2-2-2-3.

Another example to consider is (48), in which a 3-3 sequence need not undergo T3S.

(48) 'Old Li buys books.'
      Old Li buy book

    x   x
[[Lao Li] [mai shu]]

(3	3)	3	(1 Ø)	Foot (based on phrasal stress)
(2	3)	3	(1 Ø)	T3S cycle 1 (no effect for 1-Ø)
(2	3)	3	(1 Ø)	T3S cycle 2 (no effect)

Two of the syllables get phrasal stress, which create two feet. The first undergoes T3S and gives 2-3. For the second foot, T3S is not applicable. T3S then checks *mai shu* but produces no change either. This still leaves a 3-3 sequence over *Li mai,* but T3S is not required here because *mai* is not syntactically adjacent to *Li*.

Now consider another pair of expressions that have the same tree structure and input tones but different tone patterns, shown in (49) and (50).

(49) 'Dogs are smaller than horses'
      dog than horse small

    x   x
[gou [[bi ma] xiao]]

(3	3)(3	3)	Foot (based on phrasal stress)
(2	3)(2	3)	T3S

(50) 'Dogs are very easy to raise'
      dog very easy raise

    x   x
[gou [[hen hao] yang]]

(3 Ø)	(3	3)	3	Foot (based on phrasal stress)
(3 Ø)	(2	3)	3	T3S cycle 1
(3 Ø)	(2	2)	3	T3S cycle 2
(V Ø)	(2	2)	3	T3S cycle 3

In (49), *ma* is the nonhead of [*bi ma*], so it has stress. Next, [*bi ma*] is the nonhead of [[*bi ma*] *xiao*], so it should have stress, which is already true. Finally, the subject is not the head of a sentence, so it also has stress. The two stresses create two disyllabic feet, which gives 2-3-2-3. In (50), *hen* is the nonhead of [*hen hao*], so it has stress. [*hen hao*] is the nonhead of [[*hen hao*] *yang*], so it should have stress, which is already true. Finally, the subject also has stress. Now the subject is monosyllabic, but it is before a major phrase boundary, and so an empty beat is available. Thus, there are two feet. After three cycles of T3S, the result is V-2-2-3.

Finally, consider why emphasis can affect T3S. In the present analysis, the reason is straightforward: emphasis is stress, which affects foot structure, which in turn affects T3S. The examples in (9) are analysed in (51) and (52).

(51) 'want to buy stocks'
      want buy stock

      <x>   x
      [xiang [mai gu-piao]]
      3   3 (3   4)   Foot cycle 1 (based on phrasal stress)
      3   3 (3   4)   T3S cycle 1 (no effect)
      (3   3) (3   4)   Foot cycle 2 (for free words)
      (2   3) (3   4)   T3S cycle 2

(52) 'want to BUY stocks'
      want BUY stock

             x   x
      [xiang [MAI gu-piao]]
      3   3 (3   4)   Foot cycle 1
      3   3 (3   4)   T3S cycle 1 (no effect)
      3   (3 3   4)   Foot cycle 2
      3   (2 3   4)   T3S cycle 2
      V   (2 3   4)   T3S cycle 3

In (51), the disyllabic object forms a foot. In [*mai gu-piao*], *gu-piao* should have more stress, which is already true. In [*xiang* [*mai gu-piao*]], [*mai gu-piao*] should have more stress, which is also already true. Now the first two words are free, so they can form another foot, and after T3S the result is 2-3-3-4. In (52), *gu-piao* forms a foot on the first cycle. Emphasis then puts stress on *mai*, and because it is monosyllabic, the stress on *gu* should be deleted (assuming that emphatic stress is stronger than other stress). The result is one foot, and cyclic T3S gives V-2-3-4. It is also possible that *mai* forms a foot with an empty beat since it is at a major syntactic boundary; this is shown in (53).

(53) 'want to BUY stocks'
      want BUY stock

```
              x    x
     [xiang [MAI  gu-piao]]
       3    (3 Ø) (3   4)        Feet
       3    (3 Ø) (3   4)        T3S cycle 1 (no effect)
       3    (2 Ø) (3   4)        T3S cycle 2
       V    (2 Ø) (3   4)        T3S cycle 3
```

On the first T3S cycle, there is no change. On the second cycle, *MAI* is not a full foot, so T3S applies again and changes it to T2. On the third cycle we get V-2-3-4, which is the same as that in (52).

We have seen that although both the stress-insensitive foot analysis and the present one build feet, they offer different foot structures in some expressions. We now ask which analysis offers better foot structures. There are three arguments for the present analysis: (1) the present foot structures are more consistent with independent stress judgements, such as those given by Chao (1968) and Hoa (1983); (2) the present foot structures are consistent with those in the analysis of the word-length problem (Chapter 7) and the word-order problem (Chapter 8); (3) the present foot structures are consistent with the analysis of tone sandhi in some other Chinese dialects, such as Nantong (Ao 1993) and Shanghai (Duanmu 1999*a*), where foot boundaries are clearly marked by tonal domains. For example, take the expression in (54) (# indicates a foot boundary).

(54) [[Lao Li] [mai jiu]] 'Old Li buys wine.'

       Lao Li # mai jiu   Chen (2000), Shih (1997)
       Lao Li # mai # jiu   Present analysis
       Lao Li # mai # jiu   Shanghai and Nantong

The stress-insensitive foot analysis predicts that the last two syllables form a foot, but the present analysis predicts that they do not. The data in Shanghai and Nantong support the present analysis.

11.6. SUMMARY

I have presented the facts of T3S and discussed three analyses: the tree-only analysis, the stress-insensitive foot analysis, and my own analysis, which is based on metrical feet. The tree-only analysis can account for some alternative patterns but cannot explain why expressions of the same tree structure and input tones can have different output patterns. In addition, it cannot explain why emphasis can affect T3S. The stress-insensitive foot analysis can account for a lot more facts, but it still has several problems: it attributes alternative patterns to speed of speech, which is a questionable claim (see Shih 1997: 85); it must assume clitics; its feet are incompatible with regular metrical feet; and it is unclear why emphasis should create a foot boundary.

My analysis is based on metrical feet that are determined by stress, which in turn is determined by the Information-Stress Principle (Chapter 6), which governs both Nonhead Stress and emphatic stress. T3S then applies cyclically from each foot. The present analysis has several merits. First, it need not assume clitics. Second, it need not link alternative patterns to different tempos of speech. Third, it explains why T3S is sensitive to emphasis: since emphasis is stress, it can affect foot boundaries, which in turn affects T3S. Fourth, the present analysis assumes regular foot structures. Finally, the foot structures are independently supported by evidence from other Chinese dialects.

12

Rhythm in Poetry

12.1. WHAT IS RHYTHM IN POETRY?

In this chapter I use 'poem' to refer to a set of two or more lines that sound rhythmic to native speakers. As an example, consider the poem 'Returning Home' in (1), written by the Tang poet He Zhizhang (659–744). The word-for-word gloss is on the right and my translation is under the Chinese text.

(1) shao-xiao li jia lao-da hui   young leave home old return
     xiang yin wu gai bin-mao shuai   native accent no change hair fade
     er-tong xiang-jian bu xiang-shi   children see not recognize
     xiao wen ke cong he-chu lai   smile ask guest from where come

    'I left home young and return old
    My native accent unchanged, but my hair fading
    Children see me but do not recognize me
    They smile and ask, "Guest, where are you from?" '

The poem sounds rhythmic to modern native speakers (regardless of how it sounded in the past, although I assume it must have sounded good, too). The question is why. Several considerations quickly come to mind, given in (2), where A is an A-tone; B is a B-tone; R is a rhyming syllable; and X is any syllable.

(2) Line length: Each line has seven syllables.
    Rhyming: Even lines rhyme on the last syllable.
    Tonal pattern: Tones alternate in a specific way as follows:
                       XBXAXBX
                       XAXBXAR
                       XAXBXAX
                       XBXAXBR

The first two considerations need no elaboration. The tonal alternation is a special requirement for certain Tang poems, which is often discussed in the literature. In simple terms, lexical tones are divided into two types, A (called *Ping* 'level' in Chinese) and B (called *Ze* 'deflected' in Chinese). Some positions in a poem require A, some require B, and some can be either tone. The required pattern for the given poem is as given above, which the poem satisfies. To test which of the factors play a role, I changed the second and fourth lines (both are still grammatical), shown in (3), and the poem does not sound rhythmic any more.

(3) shao-xiao li jia # lao-da hui   young leave home # old return
     yin ru jiu # fa-mao quan shuai   accent as before # hair all fade
     er-tong xiang-jian # bu xiang-shi   children see # not recognize
     wen ke-ren # he-chu er-lai   ask guest # where come

     Length/Tone/Rhyming   Syntax?
     XBXAXBX   4-3
     XAXBXAR   3-4
     XAXBXAX   4-3
     XBXAXBR   3-4

The line length, tonal pattern, and rhyming are the same in (3) and (1). So none of them explains why (1) is rhythmic, or why (3) is not. It can be noted though that the lines have different locations of a major syntactic break, shown by #. In particular, the break splits the seven syllables into 4-3 for the first and third lines in (3) but 3-4 for the second and fourth lines. So perhaps the inconsistency of the syntactic break is the reason for the lack of rhythm in (3). But now consider (4), where I changed the first and third lines (both still being grammatical). The poem still does not sound rhythmic.

(4) *wo yuan li jia # lao zai hui*   I far leave home # old then return
     xiang yin wu gai # bin-mao shuai   native accent no change # hair fade
     tong xiang-jian hou # bu xiang-shi   children see after # not recognize
     xiao wen ke # cong he-chu lai   smile ask guest # from where come

     Length/Tone/Rhyming   Syntax?
     XBXAXBX   4-3
     XAXBXAR   4-3
     XAXBXAX   4-3
     XBXAXBR   3-4

There is no problem with line length, tonal pattern, or rhyming in (4). In addition, the changed lines (first and third) are both 4-3 with regard to major syntactic breaks, as the original first and third lines are. So syntax cannot explain why (4) is non-rhythmic after all. Indeed, the fourth line in (4) is the original one, yet its syntax is 3-4. This means that 3-4 can pair with 4-3 in a rhythmic poem, as in the original (1), and syntax cannot be a deciding factor. Therefore, we still do not understand why (1) is rhythmic and why (3) and (4) are not.

Modern verse presents the same problem. Consider the lines in (5), which sound rhythmic, and those in (6), which do not. The two pairs of lines differ only in one syllable in the second line, which is underlined.

(5) deng wo zheng-dao da qian shi   wait I make big money time
     mai liang qi-che # song-gei ni   buy a car # give you
     'Wait till the time I make big money
     I'll buy a car to give you.'

(6) deng wo zheng-dao da qian shi   wait I make big money time
     mai xin qi-che # song-gei ni   buy new car # give you

In modern poems, there is no requirement on tonal patterns. In addition, there is no difference in rhyming, line length, or major syntactic breaks between (5) and (6). Therefore, none of the factors explains why (5) is rhythmic but (6) is not.

A person with some knowledge of English poetry might suggest that we have overlooked an important factor, namely, stress. Should that not be the first thing to consider? Surprisingly, other than Duanmu (2004), no previous work on Chinese poetry has offered an account of rhythm in terms of stress. There is a good reason for the lack of discussion on stress in Chinese poetry. In English, poetic meter is indeed based on stress, but it is usually based on word stress. In addition, Kiparsky (1977) argues that monosyllables are not marked with word stress, so they can be used in any position. If so, most Chinese poems ought to be rhythmic because most Chinese words are monosyllables, but clearly the prediction is incorrect. It is worth noting, too, that stress judgement in Chinese can be hard to obtain, and confusion is not uncommon. For example, Chen (1979) suggests that the rhythm of Tang poems is (WS)(WS)..., where S is a strong position, W a weak position, and (WS) a foot. However, D. Liu (1927), a poet himself, suggests that the same poems are (SW)(SW)... instead. In summary, Chinese speakers have a good judgement on whether a poem is rhythmic or not, but the explanation for the judgement is far from obvious.

12.2. IS RHYTHM DETERMINED BY THE SYNTACTIC TREE?

L. Wang (1958) offers an extensive discussion of prosody in classic Chinese verse, but his main focus is on tonal requirements. D. Liu

(1927) and Schlepp (1980) propose that the rhythm in Chinese poems is (SW)(SW)..., but they offer no discussion on why some poems are rhythmic and some are not.

A more serious proposal is offered by Chen (1979, 1980). He argues that whereas English rhythm is based on stress, Chinese rhythm is based on tone and a match between the syntactic tree and the prosodic tree. The tonal requirement applies only to one style of classic poetry. The tree-matching requirement should apply to all poems. The idea of tree-matching is illustrated in (7) with a seven-syllable line.

(7)   Prosody–syntax match (Chen 1979)

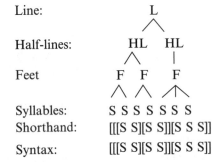

Line:	L
Half-lines:	HL HL
Feet	F F F
Syllables:	S S S S S S
Shorthand:	[[[S S][S S]][S S S]]
Syntax:	[[[S S][S S]][S S S]]

Chen assumes that the prosody of a line consists of a hierarchy of four categories which are organized in a tree or, equivalently, in layered brackets. A similar view has been expressed more recently by Golston (1998) and Golston and Riad (2005). Chen further proposes that, for a line to be rhythmic, its syntactic brackets should match the prosodic brackets.

To check whether the theory works, Chen (1979) examined 100 lines of Tang poems, which all sound rhythmic to modern speakers. The result is mixed. On the positive side, about 50 per cent of the lines show a perfect prosody–syntax match, which seems to support the claim that the perfect syntax is [[2 2] 3]. On the downside, Chen's analysis predicts that the other 50 per cent of the lines should sound marginal or non-rhythmic, but the prediction is not borne out.

To account for the problem, Chen suggests that the rhythm of a line need not be perfect. Instead, rhythm is gradient and measurable. In particular, a perfect line should show a perfect syntax–prosody match. The next best line should have just one pair of mismatched brackets. The third best line should have just two pairs of mismatched brackets. And so on. Chen shows that in his corpus it is indeed true that the more mismatches a line has, the less frequently it occurs. However, there is no evidence from speaker judgement that lines with mismatches are less rhythmic. In any case, the claim that 50 per cent of the lines in Tang poems are rhythmically defective seems highly unlikely, because Tang poems are considered to be among the best in Chinese literature, and most of them still sound perfectly rhythmic to modern speakers.

Perhaps Chen's corpus was too small. In order to check how his theory works for a larger corpus, I coded 231 poems by hand (Duanmu 2004), with a total of 1,460 lines, from the popular *Anthology of 300 Tang Poems*. 117 of the poems have five syllables per line, and 114 of the poems have seven syllables per line. The results do not seem to support Chen's theory. Consider the data in (8), from seven-syllable lines.

(8)	Pattern	Tree	Freq.	%	Mismatches
	1	[[2 2][1 2]]	215	32.0%	0
	2	[[2 2][2 1]]	119	17.7%	0
	3	[2 [1 [1 [2 1]]]]	63	9.4%	2
	4	[2 [2 [1 2]]]	47	7.0%	1
	5	[[1 [1 2]][1 2]]	43	6.4%	1
	6	[1 [1 [2 [1 2]]]]	26	3.9%	2
	18	[[[2 2] 1] 2]	2	0.3%	1
	19	[[[2 2] 2] 1]	2	0.3%	1
	26	[2 [[2 2] 1]]	2	0.3%	2

As in Chen's own corpus, only patterns 1 and 2 are perfect, which cover 50 per cent of the lines. In addition, pattern 3 has two mismatches, yet it is more frequent than patterns 4, 5, 18, and 19, which have only one mismatch. Moreover, although patterns 3 and 26 both have two mismatches, one occurs 63 times while the other just two.

In conclusion, there does not seem to be a direct relation between the frequency of a line type and the match (or mismatch) between its syntax and the proposed prosodic tree. In addition, there is no evidence that 50 per cent of the lines in Tang poems are rhythmically bad. Finally, there is no evidence that less frequent line types are rhythmically worse than more frequent ones.

12.3. STRESS PATTERN, TEMPLATE, AND THEIR MAPPING

In this section I offer a theory of poetic rhythm in terms of stress. I argue that the model for English can be applied to Chinese as well. I also argue that whereas word stress plays the major role in English poetry, it is phrasal stress that is the key to the understanding of rhythm in Chinese poetry.

Following Halle and Keyser (1971), most generative models on poetic meter assume three elements (Kiparsky 1975, 1977; Hayes 1989*b*; Golston 1998; Rice 2000; Fabb 2002; Golston and Riad 2005), which are given in (9).

(9) Template for a poem (e.g. SWSWSWS);
     stress pattern of a line;
     stress-template mapping.

The template is an ideal form for each type of poem; it is made of a string of S and W positions, where S is strong and W is weak. If we tap every other syllable, S positions are where taps can fall, and W positions are where taps cannot fall.

The stress pattern of a line is determined by rules for word stress and phrasal stress. For Chinese I will assume the rules discussed in Chapter 6.

According to Halle and Keyser (1971: 169), the most important mapping requirement between the stress pattern of a line and the template is given in (10) and (11). For ease of exposition, I have slightly modified the original wording.

(10) Each stress maximum in a line must fill an S position in the template.

(11) Stress maximum: A stressed syllable not next to a stressed syllable

Requirement (10) holds for stressed syllables only, and there is no corresponding requirement for unstressed syllables to fill just W positions. In other words, unstressed syllables are allowed to fill either S or W positions. It is also possible to omit (11) and simplify (10). In particular, if we assume that a foot must always be binary, there will be no adjacent stressed syllables, and every stressed syllable is a stress maximum. Therefore, we can state the requirement on stress-template mapping in (12).

(12) *Stress-template mapping*
     Each stressed syllable in a line must fill an S position in the template. Each W position in the template must be filled by an unstressed syllable.

In (13) I show a sample template and three sample lines to illustrate the stress-template mapping. I use X for a stressed syllable and x for an unstressed one. The syllable of interest in line 2 and 3 are underlined.

(13) Template: S   W   S   W   S
      Line 1:   X   x   X   x   X   Good
      Line 2:   X   x   <u>x</u>   x   X   Good (x can be in S)
      Line 3:   x   <u>X</u>   x   x   X   Bad (X in W)

Both line 1 and line 2 are good, but line 3 is bad because the second syllable is stressed yet it is in a W position.

Let us now consider the analysis of some poems we saw earlier. First, consider (1), analysed in (14). Based on tapping, I assume that the template of this poem is SWSWSWS.

(14) Template: S W S W S W S
      Line 1:   X x X x X x X
      Line 2:   X x X x X x X
      Line 3:   X x X x x x X
      Line 4:   X x X x X x X

shao-xiao li jia lao-da hui   young leave home old return
xiang yin wu gai bin-mao shuai   native accent no change hair fade
er-tong xiang-jian bu xiang-shi   children see not recognize
xiao wen ke cong he-chu lai   smile ask guest from where come

Let me go through the example in detail. Recall that a disyllabic unit can be xX in final position but Xx in non-final positions (Chapter 6). In line 1, 'young' and 'old' are disyllabic and non-final, and so their stress is Xx. In 'leave home', 'home' can be assigned phrasal stress if it is final, but here it is followed by a stressed syllable. Therefore, 'home' cannot carry the phrasal stress because it cannot form a binary foot. Instead, 'leave home' can be treated as a disyllabic compound (owing to Foot Shelter), whose stress is Xx. Alternatively, 'leave home' can remain as unstressed words xx, without phrasal stress, in which case they can still fill SW. Finally, 'return' is line-final and can form a foot with an empty beat, and so it is X (or XØ, strictly speaking).

In line 2, 'native accent', 'no change', and 'hair' are all disyllabic, and so they are all Xx. The final syllable 'fade' is X, because it can form a foot with an empty beat.

In line 3, 'children' and 'see' are disyllabic, so both are Xx. The word 'not' is probably a syntactic head (of a negative phrase), so it has no phrasal stress. Finally, the disyllabic 'recognize' is in final position and can have the stress pattern xX.

In line 4, if 'smile' is an adverbial, it has phrasal stress; otherwise it can be unstressed. In 'ask guest', 'guest' has phrasal stress and can form a foot with 'from', which has no stress. The object of 'from', 'where' has phrasal stress and can be Xx. Finally, 'come' is line-final and can form a foot with an empty beat, and so it is X. An examination of the stress patterns shows that all of them can map to the template.

Next consider the four lines I revised for the poem in (1). The stress pattern of the first line is shown in (15), against the template for (1). For

ease of reading I have underlined the offending position in the stress line,
namely, a stressed syllable X that is aligned with W. I have also underlined
syntactic nonheads that receive phrasal stress. The subject 'I' is a pronoun
and has no phrasal stress even though it is a syntactic nonhead.

(15)   Template: S   W   S   W   S   W   S
       Stress: x $\underline{X}$ x   x   X   x   X

       wo yuan li jia lao zai hui
       I far leave home old then return
       'I left home far behind and return in old age'

The words 'home' and 'old' are both syntactic nonheads, but they cannot
both have phrasal stress because 'home' cannot form a binary foot, unless
a pause is introduced after 'home'. Thus, only 'old' has phrasal stress. The
line is bad because there is an offending syllable 'far', which is an adverbial and has phrasal stress, but it is in W.

   Let us turn now to the second line I revised for the poem in (1). The
stress pattern is shown in (16), against the template for (1).

(16)   Template: S   W   S   W   S   W   S
       Stress: X   x   x $\underline{X}$ x   x   X

       yin ru jiu fa-mao quan shuai
       accent as before hair all fade
       'My accent is as before, but my hair has all faded.'

This line also has an offending word 'hair', which has the stress pattern
Xx, yet it fills WS, which violates stress-template mapping. We also note
that 'before' and 'hair' are adjacent and cannot both carry phrasal stress,
because 'before' cannot form a binary foot, unless a pause is introduced
after it. Indeed, even if the line is not used in a poem, it sounds bad unless
there is a pause after 'before'. Finally, in 'all fade', 'all' is an adverbial
and can have phrasal stress. If it does, it creates another violation of stress-
template mapping, because it is in W. Alternatively, 'all fade' can be
treated as a disyllabic word, which can be xX in a pre-pause position.

   The third line I revised for the poem in (1) is shown in (17).

(17)   Tong xiang-jian hou bu xiang-shi.
       children see after not recognize
       'After the children see me, they do not recognize me.'

This line is phonologically bad even if it is not used in a poem. The
problem is in the first two words. The verb 'see' is disyllabic and has
the word stress pattern Xx. The subject 'children' is a syntactic nonhead

and has phrasal stress, but because the next syllable is stressed, 'children' cannot carry phrasal stress, because it cannot form a binary foot, unless a pause is introduced after it. In fact, because 'children' has a disyllabic pseudo-compound *er-tong*, the monosyllabic *tong* should be avoided in this environment (Chapter 7).

The analysis of the fourth line is shown in (18), against the template for (1).

(18) Template: S   W   S   W   S   W   S
      Stress: x   X̲   x   X̲   x   x   X

      wen k̲e̲-r̲e̲n̲ h̲e̲-c̲h̲u̲ er-lai
      ask guest where come
      'They ask the guest, "Where are you from?" '

The two syntactic nonheads 'guest' and 'where' both have phrasal stress and each can form a foot. This creates two stressed syllables in W positions, which violates stress-template mapping.

We now return to the lines in (19), which are rhythmic, and the analysis shows the same. The syntactic nonheads are underlined.

(19) Template: S   W   S   W   S   W   S
      Line 1:   x   x   X   x   X   x   X
      Line 2:   x   x   X   x   X   x   X

      deng wo zheng-dao d̲a̲ qian shi   wait I make b̲i̲g̲ money time
      mai liang q̲i̲-c̲h̲e̲ song-gei ni   buy a c̲a̲r̲ give you
      'Wait till I make big money.
      I'll buy a car for you.'

In line 1, the pronoun 'I' has no phrasal stress. In the compound 'big money', 'big' has phrasal stress. The disyllabic 'make' is also a foot and has word stress on the first syllable. Finally, 'time' has stress because it can form a foot with an empty beat. In line 2, 'car' is the syntactic nonhead of the classifier phrase, whose head is 'liang', and 'you' can form a foot with the empty beat. Thus, both lines match the given template. Now consider the lines in (20), which do not sound rhythmic. They differ from those in (19) only in the second syllable of line 2.

(20) Template: S   W   S   W   S   W   S
      Line 1:   x   x   X   x   X   x   X
      Line 2:   x   X̲   x   x   X   x   X

      deng wo zheng-dao d̲a̲ qian shi   wait I make b̲i̲g̲ money time
      mai x̲i̲n̲ qi-che song-gei ni   buy n̲e̲w̲ car give you

In line 2, 'new' has phrasal stress. If it overrides the word stress in 'car', which is what happens in actual pronunciation, then we have a violation of stress-template mapping, because 'new' is stressed but in W.

I have shown how stress accounts for the rhythmic patterns in several examples. It can be shown, too, that under the same analysis, over 99 per cent of the 1,460 lines (from 231 Tang poems) in the corpus of Duanmu (2004) are rhythmic. The result agrees well with the fact that most of the poems sound perfectly rhythmic to modern speakers.

12.4. IS IT EASIER TO CREATE POEMS IN CHINESE?

The analysis that over 99 per cent of the lines in Tang poems are perfectly rhythmic may seem unbelievably optimistic from the viewpoint of the English verse tradition, in which there is a general agreement that, apart from nursery rhymes perhaps, verse lines are often imperfect. For example, Golston (1998) argues that all the rules proposed by Halle and Keyser (1971) for the stress-template mapping are violated in Shakespeare's poems. In addition, many native English speakers find it difficult to judge the rhythm of English verse (thanks to Anthony Brasher and Michael Marlo for pointing this out to me), and many verse scholars doubt whether there is a clear distinction between rhythmic and non-rhythmic lines (Youmans 1989). Moreover, verse scholars can disagree on how to interpret a poet's meter (see Kiparsky 1989 for different interpretations of Hopkins's sprung rhythm).

In contrast, it is quite easy to obtain native judgement on whether a Chinese poem is rhythmic or not, be it classic or modern, and I am not aware of any serious dispute among Chinese scholars on such judgement.

It would be useful if an experiment is conducted on how much agreement English speakers have on the rhythm of various English poems, and how much agreement Chinese speakers have on the rhythm of various Chinese poems. For the limited evidence available, it seems that many English poems are not perfectly rhythmic while most Chinese poems are rhythmic. If this is the case, we must ask why. The answer, it seems to me, lies in the fact that English words have fixed length, whereas most Chinese words have flexible length (see 'the dual vocabulary' in Chapter 7). The absence of flexible word length creates several difficulties for making poems in English, shown in (21).

(21) Difficulties with fixed-length words in English.
   (a) Some words have initial stress, such as _Canada, Mexico,_ and _lion_, which do not fit templates that start with WS...
   (b) Some words have non-initial stress, such as _Chicago, America,_ and _tomorrow_, which do not fit templates that start with SW...
   (c) Some words contain XxxX, such as _fortification_ and _Mediterranean_, which do not fit templates that contain...SWSW...
   (d) Some words contain XxX, such as _revolution_ and _compensation_, which do not fit templates that contain...SWWSWW...

In contrast, the availability of flexible word length in Chinese offers various ways out of difficult situations, such as those in (22), where X is a stressed syllable and x an unstressed one.

(22) Uses of flexible word length in Chinese.
   (a) Word in W without phrasal stress: just fine.
   (b) Word in S without phrasal stress: just fine, because S does not require X; however, using a disyllabic word Xx can fill the S with X.
   (c) Word in W with phrasal stress: use a disyllabic form for the previous word, so that the current word is pushed to the next position, which is S.
   (d) Word in S with phrasal stress: just fine.

In summary, it seems to be a lot easier to make rhythmic poems in Chinese than in English. The difference can be attributed to the fact that most English words have fixed length but most Chinese words have flexible length.

It is also interesting to observe that the use of poems is more prevalent in Chinese than in English culture. For example, many texts in traditional Chinese schools used to be written in rhythmic lines; traditional civil service exams used to include poetry composition. Couplet matching and poem making used to be a popular entertainment activity in literary circles. Often at critical moments people were judged by their poetic skills, such as the selection of an heir to a religious sect, or whether someone with a capital offense should be pardoned. In modern Chinese society, the use of poems is just as widespread. For example, government documents and policies often contain or are summarized in rhythmic lines. Temples, tombs, gateways, parks, and other monuments are decorated with poems. Enter a Chinese family, and you will likely see poems in prominent positions. Indeed, a custom composed poem is a popular choice as a valued present. Finally, humorous or satirical poems are constantly produced and refined by the population, and their circulation is a favourite pastime among many Chinese people. All this seems conspicuously lacking in America—it could be a difference in culture or a difference in the flexibility of word length.

12.5. TEMPLATE TYPOLOGY

Every language probably has several types of template, or rhythmic pattern in poetry. In this section I review some template types in modern Chinese poems. All the examples are by anonymous authors and collected from open online sources. Sometimes a poem may appear in different versions, such as different words, different line length, or different number of lines. We will see an example below.

There is no poem in which each line has just one or two syllables. Also, there is no poem that has just one line. The reason seems to have to do with the nature of rhythm, which is stress alternation and repetition. A minimal stress alternation is a foot, a repetition of a foot is a line, and a repetition of a line or template is a poem. Therefore, I define the line and the poem in (23).

(23) *Definitions*

  A line is the repetition of a foot.
  A template is the rhythmic pattern of a line.
  A poem is the repetition of a template.

The definitions predict that there are poems with three syllables per line, which is true. Given the requirement that a foot must be binary, we also predict that there is only one possible template for three-syllable lines, which is (SW)(SØ). The prediction is borne out as far as I know.

For poems with four syllables per line, there are three possible templates, shown in (24), where I have included foot boundaries and the empty beat.

(24) Template types for four-syllable lines

  (SW)(SW)
  (SW)W(SØ)
  W(SW)(SØ)

An example of (SW)(SW) is shown in (25), where *le* is an aspectual particle. Since all the lines have the same stress pattern, only one stress line is shown.

(25) Template: (S W)(S W)
      Lines 1–4:   X x X x

       ji-gou he le   departments merge ASP
       dui-wu kan le   troops cut ASP
       bian-zhi jian le   size reduce ASP
       ren-xin san le   person-heart disperse ASP

'Departments were merged
Troops were cut
Size was reduced
People's loyalty dispersed.'

Each line starts with a disyllabic word, whose stress is Xx. The final particle is the head of an inflectional phrase or tense phrase, and the verb is its nonhead. Therefore it forms a foot with the verb with the stress Xx. Next consider (SW)W(SØ), exemplified in (26).

(26) Template: (S W) W (S Ø)
      Lines 1–4:   X   x   x   X   Ø

      da-dan de chi   fearless -ly eat
      xiao-xin de na   careful -ly take
      jin-shen de you   cautious -ly tour
      mi-mi de wan   secret -ly play

      'Fearlessly eat
      Carefully take
      Cautiously tour
      Secretly play'

Each line starts with a disyllabic word whose stress is Xx. The third syllable is probably the head of a functional phrase; in any case it has no stress. The final syllable is the nonhead of '-ly' and has phrasal stress, and it can form a foot with an empty beat.

Next consider the template W(SW)(SØ). I have not come across an example, but have made one up, shown in (27), which seems to be quite acceptable as far as rhythm is concerned.

(27) Template: W (S W) (S Ø)
      Lines 1–4:   x X   x   X   Ø

      dai Shanghai biao   'Wear Shanghai watch'
      qi Menggu ma   'Ride Mongolian horse'
      he Sichuan jiu   'Drink Sichuan liquor'
      chi Guangdong cai   'Eat Cantonese food'

In each line, the trisyllabic object has the stress pattern XxXØ. The verb is the syntactic head and has no phrasal stress.

Sometimes a poem can fit two templates. An example is shown in (28).

(28) Template: (S W) W (S Ø) (S W) (S W)
      Lines 1–4:   X   x   x   X   Ø   X   x   X   x

      dou shuo bu bian   all say no change
      you xia wen-jian   again issue document

gang-gang xue hui   just learn well
you shuo bu dui   again say not right

'You all say it won't change
Again you issue a new document
We have just understood it
Again you say the document is incorrect.'

In each line, the first two syllables are Xx, either because they are a disyl-labic word, or because the first syllable is an adverbial and has phrasal stress. In line 1 and 4, the last syllable is the syntactic nonhead of a 'nega-tion phrase', and in line 3 the last syllable is the syntactic nonhead of a verb-complement structure; so the last two syllables can be xX in these lines. In line 2 the last two syllables are a disyllabic word, which can be xX in final position. Thus, all the lines can be XxxXØ and map to (SW)W(SØ). Alternatively, the last two syllables can be treated as a disyl-labic word and take the stress pattern Xx, and so the lines can be XxXx and can map to (SW)(SW).

Let us now consider poems with five syllables per line. There are six possible templates, shown in (29).

(29)   Template types for five-syllable lines

        (SW)(SW)(SØ)
        (SW)(SW)W
        (SW)W(SW)
        W(SW)W(SØ)
        W(SW)(SW)
        (SW)WW(SØ)

An example of (SW)(SW)(SØ) is shown in (30).

(30)   Template: (S W) (S W) (S Ø)
        Lines 1–4:   X   x   X   x   X Ø

        chun-tian li-yu fei   spring carp fat
        xia xiang he liang bei   go-to country drink some cup
        qiu-tian pang-xie xian   autumn crab fresh
        xia xiang jie-jie chan   go-to country treat craving

        'In spring carps are fat
        Let's go to the countryside and have some drinks
        In autumn crabs are fresh
        Let's go to the countryside and treat our craving appetite.'

In line 1 and 3, each disyllabic word has the stress pattern Xx, and the final syllable can form a foot with an empty beat. In line 2, the first two

(16)   [[Lao3 Li3] [mai3 jiu3]] 'Old Li buys wine'
       [[2 3] [2 3]]   Cycle 1
       [[2 2] [2 3]]   Cycle 2 (optional)

The first cycle includes *Lao Li* and *mai jiu*, which both undergo T3S. On cycle 2, T3S looks at *Li* and *mai*. Since *mai* is now T2, T3S is optional (see (14*b*)). If it applies, we get 2-2-2-3, otherwise we get 2-3-2-3.

Like C. Cheng (1973), Shen's analysis cannot explain (7), where expressions of the same tree structure and input tones can have different output patterns. J. Shen is aware of some such examples and offers a meaning-based remedy, which does not provide much insight. Also, neither Cheng nor Shen discusses why T3S is sensitive to emphasis (see (9)).

11.4. THE STRESS-INSENSITIVE FOOT ANALYSIS

The stress-insensitive foot analysis has been developed in a series of works, notably Shih (1986, 1997) and Chen (2000). The analysis is summarized in (17).

(17)   (*a*) Place a foot boundary before a syllable with emphatic stress.
       (*b*) Build disyllabic feet left-to-right for polysyllabic words.
       (*c*) Build feet cyclically for compounds.
       (*d*) Build disyllabic feet at the lowest branches.
       (*e*) Build disyllabic feet left-to-right for other syllables.
       (*f*) Join free syllables to neighbouring feet.
       (*g*) T3S applies cyclically in a foot (and optionally across feet).
       (*h*) At higher speed, T3S can apply to a larger tree node in one step.

Although (17*a*) refers to stress, Shih (1997: 84) remarks that the foot in her analysis is otherwise simply a group of syllables and no claim is made about stress. Similarly, Chen (2000) says that the foot in his analysis is not a metrical foot, because the latter is based on stress, whereas the former is not. To see why their feet are not sensitive to stress, consider the examples in (18), where S is metrically strong and W is metrically weak.

(18)   (SW)   ma-ma   'mom'
       (WS)   bo-luo   'pineapple'
                     mai jiu   'buy wine'
       (SWS)   bo-lou kuai   'pineapple cube'
                     sheng-chan jiu   'produce wine'
       (WSW)   jiao ma-ma   'call mom'
       (WSWS)   chi bo-lou kuai 'eat pineapple cube'

syllables can be treated as a disyllabic word, which will be Xx. The verb 'drink' has no phrasal stress. The indefinite quantifier 'some' is unstressed, probably because it is the head of a determiner or quantifier phrase. The final syllable 'cup' has phrasal stress and can form a foot with an empty beat. In line 4, the first two syllables are the same as in line 2. The disyllabic verb 'treat' is Xx, and the object 'craving' has phrasal stress and forms a foot with an empty beat. Thus, all lines can map to the template.

Next, consider (SW)(SW)W. I have not come across an example, but it is easy to create one for this template. The one in (31) was made by me. The last two syllables are both aspect markers.

(31) Template: (S W) (S W) W
      Lines 1–3:   X   x   X   x   x

      xiao-shuo du guo le   novel read ASP ASP
      dian-ying kan guo le   movie see ASP ASP
      yin-yue ting guo le   music hear ASP ASP

      'I have read the novel
      I have seen the movie
      I have listened to the music.'

In all the lines, the first word is a disyllabic foot. The aspect markers are heads of some inflectional or tense phrases and the verb is their nonhead. Therefore, the verb has phrasal stress and the aspects do not, and all lines are XxXxx.

An example of (SW)W(SW) is shown in (32), where *de* means something like 'the one that is …'.

(32) Template: (S W) W (S W)
      Lines 1–4:   X   x   x   X   x

      ding de shi piao-zi   aim DE is money
      mou de shi fang-zi   seek DE is house
      bao de shi wei-zi   protect DE is position
      wei de shi hai-zi   serve DE is child

      'What is aimed at is money
      What is sought after is a house
      What is protected is one's position
      The person this is for is one's child.'

In all lines, *de* is the head of a nominal structure and the preceding verb is its nonhead, so the verb has phrasal stress and *de* does not. The verb 'is' is the head of a verb phrase and has no phrasal stress, and its object has the stress pattern Xx in the given cases, because the second syllable is a light syllable.

Next, consider W(SW)W(SØ). An example is shown in (33).

(33)   Template: W (S W) W   (S   Ø)
       Lines 1–4:   x   X   x   x   X   Ø

       pa xiaojie you bing   fear girl has disease
       pa qingren huai yun   fear lover get pregnant
       pa qunzhong xie xin   fear public write letter
       pa laopo zi jin   fear wife self end

       'They fear the girls (they meet) have sexual diseases
       They fear their lovers would get pregnant
       They fear the public would write complaint letters
       They fear their wives would commit suicide.'

The same pattern can be seen in the constructed example in (34). This is the same poem I used earlier, except that I added *de* between the last two words of each line, so that the nominal now means 'N's N', instead of a compound [N N].

(34)   Template: W (S W) W   (S   Ø)
       Lines 1–4:   x   X   x   x   X   Ø

       dai Shanghai de biao   'Wear Shanghai's watch'
       qi Menggu de ma   'Ride Mongolia's horse'
       he Sichuan de jiu   'Drink Sichuan's liquor'
       chi Guangdong de cai   'Eat Canton's food'

In all lines, the verb has no phrasal stress, nor does *de*, which serves as the head of a possessive phrase. The disyllabic noun is Xx and the final noun forms a foot with an empty beat.

The example in (35) shows W(SW)(SW)

(35)   Template: W (S W) (S   W)
       Lines 1–4:   x   X   x   X   x

       jian wen-ti bi yan   see problem close eye
       jian chao-piao hong yan   see money red eye
       jian xuan-ju sha yan   see election shock eye

       'Seeing problems the eyes are closed
       Seeing money the eyes are green
       Seeing election results the eyes are shocked.'

In each line the first verb has no phrasal stress, and the disyllabic noun is Xx. The last two syllables are VO, where phrasal stress should go to O.

However, since the lines are parallel, the verb has contrastive stress, and therefore the last two syllables are Xx.

Finally, consider (SW)WW(SØ). An example is shown in (36), where the line-final rhyme [-anr] is realized as [-aɚ].

(36) Template: (S W) W   W (S Ø)
      Lines 1–4:   X   x   x   x X Ø

huai dandan dang guanr	bad egg be official
men dandan shang banr	stupid egg go-to work
jing dandan bai tanr	smart egg start business
hun dandan tou qianr	aimless egg steal money

'Bad guys are officials
Stupid guys go to work
Smart guys start a business
Aimless guys steal money.'

One can easily construct more examples of (SW)WW(SØ). An example is shown in (37).

(37) Template: (S W) W   W (S Ø)
      Lines 1–2:   X   x   x   x X Ø

wan guo de ren duo	play ASP DE person many
ying guo de ren shao	win ASP DE person few

'Those who played are many
Those who won are few.'

As I discussed earlier, some poems fit two different templates. The same is true for poems with five syllables per line—an example is shown in (38), which is another version of the one we saw in (28). The version in (38) has an extra aspect marker at the end of each line, as well as a few different words (e.g. 'policy' for 'document')

(38) Template: (S W) W (S W)   (S W) (S W) W
      Lines 1–4:   X   x   x   X   x   X   x X   x   x

shuo hao bu bian le	say final no change ASP
you lai zheng-ce le	again come policy ASP
zheng-ce xue tou le	policy learn thorough ASP
you shuo bu gan le	again say not do ASP

'You say it is final that there won't be changes
Again you issue a new policy
We have learned the policy thoroughly
Again you say we won't implement it.'

The variation again comes from the optional stress pattern of a disyllabic unit (here the third and fourth syllables), which can be xX when it is final or before a light syllable, which gives (SW)W(SW), or Xx, which gives (SW)(SW)W.

As expected, longer lines have even more possible template patterns. For lack of space, I do not review them here.

12.6. APPROACHES TO TEMPLATE TYPOLOGY

A theory of metrical templates should explain which patterns are possible and which are not. In this section I discuss three proposals. The first is offered by Fabb (2002) and Fabb and Halle (2005). In this approach, a template (or metric structure) is built for a line by a set of rules; different templates are built by different sets of rules. The second approach is offered by Golston (1998) and Golston and Riad (2005), according to which templates are determined by a set of ranked constraints. For illustration, let us assume the metrical categories used in Chen, which are shown in (39), and the ranked constraints in (40), which are slightly modified from those proposed in Golston and Riad (2005).

(39)   Metrical categories: the syllable, the foot, the half-line, and the line.

(40)   Constraints on templates

Foot-Binarity: the foot must be binary.
Half-line-Binarity: the half-line must be binary.
Line-Binarity: the line must be binary.
Exhaustivity: every metrical category must be dominated by a higher category.
No-Lapse: Adjacent un-dominated categories are not allowed.

Ranking

Foot-Binarity, No-Lapse>>Half-line-Binarity, Line-Binarity, Exhaustivity

According to the given constraints, the ideal template would be made of eight syllables (or seven plus an empty beat), four feet, and two half-lines. On the other hand, all the templates we discussed above would be imperfect. In (41) I show the analysis of the perfect template, along with some imperfect ones. I use parentheses for foot boundaries, square brackets for half-line boundaries, curly brackets for line boundaries, and abbreviations for constraint names.

(41) Ranked constraints

	F-B	N-L	HL-B	L-B	Exh.
{[(SW)(SW)][(SW)(SW)]}					
{[(S)(SW)][(SW)(SW)]}	*				
{[(SW)(SW)][(SØ)]}			*		
{[(SW)][(SW)W]}			**		*
{[(SW)W][(SW)]}			**		*
{[W(SW)][W(SØ)]}			**		**
{[W(SW)(SW)]}				*	*
{[WW(SW)(SØ)]}		*		*	**

The analysis has three problems. First, it predicts that some real templates are imperfect, including all those we saw for four- and five-syllable poems. The prediction is purely theory-internal because there is no other evidence, such as speaker judgement. Secondly, since every constraint is in principle violable, there is no theoretical distinction between possible and impossible templates. And thirdly, it is hard to tell which of the imperfect forms are better (or invoke less serious violations) than others. The reason is that there is no pre-determined ranking of the constraints, and so every ranking offers a different prediction of which templates are better than others. A common answer to this problem is that we can look at statistical frequency and assume that more frequent templates are metrically better than less frequent ones (Halle and Keyser 1971; Kiparsky 1975, 1977; Chen 1979; Youmans 1989; Golston 1998). Then we can rank the constraints accordingly so that frequent templates have less serious violations than infrequent ones. However, it is possible that for non-phonological reasons some structures are inherently less common and may either occur rarely in a corpus or not at all. In other words, there is a flaw in the common belief that 'patterns found in the corpus are grammatical, while those absent from the corpus are ungrammatical', as Rice (2000: 330) puts it, where 'grammatical' means 'metrical'. The premise assumes that phonology is the only factor that affects frequency, that all phonologically good structures are equally common, and that any corpus will contain all phonologically good structures at equal frequencies. It is similar to saying that 'all grammatical sentences are equally frequent', 'less frequent sentences are less grammatical', and 'sentences absent from a corpus are ungrammatical'. The claim is obviously incorrect and inconsistent with a fundamental goal of generative linguistics, which is to account not only for existing structures but also for possible new structures (Chomsky 1957).

The third approach, which I argue for, assumes that there is a distinction between possible and impossible templates. In addition, all occurring templates are good; in other words, a template is either good or bad. The key in this analysis is to identify those constraints that are inviolable. I suggest that, of the constraints just discussed, only one is relevant, namely, Foot-Binarity (obviously, we also need a few other constraints not discussed here, such as for a stressed syllable to be heavy). In (42) I show some examples, where √ indicates an occurring template, X indicates a bad template, and a question mark indicates a non-occurring template that is theoretically possible.

(42)   Inviolable constraints only

		F-B
√	(SW)(SW)(SW)(SW)	
X	(S)(SW)(SW)(SW)	*
√	(SW)(SW)	
√	(SW)W(SØ)	
√	W(SW)(SØ)	
√	(SW)(SW)(SØ)	
√	(SW)(SW)W	
√	(SW)W(SW)	
√	W(SW)W(SØ)	
√	W(SW)(SW)	
√	(SW)WW(SØ)	
?	WW(SW)(SØ)	

Given the definition that a line has at least two feet, the analysis predicts that there is only one possible template for three-syllable lines (not shown), three possible templates for four-syllable lines, and at least six possible templates for five-syllable lines. A central property of my analysis is that, because there are fewer constraints, there are many ways to satisfy them, so that many templates are equally good. The last template in (42) is not found; it seems to violate the constraint No-Lapse. However, No-Lapse is violated by the pattern (SW)WW(SØ), which occurs anyway. In addition, No-Lapse is violated by such English words as *presidency*, which is (SW)WW. But without No-Lapse, how do we account for the lack of WW(SW)(SØ)? I suggest that not all zero-occurrences are due to metrical reasons. In particular, the absence of WW(SW)(SØ) is probably due to the fact that Chinese syntax is rarely head-initial, so an expression rarely starts with two functional words. Similarly, while (SW)WW(SØ) is found, it is not frequent, because it is uncommon to have three adjacent unstressed syllables in a sentence, such as a string of three function words, even in non-poetry. But it is possible to make up such poems that contain a string of three unstressed syllables. A example is shown in (43), made by myself.

(43) Template: W (S W) W W (S W)
       Lines 1–4:   x X   x   x   x   X   x

       you piao-zi de ren le le   have money DE person happy ASP
       you fang-zi de ren ji le   have house DE person anxious ASP
       you che-zi de ren duo le   have car DE person increase ASP
       you hai-zi de ren shao le   have child DE person decrease ASP

       'Those who have money are happy
       Those who have houses are anxious
       Those who have cars are increasing
       Those who have children are decreasing'

The first syllable is the head of a verb phrase and has no phrasal stress; the third syllable is unstressed because all the disyllabic nouns here are lexically Xx; the fourth and last syllables have no stress because they are both function words; the sixth syllable is stressed because it is the nonhead of an aspectual phrase; the fifth syllable has no stress because it is like a generic pronoun 'one who...', and because it is before a stressed syllable. Another reason for stress to fall on the second and sixth syllables only is that they have contrastive stress in the given lines, whereas other syllables do not.

   In summary, my analysis seems to be the simplest. It assumes fewer constraints (or rules), and correctly predicts possible and impossible patterns.

12.7. THE PROSODIC HIERARCHY

Chen (1979) proposes that the prosody of a poetic line is organized as a hierarchy of categories. Golston (1998) and Golston and Riad (2005) hold a similar view, although they have added a category, following the theory of prosodic phonology (Selkirk 1986; Nespor and Vogel 1986). A comparison of the categories is shown in (44), along with the ones assumed in the present study.

(44)	This book	Chen (1979)	Golston and Riad (2005)
		Line	Intonational phrase
		Half-line	Phonological phrase
	Syllabic foot	Foot	Prosodic word
	Syllable	Syllable	Moraic trochee
	Mora	Mora	

Like Golston and Riad (2005), I assume that Chinese counts moras and builds moraic feet for heavy syllables (Chapter 6). And like Chen (1979) I assume that Chinese builds syllabic feet (Chapter 6). There are two reasons why the Chinese syllabic feet are not prosodic words: they are based on stress assignment (Chapter 6), and prosodic words are difficult to define. According to Selkirk (1986) and Hayes (1989b), a prosodic word is a lexical word plus adjacent function words. However, polysyllabic words and compounds present a problem. According to Selkirk's definition, a polysyllabic word is one prosodic word, but in Chinese it can form two or more syllabic feet (Chapter 6). Similarly, if lexical words do not include compounds (Hanson and Kiparsky 1996: 291), prosodic words will be too small in Chinese: they are basically monosyllables, whereas syllabic feet are disyllabic. If lexical words include compounds, prosodic words will often be more than a syllabic foot. For example, the compound [NN NN] is one prosodic word but two syllabic feet.

I have also avoided using the phonological phrase and the intonational phrase for two reasons: they do not seem to play an obvious role in accounting for rhythm in Chinese and they are hard to define. According to Selkirk (1986) and Hayes (1989b), phonological phrases are delimited by XP boundaries, which again gives undesirable results. For example, consider the line in (45), from a real Tang poem (line 1, poem 186, in the anthology *300 Tang Poems*, edited by Qiu 1976).

(45) feng ji   tian gao   yuan xiao ai
      wind fast sky high   ape   cry sad
      'The wind is fast, the sky is high, and the ape cry is sad.'

This line is made of three clauses [[N V][N V][NN V]], which gives six phonological phrases. However, a line is supposed to be made of just two phonological phrases (or half-lines).

A central claim of prosodic phonology is that phonological rules do not refer to syntax directly, but only to prosodic categories. However, phonological rules must refer to syntax in some ways, such as in defining prosodic categories. This kind of reference is thought to be 'indirect'. According to Hayes (1989*b*: 205), direct reference to syntax means referring to syntactic categories, such as N, NP, V, and VP, and indirect reference means referring to syntactic levels (such as X^0 and XP). In the present analysis, the phrasal stress rule refers to syntactic heads vs. nonheads, that is, X^0 vs. XP. Therefore, the present analysis makes no more reference to syntax than prosodic phonology. But once stress and foot structure are determined, there does not seem to be any need for other phonological categories, as far as Chinese is concerned. Therefore, my analysis is simpler than prosodic phonology and avoids the problems in defining prosodic categories beyond the syllabic foot.

12.8. SUMMARY

Rhythm in Chinese poems involves more than rhyming, line length, tonal requirements, and syntactic brackets. Just as in English, rhythm is primarily based on the stress pattern of a line, which must be mapped to the template for the poem (Halle and Keyser 1971).

I have also suggested that Chinese poems in general seem to be more rhythmic than English poems. The reason is probably due to the fact that English words have a fixed length so that there is no easy way to shift the stress position in a polysyllabic word. In contrast, Chinese has a dual vocabulary (Chapter 7), in which many words have a monosyllabic and a disyllabic length. The dual vocabulary offers an easy way to adjust word and line length as well as shifting the location of stress. Moreover, the phonological difference in word-length flexibility may have created what seems to be a cultural difference; in Chinese society the use of poetry prevails, by the educated and the populace alike, whereas in English-speaking societies the use and appreciation of poetry seem to be limited to the literary elite.

Finally, I have shown different types of poetic template in Chinese and compared three ways to account for them. The simplest analysis, I propose, is to use only those constraints that are truly inviolable. Variations in template types are better accounted for by the claim that the constraints can be satisfied in different ways, rather than the claim that all constraints are violable and defective templates can be routinely tolerated (Golston and Riad 2005).

13

Connected Speech and Other Dialects

13.1. INTRODUCTION

In this chapter I discuss some sound changes in connected speech, major phonological processes in other Chinese dialects, and Taiwanese accented SC. I use connected speech to refer to speech that occurs at natural speed, such as spontaneous conversations or narratives. This section is not meant to be a detailed review or analysis of connected speech; its purpose is to show the kind of changes that occur by listing some examples, transcribed in phonetic symbols. Tones are marked when relevant (see Chapter 10 for representation of tone). Vowel length is not always indicated.

13.2. CONSONANT REDUCTION

I use consonant reduction to refer to the process in which voiceless stops (especially unaspirated ones) become voiced stops, which in turn become fricatives, which in turn become approximants. This occurs on unstressed syllables in SC. Some of the steps can also be called spirantization. Consonant reduction has been noted before, for example by Chao (1968: 38) and S. Xu (1980: 159). Some examples are shown in (1) (for transcription, see Chapters 2 and 3).

(1) [p, t, k, ʦ]   →   [b, d, g, ʣ̢]
     [li-pa]   →   [li-ba]   'fence'
     [ti-ti]   →   [ti-di]   'younger brother'
     [kɤ-kɤ]   →   [kɤ-gə]   'older brother'
     [kan-ʦə]   →   [kan-ʣə]   'do ASP (doing it)'

     [ʂ, xʷ, ç]   →   [z̢, w, j]
     [pau-ʂaŋ]   →   [pau- z̢ə̃]   'in the newspaper'
     [çau-xʷo-ʦʰɤ]   →   [çau-wo-ʦʰɤ]   'small train'
     [waŋ-çan-ʂən]   →   [wã-jə̃ -z̢ə̃]   'Wang mister (Mr. Wang)'

[k, tʂ, tʂʰ]   →   [ɣ, z̞, z̞]
[kaŋ-kaŋ-tɕʰʷy]   →   [kã-ɣã-tɕʰʷy]   'just went'
[pu-tʂz̞-tau]   →   [pu-z̞-tau]   'don't know'
[ʂəŋ-tʂʰan-ɕan]   →   [ʂə̃-zã-ɕan]   'production line'

Consonant reduction seems to be easier in the second position of a trisyllabic expression than in the second position of a disyllabic expression. We have seen [xʷ, ɕ, k, tʂ, tʂʰ] become [w, j, ɣ, z̞, z̞], respectively, in the middle of a trisyllabic expression. The same process is harder in a disyllabic expression, even if the second syllable is unstressed, as shown in (2).

(2) [xʷ, ɕ, k, tʂ]   →   ?[w, j, ɣ, z̞]
     [kʷai-xʷo]   →   ?[kʷai-wo]   'happy'
     [ɕin-ɕan]   →   ?[ɕĩ-jã]   'fresh'
     [tʂəi-kə]   →   ?[tʂəi-ɣə]   'this one'
     [pau-tʂz̞]   →   ?[pau-z̞]   'newspaper'

It is harder to find examples of reduced [pʰ, tʰ, tsʰ, kʰ, s, f], all of which are aspirated; instead, aspirated consonants tend to devoice the following vowel, to be discussed in section 13.4. Sometimes a consonant can be deleted altogether; see section 13.5.

13.3. DE-STRESSING AND RHYME REDUCTION

De-stressing is used here to refer to the process in which an underlying full syllable becomes weak and toneless. It is often accompanied by the loss of the coda slot, and the vowel reduces towards schwa. The process has also been observed in read speech (M. Lin and Yan 1988). Two examples are shown in (3) (Ø indicates absence of tone).

(3) [an] → [ɔ̃]
     H-H   H-Ø
     [tʂʰʷən-tʰʲan]   →   [tʂʰʷən-tʰʲɔ̃]   'spring-day (spring)'
     [əu] → [o]
     HL-LH   HL-Ø
     [muu-tʰəu]   →   [muu-tʰo]   'wood'
     [ai] → [ɛ]
     L-HL   L-Ø (L-H)
     [nau-tai]   →   [nau-dɛ]   'head'

In 'head', the second syllable also loses its original tone, giving L-Ø, which is realized as L-H in SC (see Chapter 10). In connected speech the percentage of syllables that are unstressed and toneless is rather large. For example, in the corpus of Duanmu *et al.* (1998), about one third of all syllables are unstressed and toneless. This is considerably higher than the percentage of weak syllables in written texts, which is estimated to be between 15 and 20 per cent (W. Li 1981: 35). The increase probably comes from the de-stressing of underlyingly full syllables.

13.4. VOWEL DEVOICING AND VOICELESS SYLLABLES

A high vowel after an aspirated onset, including voiceless fricatives, aspirated stops, and aspirated affricates, can be devoiced or deleted when (*a*) it is unstressed or (*b*) it has a low tone. Case (*a*) often happens to the second syllable of a disyllabic word, case (*b*) can occur on any syllable. Some examples are shown in (4) (vowel length not shown). When a vowel is devoiced, the tone cannot be heard, which is indicated by Ø.

(4)

		HL-L		HL-Ø	
[ʋ] → [f]		[təu-fʋ]	→	[tou-ff]	'tofu'
		H-HL		H-Ø	
		[ʂʐ̩-fʋ]	→	[ʂʐ̩-ff]	'master'
		HL-H		HL-Ø	
		[tʂaŋ-fʋ]	→	[tʂaŋ-ff]	'husband'
		HL-L		HL-Ø	
[z̩] → [ʂ]		[lʲi-ʂz̩]	→	[lʲi-ʂʂ]	'history'
		HL-L		HL-Ø	
[i] → [ɕ]		[i-tɕʰi]	→	[i-tɕʰɕ]	'together'
		L-HL		Ø-HL	
		[tɕʰi-tʷuŋ]	→	[tɕʰɕ-tʷuŋ]	'start'
		H-H		H-Ø	
		[tuŋ-ɕi]	→	[tuŋ-ɕɕ]	'thing'
		HL-LH		HL-Ø	
		[wən-tʰʲi]	→	[wən-tʰʲɕ]	'question'
		H-L		H-Ø	
[y] → [ɕʷ]		[tʂəŋ-tɕʰʷy]	→	[tʂəŋ-tɕʰʷɕʷ]	'strive for'
		L-H		Ø-H	
		[ɕʷy-tʷo]	→	[ɕʷɕʷ-tʷo]	'many'

	H-HL		H-Ø	
	[t̠s̪ʰʷu-t̠ɕʰʷy]	→	[t̠s̪ʰʷu-t̠ɕʰʷɕʷ]	'go out'
	L-LH		Ø-LH	
[ɤ] → [x]	[kʰɤ-nəŋ]	→	[kʰx-nəŋ]	'possible'
	L-HL		Ø-HL	
[u] → [xʷ]	[ṣʷu-t̠ɕa]	→	[ṣʷxʷ-t̠ɕa]	'summer vacation'
	HL-HL		HL-Ø	
	[sʷan-ṣʷu]	→	[sʷan-ṣʷxʷ]	'arithmetic'
	H-L		H-Ø	
	[ɕin-kʰʷu]	→	[ɕin-kʰʷxʷ]	'working hard'
	L-HL		Ø-HL	
	[tʰʷu-tʲi]	→	[tʰʷxʷ-tʲi]	'land'
	L-HL		Ø-HL	
	[kʰʷu-nan]	→	[kʰʷxʷ-nan]	'suffering'

Strictly speaking, [ɤ] is a mid vowel, but since SC does not have the corresponding high vowel [ɯ], [ɤ] is often realized as [ɯ], which is probably why it can devoice. The vowel [ʊ] is a variant of [u] and occurs after [f]. Devoiced [ʊ, z̩, i, y, ɤ, u] sound like [f, ṣ, ɕ, ɕʷ, x, xʷ], respectively. The devoiced syllables have similar durations as the originals (all of which should be CVX, at least in initial position, although rhyme length is not always indicated in the above transcription), and therefore they still sound like separate syllables. Also, the syllables [ff, ṣṣ, t̠ɕʰɕ, ɕɕ, tʰʲɕ, t̠ɕʰʷɕʷ, ɕʷɕʷ, kʰʷxʷ, tʰʷxʷ] can be transcribed as [f, ṣ, t̠ɕʰ, ɕ, tʰʲ, t̠ɕʰʷ, ɕʷ, kʰʷ, tʰʷ], respectively, since the rhyme is basically the prolongation of the onset. The syllable [ṣʷxʷ] should be transcribed as is. The syllabic consonant [z] can also be devoiced under similar conditions. Some examples are shown in (5).

(5)		HL-L		HL-Ø	
	[z] → [s]	[ṣaŋ-tsʰz]	→	[ṣaŋ-tsʰs]	'last time'
		HL-H		HL-Ø	
		[i-sz]	→	[i-ss]	'meaning'
		L-HL		Ø-HL	
		[tsʰz-tʲi]	→	[tsʰs-tʲi]	'this place'

Again, [tsʰs, ss] can be transcribed simply as [tsʰ, s], but they still sound like separate syllables.

When the onset consonant is not aspirated, as in (6), or when the syllable does not have a low tone, as in (7), vowel deletion usually does not occur.

(6) L-HL   Ø-HL
     [kʷu-ʎi]   →   ?[kʷxʷ-ʎi]   'encourage'

     L-HL   Ø-HL
     [tʲi-ça]   →   ?[tʲç-ça]   'underneath'

(7) H-HL   Ø-HL
     [kʰʷu-tsau] → *[kʰʷxʷ-tsau]   'boring'

     LH-HL   Ø-HL
     [tʰʷu-xʷa] → *[tʰʷxʷ-xʷa]   'painting'

     HL-LH   Ø-LH
     [kʰʷu-faŋ] → *[kʰʷxʷ-faŋ]   'storage house'

The devoicing of non-high vowels is less common but can occur, again with an L tone and an aspirated onset. Two examples are shown in (8).

(8) HL-L   HL-Ø
     [y-tsʰaŋ]   → [y-tsʰą̊]   'bathing place'

     LH-L   LH-Ø
     [xən-xau]   → [xən-xa̯u̥]   'very good'

   Linguists are divided on the analysis of voiceless syllables. Some believe that every syllable must have a vowel (Cheung 1986; Hsueh 1986; Coleman 1996, 2001). On this view, voiceless syllables either have a voiceless vowel, or have a vowel that overlaps with a consonant such that the articulation of the vowel is hidden behind the articulation of the consonant (Coleman 2001). It is interesting to note that in Coleman's analysis of Berber, when the vowel is not heard, it is thought to be covered by the following conso-nant, which cannot be the case in SC, where there is no following conso-nant in voiceless syllables. Other linguists believe that not all syllables need to have a vowel, or even a voiced sound (Chao 1968; Dell and Elmedlaoui 1985, 1996, 2003; Ramsey 1987). On this view, it is not always necessary to assume a voiceless or hidden vowel. I do not intend to settle the dispute here; instead, I describe the facts as phonetically accurately as possible.

   There has not been much discussion of vowel devoicing in SC, a lot less than, say, in Japanese. The reason, I suspect, is that vowel devoicing is optional in SC, probably because most SC syllables are heavy and tend to retain some stress.

13.5. SYLLABLE MERGER

In syllable merger, two (or more) syllables merge into one. I offer some examples to indicate the kind of mergers that occur. First, consider the data in (9). (Tone 3 Sandhi has been taken into consideration in the tonal representation.)

(9) LH-L   HL
     [sʷo-i]   →   [sʷəi]   'therefore'

     HL-HL   HL
     [tɕəu-jau]   →   [tɕau]   'will (soon)'

     HL L HL-H   HL HL-Ø
     [pu xau i-sz] →   [pau i-s]   'not good meaning (embarrassed)'

     L-LH-HL   L-HL
     [jəu-ʂz̩-xəu]   →   [jəu-ʂəu]   'sometimes'

The merged syllables sound like one syllable in that if they are played alone, they sound the same as a monosyllabic word. For example, the merged [sʷəi] 'therefore' sounds the same as [sʷəi] 'age', the merged [tɕau] 'will (soon)' sounds [tɕau] 'shout'.

Sometimes the result of a syllable merger does not quite sound like a single syllable. For example, consider the cases in (10).

(10) LH-L   HL
      [kʰɤ-i]   →   [kʰəi]   'can'

      LH-HL   HL
      [pu-xʷəi]   →   [pʷəi]   'can't be'

      L-LH   LH
      [wo-mən]   →   [wom]   'we'

      HL-H   HLH
      [ta-tɕa]   →   [taa]   'everybody'

      L-HL   LHL
      [pʲi-tɕau]   →   [pʲiau]   'comparatively'

In the first three expressions, the result of merger seems to be a syllable, yet SC has no such syllables. In particular, SC has [kʰəi] with H tone but not with HL tone. Similarly, SC has no [pʷəi] or [wom] with any tone. For the last two expressions, the result of merger sounds somewhat like two syllables, since it has kept both of the input tones and it is longer than a single syllable. On the other hand, the middle consonant is completely deleted, so that acoustically (such as on a spectrogram), the result looks like a single syllable (except it is rather long).

It is interesting to ask whether merger can create syllables that are ill-formed, such as those that violate Rhyme-Harmony (see Chapter 3). If it cannot then we have found an important conclusion that merger can only create syllables that are theoretically possible.

13.6. PHONOLOGICAL PROCESSES
IN OTHER DIALECTS

The phonological processes reviewed here are those that have attracted considerable attention in recent literature. They do not represent all phonological problems in Chinese dialects—perhaps only a fraction of them, since many dialects have not been studied in detail.

13.6.1. Tone sandhi in Wu dialects

The Wu dialects, such as Suzhou, Wuxi, Shanghai, Tangxi (Tangsic), Nantong, Danyang, and Chongming, are spoken in the area around Shanghai. According to J. Yuan (1989), the defining characteristic of Wu dialects is a contrast between voiced and voiceless obstruents. However, the best-known phonological process of this dialect family is left-dominant tone sandhi (found mostly in northern Wu dialects), by which the initial syllable determines the tonal pattern of the entire domain. For illustration, consider the Shanghai data in (11) and (12), transcribed in phonetic symbols, where tonal register is ignored.

(11) HL   LH   HL   LH
      [se]   [sz]   [pe]   [bø]
      'three'   'four'   'cup'   'plate'

(12) H-L   H-L   L-H   L-H
      [se-pe]   [se-bø]   [sz-pe]   [sz-bø]
      'three cups' 'three plates' 'four cups' 'four plates'

Example (11) shows some monosyllabic words in isolation. Example (12) gives their disyllabic combinations, where the initial syllable determines the tone pattern of the expression, regardless of the tone of the second syllable.

The Wu tone sandhi raises two questions; why do Wu dialects have such tone sandhi? And, what determines the domain of tone sandhi? In traditional literature, there has been no answer to the first question beyond a typological classification (Yue-Hashimoto 1987). For the second question, various answers have been proposed, from functional considerations (e.g. Kennedy 1953) to prosodic categories (Selkirk and T. Shen 1990), but various problems remain.

A different proposal is made in Duanmu (1990), elaborated in Duanmu (1993, 1999a). It is based on two observations: northern Wu dialects have no diphthongs or contrastive codas, so all their syllables can be considered light or unspecified for weight; and in all Chinese dialects an unstressed syllable loses its underlying tone. The observations lead to the following analysis. First, since syllables in northern Wu dialects are light, each syllable cannot form a bimoraic foot by itself and so it lacks stress, unless it occurs in a stressed position, which is the initial position of a domain. Thus, noninitial syllables lose their underlying tones while initial syllables retain their underlying tones, which determine the pitch pattern of the domain. Second, a tonal domain is a stress domain, or a foot. The foot is determined by moraic trochee, syllabic trochee, and phrasal stress assignment above the word level (Duanmu 1999a, and Chapter 6). The same analysis applies to non-Wu dialects such as SC. Since full SC syllables are heavy, they each form a moraic foot and have stress, so they each can retain its underlying tone. This prevents left-dominant tone sandhi from occurring across full syllables.

It is interesting to note that southern Wu dialects have diphthongs (J. Yuan 1989), so they have underlyingly heavy syllables, which can keep their underlying tones and prevent left-dominant tone sandhi. As expected, left-dominant tone sandhi does not actively occur in southern Wu dialects.

13.6.2. Tone sandhi in Min dialects

The Min dialects are spoken in Fujian Province and Taiwan. The most interesting phonological problem is that each full syllable has two lexical tones. One can be called final tone, which is used when the syllable occurs in isolation or when it is the last full syllable in a domain. The other can be called nonfinal tone, which is used in nonfinal positions. For example, the Xiamen dialect (also called Taiwanese) has seven tonal categories, so there are seven final and seven non-final tones (some of which are identical), shown in (13). The transcription is based on J. Yuan (1989: 244–5), using the digit system of Chao (1930) (see Chapter 10).

(13)

	T1	T2	T3	T4	T5	T6	T7
Final	55	24	51	11	33	32	5
Nonfinal	33	33	55	51	22	5	1

The tone of a syllable when it is spoken in isolation is called the citation tone. In traditional literature, the citation tone is usually seen as the basic tone. Since the final tone in Min dialects is the same as the citation tone, some people consider the nonfinal tone to be derived, or the sandhi tone (e.g. Chen 1987, 2000). And since the final tone remains unchanged (from the citation tone) and the nonfinal tones change,

Min dialects are said to have right-dominant tone sandhi. On the other hand, some linguists argue that nonfinal tones in Min are basic and final tones are derived (e.g. Woo 1969; M. Hashimoto 1982; Ting 1982).

Some linguists have explored whether there is a systematic relation between final tones and nonfinal tones in Min (e.g. W. Wang 1967; Chen 1987; Tsay 1990, 1991), but the relation is probably a matter of historical residue. Yue-Hashimoto (1986: 167) made an interesting observation. She pointed out that non-final tones in Min dialects are largely consistent with the generalization of voiceless–high and voiced–low, that is to say, syllables whose onsets are historically voiceless have higher tones and syllables whose onsets are historically voiced have lower tones (see Chapter 10). In contrast, final tones often violate the generalization. It is possible, therefore, that what happened to Min dialects is a tonal reversal on the final syllable (what Yue-Hashimoto calls tonal flip-flop).

The issue of more interest, and of a more complex nature, is how to determine a tonal domain, that is, where to use the final tone and where to use the nonfinal tone (see R. Cheng 1968, 1973; J. Lin 1994; Chen 1987, 2000). According to Chen (1987, 2000), the domains are sensitive primarily to syntactic boundaries, but also to various other factors, such as phonological rhythm, recitation style, idioms, and the syntactic notion of lexical government.

13.6.3. Tone sandhi in Tianjin

Interest in Tianjin tone sandhi was sparked by an article by X. Li and Liu (1985). Many discussions soon followed (for a review, see Chen 2000: ch. 3 and Ma 2005). Tianjin has three tone-sandhi rules. The result of one rule can create a condition for another. In other words, the rules can inter-act with each other. The challenge is to determine how they interact, and whether the rules apply left-to-right, right-to-left, or cyclically, especially in long expressions.

13.6.4. Rhyme changes

One case of rhyme change is the [ɚ]-suffix in SC (Chapter 9). Some other dialects, too, have been reported to have affix-triggered rhyme changes, which may surface as either one or two syllables. A lot of data can be found in the journal *Zhongguo Yuwen*. For some analyses, see Y. Lin (1989: ch. 3, 1993), Duanmu (1990: ch. 3), and H. Wang (1999: ch. 9).

13.6.5. **Language games**

Language games refer to disguised languages. They can be used either by children or by adults. The most common Chinese language games are Fanqie languages, in which a syllable is first copied into two, then the onset of one of them is modified, and finally the rhyme of the other is modified (see Chapter 4 for some examples). An early study of Fanqie languages is Chao (1931). Formal studies include Yip (1982), Bao (1990*b*), and Duanmu (1990). The analysis of language games has implications for syllable structure and the feature composition of sounds, including the status of the prenuclear glide: is it in the rhyme, in the onset, in both, or in neither.

13.7. TAIWANESE ACCENTED STANDARD CHINESE

As mentioned in Chapter 1, most speakers of SC do not have a perfect accent—the accent of a Beijing speaker, or that of a news reader on a national TV or radio station. It is therefore often easy to identify from which region a person comes by his or her accent. In this section I discuss one accent in some detail—the accent of Taiwanese speakers of SC. The purpose is to give a picture of what linguistic factors, especially phonological ones, are involved in an accent. The data are from Duanmu *et al.* (1998).

Taiwanese accented SC (TWSC) is loosely defined as the SC spoken by people (*a*) who grew up in Taiwan and (*b*) whose first dialect is Taiwanese (Southern Min). Of course, not everyone who grew up in Taiwan and whose first dialect is Taiwanese has such an accent. However, there are some features that are shared by most Taiwanese speakers of SC, which make the accent rather distinctive. I will discuss the accent from five aspects: lexicon, stress, tone, segmental differences, and consonant reduction and syllable merger.

13.7.1. **Lexicon**

Certain expressions are characteristic of Taiwanese speakers of SC. Some are shown in (14).

(14) (*a*) Interjection
        [xo] or [ho], indicating friendliness
     (*b*) The reduplicated L-LH form for kinship terms
        HL   L-LH
        [pa] → [pa-pa]   'dad'

H   L-LH
[ma] → [ma-ma] 'mom'

(c) Words with different tones from SC

H-LH
[tɕau-ɕʷe]   'teaching' (the tone in SC is HL-LH)

(d) English vocabulary

The interjection in (14a) is not used in SC, but some Taiwanese speakers use it a lot, scattered frequently throughout a conversation. It would be interesting to find out which locations are possible sites for [xo], although it appears to occur at phrase boundaries. The reduplicated form in (14b) is another feature of Taiwanese accented SC. The words in (14c) also occur in SC, but with different tones. Finally, Taiwanese speakers often mix in English words when they speak SC. In contrast, speakers from the Mainland use English words a lot less, at least until quite recently. This seems to be a reflection of how much contact there is with western culture. For example, Hong Kong Chinese has a very high percentage of English words. Some English words are beginning to enter SC, especially in the speech of young people, such as [si-ti] 'CD', [tʰi-vi] 'TV', [kʰu] 'cool', and [ɕəu] 'show'.

13.7.2. Stress

In SC, de-stressing is quite common (see above). In Taiwanese accented SC (TWSC), de-stressing occurs less frequently. Some examples are shown in (15).

(15)   TWSC   SC
        LH-H   LH-Ø
        [mʲan-xʷa] [mʲan-xʷa] 'cotton'

        H-HL   H-Ø
        [tsɯ-tau]   [tʂz̩-tɔ]   'know'

        LH-H   H-Ø
        [ɕʷe-səŋ]   [ɕʷe-ʂə̃]   'student'

Since de-stressing is accompanied by tone loss, it is quite obvious to the ear. Besides stress, there are segmental differences between TWSC and SC in (15), to be discussed below.

13.7.3. Tone

A major characteristic of TWSC is the use of L at a phrase boundary for what is LH or H in SC. Some examples are shown in (16).

(16) TWSC   SC

L-L   L-H
[tsəu-lə]   [tsəu-lə]   'walk ASP (left)'

LH-L-L   LH-L-H
[xai-xau-la]   [xai-xau-la]   'still good ASP (not bad)'

LH-L-L   LH-L-H
[xən-tɕəu-lə]   [xən-tɕəu-lə]   'very long ASP'

L-L   L-LH
[kʰɤ-nəŋ]   [kʰɤ-nəŋ]   'maybe'

HL-L   HL-LH
[tʰai-fəi]   [tʰai-fəi]   'too fat'

H-L   H-LH
[ɕa-zən]   [ɕa-zən]   'shrimp (without shell)'

The change of LH to L can create ambiguities, in that an underlying T2 (LH) can sound the same as an underlying T3 (L), as observed by Lo (2005). Some examples are shown in (17), transcribed in Pinyin, thanks to Hui-Ju Hsu (personal communications).

(17) H-LH → H-L   =   H-L
     sheng-huo   sheng huo
     grow-live   grow fire
     'to live'   'to start fire'

     HL-LH → HL-L   =   HL-L
     lu ying   lu ying
     open camp   record picture
     'to camp'   'to record pictures'

The preference for L can sometimes override Tone 3 Sandhi (T3S), by which underlying L-L change to LH-L (see Chapter 11). Consider the examples in (18).

(18) TWSC   SC

LH-L-L-LH   LH-LH-L-LH
[xən-tɕəu i-tɕʰan]   [xən-tɕəu i-tɕʰan]   'very-long ago'

L-L-H   LH-L-H
[wo i-tɕəŋ]   [wo i-tɕəŋ]   'I already'

H-L-L   H-LH-L
[pʰʷo xən-təu]   [pʰʷo xən-təu]   'slope (is) very-steep'

In the first example, T3S is optional over the second and third syllables (because they lie in separate feet), but it usually applies in SC and not in TWSC. In the last two examples, T3S applies in SC, but it fails to in TWSC.

Lo (2005) reports an interesting additional rule for some TWSC speakers. When a T3-T2 sequence changes to T3-T3 by final lowering, they may undergo T3S and become T2-T3. Some examples are shown in (19).

(19) SC   Final lowering   T3S
      L-LH   →   L-L   →   LH-L
      [pən-lai]
      'originally'

      L-LH   →   L-L   →   LH-L
      [ni lai]
      'you come'

      L-LH   →   L-L   →   LH-L
      [xən tɕʰʲaŋ]
      'very strong'

It is worth asking whether the change in (19) is due to the chain tone sandhi effect as suggested by Lo, or whether it is because the speakers simply pronounced a full T3 rather than T2 (i.e. 214 rather than 35) before the final syllable.

13.7.4. Segmental differences

Most TWSC speakers do not have the retroflex series or the front round vowel or glide. In addition, many of them pronounce the syllabic [z] with a velar quality, either [ɯ] or [zˠ]. Some examples are shown in (20).

(20) Correspondence   Examples

SC	TWSC	SC	TWSC	
[tʂ]	[ts]	[tʂˠ]	[tsˠ]	'this'
[tʂʰ]	[tsʰ]	[tʂʰaŋ]	[tsʰaŋ]	'long'
[ʂ]	[s]	[ʂau]	[sau]	'less'
[ʐ]	[z]	[ʐaŋ]	[zaŋ]	'let'
[ʐ]	[l]	[ʐəŋ]	[ləŋ]	'throw'
[y]	[i]	[y]	[i]	'language'
[ɚ]	[ɤ]	[ɚ]	[ɤ]	'child'
[z] (syllabic)	[ɯ] or [zˠ]	[sz]	[sɯ] or [szˠ]	'four'

In addition, the oral closure of the nasal codas [n, ŋ] is often incomplete in SC (Y. Xu 1986; J. Wang 1993), especially after a low vowel, but their closure is often rather firm in TWSC (but see consonant reduction below). An example is shown in (21), where [a] is front (and can be transcribed as [æ]) owing to the influence of [n] (with or without closure).

(21) TWSC   SC
      [tɕin-nʲan] [tɕin-nʲã] 'this year'

13.7.5. Consonant reduction and syllable merger

As in SC, consonant reduction and syllable merger also occurs in TWSC, as shown in (22).

(22) H-L   HL
      [təu-jəu]   →   [təu]   'all have'
      L-H   LH
      [pa-tʰa]   →   [pa]   'take/cause it'
      L-LH   LH
      [wo-xai]   →   [wai]   'I still'
      HL-L-LH   HL
      [na-wo-mən] →   [nom]   'then we'

But because of their segmental differences, the result of weakening and merger in TWSC is not always the same as that in SC. Compare the examples among SC, TWSC, and reduced TWSC (weakened or merged) in (23).

(23) SC   TWSC   Reduced TWSC   Gloss
      L-HL   L-HL   HL
      [tʂz̩-jau]   [tsz-jau]   [tɕau]   'if'
      H-LH   H-LH   H-H
      [taŋ-ʐan]   [taŋ-zan]   [tã-æ̃] high tone 'of course'
      LH-HL   LH-HL   LH-HL
      [ʐan-xəu]   [zan-xəu]   [zæ̃-ɣəu]   'then'
      HL-HL   HL-HL   HL
      [tʂɤ-jaŋ]   [tsɤ-jaŋ]   [tɕaŋ]   'this way'
      HL-L   HL-L   HL
      [tʂɤ-tʂuŋ]   [tsɤ-tsuŋ]   [tsuŋ]   'this kind'

The reduced TWSC forms differ from those in SC (not given) because TWSC lacks retroflex sounds. In fact, TWSC has more extensive consonant reduction than SC in that reduction can occur on stressed syllables in TWSC, whereas in SC it occurs mostly on unstressed syllables. This is exemplified in (24).

(24) Consonant reduction on stressed syllables in TWSC
      HL-HL   HL-HL
      [ta-kai]   → [ta-ɣai]   'probably'

H-H		H-H		
[kʷan-kʷaŋ]	→	[kʷan-waŋ]	'sightseeing'	
HL-HL		HL-HL		
[pau-kau]	→	[pau-ɣau]	'report'	
HL-H		HL-H		
[wəi-səŋ]	→	[wəi-zəŋ]	'health'	
H-HL		H-HL		
[kʰai-faŋ]	→	[kʰai-vaŋ]	'open-up'	
H-HL		H-HL		
[tɕi-xʷəi]	→	[tɕi-wəi]	'chance'	
HL-L-LH		HL-L-LH		
[pu-ɕaŋ-xʷo]	→	[pu-ɕaŋ-wo]	'not want (to) live'	

In the above examples, the last syllable kept its tone, indicating that there is no de-stressing, yet consonant reduction has occurred, affecting both stops and fricatives. Sometimes a consonant in initial position can also reduce in TWSC, as shown in (25).

(25) [xən-dʷo] → [ɦən-dʷo]   'many
      [zan-xəu] → [ã-əu]   'afterwards'
      [kʰɤ-sɯ]   → [ɤ-sɯ]   'but'
      [tʰa]   → [ɦa] or [a] 'he'

Consonant reduction and syllable mergers do not seem to present a problem for listening. In fact, many cases of consonant reduction and syllable merger were not noticed until they were examined on a spectrogram or played back in isolation. This shows that the context can compensate for the loss of phonetic cues.

13.8. SUMMARY

This is a brief survey of connected speech and phonetic and phonological processes in other varieties of Chinese. It intends to point to several interesting areas of research that cannot be covered in the present study.

14

Theoretical Implications

After reading the preceding chapters, theoretically oriented readers might ask two questions: What general principles does the book claim to have found? How do we evaluate the predictions?

As stated in the original preface, I believe that there are linguistic laws (universals) that apply to all human languages. A major goal of my research is to look for such universals. In this regard, I share the theoretical position of generative linguistics.

I proposed some generalizations for Standard Chinese, but I did not always claim whether the proposals are universal. The main reason was that the subject of the book was on Chinese and there was little space to discuss other languages. Besides, there are enough problems to solve in Chinese, a tall order by itself.

But it is likely that some of my proposals have broader implications. Let me give two examples: stress and syllable structure. English Stress is intuitively clear most of the time and has been studied extensively. In contrast, stress in Chinese is intuitively unclear most of the time, and many linguists believe that Chinese has no stress. I have argued instead that Chinese in fact has the same stress pattern as English. This result, if correct, is unlikely to be an accident, to which I will return.

Compared with stress, syllable structure is less obvious in English. In particular, there are two difficulties. The first problem is that linguists are not always sure where syllable boundaries are in the middle of a word. For example, a word like *city* has been analyzed as *cit.ty* (Kahn 1976; Burzio 1994; Hammond 1997), *cit.y* (Selkirk 1982; Hammond 1999), and *ci.ty* (Halle and Vergnaud 1987; Hayes 1995). Secondly, linguists are not sure how to treat consonant clusters that occur at word edges. For example, are all the sounds in *sixths* in one syllable (Fudge 1968; Kahn 1976; Selkirk 1982), or are the suffixes *-th-s* outside the basic syllable (Borowsky 1989; Pierrehumbert 1994)? Are all the sounds in *lisp* in one syllable, or is [p] in another syllable *lis.p*Ø, where Ø is a 'zero vowel' (Burzio 1994; Harris 1994)? Because of such uncertainties, some linguists believe that syllable boundaries are not determined by linguistic principles but by expedient conjectures that are based on consonant cluster patterns at word edges (Steriade 1999; Blevins 2003; and references therein).

In contrast to English, syllable boundaries are unambiguous in Chinese, where it is possible to study actual and missing syllables and constraints on sound combinations within a syllable. Having done so, and looking back at English, I see a similar pattern. Specifically, Borowsky (1989) has argued that, if we treat word-edge effects separately, then the maximal English rhyme is VX, which is similar to that in Chinese. In addition, if we leave aside the initial [s] (which remains a problem for any syllable theory), then the maximal English syllable is CRVX, where R is [l], [r], [w], or [j]. This is similar to the Chinese CGVX. Moreover, just as CG can be analysed as a single complex sound (Chapters 2 and 3), so can CR (Duanmu 2002). Thus, in both languages, we are essentially looking at a CVX syllable.

The examples show that the understanding of stress in English helps the understanding of stress in Chinese. In turn, the understanding of the syllable in Chinese helps the understanding of the syllable in English. In both cases, the two languages turn out to be similar, even though they appear to be different.

But even so, it is still a long way from showing that all languages are similar. What is the reason to believe that they are? Let us look at stress and foot types in more detail. Most linguists believe that languages can differ in stress and foot types, such that some languages have trochaic feet (stress on the first beat of a foot), some have iambic feet (stress on the second beat of a foot), and some have no stress. The differences have often been used to argue for the Principles-and-Parameters model (Chomsky 1981), according to which languages share certain universals (principles) but can differ in systematic ways (parameters). In addition, parametric differences do not need further explanation. For example, once we decide that some languages have syllabic feet, some moraic feet, and some no stress, there is nothing to explain beyond that. There is, however, another possibility, namely, that all languages have stress and all feet are trochaic. There are four arguments for the alternative. In the first place, languages that are thought to have no stress are generally tone languages, including Chinese. I have argued why stress is not intuitively obvious in Chinese and how stress can be detected in other ways. It remains to be shown whether other tone languages can be analysed in the same way. Secondly, if Chinese has syllabic trochee, as I have argued, it is likely to be innate, because it is not obvious how the pattern could have been learned (since stress is not obvious in Chinese). Thirdly, according to Hayes (1995), most languages have trochaic feet. In the small number of languages that are thought to have iambic feet, the evidence is, in my view, not compelling. Finally, according to a survey of 444 languages by Hyman (1977), there are languages in which stress is regularly on the first, second, or third syllable from the end of a word, or on the first or second syllable from the beginning of a word, but there is no language in which stress is regularly on the third syllable from the beginning of a word. This is shown in (1). (Of the remaining 138 languages, 129 are thought to have no stress, including Chinese, and 9 have stress on heavy syllables in variable locations.)

(1) Stress location   Number of languages (total 306)

First from left:	114
Second from left:	12
Third from left:	None
Third from right:	6
Second from right:	77
First from right:	97

The pattern can be accounted for in terms of syllabic trochee. Following a standard assumption, one syllable can be skipped at word edges and an empty beat Ø is available at the end of a word. The analysis is shown in (2), where S is a stressed syllable, s an unstressed syllable, and <s> is a skipped syllable.

(2) Analysis of (1) in syllabic trochee (# indicates word boundary)

First from left:	#(Ss)…
Second from left:	#<s>(Ss)…
Third from left:	Not possible
Third from right:	…(Ss)<s>#
Second from right:	…(Ss)#
First from right:	…(SØ)#

The analysis correctly predicts that no language can regularly have stress on the third syllable from the beginning. If there are iambic feet, it should be possible to have stress on the third syllable, as shown in (3).

(3) Syllabic iamb
     Third from left: #<s>(sS)…

The lack of the pattern in (3) argues against iambic feet as a natural foot type.

I have made a proposal according to which there are only phonological universals and no phonological parameters. Three questions immediately arise. How do languages differ? What are the implications for current theories? And, how does the new approach guide linguistic research?

For the first question, I suggest that there are three ways in which languages can differ arbitrarily, in the sense that the differences require no linguistic explanation. First, the association between sound and meaning is arbitrary. For example, there is no linguistic explanation why 'cat' is called [kæt] in English but [mau] in Chinese. Secondly, a language can arbitrarily choose any number of items to use out of a universal inventory. For example, English uses over ten vowels but Standard Chinese uses five. Thirdly, when there are different ways to satisfy a linguistic requirement, a language can arbitrarily choose which ways to use. For example, if the only foot type is trochaic, and if stress must fall on a real syllable, there are two ways to satisfy the requirement in a disyllabic word: (Ss) and s(SØ). A language can choose (Ss) only, or s(SØ) only, or both. English uses both, as in *Holland* vs. *Japan*. Similarly, for a trisyllabic word there are (at least) three ways to satisfy the requirement, (Ss)s, s(Ss), and (Ss)(SØ), and English uses all the three ways (*Canada, banana,* and *Tennessee*).

For the second question, let us consider the implications for two current theories, Principles-and-Parameters theory and Optimality Theory. The Principles-and-Parameters approach makes three assumptions: language universals (principles), limited language differences (parameters), and arbitrary language differences (such as the association between sound and meaning or the selection of a phonemic inventory). My proposal eliminates the parameters and hence simplifies the theory. For Optimality Theory, the implication is also significant. A central assumption in Optimality Theory is that any linguistic requirement can be violated. This means that there are no genuine linguistic universals. If there are genuine linguistic universals that are inviolable in any language, the theoretical basis of Optimality Theory may need to be reconsidered.

Consider how theories guide research. Ideally, when we see a difference between two languages, a theory can tell us whether the difference is arbitrary, hence no linguistic explanation is needed, or whether the difference is unexpected and an explanation *is* needed. Consider stress and foot types again. At first sight, English has stress and Chinese does not. Should we seek an explanation? The Principles-and-Parameters approach does not offer a guide, because it assumes that languages can differ in stress, and so there is nothing more to explain. Optimality Theory offers no guide either, because it also assumes that languages can differ in stress. Now, having found that Chinese and English in fact both have stress and both have trochaic feet, how do the theories evaluate the result? For both theories, the result is trivial and accidental, because languages can differ in stress, and Chinese and English just happen to be the same. What do we expect when we look at other languages? Neither theory offers any guide either, because the next language could be the same as Chinese and English, or it could be different.

In contrast, the approach I outlined offers a better guide for research at all stages. For example, if we assume that all languages have stress and trochaic feet, then when we see that Chinese does not appear to have stress, we must ask why and look for an answer (in this case, the answer is that tone obscures the main cue for stress). If a new foot structure is needed for Chinese—one that contains both moraic trochee and syllabic trochee (see the Dual Trochee in Chapter 6), then we must ask whether the same is needed for English (and other languages). If the answer is yes, then we have made a significant discovery; if it is no, then we must reexamine the foot structure in Chinese. In this regard, the new theory makes more explicit and falsifiable predictions and sets a higher standard.

I have also been asked another interesting question. If all languages observe the same phonological principles, is it misleading to write a book on the phonology of Chinese as if Chinese has its own phonology? Shouldn't one focus on the phonology of all languages instead? The answer is that the phonology of Chinese is like the physics of the Amazon River—both studies involve applying a general science to a particular case. While the principles of the science remain true, they can interact with other factors for each particular case in unique ways. In the case of the river, physics interacts with ecology and human settlement, among other things, and in the case of language, phonology interacts with arbitrary choices of speakers and other social issues. In this regard, the study of a language or a river is like the study of natural history or evolution, as suggested by Blevins (2003). It offers no less a challenge than the theory itself.

Two other questions may be raised for the present theory: Can linguistic laws change, given that languages do? And if all languages observe the same linguistic laws, what is the value of studying different languages or preserving endangered ones?

The answer to the first question can be given with an analogy. The course of a river can change through time, but it does not mean that physical laws have changed. Similarly, languages can change for various non-linguistic reasons, and it does not mean that linguistic laws have changed. For example, a language may shift stress in a trisyllabic word from (Ss)s to s(Ss), both of which satisfy the syllabic trochee. Similarly, a language may acquire a new vowel through borrowing, which may trigger other adjustments in the sound system, even though linguistic laws remain the same.

The answer to the second question can also be given with an analogy. Since all national parks observe the same physical laws, what is the value of keeping them all? The answer is that each landscape offers a unique record of history, and humans value such histories. Similarly, each language is a unique record of the people who use it and of their culture, and humans value such records.

APPENDIX: FULL SYLLABLES
IN STANDARD CHINESE

Notes

1. The list, below, represents all full syllables in *Xiandai Hanyu Cidian* 'A Modern Chinese Dictionary', compiled by the Chinese Academy of Social Sciences Institute of Linguistics (1978).
2. The syllables are listed alphabetically by Pinyin (first column). Each syllable is listed with just one tone and one meaning.
3. The character for each syllable is chosen so that (*a*) it has the same shape in both the traditional system and the simplified system and (*b*) it is a reasonably common word. When this is not possible, the traditional character is used.
4. The syllables are divided into three groups: (*a*) regular syllables (404 in all), (*b*) dialectal syllables (3 in all), and (*c*) interjections (7 in all).
5. For each syllable (except interjections), five items are provided: its Pinyin and tone (column 1), its underlying sounds in phonetic symbols (column 2), its surface sounds in phonetic symbols (column 3), its Chinese character (column 4), and its meaning (column 5). The relation between underlying sounds and surface sounds are discussed in Chapters 2 and 3.
6. For interjections, only the Pinyin and the meaning are provided.
7. *Xiandai Hanyu Cidian* 'A Modern Chinese Dictionary' lists thirty-seven weak syllables, some of which represent more than one word. They are not included here.

Regular syllables (404 in all)

al	a	aa	阿	ah
ai1	ai	ai	哀	sadness
an1	an	æn	安	peace
ang2	aŋ	aŋ	昂	spirited
ao4	au	au	傲	proud
ba1	pa	paa	八	eight
bai2	pai	pai	白	white
ban4	pan	pæn	半	half
bang4	paŋ	paŋ	棒	stick
bao2	pau	pau	薄	thin
bei3	pəi	pəi	北	north
ben4	pən	pən	笨	stupid

beng4	pəŋ	pəŋ	蹦	jump
bi3	pi	pʲii	比	compare
bian1	pian	pʲæn	編	weave
biao3	piau	pʲau	表	chart
bie2	piə	pʲee	別	other
bin1	pin	pʲin	賓	guest
bing1	piəŋ	pʲəŋ	冰	ice
bo1	pə	pʷoo	波	wave
bu4	pu	pʷuu	不	not
ca1	tsʰa	tsʰaa	擦	wipe
cai4	tsʰai	tsʰai	菜	vegetable
can1	tsʰan	tsʰæn	餐	meal
cang2	tsʰaŋ	tsʰaŋ	藏	hide
cao3	tsʰau	tsʰau	草	grass
ce4	tsʰə	tsʰɤɤ	策	strategy
cen1	tsʰən	tsʰən	參	uneven length
ceng2	tsʰəŋ	tsʰəŋ	曾	once
cha2	tʂʰa	tʂʰaa	茶	tea
chai2	tʂʰai	tʂʰai	柴	firewood
chan2	tʂʰan	tʂʰæn	蟾	toad
chang4	tʂʰaŋ	tʂʰaŋ	唱	sing
chao3	tʂʰau	tʂʰau	炒	fry
che3	tʂʰə	tʂʰɤɤ	扯	tear
chen2	tʂʰən	tʂʰən	沉	sink
cheng2	tʂʰəŋ	tʂʰəŋ	城	city
chi1	tʂʰ	tʂʰʐʐ̩	吃	eat
chong2	tʂʰuŋ	tʂʰwuŋ	虫	worm
chou2	tʂʰəu	tʂʰəu	仇	hatred
chu1	tʂʰu	tʂʰwuu	出	go out
chua1	tʂʰua	tʂʰwaa	欻	(a sound)
chuai4	tʂʰuai	tʂʰwai	踹	kick
chuan2	tʂʰuan	tʂʰwæn	船	boat
chuang1	tʂʰuaŋ	tʂʰwaŋ	窗	window
chui1	tʂʰuəi	tʂʰwəi	吹	blow
chun1	tʂʰuən	tʂʰwən	春	spring
chuo1	tʂʰuə	tʂʰwoo	戳	pierce
ci2	tsʰ	tsʰzz̩	磁	magnet
cong1	tsʰuŋ	tsʰwuŋ	匆	hurry
cou4	tsʰəu	tsʰəu	湊	gather
cu1	tsʰu	tsʰwuu	粗	thick
cuan4	tsʰuan	tsʰwæn	篡	usurp
cui4	tsʰuəi	tsʰwəi	脆	crispy
cun1	tsʰuən	tsʰwən	村	village

cuo4	tsʰuə	tsʰʷoo	錯	mistake
da4	ta	taa	大	big
dai4	tai	tai	袋	bag
dan4	tan	tæn	蛋	egg
dang4	taŋ	taŋ	蕩	swing
dao1	tau	tau	刀	knife
de2	tə	tɤɤ	德	virtue
dei3	təi	təi	得	should
den4	tən	tən	扽	yank
deng3	təŋ	təŋ	等	wait
di4	ti	tʲii	地	land
dian4	tian	tʲæn	店	store
diao4	tiau	tʲau	掉	drop
die1	tiə	tʲee	爹	dad
ding4	tiəŋ	tʲəŋ	定	decide
diu1	tiəu	tʲəu	丟	throw away
dong1	tuŋ	tʷuŋ	冬	winter
dou1	təu	təu	都	all
du2	tu	tʷuu	毒	poison
duan3	tuan	tʷæn	短	short
dui1	tuəi	tʷəi	堆	pile
dun4	tuən	tʷən	盾	shield
duo1	tuə	tʷoo	多	many
e2	ə	ɤɤ	蛾	moth
en1	ən	ən	恩	favour
eng1	əŋ	əŋ	鞥	horse reins
er4	ər	ər	二	two
fa3	fa	faa	法	law
fan3	fan	fæn	反	opposite
fang1	faŋ	faŋ	方	square
fei2	fəi	fəi	肥	fat
fen1	fən	fən	分	split
feng1	fəŋ	fəŋ	峰	peak
fo2	fə	fʷoo	佛	Buddha
fou3	fəu	fəu	否	deny
fu4	fu	fʷuu	父	father
ga1	ka	kaa	嘎	(a sound)
gai3	kai	kai	改	change
gan3	kan	kæn	敢	dare
gang3	kaŋ	kaŋ	港	harbour
gao1	kau	kau	高	tall
ge1	kə	kɤɤ	歌	song
gei3	kəi	kəi	給	give

gen1	kən	kən	根	root
geng1	kəŋ	kəŋ	耕	plough
gong1	kuŋ	kʷuŋ	工	work
gou3	kəu	kəu	狗	dog
gu3	ku	kʷuu	古	ancient
gua1	kua	kʷaa	瓜	melon
guai4	kuai	kʷai	怪	strange
guan1	kuan	kʷæn	官	official
guang1	kuaŋ	kʷaŋ	光	light
gui3	kuəi	kʷəi	鬼	ghost
gun3	kuən	kʷən	滚	roll
guo3	kuə	kʷoo	果	fruit
ha2	xa	xaa	蛤	toad
hai3	xai	xai	海	sea
han4	xan	xæn	汗	sweat
hang2	xaŋ	xaŋ	航	sail
hao3	xau	xau	好	good
he2	xə	xɤɤ	河	river
hei1	xəi	xəi	黑	black
hen3	xən	xən	很	very
heng2	xəŋ	xəŋ	横	cross
hong1	xuŋ	xʷuŋ	烘	bake
hou4	xəu	xəu	厚	thick
hu2	xu	xʷuu	湖	lake
hua1	xua	xʷaa	花	flower
huai4	xuai	xʷai	坏	bad
huan4	xuan	xʷæn	换	replace
huang2	xuaŋ	xʷaŋ	黄	yellow
hui2	xuəi	xʷəi	回	go back
hun1	xuən	xʷən	婚	marriage
huo3	xuə	xʷoo	火	fire
ji1	tsi	tɕii	基	base
jia1	tsia	tɕaa	家	home
jian4	tsian	tɕæn	建	build
jiang1	tsiaŋ	tɕaŋ	江	river
jiao1	tsiau	tɕau	教	teach
jie3	tsiə	tɕee	姐	sister
jin1	tsin	tɕin	今	today
jing4	tsiəŋ	tɕəŋ	静	quiet
jiong3	tsiuŋ	tɕʷuŋ	炯	bright
jiu3	tsiəu	tɕəu	九	nine
ju4	tsy	tɕʷyy	具	tool
juan1	tsyan	tɕʷæn	捐	donate

jue2	tsyə	tɕʷee	掘	dig
jun1	tsuin	tɕʷin	均	equal
ka3	kʰa	kʰaa	卡	card
kai3	kʰai	kʰai	凱	triumphant
kan4	kʰan	kʰæn	看	see
kang2	kʰaŋ	kʰaŋ	扛	carry on shoulder
kao3	kʰau	kʰau	考	test
ke4	kʰə	kʰɤɤ	客	guest
kei1	kʰəi	kʰəi	剋	reprimand
ken3	kʰən	kʰən	肯	willing
keng1	kʰəŋ	kʰəŋ	坑	pit
kong1	kʰuŋ	kʰwuŋ	空	empty
kou3	kʰəu	kʰəu	口	mouth
ku3	kʰu	kʰwuu	苦	bitter
kua1	kʰua	kʰwaa	夸	praise
kuai4	kʰuai	kʰwai	快	fast
kuan3	kʰuan	kʰwæn	款	fund
kuang1	kʰuaŋ	kʰwaŋ	筐	basket
kui2	kʰuəi	kʰwəi	葵	sunflower
kun3	kʰuən	kʰwən	捆	tie
kuo4	kʰuə	kʰwoo	括	brackets
la1	la	laa	拉	pull
lai2	lai	lai	來	come
lan2	lan	læn	藍	blue
lang2	laŋ	laŋ	狼	wolf
lao3	lau	lau	老	old
le4	lə	lɤɤ	肋	rib
lei2	ləi	ləi	雷	thunder
leng3	ləŋ	ləŋ	冷	cold
li3	li	lʲii	里	inside
lia3	lia	lʲaa	倆	two
lian2	lian	lʲæn	帘	curtain
liang4	liaŋ	lʲaŋ	量	amount
liao4	liau	lʲau	料	material
lie4	liə	lʲee	裂	crack
lin2	lin	lʲin	林	woods
ling2	liəŋ	lʲəŋ	零	zero
liu4	liəu	lʲəu	六	six
long2	luŋ	lʷuŋ	隆	thriving
lou4	ləu	ləu	漏	leak
lu4	lu	lʷuu	路	road
lü3	ly	lᶣyy	旅	travel
luan3	luan	lʷæn	卵	egg

lüe4	lyə	lᶣee	略	omit
lun2	luən	lʷən	輪	wheel
luo4	luə	lʷoo	落	fall
ma3	ma	maa	馬	horse
mai2	mai	mai	埋	bury
man4	man	mæn	慢	slow
mang2	maŋ	maŋ	忙	busy
mao2	mau	mau	毛	fur
mei3	məi	məi	美	beautiful
men2	mən	mən	門	door
meng3	məŋ	məŋ	猛	fierce
mi3	mi	mʲii	米	rice
mian2	mian	mʲæn	棉	cotton
miao3	miau	mʲau	秒	second
mie4	miə	mʲee	篾	bamboo strip
min2	min	mʲin	民	people
ming2	miəŋ	mʲəŋ	名	name
miu4	miəu	mʲəu	謬	fallacy
mo4	mə	mʷoo	末	last
mou2	məu	məu	牟	gain (profit)
mu4	mu	mʷuu	目	eye
na2	na	naa	拿	take
nai3	nai	nai	奶	milk
nan2	nan	næn	男	man
nang2	naŋ	naŋ	囊	bag
nao4	nau	nau	腦	head
ne4	nə	nɤɤ	那	that
nei4	nəi	nəi	內	internal
neng2	nəŋ	nəŋ	能	can
ni3	ni	nʲii	你	you
nian2	nian	nʲæn	年	year
niang2	niaŋ	nʲaŋ	娘	mother
niao3	niau	nʲau	鳥	bird
nie1	niə	nʲee	捏	knead with fingers
nin2	nin	nʲin	您	you
ning2	niəŋ	nʲəŋ	凝	solidify
niu2	niəu	nʲəu	牛	cow
nong4	nuŋ	nʷuŋ	弄	play with
nou4	nəu	nəu	耨	weeding
nu4	nu	nʷuu	怒	anger
nü3	ny	nᶣyy	女	women
nuan3	nuan	nʷæn	暖	warm
nüe4	nyə	nᶣee	虐	cruel

nun2	nuən	nʷən	麿	fragrant
nuo2	nuə	nʷoo	挪	move
ou3	əu	əu	偶	even
pa4	pʰa	pʰaa	怕	afraid
pai1	pʰai	pʰai	拍	pat
pan4	pʰan	pʰæn	判	judge
pang4	pʰaŋ	pʰaŋ	胖	fat
pao3	pʰau	pʰau	跑	run
pei2	pʰəi	pʰəi	陪	accompany
pen2	pʰən	pʰən	盆	basin
peng2	pʰəŋ	pʰəŋ	朋	friend
pi2	pʰi	pʰjii	皮	skin
pian4	pʰian	pʰjæn	片	flake
piao1	pʰiau	pʰjau	漂	float
pie1	pʰiə	pʰjee	撇	cast aside
pin1	pʰin	pʰjin	拼	piece together
ping2	pʰiəŋ	pʰjəŋ	瓶	vase
po1	pʰə	pʰwoo	坡	slope
pou1	pʰəu	pʰəu	剖	dissect
pu3	pʰu	pʰwuu	普	ordinary
qi1	tsʰi	tɕʰii	七	seven
qia1	tsʰia	tɕʰa	掐	pinch
qian2	tsʰian	tɕʰæn	前	front
qiang1	tsʰiaŋ	tɕʰaŋ	腔	cavity
qiao1	tsʰiau	tɕʰau	敲	knock
qie1	tsʰiə	tɕʰee	切	cut
qin2	tsʰin	tɕʰin	琴	string instrument
qing2	tsʰiəŋ	tɕʰəŋ	情	feeling
qiong2	tsʰiuŋ	tɕʰwuŋ	窮	poor
qiu1	tsʰiəu	tɕʰəu	秋	autumn
qu4	tsʰy	tɕʰwyy	去	go
quan2	tsʰyan	tɕʰwæn	全	whole
que4	tsʰyə	tɕʰwee	雀	bird
qun2	tsʰuin	tɕʰwin	群	group
ran3	ẓan	ẓæn	染	dye
rang3	ẓaŋ	ẓaŋ	嚷	shout
rao4	ẓau	ẓau	繞	circle around
re4	ẓə	ẓɤɤ	熱	hot
ren2	ẓən	ẓən	人	person
reng1	ẓəŋ	ẓəŋ	扔	throw
ri4	ẓ̩	ẓ̩ẓ̩	日	sun
rong2	ẓuŋ	ẓʷuŋ	融	melt
rou4	ẓəu	ẓəu	肉	meet

ru4	ʐu	ʐʷuu	入	enter
ruan3	ʐuan	ʐʷæn	軟	soft
rui3	ʐuəi	ʐʷəi	蕊	stamen/pistil
run4	ʐuən	ʐʷən	潤	moist
ruo4	ʐuə	ʐʷoo	弱	weak
sa3	sa	saa	洒	sprinkle
sai4	sai	sai	塞	stuff in
san1	san	sæn	三	three
sang1	saŋ	saŋ	桑	mulberry
sao3	sau	sau	嫂	sister-in-law
se4	sə	sɤɤ	色	colour
sen1	sən	sən	森	forest
seng1	səŋ	səŋ	僧	monk
sha1	ʂa	ʂaa	沙	sand
shai4	ʂai	ʂai	晒	sunbathe
shan1	ʂan	ʂæn	山	mountain
shang4	ʂaŋ	ʂaŋ	上	up
shao3	ʂau	ʂau	少	few
she2	ʂə	ʂɤɤ	舌	tongue
shei2	ʂəi	ʂəi	誰	who
shen1	ʂən	ʂən	深	deep
sheng1	ʂəŋ	ʂəŋ	升	rise
shi2	ʂ	ʂʐʐ̩	十	ten
shou3	ʂəu	ʂəu	手	hand
shu3	ʂu	ʂʷuu	鼠	rat
shua1	ʂua	ʂʷaa	刷	brush
shuai3	ʂuai	ʂʷai	甩	throw away
shuan1	ʂuan	ʂʷæn	栓	fasten
shuang1	ʂuaŋ	ʂʷaŋ	霜	frost
shui1	ʂuəi	ʂʷəi	水	water
shun3	ʂuən	ʂʷən	瞬	wink
shuo1	ʂuə	ʂʷoo	說	speak
si4	s	szz̩	四	four
song4	suŋ	sʷuŋ	送	send
sou4	səu	səu	嗽	cough
su4	su	sʷuu	速	speed
suan1	suan	sʷæn	酸	sour
sui2	suəi	sʷəi	隨	follow
sun1	suən	sʷən	孫	grandchild
suo3	suə	sʷoo	索	search
ta1	tʰa	tʰaa	她	she
tai1	tʰai	tʰai	胎	embryo
tan3	tʰan	tʰæn	毯	blanket

tang2	tʰaŋ	tʰaŋ	糖	sugar
tao2	tʰau	tʰau	逃	escape
te4	tʰə	tʰɤɤ	特	special
tei1	tʰəi	tʰəi	忒	(a sound)
teng2	tʰəŋ	tʰəŋ	疼	pain
ti2	tʰi	tʰʲii	堤	dam
tian1	tʰian	tʰʲæn	天	sky
tiao4	tʰiau	tʰʲau	跳	jump
tie1	tʰiə	tʰʲee	贴	stick on
ting2	tʰiəŋ	tʰʲəŋ	停	stop
tong2	tʰuŋ	tʰʷuŋ	同	same
tou2	tʰəu	tʰəu	投	cast
tu3	tʰu	tʰʷuu	土	mud
tuan1	tʰuan	tʰʷæn	湍	fast water
tui1	tʰuəi	tʰʷəi	推	push
tun1	tʰuən	tʰʷən	吞	swallow
tuo1	tʰuə	tʰʷoo	脱	take off
wa3	ua	waa	瓦	tile
wai4	uai	wai	外	outside
wan2	uan	wæn	完	finish
wang4	uaŋ	waŋ	忘	forget
wei4	uəi	wəi	位	seat
wen2	uən	wən	蚊	mosquito
weng1	uəŋ	wəŋ	翁	old man
wo3	uə	woo	我	I
wu3	u	uu	五	five
xi1	si	ɕii	西	west
xia4	sia	ɕaa	下	down
xian1	sian	ɕæn	先	ahead
xiang1	siaŋ	ɕaŋ	香	good smell
xiao3	siau	ɕau	小	small
xie1	siə	ɕee	些	some
xin1	sin	ɕin	心	heart
xing2	siəŋ	ɕəŋ	形	shape
xiong1	siuŋ	ɕʷuŋ	胸	chest
xiu1	siəu	ɕəu	修	repair
xu1	sy	ɕʷyy	虚	empty
xuan2	syan	ɕʷæn	旋	spiral
xue1	syə	ɕʷee	削	peel
xun4	suin	ɕʷin	迅	fast
ya3	ia	jaa	雅	refined
yan3	ian	jæn	眼	eye
yang2	iaŋ	jaŋ	羊	sheep

yao4	iau	jau	要	want
ye4	iə	jee	夜	night
yi1	i	ii	一	one
yin1	in	in	音	sound
ying3	iəŋ	jəŋ	影	shadow
yong4	iuŋ	jʷuŋ	用	use
you3	iəu	jəu	有	have
yu3	y	yy	雨	rain
yuan2	yan	ɥæn	原	field
yue4	yə	ɥee	月	moon
yun2	yin	ɥin	云	cloud
za2	tsa	tsaa	砸	pound
zai4	tsai	tsai	再	again
zan2	tsan	tsæn	咱	we
zang4	tsaŋ	tsaŋ	葬	bury
zao3	tsau	tsau	早	early
ze2	tsə	tsɤɤ	責	duty
zei2	tsəi	tsəi	賊	thief
zen3	tsən	tsən	怎	how
zeng1	tsəŋ	tsəŋ	增	add
zha4	tʂa	tʂaa	炸	explode
zhai3	tʂai	tʂai	宅	residence
zhan4	tʂan	tʂæn	站	stand
zhang4	tʂaŋ	tʂaŋ	丈	3.3 metres
zhao3	tʂau	tʂau	找	look for
zhe2	tʂə	tʂɤɤ	折	break
zhei4	tʂəi	tʂəi	這	this
zhen1	tʂən	tʂən	真	true
zheng4	tʂəŋ	tʂəŋ	正	upright
zhi1	tʂ	tʂz̻	知	know
zhong4	tʂuŋ	tʂʷuŋ	重	heavy
zhou1	tʂəu	tʂəu	周	week
zhu3	tʂu	tʂʷuu	主	master
zhua1	tʂua	tʂʷaa	抓	catch
zhuai4	tʂuai	tʂʷai	拽	drag
zhuan4	tʂuan	tʂʷæn	僎	compose
zhuang4	tʂuaŋ	tʂʷaŋ	壯	strong
zhui1	tʂuəi	tʂʷəi	追	chase
zhun3	tʂuən	tʂʷən	准	accurate
zhuo1	tʂuə	tʂʷoo	桌	table
zi4	ts	tszz	字	character
zong1	tsuŋ	tsʷuŋ	宗	ancestor
zou3	tsəu	tsəu	走	walk

zu2	tsu	tsʷuu	足	foot
zuan4	tsuan	tsʷæn	纂	edit
zui3	tsuəi	tsʷəi	嘴	mouth
zun1	tsuən	tsʷən	鳟	trout
zuo4	tsuə	tsʷoo	坐	sit

Dialectal (three in all)

dia3	tia	tʲaa	嗲	spoiled voice
fiao4	fiau	fʲau	覅	not want
rua2	ʐua	ʐʷaa	挼	wrinkle

Interjections (seven in all; some may represent more than one word)

hm4	(showing contempt)
hng4	(showing contempt)
m2	(expecting an answer)
n4	yes
ng4	yes
o3	(showing surprise)
yo1	(showing surprise)

REFERENCES

Chinese first names are written as a single word without a hyphen, such as *Dexi Zhu* (not *De Xi Zhu*, *De-Xi Zhu*, or *De-xi Zhu*), unless an author's name is conventionally spelled with a hyphen, such as *Yuen-Ren Chao* (not *Yuenren Chao*). When the first name has a hyphen, both syllables are capitalized, such as *Chin-Chuan Cheng* (not *Chin-chuan Cheng*). Works in Chinese are given an English entry followed by a Chinese entry.

ABERCROMBIE, DAVID (1967). *Elements of General Phonetics* (Chicago: Aldine).

ABNEY, STEVEN (1987). 'The English Noun Phrase in its Sentential Aspect', doctoral dissertation, MIT, Cambridge, Mass.

AO, BENJAMIN X. P. (1992). 'The Non-uniqueness Condition and the Segmentation of the Chinese Syllable', *Working Papers in Linguistics*, 42: 1–25 (Ohio State University).

——(1993). 'Phonetics and Phonology of Nantong Chinese', doctoral dissertation, Ohio State University, Columbus.

ARCHANGELI, DIANA (1988). 'Aspects of Underspecification Theory', *Phonology*, 5: 183–207.

BAAYEN, R. HARALD, PIEPENBROCK, RICHARD, and GULIKERS, L. (1993). *The CELEX Lexical Database (CD-ROM)* (Philadelphia, PA: Linguistic Data Consortium, University of Pennsylvania).

BAILEY, CHARLES-JAMES NICE (1978). *Gradience in English Syllabification and a Revised Concept of Unmarked Syllabification* (Indiana University Linguistics Club, Bloomington).

BAO, ZHIMING (1990*a*). 'On the Nature of Tone', doctoral dissertation, MIT, Cambridge, Mass.

——(1990*b*). 'Fanqie Languages and Reduplication', *Linguistic Inquiry*, 21.3: 317–50.

——(1999). *The Structure of Tone* (New York: Oxford University Press).

BATES, DAWN (1988). 'Prominence Relations and Structures in English Compound Morphology', doctoral dissertation, University of Washington, Seattle.

BAXTER, WILLIAM (1992). *A Handbook of Old Chinese Phonology* (Berlin: Mouton de Gruyter).

BECKMAN, MARY (1986). *Stress and Non-stress Accent* (Dordrecht: Foris).

——and PIERREHUMBERT, JANET (1986). 'Intonation Structure in Japanese and English', *Phonology Yearbook*, 3: 255–309.

BLEVINS, JULIETTE (1995). 'The Syllable in Phonological Theory', in John Goldsmith (ed.), *The Handbook of Phonological Theory* (Cambridge, Mass.: Blackwell), 206–44.

——(2003). *Evolutionary Phonology: The Emergence of Sound Patterns* (Cambridge: Cambridge University Press).

BOLINGER, DWIGHT (1967). 'Adjectives in English: Attribution and Predication', *Lingua*, 18: 1–34.

BOOIJ, GEERT (1988). 'The Relation between Inheritance and Argument Linking: Deverbal Nouns in Dutch', in Martin Everaert *et al.* (eds.), *Morphology and Modularity: In Honour of Henk Schultink* (Dordrecht: Foris), 57–74.

Borowsky, Toni (1989). 'Structure Preservation and the Syllable Coda in English', *Natural Language and Linguistic Theory*, 7: 145–66.

Broselow, Ellen (1995). 'Skeletal Positions and Moras', in John Goldsmith (ed.), *The Handbook of Phonological Theory* (Cambridge, Mass.: Blackwell), 175–205.

Bybee, Joan (2001). *Phonology and Language Use* [Cambridge Studies in Linguistics 94] (Cambridge: Cambridge University Press).

Burzio, Luigi (1994). *Principles of English Stress* (Cambridge: Cambridge University Press).

——(1996). 'Surface Constraints versus Underlying Representation', in Jacques Durand and Bernard Laks (eds.), *Current Trends in Phonology: Models and Methods*, vol. i (Salford: European Studies Research Institute, University of Salford Publications), 123–41.

Cao, Yun (1987). 'Beijinghua tɕ zu shengmu de qianhua xianxiang' [The fronting of the tɕ series of onsets in Beijing Mandarin], *Yuyan Jiaoxue Yu Yanjiu*, 1987.3: 84–91.
[曹耘, 1987, '北京話 tɕ 組 聲母 的 前化 現象', <語言 教學 與 研究> 1987.3: 84–91.]

Cen, Qixiang (1956). 'Guanyu Hanyu goucifa de jige wenti' [Some problems concerning Chinese word structure], *Zhongguo Yuwen*, 1956.12: 12–14.
[岑麒祥, 1956, '關於漢語構詞法的幾個問題', <中國 語文> 1956.12: 12–14.]

Chan, Marjorie K. M. (1985). 'Fuzhou Phonology: A Non-linear Analysis of Tone and Stress', doctoral dissertation, University of Washington, Seattle.

——(1991). 'Contour-tone Spreading and Tone Sandhi in Danyang Chinese', *Phonology*, 8.2: 237–59.

Chang, Kun (1953). 'On the Tone System of the Miao-Yao Languages', *Language*, 29.3: 374–8.

Chao, Yuen-Ren (1927). *Guo Yin Xin Shi Yun* [A New Vocabulary of Rhymes] (Shanghai: Commercial Press).
[趙元任, 1927, <國音新詩韻>, 上海: 商務印書館.]
——(1930). 'A System of Tone Letters', *Le maître phonétique*, 45: 24–7.
——(1931). 'Fanqie yu ba zhong' [Eight types of Fanqie languages], *Bulletin of the Institute of History and Philology, Academia Sinica*, 2.3: 312–54.
[趙元任, 1931, '反切語八種', < 中央研究院歷史語言研究所集刊> 2.3: 312–54.
——(1933). 'Tone and Intonation in Chinese, *Bulletin of the Institute of History and Philology, Academia Sinica*, 4.2: 121–134.
——(1934). 'The Non-uniqueness of Phonemic Solutions of Phonetic Systems', *Bulletin of the Institute of History and Philology, Academia Sinica*, 4.4: 363–97. Reprinted in Martin Joos (ed.), *Readings in Linguistics I* (Chicago: University of Chicago Press, 1957), 38–54.
——(1948). 'The Voiced Velar Fricative as an Initial in Mandarin', *Le Maître phonétique*, 89: 2–3.
——(1968). *A Grammar of Spoken Chinese* (Berkeley and Los Angeles: University of California Press).
——(1973). 'Chinese as a Symbolic System', in Richard B. Mather (ed.), *Papers of the C.I.C. Far Eastern Language Institute,* vol. iv (Ann Arbor, MI: Panel on Far Eastern Language Institutes of the Committee on Institutional Cooperation), 1–9.
——(1979). *Hanyu Kouyu Yufa* [A Grammar of Spoken Chinese], trans. Shuxiang Lü (Beijing: Shangwu Yinshuguan).
[趙元任, 1979, <漢語 口語 語法>, 呂叔湘譯, 北京: 商務印書館.]

CHEN, MATTHEW (1979). 'Metrical Structure: Evidence from Chinese Poetry', *Linguistic Inquiry*, 10: 371–420.

——(1980). 'The Primacy of Rhythm in Verse: A Linguistic Perspective', *Journal of Chinese Linguistics*, 8: 15–41.

——(1984). 'Abstract Symmetry in Chinese Verse', *Linguistic Inquiry*, 15.1: 167–70.

——(1987). 'The Syntax of Xiamen Tone Sandhi', *Phonology Yearbook*, 4: 109–49.

——(2000). *Tone Sandhi: Patterns across Chinese Dialects*, Cambridge Studies in Linguistics 92 (Cambridge: Cambridge University Press).

CHENG, AIWEN, and YU, PING (1979). 'Binglie shuangyinci de zi xu' [Word order in disyllabic coordinate expressions], *Zhongguo Yuwen*, 1979.2 (149): 101–5.

[陈爱文, 于平, 1979, '并列双音词的字序', <中國 語文>, 1979.2 (149): 101–5.]

CHENG, CHIN-CHUAN (1973). *A Synchronic Phonology of Mandarin Chinese*. Monographs on Linguistic Analysis 4 (The Hague: Mouton).

CHENG, ROBERT L. (1966). 'Mandarin Phonological Structure', *Journal of Linguistics*, 2.2: 135–262.

——(1968). 'Tone Sandhi in Taiwanese', *Linguistics*, 41: 19–42.

——(1973). 'Some notes on Tone Sandhi in Taiwanese', *Linguistics*, 100: 5–25.

CHEUNG, KWAN-HIN (1986). 'The Phonology of Present-Day Cantonese', doctoral dissertation, University of London.

Chinese Academy of Social Sciences Institute of Linguistics (1978). *Xiandai Hanyu Cidian* [A Dictionary of Modern Chinese] (Beijing: Shangwu Yinshuguan).

[中國社會科學院語言研究所詞典編輯室編, 1978, <現代 漢語 詞典>, 北京: 商務印書館.]

Chinese Ministry of Education (2004). 'Zhongguo yuyan wenzi shiyong qingkuang diaocha bufen shuju' [Survey of language use in China: partial data], [http://www.china-language.gov.cn/doc/zhongguodiaocha2004-12/shujv.doc].

[中国教育部语言文字应用研究所, 2004, '中国语言文字使用情况调查部分数据'.]

CHOMSKY, NOAM (1957). *Syntactic Structures* (The Hague: Mouton).

——(1964). *Current Issues in Linguistic Theory* (The Hague: Mouton).

——(1981). *Lectures on Government and Binding* (Dordrecht: Foris).

——(1986). *Knowledge of Language: Its Nature, Origin, and Use* (New York: Prager).

——(1994). *Bare Phrase Structure*, MIT Occasional Papers in Linguistics 5 (Cambridge, Mass.: MIT; distributed by MIT Working Papers in Linguistics).

——and HALLE, MORRIS (1968). *The Sound Pattern of English* (New York: Harper & Row).

CHU, MIN, and LÜ, SHUNAN (1996). 'A Text-to-Speech Synthesis with High Intelligibility and Naturalness for Chinese', *Chinese Journal of Acoustics*, 15.1: 81–90.

CHUNG, RAUNG-FU (1996). *The Segmental Phonology Southern Min in Taiwan* (Taipei: Crane Publishing Company).

CINQUE, GUGLIELMO (1993). 'A Null Theory of Phrase and Compound Stress', *Linguistic Inquiry*, 24.2: 239–97.

CLEMENTS, G. N. (1985). 'The Geometry of Phonological Features', *Phonology Yearbook*, 2: 225–52.

——and HUME, ELIZABETH (1995). 'The Internal Organization of Speech Sounds', in John Goldsmith (ed.), *The Handbook of Phonological Theory* (Cambridge, Mass.: Blackwell), 245–306.

COLEMAN, JOHN (1996). 'Declarative Syllabification in Tashlhit Berber', in Jacques Durand and Bernard Laks (eds.), *Current Trends in Phonology: Models and Methods*, vol. i

(Salford: European Studies Research Institute, University of Salford Publications), 175–216.

——(2001). 'The Phonetics and Phonology of Tashlhiyt Berber Syllabic Consonants', *Transactions of the Philological Society*, 99.1: 29–64.

DA, JUN (1998). 'Chinese Text Computing', http://lingua.mtsu.edu/chinese-computing/. (Murfreesboro, TN: Department of Foreign Languages and Literatures, Middle Tennessee State University).

DAI, JOHN XIANGLING (1990). 'Historical Morphologization of Syntactic Words: Evidence from Chinese Derived Verbs', *Diachronica*, 7.1: 9–46.

——(1992). 'Chinese Morphology and its Interface with the Syntax', doctoral dissertation, Ohio State University, Columbus.

DE LACY, PAUL (2002). 'The Interaction of Tone and Stress in Optimality Theory', *Phonology*, 19.1: 1–32.

DELL, FRANÇOIS (2004). 'On Unwarranted Claims about Stress and Tone in Beijing Mandarin', *Cahiers de Linguistique Asie Orientale* (Paris), 33.1: 33–63.

——and ELMEDLAOUI, MOHAMED (1985). 'Syllabic Consonants and Syllabification in Imdlawn Tashlhiyt Berber', *Journal of African Languages and Linguistics*, 7: 105–30.

—— ——(1996). 'Nonsyllabic Transitional Vocoids in Imdlawn Tashlhiyt Berber', in Jacques Durand and Bernard Laks (eds.), *Current Trends in Phonology: Models and Methods*, vol. i (Salford: European Studies Research Institute, University of Salford Publications), 217–44.

—— ——(2003). *Syllables in Tashlhiyt Berber and in Moroccan Arabic*, Kluwer International Handbooks in Linguistics, vol. ii (Dordrecht and Boston: Kluwer Academic Publishers).

DOBSON, W. A. C. H. (1959). *Late Archaic Chinese: A Grammatical Study* (Toronto: University of Toronto Press).

DONG, SHAOWEN (1958). *Yuyin Changtan* [Introduction to Phonetics] (Beijing: Wenhua Jiaoyu Chubanshe).

[董少文, 1958, <語音 常談>, 北京: 文化 教育 出版社.]

DUANMU, SAN (1989). 'Cyclicity and the Mandarin Third Tone Sandhi', MS, MIT.

——(1990). 'A Formal Study of Syllable, Tone, Stress and Domain in Chinese Languages', doctoral dissertation, MIT, Cambridge, Mass.

——(1993). 'Rhyme Length, Stress, and Association Domains', *Journal of East Asian Linguistics*, 2.1: 1–44.

——(1994). 'Against Contour Tone Units', *Linguistic Inquiry*, 25.4: 555–608.

——(1996). 'Tone: An Overview', *Glot International*, 2.4: 3–10.

——(1997). 'Phonologically Motivated Word Order Movement: Evidence from Chinese Compounds', *Studies in the Linguistic Sciences*, 27.1: 49–77.

——(1998). 'Wordhood in Chinese', in Jerome L. Packard (ed.), *New Approaches to Chinese Word Formation: Morphology, Phonology and the Lexicon in Modern and Ancient Chinese* (Berlin: Mouton de Gruyter), 135–96.

——(1999a). 'Metrical Structure and Tone: Evidence from Mandarin and Shanghai', *Journal of East Asian Linguistics*, 8.1: 1–38.

——(1999b). 'Stress and the Development of Disyllabic Words in Chinese', *Diachronica*, XVI: 1.1–35.

——(1999c). 'The syllable in Chinese', in Harry van der Hulst and Nancy Ritter (eds.), *The Syllable: Views and Facts*. Studies in Generative Grammar 45 (Berlin: Mouton de Gruyter), 477–99.

——(2000). *The Phonology of Standard Chinese* (Oxford: Oxford University Press).

——(2002). 'Two theories of onset clusters', *Shengyun Luncong* [Chinese Phonology], 11: 97–120.

——(2003). 'The Syllable Phonology of Mandarin and Shanghai', *Proceedings of the Fifteenth North American Conference on Chinese Linguistics* (Los Angeles: University of Southern California Press), 86–102.

——(2004). 'A Corpus Study of Chinese Regulated Verse: Phrasal Stress and the Analysis of Variability', *Phonology*, 21.1: 43–89.

——(2005). 'The Tone-Syntax Interface in Chinese: Some Recent Controversies', in Shigeki Kaji (ed.), *Proceedings of the Symposium "Cross-Linguistic Studies of Tonal Phenomena, Historical Development, Tone–Syntax Interface, and Descriptive Studies", December 14–16, 2004* (Tokyo: Institute for the Study of Languages and Cultures of Asia and Africa, Tokyo University of Foreign Studies), 221–54.

——and LU, BINGFU (1990). 'Word Length Variations in Chinese', MS, MIT and University of Connecticut.

——WAKEFIELD, GREGORY H., HSU, YIPING, CRISTINA, G., and QIU, SHANPING (1998). 'Taiwanese Putonghua speech and transcript corpus', *Linguistic Data Consortium*.

FABB, NIGEL (2002). *Language and Literary Structure: The Linguistic Analysis of Form in Verse and Narrative* (Cambridge and New York: Cambridge University Press).

——and HALLE, MORRIS (2005). 'Pairs and Triplets: A Theory of Metrical Verse', paper presented at the International Conference "Typology of Poetic Forms", École des Hautes Études en Sciences Sociales, Paris.

FAN, JIYAN (1958). 'Xing-ming zuhe jian "de" zi de yufa zuoyong' [The grammatical function of 'de' in adjective-noun constructions]. *Zhongguo Yuwen*, 1958.5: 213–17.

[范繼淹, 1958, '形-名組合間 "的" 字的語法 作用, <中國 語文> 1958.5: 213–17.]

FENG, LONG (1985). 'Beijinghua yuliu zhong shengyundiao de shichang' [Duration of initials, finals, and tones in Beijing dialect], in Tao Lin and Lijia Wang (eds.), *Beijing Yuyin Shiyanlu* [Working Papers in Experimental Phonetics] (Beijing: Beijing University Press), 131–95.

[馮隆, 1985, '北京話語流中聲韻調的時長', <北京 語音 實驗錄>, 林燾, 王理嘉, 等 著, pp. 131–95. 北京: 北京 大學出版社.]

FENG, SHENGLI (1997). *Hanyu de Yunlu, Cifa yu Jufa* [Interactions between Morphology, Syntax and Prosody in Chinese] (Beijing: Beijing University Press).

[馮勝利, 1997, <漢語 的 韻律, 詞法 與 句法>, 北京: 北京大學出版社.]

——(1998a). 'Lun Hanyu de "ziran yinbu" [On 'natural feet' in Chinese], *Zhongguo Yuwen*, 1998.1 (262): 40–7.

[馮勝利, 1998a, '論 漢語 的 "自然 音步", <中國 語文> 1998.1 (262): 40–7.]

——(1998b). 'Prosodic Structure and Compound Words in Classical Chinese', in Jerome L. Packard (ed.), *New Approaches to Chinese Word Formation: Morphology, phonology and the lexicon in modern and ancient Chinese* (Berlin: Mouton de Gruyter), 197–260.

——(2004). 'Dong bin daozhi yu yunlu goucifa' [Verb-object inversion and prosodic morphology]. *Yuyan Kexue*, [Linguistic Science] 3.3 (May 2004): 12–20.

[馮勝利, 2004, '動賓倒置與韻律構詞法', <語言科学>, 3.3 (May 2004): 12–20.]

FIDELHOLTZ, JAMES L. (1975). 'Word frequency and vowel reduction in English', in *Papers from the 11th Regional Meeting of the Chicago Linguistic Society*, CLS 11 (Chicago: Chicago Linguistic Society), 200–13.

FIRTH, J. R. (1957). *Papers in Linguistics 1934–57* (London: Oxford University Press).

——and ROGERS, B. B. (1937). 'The Structure of the Chinese Monosyllable in a Hunanese Dialect (Changsha)', *Bulletin of the School of Oriental Studies*, 8.4: 1055–74.

FRY, DENNIS B. (1958). 'Experiments in the Perception of Stress', *Language and Speech*, 1: 126–52.

FU, JINGQI (1990). 'Labial–Labial Cooccurrence Restrictions and Syllabic Structure', *Proceedings of the 1st Meeting of the Formal Linguistic Society of Mid America* (May, University of Wisconsin, Madison), 129–44.

FU, MAOJI (1956). 'Beijing hua de yinwei he pinyin zimu' [Phonemes and Pinyin symbols in the Beijing speech]. *Zhongguo Yuwen*, 1956.5: 3–12.

[傅懋勣, 1956, '北京 話 的 音位 和 拼音 字母', <中國 語文> 1956.5: 3–12.]

FUDGE, E. C. (1968). 'Syllables', *Journal of Linguistics*, 5: 253–86.

GAO, MINGKAI, and SHI, ANSHI (1963). (*Yuyanxue Gailun* [Introduction to Linguistics] (Beijing: Zhonghua Shuju).

[高名凱, 石安石, 1963, <語言學 概論>, 北京: 中華 書局.]

GIEGERICH, HEINZ (1985). *Metrical Phonology and Phonological Structure: German and English* (Cambridge: Cambridge University Press).

GIMSON, A. C. (1979). 'The Pronunciation of English', in Patrick Hanks (ed.), *Collin's Dictionary of the English Language* (London & Glasgow: Collins), xix–xxi.

GOH, YENG-SENG (1997). *The Segmental Phonology of Beijing Mandarin* (Taipei: Crane Publishing Co).

——(2000). 'Beijinghua shi danyinjie yuyan de zhiyi' [Is Beijing Mandarin a monosyllabic language?], *Contemporary Linguistics*, 2.4: 231–47.

[吳英成, 2000, '北京話是 單音節語言的置疑', <當代語言學>, 2.4: 231–47.]

GOLDSMITH, JOHN (1976). 'Autosegmental Phonology', doctoral dissertation, MIT, Cambridge, Mass. (reproduced by the Indiana University Linguistics Club, Bloomington, Ind.).

——(1981). 'English as a Tone Language', in Didier L. Goyvaerts (ed.), *Phonology in the 1980's* (Ghent, Belgium: E. Story-Scientia), 287–308.

——(1984). 'Tone and Accent in Tonga', in G. N. Clements and John Goldsmith (eds.), *Autosegmental Studies in Bantu Tone* (Dordrecht: Foris), 19–51.

GOLSTON, CHRIS (1998). 'Constraint-Based Metrics', *Natural Language and Linguistic Theory*, 16.4: 719–70.

——and KEHREIN, WOLFGANG (1999). 'Laryngeal Contrasts', MS., California State University Fresno and Philipps University of Marburg.

——and RIAD, TOMAS (2005). 'The Phonology of Greek Lyric Meter', *Journal of Linguistics*, 41.1: 77–115.

GUO, SHAOYU (1938). 'Zhongguo yuci zhi tanxing zuoyong' [The elastic function of Chinese word length], *Yen Ching Hsueh Pao*, 24. Reprinted in Shaoyu Guo 1963: 1–40.

[郭紹虞, 1938, '中國語詞之彈性作用', <燕京學報> 24. 收入 郭紹虞, 1963: 1–40.]

——(1963). *Yuwen Tonglun* [Collected Essays on Chinese Language and Literature] (Hong Kong: Taiping Shuju).

[郭紹虞, 1963, <語文 通論>, 香港: 太平書局.]

Guojia Yuyan Wenzi Gongzuo Weiyuanhui [National Committee on Language Affairs] (1989). *Xiandai Hanyu Tongyongzi Biao* [Common Characters in Modern Chinese] (Beijing: Yuwen Chubanshe).

[國家語言文字工作委員會, 1989, <現代漢語通用字 表>, 北京: 語文出版社.]

GUSSENHOVEN, CARLOS (1988). 'Adequacy in Intonation Analysis: The Case of Dutch', in Harry van der Hulst and Norval Smith (eds.), *Autosegmental Studies on Pitch Accent*, Linguistic Models 11 (Dordrecht: Foris), 95–122.

——(1991). 'The English Rhythm Rule as an Accent Deletion Rule', *Phonology*, 8: 1–35.

HALLE, MORRIS (1962). 'Phonology in Generative Grammar', *Word*, 18: 54–72.

——(1995). 'Feature Geometry and Feature Spreading', *Linguistic Inquiry*, 26: 1–46.

——(1998). 'The stress of English Words: 1968–98', *Linguistic Inquiry*, 29.4: 539–68.

——(2005). 'Palatalization/Velar Softening: What it Is and What it Tells us about the Nature of Language', *Linguistic Inquiry*, 36.1: 23–41.

——and CLEMENTS, G. N. (1983). *Problem Book in Phonology* (Cambridge, Mass.: MIT Press).

——and IDSARDI, WILLIAM (1995). 'General properties of stress and metrical structure', in John Goldsmith (ed.), *The Handbook of Phonological Theory* (Cambridge, Mass.: Blackwell), 403–43.

——and KEYSER, SAMUEL JAY (1971). *English Stress: Its Form, Its Growth, and Its Role in Verse* (New York: Harper and Row).

——and STEVENS, KENNETH (1971). 'A Note on Laryngeal Features', *RLE Quarterly Progress Report*, 101: 198–213 (MIT).

——, VAUX, BERT, and WOLFE, ANDREW (2000). 'On Feature Spreading and the Representation of Place of Articulation', *Linguistic Inquiry*, 31.3: 387–444.

——and VERGNAUD, JEAN-ROGER (1987). *An Essay on Stress* (Cambridge, Mass.: MIT Press).

HAMMOND, MICHAEL (1997). 'Vowel Quantity and Syllabification in English', *Language*, 73: 1–17.

——(1999). *The Phonology of English: A Prosodic Optimality Theoretic Approach* (Oxford: Oxford University Press).

HANSON, KRISTIN, and KIPARSKY, PAUL (1996). 'A Parametric Theory of Poetic Meter', *Language*, 72.2: 287–335.

HARRIS, JOHN (1994). *English Sound Structure* (Oxford: Blackwell).

HARTMAN, LAWTON M. (1944). 'The Segmental Phonemes of the Peiping Dialect', *Language*, 20: 28–42.

HASHIMOTO, ANN YUE (1969). 'The verb "to be" in Modern Chinese', in John W M Verhaar (ed.), *Twi/Modern Chinese/Arabic/*, The Verb 'be' and its synonyms: philosophical and grammatical studies, Volume 4, Foundations of language Supplementary series Volume 9 (Dordrecht: Reidel), 72–111.

HASHIMOTO, MANTARO J. (1982). 'The so-called "original" and "changed" tones in Fukienese: A case study of Chinese tone morphophonemics', *Bulletin of the Institute of History and Philology, Academia Sinica*, 53.4: 645–59.

HAYES, BRUCE (1989a). 'Compensatory Lengthening in Moraic Phonology', *Linguistic Inquiry*, 20.2: 253–306.

——(1989b). 'The Prosodic Hierarchy in Meter', in Paul Kiparsky and Gilbert Youmans (eds.), *Rhythm and Meter* (San Diego: Academic Press), 201–60.

——(1995). *Metrical Stress Theory: Principles and case studies* (Chicago: University of Chicago Press).

HE, KEKANG, and LI, DAKUI (1987). *Xiandai Hanyu San Qian Changyong Ci Biao* [Three Thousand Most Commonly Used Words in Modern Chinese] (Beijing: Beijing Shifan Daxue Chubanshe).

[何克抗, 李大魁, 主編, 1987, <現代 漢語 三 千 常用 詞 表>, 北京: 北京師範大學出版社.]

HE, YANG, and JING, SONG (1992). 'Beijinghua yudiao de shiyan tansuo' [Intonations of the Beijing dialect: an experimental exploration]. *Yuyan Jiaoxue Yu Yanjiu*, 1992.2: 71–96.

[賀陽, 勁松, 1992, '北京話 語調 的 實驗 探索', <語言教學與研究> 1992.2: 71–96.]

HE, YUANJIAN (2004). 'The Loop Theory in Chinese Morphology', *Contemporary Linguistics*, 6.3: 223–35.

[何元建, 2004, '回环理论与汉语构词法', <当代语言学>, 6.3: 223–35]

HOA, MONIQUE (1983). *L'accentuation en pékinois* (Paris: Editions Langages Croisés). (distributed by Centre de Recherches Linguistiques sur l'Asie Orientale, Paris).

HOCKETT, CHARLES F. (1947). 'Peiping Phonology', *Journal of the American Oriental Society*, 67.4: 253–67.

HOGG, RICHARD, and MCCULLY, C. B. (1987). *Metrical Phonology: A Coursebook* (Cambridge: Cambridge University Press).

HOWIE, JOHN (1976). *An Acoustic Study of Mandarin Tones and Vowels* (London: Cambridge University Press).

HSUEH, FENGSHENG (1986). *An Anatomy of the Pekingese Sound System* (Taipei: Taiwan Xuesheng Shuju).

[薛鳳生, 1986, <國語音系解析>, 台北: 台灣學生書局.]

HU, MINGYANG (1991). *Yuyanxue Lunwen Xuan* [Selected Writings in Linguistics] (Beijing: Renmin Daxue Chubanshe).

[胡明揚, 1991, <語言學 論文選>, 北京: 人民 大學 出版社.]

HU, TAN (1980). 'Zangyu (Lasa hua) shengdiao yanjiu' [A study of tone in Lhasa Tibetan], *Minzu Yuwen*, 1: 22–36.

[胡坦, 1980, '藏語 (拉薩 話) 聲調 研究', <民族 語文> 1: 22–36.]

HUANG, JAMES C.-T. (1984). 'Phrase Structure, Lexical Integrity, and Chinese Compounds', *Journal of the Chinese Language Teachers Association*, 19.2: 53–78.

HYMAN, LARRY (1977). 'On the Nature of Linguistic Stress', in Larry Hyman (ed.), *Studies in Stress and Accent*, Southern California Occasional Papers in Linguistics 4 (Los Angeles: Department of Linguistics, University of Southern California), 37–82.

——(1985). *A Theory of Phonological Weight* (Dordrecht: Foris).

——(1987). 'Prosodic Domains in Kukuya', *Natural Language and Linguistic Theory*, 5.3: 311–34.

IDSARDI, WILLIAM (1992). 'The Computation of Prosody', doctoral dissertation, MIT, Cambridge, Mass.

JACKENDOFF, RAY (1972). *Semantic Interpretation in Generative Grammar* (Cambridge, Mass.: MIT Press).

JAKOBSON, ROMAN, FANT, GUNNAR, and HALLE, MORRIS (1952). *Preliminaries to Speech Analysis: The Distinctive Features and Their Correlates* (Cambridge, Mass.: MIT Press).

JESPERSEN, OTTO (1922). *Language: Its Nature, Development and Origin* (New York: Macmillan).

JI, XIANLIN. (ed.) (1988). *Zhongguo Dabaikequanshu: Yuyan Wenzi* [Chinese Encyclopaedia: Language and Orthography] (Beijing and Shanghai: Zhongguo Dabaikequanshu Chubanshe).

[季羨林, 主 編, 1988, <中國大百科全書: 語言 文字>, 北京, 上海: 中國大百科全書出版社.]

JIA, CAIZHU (1992). 'Beijinghua de qingsheng erhuayun' [Unstressed [ɚ]-suffixed syllables in Beijing dialect], *Zhongguo Yuwen*, 1992.1 (226): 39–44.

[賈采珠, (1992), '北京話 的 輕聲 兒化韻', <中國 語文> 1992.1 (226): 39–44.]

JONES, DANIEL (1950). *The Pronunciation of English*. 3rd edn. (Cambridge: Cambridge University Press).

KAGER, RENÉ (1992). 'Are There Any Truly Quantity-Insensitive Systems?', in *Proceedings of the 18th Annual Meeting of the Berkeley Linguistics Society: General Session and Parasession on the Place of Morphology in a Grammar* (Berkeley: Berkeley Linguistics Society), 123–32.

——(1993). 'Alternatives to the Iambic-Trochee Law', *Natural Language and Linguistic Theory*, 11.3: 381–432.

KAHN, DANIEL (1976). 'Syllable-based Generalizations in English Phonology', doctoral dissertation, MIT, Cambridge, Mass.

KAISSE, ELLEN (1985). *Connected Speech* (New York: Academic Press).

KARLGREN, BERNHARD (1915–26). *Études sur la phonologie Chinoise* (Upsala: K.W. Appelberg).

——(1949). *The Chinese Language: An Essay on its Nature and History* (New York: The Ronald Press Company).

KAYNE, RICHARD S. (1994). *The Antisymmetry of Syntax* (Cambridge, Mass.: MIT Press).

KENNEDY, GEORGE A. (1953). 'Two Tone Patterns in Tangsic', *Language*, 29.3: 367–73.

KENSTOWICZ, MICHAEL (1987). 'Tone and Accent in Kizigua: A Bantu Language', in P-M. Bertinetto and M. Loporcaro (eds.), *Certamen Phonologicum* (Turin: Rosenberg & Sellier), 177–88.

——(1994). *Phonology in Generative Grammar* (Oxford: Blackwell).

KENYON, JOHN SAMUEL, and KNOTT, THOMAS ALBERT (1944). *A Pronouncing Dictionary of American English* (Springfield, Mass.: Merriam).

KEYSER, SAMUEL JAY, and STEVENS, KENNETH N. (1994). 'Feature Geometry and the Vocal Tract', *Phonology*, 11.2: 207–36.

KIM, HYO-YOUNG (2000). 'Flexibility of English Stress', doctoral dissertation, University of Michigan, Ann Arbor.

KIPARSKY, PAUL (1975). 'Stress, Syntax, and Meter', *Language*, 51: 576–616.

——(1977). 'The Rhythmic Structure of English Verse', *Linguistic Inquiry*, 8: 189–247.

——(1989). 'Sprung Rhythm', in Paul Kiparsky and Gilbert Youmans (eds.), *Rhythm and Meter* (San Diego: Academic Press), 305–40.

KISSEBERTH, CHARLES, and CASSIMJEE, FARIDA (1992). 'Tone and Metrical Structure in Shinjazidja', paper presented at CLS 28, Chicago.

KLATT, DENNIS H (1975). 'Vowel Lengthening is Syntactically Determined in a Connected Discourse', *Journal of Phonetics*, 3.3: 129–140.

——(1976). 'Linguistic Uses of Segmental Duration in English: Acoustic and Perceptual Evidence', *Journal of the Acoustical Society of America*, 59.5: 1208–21.

KRATOCHVIL, PAUL (1968). *The Chinese Language Today* (London: Hutchinson).

——(1970). Review of Y. R. Chao, *A Grammar of Spoken Chinese, Language*, 46.2: 513–524.

KUBOZONO, HARUO (2003). 'The Syllable as a Unit of Prosodic Organization in Japanese', in Caroline Féry and Ruben van de Vijver (eds.), *The Syllable in Optimality Theory* (Cambridge: Cambridge University Press), 99–122.

LADD, DWIGHT ROBERT (1980). *The Structure of Intonational Meaning: Evidence from English* (Bloomington: Indiana University Press).

LADEFOGED, PETER (2001). *Vowels and Consonants: An Introduction to the Sounds Of Languages* (Malden, Mass.: Blackwell).

——and HALLE, MORRIS (1988). 'Some Major Features of the International Phonetic Alphabet', *Language*, 64.3: 577–82.

LAUGHREN, MARY (1984). 'Tone in Zulu Nouns', in G. N. Clements and John Goldsmith (eds.), *Autosegmental Studies In Bantu Tone* (Dordrecht: Foris), 183–234.

LEBEN, WILLIAM (1973). 'Suprasegmental Phonology', doctoral dissertation, MIT, Cambridge, Mass.

LI, CHARLES N. and THOMPSON, SANDRA A. (1981). *Mandarin Chinese: A Functional Reference Grammar.* (Berkeley and Los Angeles: University of California Press).

LI, FANG-KUI (1966). 'The Zero Initial and the Zero Syllabic', *Language*, 42: 300–2.

LI, LINGDING (1990). 'Dongci fenlei yanjiu shuolue' [A brief discussion on verb classification], *Zhongguo Yuwen*, 1990.4: 248–57.

[李臨定, 1990, '動詞 分類 研究 說略', <中國 語文> 1990.4: 248–57.]

LI, PAUL JEN-KUEI (1985). 'A Secret Language in Taiwanese', *Journal of Chinese Linguistics*, 13: 91–121.

LI, RONG (1983). 'Guanyu fangyan yanjiu de ji dian yijian' [Some comments on dialectal studies], *Fangyan*, 1983.1: 1–15.

[李榮, 1983, '關於 方言 研究 的 幾 點 意見', <方言> 1983.1: 1–15.]

LI, SIJING (1986). *Hanyu "er" [ɚ] Yin Shi* [The History of the Sound [ɚ] in Chinese] (Beijing: Shangwu Yinshuguan).

[李思敬, 1986, <漢語 "兒" [ɚ] 音 史>, 北京: 商務 印書館.]

LI, WEIMIN (1981). 'Shi lun qingsheng he zhongyin' [A preliminary discussion on stressless and stressed syllables], *Zhongguo Yuwen*, 1981.1: 35–40.

[厲爲民, 1981, '試 論 輕聲 和 重音', <中國 語文> 1981.1: 35–40.]

LI, XINGJIAN, and LIU, SIXUN (1985). 'Tianjin fangyan de liandu biandiao' [Tone sandhi in Tianjin dialect], *Zhongguo Yuwen*, 1985.1: 76–80.

[李行健, 劉思訓, 1985, '天津方言的連讀 變調', <中國 語文> 1985.1: 76–80.]

LI, ZHENJIE, and BAI, YUKUN (ed.) (1987). *Zhongguo Baokan Xin Ciyu* [New Chinese Press Terms] (Beijing: Huayu Jiaoxue Chubanshe).

[李振杰, 白玉崑, 等 編, 1987, <中國 報刊新詞語>, 北京: 華語教學出版社.]

LIBERMAN, ALVIN M., and MATTINGLY, IGNATIUS G. (1985). 'The Motor Theory of Speech Perception Revised', *Cognition*, 21: 1–36.

LIBERMAN, MARK (1975). 'The Intonational System of English', doctoral dissertation, MIT, Cambridge, Mass.

——and PRINCE, ALAN (1977). 'On Stress and Linguistic Rhythm', *Linguistic Inquiry*, 8.2: 249–336.

LIEBER, ROCHELLE (1983). 'Argument Linking and Compounds in English', *Linguistic Inquiry*, 14.2: 251–85.

LIN, JO-WANG (1994). 'Lexical Government and Tone Group Formation in Xiamen Chinese', *Phonology*. 11: 237–75.

LIN, MAOCAN, and YAN, JINGZHU (1980). 'Beijinghua qingsheng de shengxue xingzhi' [Acoustic characteristics of neutral tone in Beijing Mandarin], *Fangyan*, 1980.3: 166–78.

[林茂燦, 顏景助, 1980, '北京話輕聲的聲學性質', <方言> 1980.3: 166–78.]

—— ——(1988). 'The Characteristic Features of the Final Reduction in the Neutral-tone Syllable of Beijing Mandarin', *Phonetic Laboratory Annual Report of Phonetic Research*

(Beijing: Phonetic Laboratory, Institute of Linguistics, Chinese Academy of Social Sciences), 37–51.

—— —— and SUN, GUOHUA (1984). 'Beijinghua liangzizu zhengchang zhongyin de chubu shiyan' [Preliminary experiments on the normal stress in Beijing disyllables], *Fangyan*, 1984.1: 57–73.

[林茂燦, 顏景助, 孫國華, 1984, '北京話兩字組正常重音的初步實驗', <方言> 1984.1: 57–73.]

LIN, TAO, and SHEN, JIONG (1995). 'Beijinghua er hua yun de yuyin fenqi' [Variations in the [er]-suffixed rhymes in the Beijing dialect], *Zhongguo Yuwen*, 1995.3: 170–9.

[林燾, 沈炯, 1995, '北京話兒化韻的語音分歧', <中國 語文> 1995.3: 170–9.]

LIN, YEN-HWEI (1989). 'Autosegmental Treatment of Segmental Processes in Chinese Phonology', doctoral dissertation, University of Texas, Austin.

——(1993). 'Degenerate Affixes and Templatic Constraints: Rhyme Change in Chinese', *Language*, 69.4: 649–82.

——(1997). 'Assimilation in Mandarin and Feature Class Theory', paper presented at NACCL9, University of Victoria, Canada.

LIU, DABAI (1927). 'Zhongguo jiu shipian zhong de shengdiao wenti' [Questions concerning the tones of classical Chinese poetry], *Xiaoshuo Yuebao* 17, Supplement. Reprinted in Qichao Liang (ed.), *Zhongguo Wenxue Yanjiu* [Studies in Chinese Literature] (Kyoto: Zhongwen Chubanshe, 1971), 149–208.

[劉大白, 1927, '中國舊詩篇中的聲調問題', <小學說月報, 增刊>. 重印于 梁啟超, 1971, <中國文學研究>, 京都: 中文出版社, 149–208.]

LIU, FENG-HSI (1980). 'Tone Sandhi in Mandarin Chinese', paper presented at the Summer Meeting of the Linguistic Society of America, University of New Mexico, Albuquerque.

——(1992). 'Verb and Syllable in Chinese', paper presented at the 25th International Conference on Sino-Tibetan Languages and Linguistics, Berkeley.

LIU, NIANHE (1944). 'Chengdu ertong jian de mimi yu' [A secret language among Chengdu children], *Bulletin of Chinese Studies*, 4.2: 69–78.

[劉念和, 1944, '成都兒童間的秘密語', <中國文化研究匯刊> 4.2: 69–78.]

LIU, ZEXIAN (1957a). 'Beijinghua li jiujing you duoshao yinjie?' [How many syllables are there in the Beijing dialect?], *Zhongguo Yuwen*, 1957.2: 1–8.

[劉澤先, 1957a, '北京話裡究竟有多少音節?', <中國 語文> 1957.2: 1–8.]

——(1957b). 'Beijinghua li jiujing you duoshao yinjie? (ji wan)' [How many syllables are there in the Beijing dialect? (continued)], *Zhongguo Yuwen*, 1957.3: 17–23.

[劉澤先, 1957b, '北京話裡究竟有多少音節? (繼完)', <中國 語文> 1957.3: 17–23.]

LIU, ZHENGTAN, GAO, MINGKAI, MAI, YONGQIAN, and SHI, YOUWEI (1984). *Hanyu Wailaici Cidian* [A Dictionary of Loan Words and Hybrid Words in Chinese] (Shanghai: Shanghai Cishu Chubanshe).

[劉正埮, 高名凱, 麥永乾, 史有爲, 1984, <漢語外來詞詞典>, 上海: 上海 辭書 出版 社.]

LO, CHIN-CHENG (2005). 'The Falling of the Rising Tone: The Second Tone Sandhi in the Mandarin Chinese Spoken by Southern Min Speakers in Taiwan', paper presented at The First Theoretical Phonology Conference, National Chengchi University, Taipei, May.

LOWENSTAMM, JEAN (1996). 'CV as the Only Syllable Type', in Jacques Durand and Bernard Laks (eds.), *Current Trends in Phonology, Models and Methods*, vol. ii (Salford: European Studies Research Institute, University of Salford Publications), 419–43.

LOWENSTAMM, JEAN (1999). 'The Beginning of the Word', in John R. Renison and Klaus Kühnammer (eds.), *Phonologika 1996: Syllables!?* (The Hague: Thesus), 153–66.

LU, BINGFU (1989). 'Hanyu dingyu de fenlei ji yuxu' [Classes and order of nominal modifiers in Chinese], *Hua Wen Shi Jie*, 1989.4: 44–52.

[陸丙甫, 1989, '漢語定語的分類及語序', <華文世界>, 1989.4: 44–52.]

——(1990). 'The Structure of Chinese Nominal Phrases', MA thesis, University of Connecticut. (Published in *Comparative Studies on the Structure of Noun Phrases*, Research Report (PI: Mamuoru Saito), Department of Linguistics, University of Connecticut, Storrs, 1–50.)

LÜ, SHUXIANG (1963). 'Xiandai Hanyu dan shuang yinjie wenti chu tan' [A preliminary study of the problem of mono- and disyllabic expressions in modern Chinese], *Zhongguo Yuwen*, 1963.1: 11–23.

[呂叔湘, 1963, '現代漢語單雙音節問題初探', <中國 語文> 1963.1: 11–23.]

——(1979). *Hanyu Yufa Fenxi Wenti* [Problems in the Analysis of Chinese Grammar] (Beijing: Shangwu Yinshuguan).

[呂叔湘, 1979, <漢語 語法 分析 問題>, 北京: 商務 印書館.]

——(1981). *Yuwen Chang Tan* [Remarks on Language] (Beijing: San Lian Shudian).

[呂叔湘, 1981, <語文常談>, 北京: 三 聯 書店.]

——(1990). *Lü Shu-Xiang Wen Ji 2* [Collected Papers by Lü Shu-Xiang, vol. ii] (Beijing: Shangwu Yinshuguan).

呂叔湘, 1990, <呂叔湘 文集 2>, 北京: 商務 印書館.]

LU, ZHIWEI (1964). *Hanyu de Goucifa* [Chinese Morphology], rev. edn. (Beijing: Kexue Chubanshe).

[陸志偉, 等著, 1964, <漢語的構詞法>, 修訂本, 北京: 科學 出版社.]

LUO, CHANGPEI, and WANG, JUN (1981). *Putong Yuyinxue Gangyao* [Outline of General Phonetics], new edn. (Beijing: Shangwu Yinshuguan). (First pub. Beijing: Kexue Chubanshe, 1957.)

[羅常培, 王均, 1981, <普通 語音學 綱要(新版)>, 北京: 商務印書館. (第一版1957年, 北京: 科學 出版社.)]

MA, QIUWU (2005). 'Zai lun "Tianjinhua liandu biandiao zhi mi"' [More on 'the paradox of Tianjin tone sandhi'], *Contemporary Linguistics*, 7.2: 97–106.

[马秋武, 2005, 再论"天津话连读变调之谜", <当代语言学>, 第7卷, 2005年02期, 97–106.]

McCARTHY, JOHN (1988). 'Feature Geometry and Dependency: A Review', *Phonetica*, 43: 1988; 45: 84–108.

——and PRINCE, ALAN (1986). 'Prosodic Morphology', MS, University of Massachusetts, Amherst and Brandies University.

McCAWLEY, JAMES D. (1968). *The Phonological Component of a Grammar of Japanese* (The Hague: Mouton).

——(1978). 'What Is a Tone Language?', in Victoria A. Fromkin (ed.), *Tone: A Linguistic Survey* (New York: Academic), 113–31.

——(1992). 'Justifying Part-of-Speech Assignments in Mandarin Chinese', *Journal of Chinese Linguistics*, 20.2: 211–46.

MANASTER-RAMER, ALEXIS (1995). 'L'arbitraire de Chine', *Journal of East Asian Linguistics*, 4: 1–11.

MARTIN, SAMUEL E. (1957). 'Problems of Hierarchy and Indeterminacy in Mandarin Phonology', *Bulletin of the Institute of History and Philology, Academia Sinica*, 29: 209–29.

MEI, TSU-LIN (1977). 'Tones and Tone Sandhi in 16th Century Mandarin', *Journal of Chinese Linguistics*, 5: 237–60.

MEREDITH, SCOTT (1990). 'Issues in the Phonology of Prominence', doctoral dissertation, MIT, Cambridge, Mass.

MESTER, R. ARMIN (1994). 'The Quantitative Trochee in Latin', *Natural Language and Linguistic Theory*, 12: 1–61.

MILLIKEN, STUART (1989). 'Why There is No Third Tone Sandhi Rule in Standard Mandarin', paper presented at the Tianjin International Conference on Phonetics and Phonology, Tianjin Normal University, June 7–10.

NESPOR, MARINA, and VOGEL, IRENE (1986). *Prosodic Phonology* (Dordrecht: Foris).

NI, HAISHU (1948). *Zhungguo pinjin wenz yndung de giandand lish (Zhongguo Pinyin Wenzi Yundong Shi Jianbian)* [A Short History of the Movement for Alphabetical Writing in Chinese] (Shanghai: Shidai Shubao Chubanshe).
[倪海曙, 1948, <中國拼音文字運動史 (簡編)>, 上海: 時代 書報 出版社.]

PADGETT, JAYE (1995). *Stricture in Feature Geometry*, Dissertations in Linguistics (Stanford, CA: Center for the Study of Language and Information, Stanford University).

PAUL, WALTRAUD (2005). 'Adjectival Modification in Mandarin Chinese and Related Issues', *Linguistics*, 43.4: 757–93.

PIERREHUMBERT, JANET (1980). 'The Phonetics and Phonology of English Intonation', doctoral dissertation, MIT, Cambridge, Mass.

——(1994). 'Syllable Structure and Word Structure: A Study of Triconsonantal Clusters in English', in Patricia A. Keating (ed.), *Phonological Structure and Phonetic Form, Papers in Laboratory Phonology III* (Cambridge and New York: Cambridge University Press), 168–88.

PIKE, KENNETH (1947). *Phonemics: A Technique for Reducing Languages to Writing* (Ann Arbor: University of Michigan Press).

——(1948). *Tone Languages* (Ann Arbor: University of Michigan Press).

POLLOCK, JEAN-YVES (1989). 'Verb Movement, Universal Grammar, and the Structure of IP', *Linguistic Inquiry*, 20: 365–424.

POSER, WILLIAM (1984). 'The Phonetics and Phonology of Tone and Intonation in Japanese', doctoral dissertation, MIT, Cambridge, Mass.

——(1990). 'Evidence for Foot Structure in Japanese', *Language*, 66: 78–105.

PRINCE, ALAN (1980). 'A Metrical Theory for Estonian Quantity', *Linguistic Inquiry*, 11: 511–62.

——(1990). 'Quantitative consequences of rhythmic organization', in *Papers from the 26th Regional Meeting of the Chicago Linguistic Society*, ii: *The Parasession on the Syllable in Phonetics and Phonology*, CLS 26 (Chicago: Chicago Linguistic Society 1992), 355–98.

——and SMOLENSKY, PAUL (1993). 'Optimality: Constraint Interaction in Generative Grammar', MS, Rutgers University and University of Colorado.

PROKOSCH, EDUARD (1939). *A Comparative Germanic Grammar* (Philadelphia, PA: Linguistic Society of America).

PULLEYBLANK, DOUGLAS (1986). *Tone in Lexical Phonology* (Dordrecht: Reidel).

PULLEYBLANK, EDWIN G. (1984). 'Vowelless Chinese? An Application of the Three-Tiered Theory of Syllable Structure', in *Proceedings of the Sixteenth International Conference on Sino-Tibetan Languages and Linguistics*, vol. ii (Seatle: University of Washington), 568–619.

Qiu, Xieyou (1976). *Xin Yi Tang Shi San Bai Shou* [New Translation of 300 Tang Poems] (Taipei: Sanmin Shuju).
[邱燮友, 1976, <新譯唐詩三百首>, 台北: 三民書局.]

Quirk, Randolph, Greenbaum, Sidney, Leech, Geoffrey, and Svartvik, Jan (1972). *A Grammar of Contemporary English* (New York: Seminar Press).

Ramsey, S. Robert (1987). *The Languages of China* (Princeton: Princeton University Press).

Rice, Curt (2000). 'Generative Metrics', in Lisa Lai-Shen Cheng and Rint Sybesma (eds.), *The First Glot International State-of-the-Article Book: The Latest in Linguistics* (Berlin: Mouton de Gruyter), 329–47.

Ritter, Elizabeth (1991). 'Two Functional Categories in Noun Phrases: Evidence from Modern Hebrew', in Susan D. Rothstein (ed.), *Perspectives on Phrase Structure: Heads and Licensing*, Syntax and Semantics 25 (San Diego: Academic), 37–62.

Sagey, Elizabeth (1986). 'The Representation of Features and Relations in Nonlinear Phonology', doctoral dissertation, MIT, Cambridge, Mass.

Schlepp, Wayne (1980). 'Tentative Remarks on Chinese Metrics', *Journal of Chinese Linguistics*, 8: 59–84.

Selkirk, Elisabeth (1982). *The Syntax of Words* (Cambridge, Mass.: MIT Press).

——(1984). *Phonology and Syntax: The Relation between Sound and Structure* (Cambridge, Mass.: MIT Press).

——(1986). 'On Derived Domains in Sentence Phonology', *Phonology Yearbook*, 3: 371–405.

——and Shen, Tong (1990). 'Prosodic Domains in Shanghai Chinese', in Sharon Inkelas and Draga Zec (eds.), *The Phonology-Syntax Connection* (Stanford, Calif.: CSLI, Stanford University, distributed by University of Chicago Press), 313–37.

Shanghai Guji Chubanshe (1989). *Shiyun Xinbian* [A New Rhyming Book] (Shanghai: Shanghai Guji Chubanshe).
[上海 古籍 出版社, 1989, <詩韻 新編>, 上海: 上海 古籍 出版社.]

Shannon, Claude E. (1948). 'The Mathematical Theory of Communication', *Bell System Technical Journal*, 27 (July and October): 379–423 and 623–56.

Shen, Jiong (1985). 'Beijinghua shengdiao de yinyu he yudiao' [Pitch range of tone and intonation in Beijing dialect]', in Tao Lin and Lijia Wang (eds.), *Beijing Yuyin Shiyanlu* [Working Papers in Experimental Phonetics] (Beijing: Beijing University Press), 73–130.
[沈炯, 1985, '北京話聲調的音域和語調', <北京語音實驗錄>, 林燾, 王理嘉, 編, pp. 73–130, 北京: 北京大學出版社.]

——(1987). 'Beijinghua hekouhu ling shengmu de yinyu fenqi' [Phonetic differences of zero initials beginning with [u] in the Beijing dialect], *Zhongguo Yuwen*, 1987.5: 352–62.
[沈炯, 1987, '北京話合口呼零聲母的語音分歧', <中國語文> 1987.5: 352–62.]

——(1994). 'Beijinghua shangsheng liandu de diaoxing zuhe he jiezou xingshi' [Tonal patterns and rhythmic structure in successive third tones in the Beijing dialect], *Zhongguo Yuwen*, 1994.4: 274–81.
[沈炯, 1994, '北京話上聲連讀的調型組合和節奏形式', <中國語文> 1994.4: 274–81.]

Shen, Susan Xiaonan (1989). 'Interplay of the four citation tones and intonation in Mandarin Chinese', *Journal of Chinese Linguistics*, 17.1: 61–73.

Shen, Tong (1981). 'Lao pai Shanghai fangyan de liandu biandiao' [Tone sandhi in Old Shanghai], *Fangyan*, 1981.2: 131–44.
[沈同, 1981, '老派上海方言的連讀變調', <方言> 1981.2: 131–44.]

SHI, DINGXU (2003). 'Hanyu de ding zhong guanxi dong-ming fuheci' [Chinese Modifier-Modifiee V-O Compounds], *Zhongguo Yuwen*, 2003.6 (297): 483–95.

[石定栩, 2003, '汉语的定中关系动-名复合词', <中国语文>, 2003.6 (297): 483–95.]

SHI, FENG, SHI, LING, and LIAO, RONGRONG (1987). 'An experimental analysis of the five level tones of the Gaoba Dong language', *Journal of Chinese Linguistics*, 15.2: 335–61.

SHIH, CHILIN (1986). 'The prosodic domain of tone sandhi in Chinese', doctoral dissertation, University of California, San Diego.

——(1997). 'Mandarin Third Tone Sandhi and Prosodic Structure', in Wang Jialing and Norval Smith (eds.), *Studies in Chinese Phonology* (Berlin: Mouton de Gruyter), 81–123.

——(2005). 'Understanding Phonology by Phonetic Implementation', MS, University of Illinois Urbana-Champaigne.

SIETSEMA, BRIAN M. (1989). 'Metrical Dependencies in Tone Assignment', doctoral dissertation, MIT, Cambridge, Mass.

SPROAT, RICHARD, and SHIH, CHILIN (1991). 'The Cross-Linguistic Distribution of Adjective Ordering Restrictions', in Carol Georgopoulos and Roberta Ishihara (eds.), *Interdisciplinary Approaches to Language: Essays in honor of S.-Y. Kuroda* (Dordrecht: Kluwer Academic Publishers), 565–93.

—— ——(1996). 'A Corpus-Based Analysis of Mandarin Nominal Root Compound', *Journal of East Asian Linguistics*, 5: 49–71.

STERIADE, DONCA (1988). Review of G. N. Clements and S. J. Keyser, *CV Phonology*, *Language*, 64.1: 118–29.

——(1989). 'Affricates are Stops', paper presented at Conference on Features and Underspecification Theories, October 7–9, MIT.

——(1995). 'Underspecification and Markedness', in John Goldsmith (ed.), *The Handbook of Phonological Theory* (Cambridge, Mass.: Blackwell), 114–74.

——(1999). 'Alternatives to Syllable-Based Accounts of Consonantal Phonotactics', in Bohumil Palek, Osamu Fujimura, and Brian D Joseph (eds.), *Proceedings of the 1998 Linguistics and Phonetics Conference*, vol. i (Prague: Charles University Press (Karolinum)), 205–46.

TING, PANG-HSIN (1982). 'Some Aspects of Tonal Development in Chinese Dialects', *Bulletin of the Institute of History and Philology, Academia Sinica*, 53.4: 629–44.

TSAY, JANE S. (1990). 'The Distribution of Tone in Taiwanese', in *WECOL 1989: Proceedings of the 1989 Western Conference on Linguistics* (Fresno: Department of Linguistics, California State University), 336–46.

——(1991). 'Tone Alternation in Taiwanese', in *Arizona Phonology Conference*, vol. iv (Tucson: Department of Linguistics, University of Arizona), 76–87.

VIJVER, RUBEN VAN DE (1998). 'The Iambic Issue: Iambs as a Result of Constraint Interaction', doctoral dissertation, Vrije Universiteit Amsterdam (distributed by HIL Dissertations).

WANG, BINBIN (1998). 'Gezai zhong xi zhijian de Riben' [Japan between the east and the west], *Shanghai Wenxue*, 1998.8: 71–80.

[王彬彬, 1998, '隔在 中西 之間 的 日本', <上海 文學> 1998.8: 71–80.]

WANG, HONGJUN (1999). *Hanyu Fei Xianxing Yinxixue* [Chinese Non-linear Phonology] (Beijing: Beijing Daxue Chubanshe).

[王洪君, 1999, <漢語 非 線性 音系學>, 北京: 北京大學出版社.]

WANG, HONGJUN (2004). 'Shilun hanyu de jiezou leixing—songjin xing' [On the metrical type of Modern Standard Chinese—a type based on looseness], *Yuyan Kexue* [Linguistic Science], 3.3 (May 2004): 21–8.

[王洪君, 2004, '試論漢語的節奏類型--鬆緊型', <語言科學>, 3.3 (May 2004): 21–8]

WANG, JENNY ZHIJIE (1993). 'The Geometry of Segmental Features in Beijing Mandarin', doctoral dissertation, University of Delaware, Newark.

WANG, JING, and WANG, LIJIA (1993). 'Putonghua duo yinjie ci yinjie shi chang fenbu moshi' [The types of relative lengths of syllables in polysyllabic words in Putonghua], *Zhongguo Yuwen*, 1993.2 (233): 112–16.

[王晶, 王理嘉, 1993, '普通話 多 音節 詞 音節 時長 分佈 模式', <中國 語文> 1993.2 (233): 112–16.]

WANG, LI (1944). *Zhongguo Yufa Lilun* [Chinese Grammatical Theory] (Shanghai: Shangwu Yinshuguan).

[王力, 1944, <中國語法理論>, 上海: 商務印書館.]

——(1958). *Hanyu Shilü Xue* [Chinese Versification]. Shanghai: Xin Zhishi Chubanshe.

[王力, 1958, <漢語詩律學>, 上海: 新知識出版社.]

——(1979). 'Xiandai hanyu yuyin fenxi zhong de ji ge wenti' [Some problems in the phonetic analysis of modern Chinese], *Zhongguo Yuwen*, 1979.4: 281–6.

[王力, 1979, '現代漢語語音分析中的幾個問題', <中國 語文> 1979.4: 281–6.]

——(1980). *Hanyu Yinyun* [Chinese Phonology], 2nd edn. (Beijing: Zhonghua Shuju).

[王力, 1980, <漢語音韻>, 第二版, 北京: 中華 書局.]

WANG, LIJIA, and HE, NINGJI (1985). 'Beijinghua er-huayun de tingbian shiyan he shengxue fenxi' [Auditory discrimination experiments and acoustic analysis of Mandarin retroflex endings], in Tao Lin and Lijia Wang (eds.), *Beijing Yuyin Shiyanlu* [Working Papers in Experimental Phonetics] (Beijing: Beijing University Press), 27–72.

[王理嘉, 賀寧基, 1985, '北京話兒化韻的聽辨實驗和聲學分析', <北京 語音 實驗錄> 林燾, 王理嘉, 編, pp. 27–72, 北京: 北京大學出版社.]

——and WANG, HAIDAN (1991). 'Erhuayun yanjiu zhong de jige wenti: yu Li Sijing xiansheng shangque' [Some issues in the study of [ɚ]-suffixed syllables: comments for Mr. Sijing Li], *Zhongguo Yuwen*, 1991.2 (221): 96–103.

[王理嘉, 王海丹, 1991, '兒化韻研究中的幾個問題: 與李思敬先生商榷', <中國 語 文> 1991.2 (221): 96–103.]

WANG, WILLIAM S.-Y. (1967). 'Phonological Features of Tone', *International Journal of American Linguistics*, 33.2: 93–105.

——and KUNG-PU LI (1967). 'Tone 3 in Pekinese', *Journal of the Speech and Hearing Research*, 10.3: 629–36.

WANG, XUDONG (1992). 'Beijinghua de qingsheng qu hua jiqi yingxiang' [The change of weak syllables to fourth tone syllables and its consequences], *Zhongguo Yuwen*, 1992.2 (227): 124–8.

[王旭東, 1992, '北京話的輕聲去化及其影響', <中國語文> 1992.2 (227): 124–8.]

WHALEN, D. H., and BEDDOR, PATRICE S. (1989). 'Connections between Nasality and Vowel Duration and Height: Elucidation of the Eastern Algonquian Intrusive Nasal', *Language*, 65.3: 457–86.

WIESE, RICHARD (1996). 'Phrasal Compounds and the Theory of Word Syntax', *Linguistic Inquiry*, 27: 183–93.

——(1997). 'Underspecification and the Description of Chinese Vowels', in Wang Jialing and Norval Smith (eds.), *Studies in Chinese Phonology* (Berlin: Mouton de Gruyter), 219–49.

WILLIAMS, EDWIN (1976). 'Underlying Tone in Margi and Igbo', *Linguistic Inquiry*, 7.3: 436–68.

WILLIAMS, S. WELLS (1889). *A Syllabic Dictionary of the Chinese Language: Arranged according to the Wu-Fang Yuan Yin, with the Pronunciation of the Characters as Heard in Peking, Canton, Amoy, and Shanghai* (Shanghai: American Presbyterian Mission Press).

WONG, PATRICK C. M., and RANDY L. DIEHL. 2002. 'How Can the Lyrics of a Song in a Tone Language be Understood?', *Psychology of Music*, 30.2: 202–9.

WOO, NANCY (1969). 'Prosody and Phonology', doctoral dissertation, MIT, Cambridge, Mass.

WRIGHT, MARTHA (1983). 'A Metrical Approach to Tone Sandhi in Chinese Dialects', doctoral dissertation, University of Massachusetts, Amherst.

XU, BAOHUA, TANG, ZHENZHU, and QIAN, NAIRONG (1981). 'Xin pai Shanghai fangyan de liandu biandiao' [Tone sandhi in New Shanghai], *Fangyan*, 1981.2: 145–55.
[許寶華, 湯珍珠, 錢乃榮, 1981, '新派上海方言的連讀變調', <方言> 1981.2: 145–55.]

—— —— YOU, RUJIE, QIAN, NAIRONG, SHI, RUJIE, and SHEN, YAMING (1988). *Shanghai Shiqü Fangyan Zhi* [Urban Shanghai Dialects] (Shanghai: Shanghai Jiaoyu Chubanshe).
[許寶華, 湯珍珠, 游汝杰, 錢乃榮, 石汝杰, 沈亞明, 1988, <上海市區方言志>. 上海: 上海教育出版社.]

XU, SHIRONG (1957). 'Beijinghua li de tuci he tuyin' [Native words and sounds in the Beijing dialect], *Zhongguo Yuwen*, 1957.3: 24–7.
[徐世榮, 1957, '北京話裡的土詞和土音', <中國語文> 1957.3: 24–7.]

——(1980). *Putonghua Yuyin Zhishi* [Phonology of Standard Chinese] (Beijing: Wenzi Gaige Chubanshe).
[徐世榮, 1980, <普通話語音知識>, 北京: 文字改革出版社.]

——(1982). 'Shuangyinjie ci de yinliang fenxi' [A quantitative analysis of disyllabic words], *Yuyan Jiaoxue Yu Yanjiu*, 1982.2: 4–19.
[徐世榮, 1982, '双音节词的音量分析', <语言教学与研究>, 1982年第2期, 4–19.]

XU, YI (1986). 'Putonghua yinlian de shengxue yuyin texing' [Acoustic properties of syllable junctures in Standard Chinese], *Zhongguo Yuwen*, 1986.5 (194): 353–60.
[許毅, 1986, '普通話音聯的聲學語音特性', <中國語文>, 1986.5 (194): 353–60.]

——(1999). 'F0 Peak Delay: When, Where, and Why It Occurs', in John Ohala (ed.), *International Congress of Phonetic Science 1999* (San Francisco), 1881–84.

—— and WANG, MAOLIN (2005). 'Phonetic Coding for Syllable Grouping in Mandarin', paper presented at The 149th Meeting of The Acoustical Society of America, 16–20 May 2005, Vancouver, Canada.

XU, ZHENG (2005). 'On the formation of adjective-noun combinations in Mandarin Chinese', paper presented at The 17th North American Conference on Chinese Linguistics, 24–6 June 2005, Monterey, California.

YAN, JINGZHU, and LIN, MAOCAN (1988). 'Beijinghua sanzizu zhongyin de shengxue biaoxian' [Acoustic characteristics of the stress in Beijing trisyllables], *Fangyan*, 1988.3: 227–37.
[顏景助, 林茂燦, 1988, '北京話三字組重音的聲學表現', <方言> 1988.3: 227–37.]

YAN, SEN (1981). 'Gao'an (Laowu Zhoujia) fangyan de yuyin xitong' [The sound system of the Gao'an (Laowu Zhoujia) dialect], *Fangyan*, 1981.2: 104–21.
[顏森, 1981, '高安 (老屋周家) 方言的語音系統', <方言> 1981.2: 104–21.]

YANG, SHUN'AN (1992). 'Beijinghua duoyinjie zuhe yunlu tezheng de shiyan yanjiu' [An experiment on the prosody of polysyllables in the Beijing dialect], *Fangyan*, 1992.2: 128–37.

[楊順安, 1992, '北京話多音節組合韻律特徵的實驗研究', <方言> 1992.2: 128–37.]

YIN, YUEN-MEI (1989). 'Phonological Aspects of Word Formation in Mandarin Chinese', doctoral dissertation, University of Texas at Austin.

YIN, ZUOYAN (1982). 'Guanyu Putonghua shuangyin changyong ci qingzhongyin de chubu kaocha' [A preliminary study of accents and atonics in disyllabic words in common use], *Zhongguo Yuwen*, 1982.3 (168): 168–73.

[殷作炎, 1982, '關於普通話雙音常用詞輕重音的初步攷察', < 中國 語文> 1982.3 (168): 168–173.]

YIP, MOIRA (1980). 'Tonal Phonology of Chinese', doctoral dissertation, MIT, Cambridge, Mass.

——(1982). 'Reduplication and C-V Skeleta in Chinese Secrete Languages', *Linguistic Inquiry*, 13: 637–61.

——(1989). 'Contour Tones', *Phonology*, 6: 149–74.

——(1992). 'Prosodic Morphology in Four Chinese Dialects', *Journal of East Asian Linguistics*, 1.1: 1–35.

——(1994). 'Isolated Uses Of Prosodic Categories', in Jennifer Cole and Charles Kisseberth (eds.), *Perspectives in Phonology*, CSLI Lecture Notes No.51 (Stanford, Calif.: CSLI, Stanford University), 293–311.

——(2002). *Tone* (Cambridge, UK: Cambridge University Press).

YOU, RUJIE, QIAN, NAIRONG, and GAO, ZHENGXIA (1980). 'Lun Putonghua de yinwei xitong' [On the phonemic system of Standard Chinese], *Zhongguo Yuwen*, 1980.5 (158): 328–34.

[游汝杰, 钱乃荣, 高钲夏, '论普通话的音位系统', <中國語文>, 1980.5 (158): 328–34.]

YOUMANS, GILBERT (1989). 'Introduction: Rhythm and Meter', in Paul Kiparsky and Gilbert Youmans (eds.), *Rhythm and Meter* (San Diego: Academic Press), 1–14.

YU, GENYUAN (editor-in-chief) (1993). *1992 Hanyu Xin Ciyu* [1992 New Chinese Terms] (Beijing: Beijing Yuyan Xueyuan Chubanshe).

[于根元, 主編, 1993, <1992 漢語新詞語>, 北京: 北京語言學院出版社.]

YUAN, JIAHUA (1989). *Hanyu Fangyan Gaiyao* [Outline of Chinese Dialects], 2nd edn. (Beijing: Wenzi Gaige Chubanshe).

[袁家驊, 1989, <漢語方言概要>, 第二版, 北京: 文字改革出版社.]

YUAN, YULIN (1999). 'A cognitive explanation of the order of modifiers and its implication', *Social Science in China*, 1999.2: 185–201.

[袁毓林, 1999, '定语顺序的认知解释及其理论蕴涵', <中国社会科学> 第2期, 185–201页.]

YUE-HASHIMOTO, ANNE O. (1986). 'Tonal Flip-Flop in Chinese Dialects', *Journal of Chinese Linguistics*, 14.2: 161–83.

——(1987). 'Tone Sandhi Across Chinese Dialects', in Chinese Language Society of Hong Kong (ed.), *Wang Li memorial volumes: Chinese volume* (Hong Kong: Joint Publishing Co.), 445–74.

ZEE, ERIC (2003). 'The Phonetic Characteristics of the Sounds in Standard Chinese (Beijing)', paper presented at The 15th North American Conference on Chinese Linguistics, July 11–13, Michigan State University, East Lansing, MI.

ZEMLIN, WILLARD R. (1981). *Speech and Hearing Science: Anatomy and Physiology*, 2nd edn. (Englewood Cliffs, NJ: Prentice-Hall).

ZHANG, HONGMING (1992). 'Topics in Chinese Phrasal Phonology', doctoral dissertation, University of California, San Diego.

ZHANG, JING (1957). 'Tan Beijinghua de yinwei' [On the phonemes of the Beijing dialect], *Zhongguo Yuwen*, 1957.2: 13–15.

　[張靜, 1957, '談北京話的音位', <中國 語文> 1957.2: 13–15.]

ZHANG, SHIZHAO (1907). *Zhongdeng Guowen Dian* [Intermediate Chinese Grammar] (Shanghai: Shangwu Yinshuguan).

　[章士釗, 1907, <中等 國文 典>, 上海: 商務印書館.]

ZHANG, YONGMIAN (1980). 'Jindai hanyu zhong zixu duihuan de shuangyinci' [Disyllabic words with flexible word orders in Late Chinese], *Zhongguo Yuwen*, 1980.3 (156): 177–83.

　[张永绵, 1980, '近代汉语中字序对换的双音词', <中国语文>, 1980.3 (156): 177–83.]

ZHANG, ZHENGSHENG (1988). 'Tone and tone sandhi in Chinese', doctoral dissertation, Ohio State University, Columbus.

ZHOU, DIANFU, and WU, ZONGJI (1963). *Putonghua Fayin Tu Pu* [Articulatory Diagrams of Standard Chinese] (Beijing: Shangwu Yinshuguan).

　[周殿福, 吳宗濟, 編著, 1963, <普通話 發音 圖 譜>, 北京: 商務印書館.

ZHOU, REN (2005). 'Zai lun Hanyu jiezou yu yuyi, jufa de guanxi' [Another remark on the relation between rhythm and semantics-syntax], MS, Department of Chinese, Peking University.

　[周韧, 2005, '再论汉语节奏与语义、句法的关系', 手稿, 北京大学中文系.]

ZHU, DEXI (1980). *Xiandai Hanyu Yufa Yanjiu* [Studies on Modern Chinese Grammar] (Beijing: Shangwu Yinshuguan).

　[朱德熙, 1980, <现代 漢語 語法 研究>, 北京: 商務印書館.]

ZUBIZARRETA, MARIA LUISA (1998). *Prosody, Focus, and Word Order*, Linguistic Inquiry, Monograph 33 (Cambridge, Mass.: MIT Press).

ZWGW (Zhongguo Wenzi Gaige Weiyuanhui Yanjiu Tuiguang Chu [Chinese Language Reform Committee Research and Popularization Office]) (1959). *Putonghua San Qian Chang yong Ci Biao* [Three Thousand Commonly Used Words in Standard Chinese], preliminary edn. (Beijing: Wenzi Gaige Chubanshe).

　[中國文字改革委員會研究推廣處編, 1959, <普通話三千常用詞 表>, 初稿, 北京: 文字改革出版社.]

INDEX

The Index includes terms and author names that appeared in the chapters. In addition, first names and/ or initial(s) are included for all authors (as they appear in the References), even though first names are not included in the chapters and initials are used only for authors who have the same last name as someone else.